The road to Russia 2018 has been far from smooth, with calls from some English politicians for the national team to boycott the finals just the latest in a long line of controversies to dog the build-up to the competition, *writes Paul Charlton*.

There is every chance that we will see controversy during the World Cup, too – the early evidence suggests that the introduction of video assistant referees will not leave the tournament unscathed, even if it seems unlikely that VAR will follow the USA 94 golf buggy and trundle off into the dustbin of history.

But nobody ever remembers the build-up and with Qatar hosting a winter World Cup in four years – the first game will kick off in November 2022 – and the tournament expanding from 32 teams to 48 in 2026, it is likely that Russia 2018 will be remembered fondly as the last of the old-fashioned World Cups.

That this might also represent the last hurrahs for Lionel Messi and Cristiano Ronaldo only adds to the feeling that we are approaching the end of an era. They are two of the greatest players ever to lace up a pair of boots but the pair will be 35 and 37 respectively in Qatar.

Luckily, this World Cup has all the necessary ingredients to be a classic, with half a dozen serious contenders for the trophy and no shortage of talented young players looking to establish themselves on the biggest stage.

The competition is getting stronger – Chile, Italy and Holland are among those to miss out – which compounds the belief that a couple of genuine dark horses could emerge. Make no mistake, this is a tournament to look forward to, even before you've had a bet. Here's to a profitable World Cup!

Edited by
Paul Charlton & Mark Langdon

Contributors
*Paul Charlton, Dan Childs,
Michael Cox, Mark Langdon,
Steve Davies*

Data
Chris Mann

Sub-editors
*Joe Champion, Dan Sait,
Graham Woods*

Cover design
Jay Vincent

Graphics
*Liam Hill, Sam Creedon,
Shane Tetley*

Published in 2018 by Racing Post Books
*27 Kingfisher Court, Hambridge Road,
Newbury RG14 5SJ*

Copyright © Racing Post 2018

*A catalogue record for this book is
available from the British Library.*

ISBN 978-1- 910497-53- 1

Printed in Great Britain by Buxton Press

CONTENTS

Mark Langdon's group previews & team profiles

OUTRIGHT WINNER

Classy Spain the value to recapture former glories

Brazil 2014 was labelled a tournament too far for **Spain**, who crashed out at the group stage, but the Iberians have impressed on the road to Russia 2018 and look decent value to lift the trophy, *writes Dan Childs*.

There is a wide-open feel to the competition with numerous contenders and no single outstanding candidate.

Holders Germany share favouritism with five-time winners Brazil but at least eight nations have a realistic chance, including Gareth Southgate's England.

Eighth in the betting are European champions Portugal.

They will always be competitive while Cristiano Ronaldo remains in the world-class bracket and there are signs of the next generation coming through with the likes of Bernardo Silva.

Portugal's problem is a tough draw in Group B with Spain, Morocco and Iran. They should finish in the top two but they have struggled against Spain in recent years, losing 1-0 in the last 16 at World Cup 2010 and losing 4-2 on penalties in the Euro 2012 semi-finals after a 0-0 draw.

Failure against Spain again would likely see them finish second in Group B and on a collision-course to face well-fancied France, the likely winners of Group C, in the quarter-finals.

The winners of Group B should get an easier route through the tournament even though 2014 runners-up Argentina are potential quarter-final opponents.

Spain can be slow starters but the draw is kinder than at Brazil 2014 and gives them time to settle into their stride.

Their potential round-of-16 opponents are Uruguay, Russia or Egypt and there is the possibility of a soft quarter-final draw if Argentina have not sorted out the mess which saw them come close to missing out on a place at the finals.

After below-par showings at the last two major tournaments Spain have been tagged as a team who are over the hill.

The 2014 tournament was a last hurrah for Xavi and Xabi Alonso but Sergio Ramos, Gerard Pique, Andres Iniesta and David Silva are still going strong and David de Gea has developed into one of the best goalkeepers in the world.

And La Roja continue to perform at a consistent level. They excelled in qualifying, taking 28 points from a possible 30 and finishing five points above second-placed Italy.

Italy are not the force they once were but Spain sent out a real statement in March when Argentina were battered 6-1 in a Madrid friendly.

Crucially they retain key members of the team who won Euro 2012, including six of the players who triumphed 4-0 over Italy in the final (Pique, Iniesta, Ramos, Sergio Busquets, Jordi Alba and Silva). That tournament-winning mentality is still in the group and could carry them a long way this summer.

Holders Germany have strong claims, but while they have reached at least the semi-finals at each of the last four World Cups, they disappointed in a 2-0 loss to France at the Euro 2016 semi-finals and have worries over a number of key

Andres Iniesta and his Spain teammates
know how it feels to win a World Cup

Photo by Clive Mason/Getty Images

players due to injuries and loss of form.

There are plusses, such as the emergence of exciting wingers Leroy Sane and Julian Brandt, but it is hard to pin down Germany's best 11 and that must be a worry for anyone wanting to back them.

Brazil have recovered from the psychological damage of their 7-1 loss to Germany in the 2014 semi-finals and topped the ultra-competitive South American qualifying group by ten points.

But key players are ageing and there is a heavy reliance on Neymar, who is battling back from surgery on his injured right foot.

France look the best value among the market's leading trio. They have a combination of exciting young players and world-class stars coming into their prime.

France will surely go close if they play to their potential but the nagging doubt is the mental side. They noticeably wilted in the Euro 2016 final against Portugal and it remains to be seen whether head coach Didier Deschamps is the right man to take them forward.

England's expectations have been played down – perhaps understandably after their dreadful showing four years ago.

There are reasons for optimism if they can get the best out of exciting talents like Raheem Sterling, Dele Alli and Harry Kane at a tournament where none of the teams look the finished article, but England are probably not even the strongest team in Group G.

Belgium have few obvious weaknesses and their star duo, Eden Hazard and Kevin De Bruyne, are having fantastic seasons in the Premier League. But they are becoming expensive to follow at major tournaments and failed to cope with the pressure when losing 3-1 to Wales in the quarter-finals at Euro 2016.

Recommendation

★★★☆☆ Spain to win the World Cup

TOP SCORER

Lukaku can make hay in group games

Brazilian sensation Ronaldo is the only player since Paolo Rossi in 1982 to finish in the clear as top goalscorer for the World Cup winners, with six-goal James Rodriguez suffering a quarter-final exit four years ago, *writes Mark Langdon*.

Belgium, who may lack the tactical nous under Roberto Martinez to lift the World Cup, have become experts at beating up weaker opponents. They scored 43 times in qualifying and **Romelu Lukaku** could fill his boots in group matches against Panama and Tunisia.

Lukaku can feed off the creativity of Eden Hazard and Kevin De Bruyne and the Red Devils should at least match their World Cup quarter-final run in 2014 and at Euro 2016.

Dangers are everywhere but Argentina have not always got the best from Lionel Messi, while if over-the-hill Portugal peaked at Euro 2016, that will hamper Cristiano Ronaldo's bid for individual glory.

Neymar carries the hopes of a nation but Brazil could share the goals around with Gabriel Jesus and Philippe Coutinho also

expected to fill a star-studded front three.

Antoine Griezmann top-scored at Euro 2016 and his French side should go well, but competition for places may yet damage the Atletico Madrid man's chances, while England and Poland may not go far enough to support bids for Harry Kane and Robert Lewandowski. Meanwhile, Spain's front man is up for grabs and probable starter Diego Costa is not the most prolific anyway.

International novice Timo Werner is not guaranteed to consistently lead Germany's line and dangerous underdogs Uruguay will surely split the goals between Luis Suarez and Edinson Cavani.

One advanced midfielder who may well land the each-way money at huge prices is great Dane **Christian Eriksen**.

Denmark have the potential to qualify from a group including France, Peru and Australia in what looks set to be a high-scoring section. The last 16 would most likely throw up a date with Argentina but, if they flop, Nigeria, Iceland or Croatia could make for a winnable knockout contest.

Set-piece master Eriksen scored 11 times in qualifying – only Lewandowski and Ronaldo notched more in Europe – and, interestingly, the Spurs schemer came to life the longer qualifying progressed.

He is capable of putting together a red-hot streak over a short period.

Recommendation

★★☆☆☆ Romelu Lukaku each-way
★☆☆☆☆ Christian Eriksen each-way

World Cup top scorers since France 1998						
Year	Top scorer	Country	Played	Scored	Golden Boot	Team Performance
2014	James Rodriguez	Colombia	5	6	✓	Quarter-finalists
2010	Thomas Muller	Germany	6	5	✓	Third place
	David Villa	Spain	7	5		**Winners**
	Wesley Sneijder	Holland	7	5		Beaten finalists
	Diego Forlan	Uruguay	7	5		Fourth place
2006	Miroslav Klose	Germany	7	5	✓	Third place
2002	Ronaldo	Brazil	7	8	✓	**Winners**
1998	Davor Suker	Croatia	7	6	✓	Third place

Romelu Lukaku
Photo by Dean Mouhtaropoulos/Getty Images

ROUTE TO THE FINAL

Group A

Russia v Saudi Arabia	14 June 4pm, Moscow, ITV
Egypt v Uruguay	15 June 1pm, Yekaterinburg, BBC
Russia v Egypt	19 June 7pm, Saint Petersburg, BBC
Uruguay v Saudi Arabia	20 June 4pm, Rostov, BBC
Saudi Arabia v Egypt	25 June 3pm, Volgograd, ITV
Uruguay v Russia	25 June 3pm, Samara, ITV

Group B

Morocco v Iran	15 June 4pm, St Petersburg, ITV
Portugal v Spain	15 June 7pm, Sochi, BBC
Portugal v Morocco	20 June 1pm, Moscow, BBC
Iran v Spain	20 June 7pm, Kazan, ITV
Iran v Portugal	25 June 7pm, Saransk, BBC
Spain v Morocco	25 June 7pm, Kaliningrad, BBC

Group C

France v Australia	16 June 11am, Kazan, BBC
Peru v Denmark	16 June 5pm, Saransk, BBC
Denmark v Australia	21 June 1pm, Samara, ITV
France v Peru	21 June 4pm, Yekaterinburg, ITV
Australia v Peru	26 June 3pm, Sochi, ITV
Denmark v France	26 June 3pm, Moscow, ITV

Group D

Argentina v Iceland	16 June 2pm, Moscow, ITV
Croatia v Nigeria	16 June 8pm, Kaliningrad, ITV
Argentina v Croatia	21 June 7pm, Nizhny Novgorod, BBC
Nigeria v Iceland	22 June 4pm, Volgograd, BBC
Iceland v Croatia	26 June 7pm, Rostov, BBC
Nigeria v Argentina	26 June 7pm, St Petersburg, BBC

Group E

Costa Rica v Serbia	17 June 1pm, Samara, ITV
Brazil v Switzerland	17 June 7pm, Rostov, ITV
Brazil v Costa Rica	22 June 1pm, St Petersburg, ITV
Serbia v Switzerland	22 June 7pm, Kaliningrad, BBC
Serbia v Brazil	27 June 7pm, Moscow, ITV
Switzerland v Costa Rica	27 June 7pm, Nizhny N, ITV

Group F

Germany v Mexico	17 June 4pm, Moscow, BBC
Sweden v South Korea	18 June 1pm, Nizhny N, ITV
South Korea v Mexico	23 June 4pm, Rostov, ITV
Germany v Sweden	23 June 7pm, Sochi, ITV
South Korea v Germany	27 June 3pm, Kazan, BBC
Mexico v Sweden	27 June 3pm, Yekaterinburg, BBC

Group G

Belgium v Panama	18 June 4pm, Sochi, BBC
Tunisia v England	18 June 7pm, Volgograd, BBC
Belgium v Tunisia	23 June 1pm, Moscow, BBC
England v Panama	24 June 1pm, Nizhny Novgorod, BBC
England v Belgium	28 June 7pm, Kaliningrad, ITV
Panama v Tunisia	28 June 7pm, Saransk, ITV

Group H

Colombia v Japan	19 June 1pm, Saransk, BBC
Poland v Senegal	19 June 4pm, Moscow, ITV
Japan v Senegal	24 June 4pm, Yekaterinburg, BBC
Poland v Colombia	24 June 7pm, Kazan, ITV
Japan v Poland	28 June 3pm, Volgograd, BBC
Senegal v Colombia	28 June 3pm, Samara, BBC

Groups are decided as follows: **1** Points **2** Goal difference **3** Goals scored. If two or more teams are still level: **4** points in games between teams concerned **5** goal difference in games between teams concerned **6** goals scored in games between teams concerned **7** Fair play in games between teams concerned, scored as follows: ▢ -1, ▧ -3, ■ -4, ▢+■ -5 **8** Lots are drawn

Pot 1		Pot 2		Pot 3		Pot 4	
Russia	Fifa Ranking 65	Spain	Fifa Ranking 8	Denmark	Fifa Ranking 19	Serbia	Fifa Ranking 38
Germany	1	Peru	10	Iceland	21	Nigeria	41
Brazil	2	Switzerland	11	Costa Rica	22	Australia	43
Portugal	3	England	12	Sweden	25	Japan	44
Argentina	4	Colombia	13	Tunisia	28	Morocco	48
Belgium	5	Mexico	16	Egypt	30	Panama	49
Poland	6	Uruguay	17	Senegal	32	South Korea	62
France	7	Croatia	18	Iran	34	Saudi Arabia	63

Seedings and Fifa Rankings are from when the World Cup draw took place (December 1 2017)

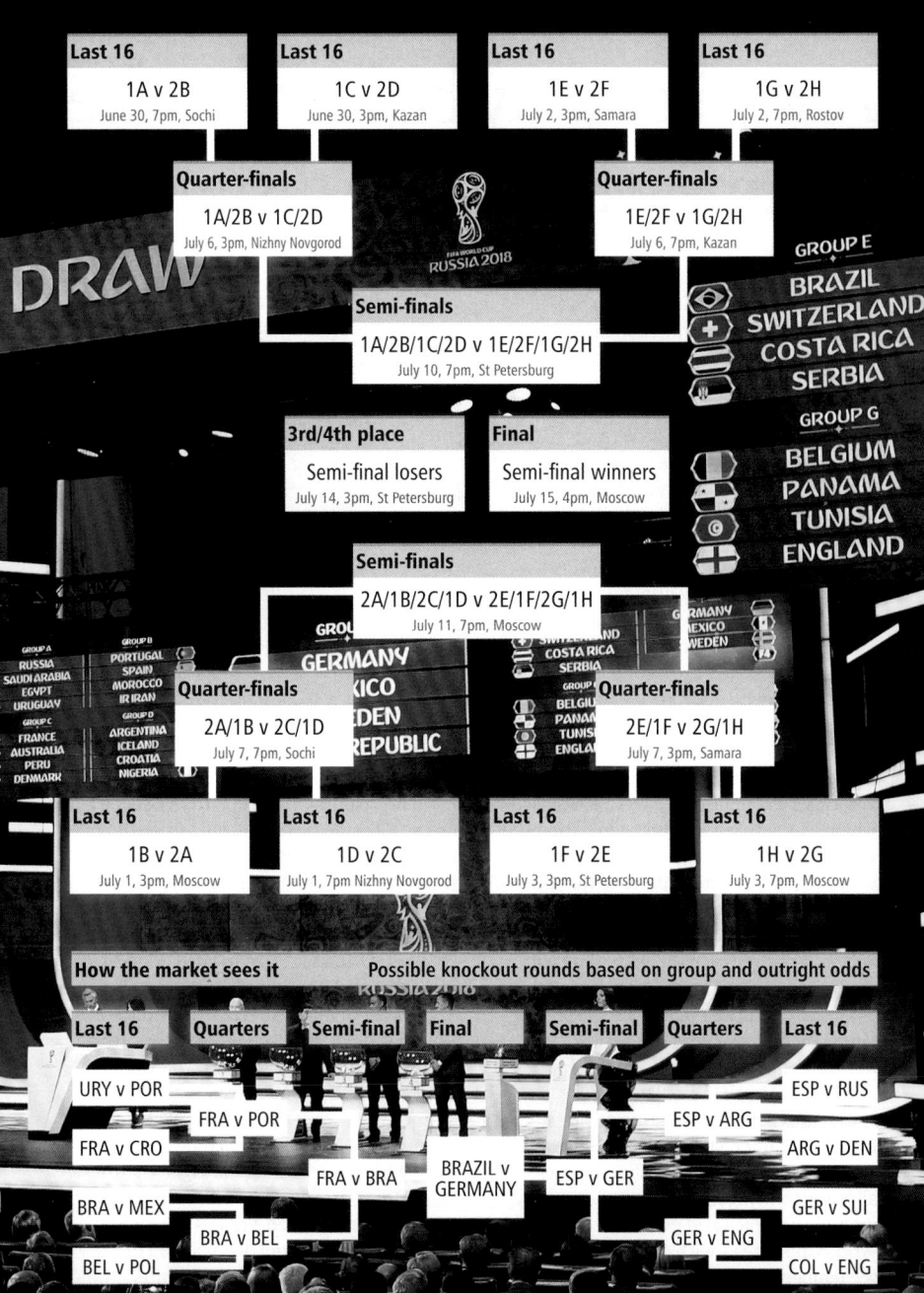

Last 16
1A v 2B
June 30, 7pm, Sochi

Last 16
1C v 2D
June 30, 3pm, Kazan

Last 16
1E v 2F
July 2, 3pm, Samara

Last 16
1G v 2H
July 2, 7pm, Rostov

Quarter-finals
1A/2B v 1C/2D
July 6, 3pm, Nizhny Novgorod

Quarter-finals
1E/2F v 1G/2H
July 6, 7pm, Kazan

Semi-finals
1A/2B/1C/2D v 1E/2F/1G/2H
July 10, 7pm, St Petersburg

3rd/4th place
Semi-final losers
July 14, 3pm, St Petersburg

Final
Semi-final winners
July 15, 4pm, Moscow

Semi-finals
2A/1B/2C/1D v 2E/1F/2G/1H
July 11, 7pm, Moscow

Quarter-finals
2A/1B v 2C/1D
July 7, 7pm, Sochi

Quarter-finals
2E/1F v 2G/1H
July 7, 3pm, Samara

Last 16
1B v 2A
July 1, 3pm, Moscow

Last 16
1D v 2C
July 1, 7pm Nizhny Novgorod

Last 16
1F v 2E
July 3, 3pm, St Petersburg

Last 16
1H v 2G
July 3, 7pm, Moscow

RUSSIA 2018
FIFA WORLD CUP

DRAW

GROUP E
BRAZIL
SWITZERLAND
COSTA RICA
SERBIA

GROUP G
BELGIUM
PANAMA
TUNISIA
ENGLAND

GROUP A
RUSSIA
SAUDI ARABIA
EGYPT
URUGUAY

GROUP B
PORTUGAL
SPAIN
MOROCCO
IR IRAN

GROUP C
FRANCE
AUSTRALIA
PERU
DENMARK

GROUP D
ARGENTINA
ICELAND
CROATIA
NIGERIA

GERMANY
MEXICO
SWEDEN
REPUBLIC

GERMANY
MEXICO
SWEDEN

SWITZERLAND
COSTA RICA
SERBIA

BELGIUM
PANAMA
TUNISIA
ENGLAND

How the market sees it   Possible knockout rounds based on group and outright odds

Last 16	Quarters	Semi-final	Final	Semi-final	Quarters	Last 16
URY v POR						ESP v RUS
	FRA v POR				ESP v ARG	
FRA v CRO						ARG v DEN
		FRA v BRA	BRAZIL v GERMANY	ESP v GER		
BRA v MEX						GER v SUI
	BRA v BEL				GER v ENG	
BEL v POL						COL v ENG

Photo by Shaun Botterill/Getty Images

Air miles may be key for the teams who go the distance

Germany took meticulousness to new heights at the last World Cup when, despite being offered their choice of the most luxurious hotels, spas and training facilities that Brazil had to offer, they chose to build their own base camp from scratch, *writes Steve Davies*.

Many in Berlin questioned the wisdom of constructing the purpose-built Campo Bahia given the time scale and that Brazil teems with stunning resorts, but those grumbles were quickly drowned out as Germany went on to win the tournament.

Having succeeded in doing it their own way four years ago it follows that few are daring to question why Germany have swapped Sochi – their training base before last summer's victorious Confederations Cup campaign – for Vatutinki, a complex used by CSKA Moscow which was still being built when nations were making their base-camp choices.

But that's German confidence for you. They've reasoned they need to be near Moscow because, by winning Group F and going on to reach the final, they will play in the Russian capital three times.

The 32 countries are inevitably spread far and wide in a country as vast as Russia with proximity to good transport links pivotal in all their planning.

Climate really isn't an issue during a Russian summer – the official online fan guide suggests supporters should cover all bases by bringing hats, sunglasses and umbrellas to each and every one of the 11 World Cup cities – with only Sochi likely to see temperatures anywhere near 30 degrees.

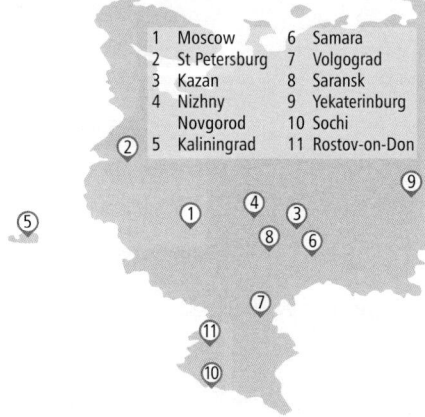

1	Moscow	6	Samara
2	St Petersburg	7	Volgograd
3	Kazan	8	Saransk
4	Nizhny Novgorod	9	Yekaterinburg
5	Kaliningrad	10	Sochi
		11	Rostov-on-Don

In an event which spans four time zones, it's travel sickness rather than sun stroke which is going to be more of an impediment to players and fans alike.

No one country is exempt from chalking up the air miles but some will fare better than others. England, for example, will travel just over 4,000 miles getting to and from their three group games from their forest retreat near St Petersburg. In contrast, Colombia's group-stage itinerary includes just 750 miles of travel.

Quite what finally determines choice of training camp, however, is anyone's guess. Was it relaxing in the lea of the oldest nuclear power station in Russia that drew Morocco to Voronezh, for example?

And presumably any welcome road-signs which proclaim war-ravaged Grozny "The Most Destroyed City on Earth" (as testified by the United Nations as recently as 2003), will be taken down ahead of Egypt's arrival in the Chechen capital.

Luzhniki Stadium, Moscow

Spartak Stadium, Moscow

Saint Petersburg Stadium

Kazan Arena

Nizhny Novgorod Stadium

Kaliningrad Stadium

Samara Arena

Volgograd Arena

Mordovia Arena, Saransk

Ekaterinburg Arena

Fisht Stadium, Sochi

Rostov Arena, Rostov-on-Don

The venues

	City	Games	Capacity	Home team	Timezone
Luzhniki Stadium	Moscow	7	80,000	Russia	BST+2
Spartak Stadium	Moscow	5	45,000	Spartak Moscow	BST+2
Saint Petersburg Stadium	St Petersburg	7	67,000	Zenit Saint Petersburg	BST+2
Kazan Arena	Kazan	6	45,000	Rubin Kazan	BST+2
Nizhny Novgorod Stadium	Nizhny Novgorod	6	45,000	Olimpiyets Nizhny Novgorod	BST+2
Kaliningrad Stadium	Kaliningrad	4	35,000	FC Baltika Kaliningrad	BST+1
Samara Arena	Samara	6	45,000	FC Krylya Sovetov	BST+3
Volgograd Arena	Volgograd	4	45,000	Rotor Volgograd	BST+2
Mordovia Arena	Saransk	4	44,000	FC Mordovia Saransk	BST+2
Ekaterinburg Arena	Yekaterinburg	4	35,000	FC Ural	BST+4
Fisht Stadium	Sochi	6	48,000	-	BST+2
Rostov Arena	Rostov-on-Don	5	45,000	FC Rostov	BST+2

ZONAL MARKING

Spain will press their claims without the ball

Looking at the runners and riders for this year's World Cup, there are probably fewer genuine contenders than in 2010 or 2014, *writes Michael Cox*.

There's Italy, no Holland – not even Chile, Ghana or the Ivory Coast, who had been considered among the dark horses ahead of the previous edition. The quality at the top of the tournament, however, appears to be stronger.

Neither the 2010 or the 2014 tournament offered many overwhelmingly impressive sides. Even the winners, Spain and Germany, were a touch underwhelming – both boasted an impressive generation of players thanks to continued investment in youth development, but Spain scored only eight goals in seven matches, and Germany only truly excelled once, in their legendary 7-1 win over Brazil.

This time, the five favourites are Spain, Germany, France, Brazil and Argentina, and all have the potential to to play genuinely good football. This could be a tournament that only truly comes alive in the latter stages.

The most unpredictable side amongst the favourites are Argentina, where Leo Messi is the bright spark in an otherwise unspectacular side lacking in genuine quality. While their manager Jorge Sampaoli might well be the competition's most talented coach, his preferred style is about pressing and attacking. That takes time on the training ground to perfect, and it also requires mobile defenders capable of playing a high line. Judging by Argentina's performance in the 6-1 thrashing by Spain in March, it could prove disastrous in Russia.

Brazil are a better side. Coutinho's quality means Neymar isn't the only source of creativity, while Willian plays a hard-working role on the right and Casemiro and Fernandinho are both top-quality holding midfielders ahead of a solid defence. Gabriel Jesus isn't quite the finished article, but at least Brazil aren't relying on Fred again.

The three European favourites, though, look particularly strong this time around.

France have their brightest generation of talent since they won the World Cup and European Championships back-to-back in 1998 and 2000, although there remains a question mark about how Didier Deschamps will structure his attack.

Southgate's three at the back could give England a tactical edge

If Gareth Southgate's England are to spring a surprise this summer, it might be because of their formation. England will probably be the only decent side fielding a three-man defence, which might cause opponents problems.

Since sealing qualification, England have played friendlies against Germany, Brazil, Holland and Italy, and have conceded just once – a debatable penalty against Italy. The three-man defence is

Antoine Griezmann prefers playing off a proper number nine, like Olivier Giroud, but this means using Kylian Mbappe out wide when he looks more suited to a central role. Deschamps has some major decisions ahead of the tournament.

The holders, Germany, have been boosted by the rise of the astonishingly quick Timo Werner since Euro 2016, and the Leipzig man seems likely to start up front. But Werner plays his best football on the counter-attack, and it's difficult to imagine Germany being allowed to play that way – opponents will defend deep against them and soak up pressure.

The defensive section of the side remains solid and

Unusually for a national team, Spain are able to press like a top club side

Photo by Denis Doyle/Getty Images

Toni Kroos is among the best controlling midfielders in this competition but, like Deschamps, Jogi Low could struggle to find the right balance.

That leaves Spain, who appear the most complete side. Julen Lopetegui is happy to overload his side with playmakers, likely to field five of Sergio Busquets, Koke, Tiago Alcantara, Andres Iniesta, David Silva and Isco. Whereas Spain have depended upon a false nine previously, now Rodrigo has emerged as a serious candidate to play up front, stretching defenders with his speed, while Diego Costa finally looks settled for his adopted country.

But Spain's real trump card is their pressing, perhaps the key concept in top-level club football recently, but often lacking at major tournaments. Spain are excellent at pressuring the opposition high up and pouncing quickly after a transition, which could them the edge over other candidates. For all their possession play, it could be Spain's attitude without the ball which helps them regain their crown.

working well, with Southgate fielding newcomers like James Tarkowski and Harry Maguire, as well as converting Kyle Walker to centre-back.

The problem, though, is further forward. The 3-4-3 has thrived in the Premier League recently because the wide players drift inside and create space on the overlap for the wing-backs. But Southgate clearly feels England aren't strong enough to play just two in central midfield, so he

has turned to 3-5-2 instead. This provides an extra man in midfield, but makes it more difficult to get players between the lines, and demands more from wing-backs.

It's been a while, too, since a genuine two-man strikeforce has thrived at the highest level. England are well-suited to playing on the break in the knockout stages, but when it comes to breaking down Tunisia and Panama, Southgate might need to field an extra attacker.

WORLD CUP JURY

Andy Brassell
European football expert

BACK GERMANY

Why Germany?

They have as many options as, say, France, but Jogi Low is far closer to knowing his best 11, and that's before you mention their experience.

Which fancied team might be vulnerable?

Argentina. They have a really tricky group and their attacking talent makes it too easy to forget how awful they were in the qualifiers.

Potential dark horse

Denmark were excellent for the second half of the qualifying campaign and have a really good set of young players around Christian Eriksen.

Who do you fancy to be top scorer?

Edinson Cavani. I think Uruguay are generally quite underrated. They have a straightforward group and Luis Suarez and Cavani are in the form of their lives.

What was your favourite World Cup?

1990. Probably because it was the first one when I watched every match but it had everything – hosts that deserved to win but didn't, the emergence of Baggio on the world stage, a great pantomime villain in Maradona and stadiums that oozed football culture.

Dan Childs
RP Sport football expert

BACK SPAIN

Why Spain?

They still have a core of tournament winners and David de Gea could make the difference in the tightest of matches.

Which fancied team might be vulnerable?

Argentina look a team of individuals. They had a tough time in qualifying and face some tricky matches against Croatia, Iceland and Nigeria in Group D.

Potential dark horse

Uruguay have a couple of world-class strikers, a decent draw and could be tough to defeat in a knockout scenario due to their rugged defence.

Who do you fancy to be top scorer?

Antoine Griezmann was the top marksman at Euro 2016 and could fill his boots against Australia, Peru and Denmark in Group C.

What was your favourite World Cup?

It has to be Italia 90 despite the pain of the penalty shootout defeat in Turin. As a Spurs fan it was great to see Paul Gascoigne playing at close to his peak and helping England to exceed expectations.

Michael Cox
Zonal Marking

BACK SPAIN

Why Spain?

They have a brilliant squad, a clear philosophy, and whereas other sides sit deep without the ball, Spain are capable of pressing high.

Which fancied team might be vulnerable?

Argentina are unpredictable. They have the world's best player, but Jorge Sampaoli wants them to play high up the pitch, and I'm not sure their defenders will cope.

Potential dark horse

They're handicapped by an extremely tough group, but I think Morocco are a decent side – six clean sheets in six qualification games tells the story.

Who do you fancy to be top scorer?

An outside bet – David Silva plays a more advanced role for Spain than Man City, has 35 international goals and is available at 175-1.

What was your favourite World Cup?

1998 was very enjoyable – all the contenders played open and attractive football, England were briefly promising and the hosts did well.

Sam Matterface
ITV World Cup commentator

BACK BRAZIL

Why Brazil?

Tite has got them defending well, they have two very good goalkeepers, some dazzling attacking talent and are much more disciplined.

Which fancied team might be vulnerable?

Argentina. I don't like the look of their group and they face a tricky opener against Iceland.

Potential dark horse

England. The draw is helpful for the top seeds so no side at huge odds will threaten but England might raise an eyebrow.

Who do you fancy to be top scorer?

Roberto Firmino. Brazil are the most attacking team and Firmino can fill his boots.

What was your favourite World Cup?

1986 – it's the first one I remember fully, Pfaff, Platini, Butrageano, Lineker, and... Maradona.

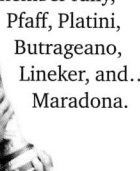

Mark O'Haire
Football betting analyst

BACK BRAZIL

Why Brazil?

It's hard to ignore the Selecao's turn around under Tite and a well-stocked squad, littered with world-class talent can go far.

Which fancied team might be vulnerable?

Argentina went through three coaches and 43 players during qualification, scoring fewer goals than Bolivia. An overreliance on Messi could hurt.

Potential dark horse

A solid base, a refreshed midfield, a deadly front two and a wonderfully competitive edge, Uruguay have been housed in arguably the weakest group.

Who do you fancy to be top scorer?

Timo Werner. The Leipzig speedster should spearhead a German side that scores goals for fun.

What was your favourite World Cup?

Forget the final and USA 94 is awash with so many iconic images. Diana Ross's penalty, Maradona's celebration, Ray Houghton's goal, I could go on...

Tim Vickery
South American journalist

BACK FRANCE

Why France?

It's close between a few of them but France's strength in depth could be the difference. If players suffer burnout they can make excellent replacements.

Which fancied team might be vulnerable?

Argentina. The group is difficult and their defence is a shambles. Just look at the way they collapsed in the November friendly defeat to Nigeria.

Potential dark horse

Uruguay have freshened up their midfield with the likes of Bentancur and Valverde who make them play plus they've still got Suarez, Cavani and Godin.

Who do you fancy to be top scorer?

Romelu Lukaku could fill his boots in that opener against Panama, who don't defend well. He will get excellent service from Hazard and De Bruyne.

What was your favourite World Cup?

1986 was the last truly great finals and it was the tournament which made me fall in love with football all over again having been music mad in my teenage years.

GROUP A

Uruguay have the firepower to disappoint the hosts

Uruguay's group price is coming under pressure but there is still enough juice left in it to back the South Americans to see off hosts Russia, Egypt and Saudi Arabia, *writes Mark Langdon*.

The key to all of this is just how much home advantage will be worth to Russia and whether they will they benefit from refereeing decisions, crowd support, familiar surroundings and other such comforts because on paper their actual team could struggle to make the last 16.

Playing at home may be decisive enough, although on value grounds there could still be some mileage in taking Egypt to finish second with Mohamed Salah showing for Liverpool that he is on the verge of moving into the world-class bracket.

However, they could both be playing catch-up to Uruguay. They are in the unique position of possessing two elite strikers and that could prove to be the difference in the race for top spot.

Edinson Cavani became Paris Saint-Germain's all-time leading scorer in January and he was the top marksman in a high-quality Conmebol qualifying field as Uruguay finished second to Brazil.

They may have even got closer to the summit had Luis Suarez not missed five matches. Even so, only Brazil scored more, only Brazil won more, and Uruguay can also boast relatively recent pedigree with a semi-final run in 2010, followed by Copa America glory in 2011.

Oscar Tabarez's outfit are not just about those two players with a rock-solid defence, led by Atletico Madrid centre-backs Diego Godin and Jose Gimenez. For Gimenez there will be plenty more tournaments but for Godin (32 years old), Suarez (31) and Cavani (31) this is likely to be their last World Cup so expect them to give everything for the cause.

Russia have the benefit of potentially getting an easy three points on the board in their opener against Saudi Arabia, but there is no desire to get involved in backing the injury-hit hosts at odds-on to overcome Egypt in the second game.

The difference in ability between the teams is not as great as the odds suggest but the short prices for Saudi Arabia to finish last are spot-on.

Saudi Arabia lost away to Japan, Australia and UAE in qualifying and won't be able to rely on their much better home form in Russia.

Photo by Ronald Martinez/Getty Images

Edinson Cavani and Luis Suarez

Recommendation

★★☆☆☆ **Uruguay to win Group A**

Group-stage performances since France 98

	Pot	P	W	Q	1998 Group	Pos	2002 Group	Pos	2006 Group	Pos	2010 Group	Pos	2014 Group	Pos
Russia	1	2	0	0	-	-	H	3	-	-	-	-	H	3
Uruguay	2	3	1	2	-	-	A	3	-	-	A	1	D	2
Egypt	3	0	0	0	-	-	-	-	-	-	-	-	-	-
Saudi Arabia	4	3	0	0	C	4	E	4	H	4	-	-	-	-

To win Group A
Win only

	Bet365	BtBrt	Betfair	Btfrd	Btwy	Boyle	Coral	Hills	Lads	P Power	Sky	188
Uruguay	11-10	Evs	Evs	Evs	11-10	21-20	Evs	5-6	10-11	Evs	Evs	Evs
Russia	5-4	11-8	11-8	13-8	11-8	6-4	6-4	7-4	13-8	6-5	6-4	6-5
Egypt	11-2	11-2	11-2	4	6	9-2	5	11-2	11-2	11-2	5	6
S Arabia	40	33	33	25	20	33	25	20	25	35	25	30

Russia v Saudi Arabia
4pm, Thursday June 14, ITV

	Bet365	BtBrt	Betfair	Btfrd	Btwy	Boyle	Coral	Hills	Lads	P Power	Sky	188
Russia	3-10	2-7	3-10	3-10	3-10	3-10	1-3	3-10	1-3	3-10	1-3	1-3
Draw	15-4	7-2	4	18-5	15-4	16-5	10-3	15-4	10-3	4	18-5	19-5
S Arabia	11	9	19-2	10	10	17-2	10	9	10	8	10	10

Egypt v Uruguay
1pm, Friday June 15, BBC

	Bet365	BtBrt	Betfair	Btfrd	Btwy	Boyle	Coral	Hills	Lads	P Power	Sky	188
Uruguay	13-20	4-6	4-5	7-10	8-11	4-6	4-6	8-11	4-6	3-4	8-11	14-19
Draw	5-2	5-2	12-5	13-5	11-4	12-5	12-5	12-5	12-5	23-10	13-5	11-4
Egypt	5	15-4	4	19-5	7-2	15-4	21-5	4	21-5	4	4	19-5

Russia v Egypt
7pm, Tuesday June 19, BBC

	Bet365	BtBrt	Betfair	Btfrd	Btwy	Boyle	Coral	Hills	Lads	P Power	Sky	188
Russia	17-20	4-5	17-20	5-6	5-6	4-5	17-20	4-5	17-20	8-11	17-20	7-8
Draw	23-10	9-4	12-5	12-5	12-5	11-5	11-5	5-2	11-5	9-4	5-2	13-5
Egypt	7-2	16-5	15-4	10-3	10-3	16-5	13-4	16-5	13-4	7-2	10-3	16-5

Uruguay v Saudi Arabia
4pm, Wednesday June 20, BBC

	Bet365	BtBrt	Betfair	Btfrd	Btwy	Boyle	Coral	Hills	Lads	P Power	Sky	188
Uruguay	2-7	2-9	3-10	1-4	1-4	2-9	1-4	2-9	1-4	1-4	1-4	3-11
Draw	4	4	4	9-2	9-2	9-2	21-5	9-2	21-5	7-2	4	23-5
S Arabia	10	10	10	11	10	11	14	10	14	9	11	21-2

Saudi Arabia v Egypt
3pm, Monday June 25, ITV

	Bet365	BetBright	Betfair	Betfred	Betway	Boyle	Hills	P Power	Sky Bet
Egypt	8-11	7-10	8-11	7-10	7-10	4-6	3-4	8-13	8-11
Draw	5-2	23-10	13-5	5-2	23-10	23-10	12-5	12-5	5-2
S Arabia	4	15-4	9-2	4	15-4	15-4	4	4	4

Uruguay v Russia
3pm, Monday June 25, ITV

	Bet365	BetBright	Betfair	Betfred	Betway	Boyle	Hills	P Power	Sky Bet
Uruguay	7-5	11-8	17-10	29-20	11-8	7-5	7-5	6-4	6-4
Russia	2	19-10	15-8	19-10	19-10	9-5	2	7-4	2
Draw	11-5	2	2	21-10	2	2	21-10	15-8	2

Prices correct March 28 2018

Profile

Since competing as Russia for the first time at USA 94 the 2018 hosts have had a miserable time of it at the World Cup, never going any further than the group stage in three attempts.

Coach Stanislav Cherchesov has been given a target of reaching the semi-final on home soil, although he said: "We should qualify for the knockout stage and then we'll see."

How they qualified

Automatically as hosts. Last year's Confederations Cup warm-up did not go well, with a group-stage elimination.

The manager

Cherchesov got the job after leading Legia Warsaw to a Polish domestic double in 2016. He walked away from Legia and Dinamo Moscow following disputes.

The squad

There have been great changes since Russia's swift Euro 2016 departure, with old stagers such as Sergei Ignashevich, the Berezutski twins and Roman Shirokov no longer around. But the squad is still heavily based around domestic players – no great surprise as footballers in Russia pay only 13 per cent tax and benefit from a rule by which at least five homegrown players need to be in every starting 11.

Cherchesov has put his trust in youth, picking offensive players in a 3-4-2-1 formation, and that was highlighted in an entertaining 3-3 friendly draw with Spain in November.

Defence remains a concern and there is a lack of experience in front of goalkeeping captain Igor Akinfeev, although Cherchesov has beefed up his options with the nationalisation of excellent Brazilian-born right wing-back Mario Fernandes and left wing-back Konstantin Rausch.

Big things are expected of midfielders Aleksandr Golovin and Aleksei

Factfile

FA founded 1912
www rfs.ru
Head coach Stanislav Cherchesov
Date qualified Qualified as hosts

Strengths

☑ Home advantage and a decent draw
☑ Golovin, Miranchuk and Dzagoev form part of a strong midfield

Weaknesses

☒ Lack international experience at centre-back
☒ Mentality – they have exited at the group stage in seven of their eight tournaments since they started competing as Russia

Star rating ★☆☆☆☆

Fixtures

1 June 14, 4pm v Saudi Arabia, Luzhniki Stadium, Moscow
2 June 19, 7pm v Egypt, Saint Petersburg
3 June 25, 3pm v Uruguay, Samara

Base Saint Petersburg
Total distance 1,850 miles

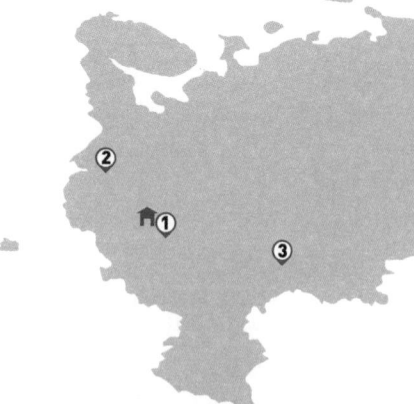

Fyodor Smolov enjoying the moment after scoring against New Zealand at the Confederations Cup

Miranchuk while fragile playmaker Alan Dzagoev will be crucial if he stays fit.

Fyodor Smolov will have to carry most of the goalscoring burden after Zenit's Aleksandr Kokorin was ruled out of the tournament with a knee injury.

Key man

Dzagoev was the joint-top goalscorer at Euro 2012 but played just 61 minutes at the 2014 World Cup before missing Euro 2016 and the 2017 Confederations Cup because of injury.

"Unfortunately, Alan is highly injury-prone," Cherchesov told Fifa.com. "He's got the whole package, good technique, pace, ability on the ball and vision."

Rising star

Aleksei Miranchuk is a dynamic goal threat from an advanced midfield position. The Lokomotiv Moscow man has a sweet left foot and has been instrumental in their title challenge.

Wildcard

How Russia could do with a defensive midfielder like Lokomotiv's Igor Denisov. However, Denisov had several bust-ups with Cherchesov during their time together at Dinamo with the player meddling in team affairs and calling the boss a "clown."

Prospects

An opener against Saudi Arabia gives Russia the perfect opportunity to grow into the tournament before the likely pivotal clash with Egypt. There are small signs of improvement but anything more than the last 16 would be outstanding.

How to back them

Russia's qualification price is tight so if anything consider them for a first-round exit. Injuries to Kokorin and centre-backs Georgi Dzhikiya and Viktor Vasin are blows.

World Cup record		Group stage(s)						Knockout rounds					
		P	W	D	L	F	A	P	W	D	L	F	A
Uruguay 1930	Did not enter	-	-	-	-	-	-	-	-	-	-	-	-
Italy 1934	Did not enter	-	-	-	-	-	-	-	-	-	-	-	-
France 1938	Did not enter	-	-	-	-	-	-	-	-	-	-	-	-
Brazil 1950	Did not enter	-	-	-	-	-	-	-	-	-	-	-	-
Switzerland 1954	Did not enter	-	-	-	-	-	-	-	-	-	-	-	-
Sweden 1958	Quarter-final	4	2	1	1	5	4	1	0	0	1	0	2
Chile 1962	Quarter-final	3	2	1	0	8	5	1	0	0	1	1	2
England 1966	Fourth place	3	3	0	0	6	1	3	1	0	2	4	5
Mexico 1970	Quarter-final	3	2	1	0	6	1	1	0	1	0	0	0
Germany 1974	DNQ (forfeit)	-	-	-	-	-	-	-	-	-	-	-	-
Argentina 1978	Did not qualify	-	-	-	-	-	-	-	-	-	-	-	-
Spain 1982	2nd group stage	5	2	2	1	7	4	-	-	-	-	-	-
Mexico 1986	Round of 16	3	2	1	0	9	1	1	0	1	0	2	2
Italy 1990	Group stage	3	1	0	2	4	4	-	-	-	-	-	-
USA 1994	Group stage	3	1	0	2	7	6	-	-	-	-	-	-
France 1998	Did not qualify	-	-	-	-	-	-	-	-	-	-	-	-
Korea/Japan 2002	Group stage	3	1	0	2	4	4	-	-	-	-	-	-
Germany 2006	Did not qualify	-	-	-	-	-	-	-	-	-	-	-	-
South Africa 2010	Did not qualify	-	-	-	-	-	-	-	-	-	-	-	-
Brazil 2014	Group stage	3	0	2	1	2	3	-	-	-	-	-	-
Totals		33	16	8	9	58	33	7	1	2	4	7	11

Competed as USSR until 1990

Continental championships (best perfomance)

Uefa European Championship	Winners (1)	1960

World Cup head-to-heads

Eusebio scored the only goal when Russia last met their possible last 16 opponents, Portugal, at the World Cup

Photo by Mirrorpix

Russia v	P	W	D	L	F	A	Latest	Russia v	P	W	D	L	F	A	Latest
Argentina	1	0	0	1	0	2	1990	Mexico	1	0	1	0	0	0	1970
Belgium	5	2	1	2	9	7	2014	Poland	1	0	1	0	0	0	1982
Brazil	3	0	0	3	1	6	1994	Portugal	1	0	0	1	1	2	1966
Colombia	1	0	1	0	4	4	1962	Serbia	1	1	0	0	2	0	1962
Croatia	1	1	0	0	2	0	1962	South Korea	1	0	1	0	1	1	2014
England	2	1	1	0	3	2	1958	Sweden	2	0	0	2	1	5	1994
France	1	0	1	0	1	1	1986	Tunisia	1	1	0	0	2	0	2002
Germany	1	0	0	1	1	2	1966	Uruguay	2	1	1	0	2	1	1970
Japan	1	0	0	1	0	1	2002								

90 mins only, includes games played as USSR and against Yugoslavia and West Germany

It's 2010 and Russia and Qatar celebrate their winning bids to host the 2018 and 2022 World Cups

Players used in friendlies in 2017-2018		Career			2017-18 friendlies			
Pos	Club	Age	P	G	P	G	🟨	🟥
GK Andrey Lunyov	Zenit	26	3	-	3	-	-	-
GK Igor Akinfeev	CSKA Moscow	32	104	-	7	-	-	-
DEF Mario Fernandes	CSKA Moscow	27	3	-	3	-	-	-
DEF Andrey Semenov	Akhmat	29	8	-	3	-	-	-
DEF Fyodor Kudryashov	Rubin	31	17	-	10	-	1	-
DEF Giorgi Dzhikiya	Spartak Moscow	24	8	-	5	-	-	-
DEF Igor Smolnikov	Zenit	29	25	-	6	-	-	-
DEF Ilya Kutepov	Spartak Moscow	24	6	-	3	-	-	-
DEF Roman Neustadter	Fenerbahce	30	6	-	2	-	-	-
DEF Roman Shishkin	FK Krasnodar	31	16	-	2	-	-	-
DEF Ruslan Kambolov	Rubin	28	2	-	1	-	-	-
DEF Viktor Vasin	CSKA Moscow	29	13	2	7	2	1	-
DEF Vladimir Granat	Rubin	31	11	1	2	-	-	-
DEF Dmitri Kombarov	Spartak Moscow	31	47	2	5	-	-	-
MID Konstantin Rausch	Dinamo Moscow	28	5	-	5	-	-	-
MID Yuri Zhirkov	Zenit	34	82	2	7	-	-	-
MID Alan Dzagoev	CSKA Moscow	27	55	9	5	-	-	-
MID Aleksandr Golovin	CSKA Moscow	22	17	2	6	-	-	-
MID Aleksandr Samedov	Spartak Moscow	33	44	6	8	-	-	-
MID Aleksey Miranchuk	Lok. Moscow	22	16	4	10	3	-	-
MID Alexandr Erokhin	Zenit	28	17	-	10	-	1	-
MID Anton Miranchuk	Lok. Moscow	22	4	-	4	-	1	-
MID Anton Shvets	Akhmat	25	1	-	1	-	-	-
MID Daler Kuzyaev	Zenit	25	4	-	4	-	1	-
MID Denis Glushakov	Spartak Moscow	31	57	5	6	-	1	-
MID Denis Cheryshev	Villarreal	27	10	1	1	-	-	-
MID Dmitriy Tarasov	Lok. Moscow	31	8	1	3	-	-	-
MID Magomed Ozdoev	Zenit	25	12	1	2	-	-	-
MID Roman Zobnin	Spartak Moscow	24	10	-	4	-	-	-
MID Vladislav Ignatjev	Lok. Moscow	31	3	-	1	-	-	-
MID Yuri Gazinskiy	FK Krasnodar	28	5	-	1	-	-	-
ATT Aleksandr Bukharov	Unattached	33	9	1	4	1	-	-
ATT Aleksandr Kokorin	Zenit	27	48	12	4	-	-	-
ATT Anton Zabolotny	Zenit	27	5	-	5	-	1	-
ATT Dmitriy Poloz	Zenit	26	15	2	6	2	-	-
ATT Fedor Smolov	FK Krasnodar	28	30	12	8	5	1	-
ATT Maksim Kanunnikov	Khabarovsk	26	12	-	2	-	-	-

Correct scores

	Competitive	Friendly
1-0	1	3
2-0	2	-
2-1	1	1
3-0*	1	2
3-1	-	-
3-2	-	-
4-0	1	1
4-1	-	-
4-2	-	2
4-3	-	-
0-0	-	2
1-1	3	3
2-2	-	-
3-3	-	2
4-4	-	-
0-1	3	1
0-2	-	1
1-2	2	2
0-3	1	1
1-3	-	2
2-3	-	-
0-4	-	-
1-4	-	-
2-4	-	1
3-4	-	1
Other	1	-

Since Brazil 2014

Half-time/full-time double results

Win/Win	5	33%	Win 1st half	6	40%
Draw/Win	1	7%	Win 2nd half	5	33%
Lose/Win	0	0%	Win both halves	3	20%
Win/Draw	1	7%	Goal both halves	3	20%
Draw/Draw	2	13%			
Lose/Draw	0	0%	**Overall**		
Win/Lose	0	0%	● Win	40%	
Draw/Lose	2	13%	● Draw	20%	
Lose/Lose	4	27%	● Lose	40%	

Overall: W6, D3, L6 in 15 completed competitive games since Brazil 2014

Under & over goals

11 (73%)	Over 1.5	4 (27%)
6 (40%)	Over 2.5	9 (60%)
2 (13%)	Over 3.5	13 (87%)
1 (7%)	Over 4.5	14 (93%)

Both teams to score

6 (40%)	Both score	9 (60%)
1 (7%)	& win	14 (93%)
2 (13%)	& lose	13 (87%)

In 15 completed competitive games since Brazil 2014

Clean sheets

5 (33%)	Clean sheets	10 (67%)
5 (33%)	Win to nil	10 (67%)

4 (27%)	Fail to score	11 (73%)
4 (27%)	Lose to nil	11 (73%)

When they score

● For ● Against

Total match goals by half

10 (59%)	1st half	7 (41%)
F		A

13 (65%)	2nd half	7 (35%)
F		A

Goals for & against by half

10 (43%)	For	13 (57%)
1st		2nd

7 (50%)	Against	7 (50%)
1st		2nd

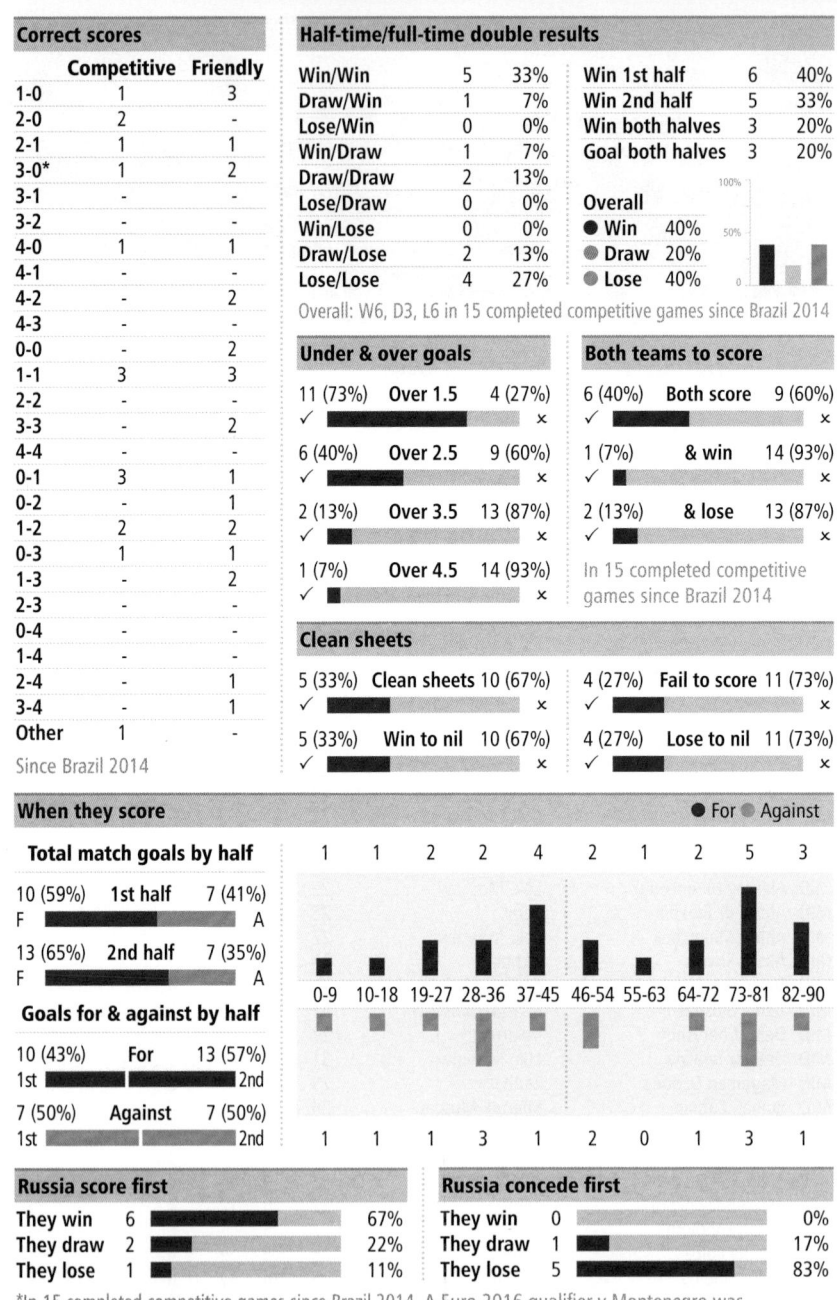

	1	1	2	2	4	2	1	2	5	3
	0-9	10-18	19-27	28-36	37-45	46-54	55-63	64-72	73-81	82-90
	1	1	1	3	1	2	0	1	3	1

Russia score first

They win	6	67%
They draw	2	22%
They lose	1	11%

Russia concede first

They win	0	0%
They draw	1	17%
They lose	5	83%

*In 15 completed competitive games since Brazil 2014. A Euro 2016 qualifier v Montenegro was abandoned after 67 minutes with the score at 0-0. Match awarded to Russia 3-0

How to read the data

The team stats in this book are intended to reflect common betting markets and include 90-minute scores in competitive games since the final of Brazil 2014.

Players used in qualifying

GK goalkeeper, DEF defender, MID midfielder, ATT attacker. Clubs current as we went to press on March 28, includes loans. Age shows players age on the day of the opening match of Russia 2018. P matches played, G goals scored.

1 Correct scores

The number of occurrences of each scoreline. Goals scored by the team being profiled are given first, whether the game was at home, away or on neutral ground, so 1-0 represents a 1-0 win, 0-1 a 1-0 loss, regardless of where the match took place. For example, since the final of Brazil 2014, Russia have won one and lost three competitive matches 1-0. Note that where a match was awarded, the official result is shown in the correct scores table but the actual result has been used to generate the stats. These scorelines are denoted by an asterisk.

2 Half-time/full-time double results

The number of occurrences of each possible combination of results at half time and full time. For example, win/win means that a team was ahead at both half time and full time. Includes stats for the related win/score by half markets.

3 Under & over goals

Games in which the total number of match goals (goals scored by the home team plus goals scored by the away team) exceeded 1.5, 2.5, 3.5 and 4.5.

4 Both teams to score, Both score & win, Both score & lose

Games in which both teams scored a goal, games in which both teams scored and the team being profiled won, games in which both teams scored and the team being profiled lost.

5 Clean sheets, Win to nil, Fail to score, Lose to nil

Games in which a team conceded no goals, won without conceding, did not score a goal and did not score a goal and were beaten.

6 Goal times

Numbers of goals scored and conceded at different

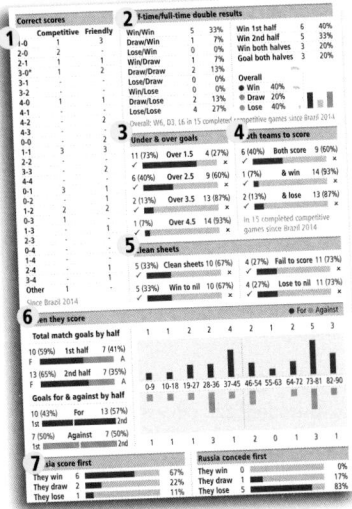

times during a team's matches. Note that 37-45 and 92-90 include added time.

7 If …

Number of games in which a team goes on to win, lose or draw after scoring or conceding the first goal.

Goalscorers

Total number of goals scored, first goal denotes first goal of game (own goals do not count – if an own goal is the first goal of a game, the first subsequent goal counts for betting purposes), anytime denotes any goalscoring appearance, % shows percentage of total team goals. Appearance details are also given for each goalscorer. Only games in qualifying for Russia 2018 are included.

Bookings

Average bookings make-ups in qualifying, 10pts for a yellow card, 25pts for red, maximum 35pts per player. Does not include cards for opponents.

Distance travelled

Three round trips, there and back again, as the crow flies from each team's basecamp to the cities where their group matches are being played, rounded to the nearest 50 miles.

Stats from Opta and Soccerbase

SAUDI ARABIA

GROUP A

Profile

Saudi Arabia will be competing in their first World Cup since 2006. High expectations from the Saudi Arabian Football Federation look unrealistic considering the Green Falcons have not won a match in three attempts since their excellent run to the last 16 at USA 94.

How they qualified

They were the only Asian nation to score in all ten of their matches in the final round of qualifying, but they lost at fellow group heavyweights Japan, Australia and UAE.

The manager

Juan Antonio Pizzi, who won the 2016 Copa America with Chile but then failed to guide them to the World Cup, was appointed just before the finals draw following a turbulent few months.

Bert van Marwijk led Saudi Arabia out of qualifying before being sacked after a dispute, while Argentinian replacement Edgardo Bauza lasted just two official November friendlies, which ended in defeats by Portugal (3-0) and Bulgaria (1-0).

The squad

A controversial agreement drawn up by the SAFF saw nine of the home-based players loaned to Spanish clubs in January, however, Saudi players have previously not had much luck abroad.

Veteran centre-back Osama Hawsawi played one league game for Anderlecht and Saeed Al-Muwallad, now with Levante, did not even get that far with Farense in Portugal after donning the club colours without an agreement with Al-Ittihad which eventually saw the deal fall through.

Mohammad Al-Sahlawi scored 16 goals in Asian qualifying, although only two of those came in the final campaign phase. The fact that eight goals came in two appearances against Timor Leste does nothing to dispel the notion that he is a flat-track bully.

Hawsawi remains a key defensive cog,

Factfile

FA founded 1956
www thesaff.com.sa
Head coach Juan Antonio Pizzi
Date qualified September 5, 2017

Strengths

☑ Decent forward options and equalled Japan's 17-goal haul in final qualifying

☑ Former striker Pizzi looks a solid managerial appointment

Weaknesses

☒ Nowhere near enough experience of football outside Saudi Arabia

☒ Don't travel particularly well

Star rating ★☆☆☆☆

Fixtures

1 June 14, 4pm v Russia, Luzhniki Stadium, Moscow

2 June 20, 4pm v Uruguay, Rostov-on-Don

3 June 25, 3pm v Egypt, Volgograd

Base Saint Petersburg

Total distance 4,650 miles

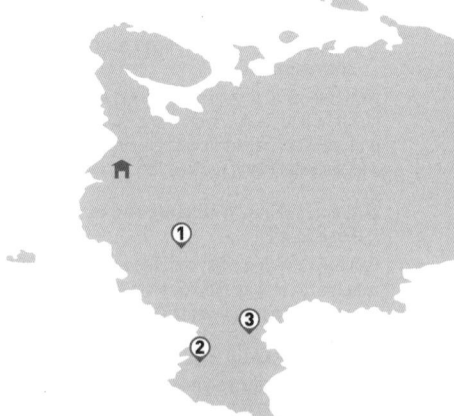

Nawaf Al-Abed is a man for the big occasion

while the versatile Yasser Al-Shahrani and midfielder Nawaf Al-Abed are also expected to be influential. All three were part of the Al-Hilal side beaten in the Asian Champions League final in November. However, many of the best players in that side are foreign so their success may not be a reliable World Cup pointer.

Key man

Nicknamed the Brave One after putting himself forward for three nerve-jangling late penalties in qualifying, Al-Abed was crucial in qualifying. As well as his spot-kicks the winger also proved decisive with both assists in a 2-2 draw with Australia.

Rising star

The speedy 23-year-old Al-Muwallad replaced Al-Sahlawi at half-time in the final qualifier against Japan and scored the goal which booked Saudi Arabia their spot in Russia.

Wild card

Former England youth international Mukhtar Ali received Saudi citizenship in 2017. The box-to-box midfielder failed to make the grade at Chelsea and is now trying to carve out a career at their unofficial feeder club Vitesse.

Prospects

Not good. Saudi Arabia's World Cup campaign is likely to be a three-and-out visit to Russia, although playing the opening game of the World Cup against the hosts on the final day of Ramadan is likely to be a fantastic occasion for the Green Falcons.

How to back them

Al-Abed to be their top scorer. The penalty taker bagged five times in the final, more difficult, round of qualifying when nobody else managed more than two goals. If Saudi Arabia score he looks the man most likely to notch.

SAUDI ARABIA

GROUP A

World Cup record

World Cup record		Group stage(s)						Knockout rounds					
		P	W	D	L	F	A	P	W	D	L	F	A
Uruguay 1930	Not part of Fifa	-	-	-	-	-	-	-	-	-	-	-	-
Italy 1934	Not part of Fifa	-	-	-	-	-	-	-	-	-	-	-	-
France 1938	Not part of Fifa	-	-	-	-	-	-	-	-	-	-	-	-
Brazil 1950	Not part of Fifa	-	-	-	-	-	-	-	-	-	-	-	-
Switzerland 1954	Not part of Fifa	-	-	-	-	-	-	-	-	-	-	-	-
Sweden 1958	Did not enter	-	-	-	-	-	-	-	-	-	-	-	-
Chile 1962	Did not enter	-	-	-	-	-	-	-	-	-	-	-	-
England 1966	Did not enter	-	-	-	-	-	-	-	-	-	-	-	-
Mexico 1970	Did not enter	-	-	-	-	-	-	-	-	-	-	-	-
Germany 1974	Did not enter	-	-	-	-	-	-	-	-	-	-	-	-
Argentina 1978	Did not qualify	-	-	-	-	-	-	-	-	-	-	-	-
Spain 1982	Did not qualify	-	-	-	-	-	-	-	-	-	-	-	-
Mexico 1986	Did not qualify	-	-	-	-	-	-	-	-	-	-	-	-
Italy 1990	Did not qualify	-	-	-	-	-	-	-	-	-	-	-	-
USA 1994	Round of 16	3	2	0	1	4	3	1	0	0	1	1	3
France 1998	Group stage	3	0	1	2	2	7	-	-	-	-	-	-
Korea/Japan 2002	Group stage	3	0	0	3	0	12	-	-	-	-	-	-
Germany 2006	Group stage	3	0	1	2	2	7	-	-	-	-	-	-
South Africa 2010	Did not qualify	-	-	-	-	-	-	-	-	-	-	-	-
Brazil 2014	Did not qualify	-	-	-	-	-	-	-	-	-	-	-	-
Totals		12	2	2	8	8	29	1	0	0	1	1	3

Continental championships (best perfomance)

AFC Asian Cup	Winners (3)	1984, 1988, 1996

World Cup head-to-heads

Saudi Arabia v	P	W	D	L	F	A	Latest	Saudi Arabia v	P	W	D	L	F	A	Latest
Belgium	1	1	0	0	1	0	1994	Morocco	1	1	0	0	2	1	1994
Denmark	1	0	0	1	0	1	1998	Spain	1	0	0	1	0	1	2006
France	1	0	0	1	0	4	1998	Sweden	1	0	0	1	1	3	1994
Germany	1	0	0	1	0	8	2002	Tunisia	1	0	1	0	2	2	2006

90 mins only

How they qualified

Group A	P	W	D	L	F	A	GD	P
Saudi Arabia	8	6	2	0	28	4	24	20
UAE	8	5	2	1	27	4	23	17
Palestine	8	4	2	2	24	5	19	14
Malaysia	8	2	0	6	7	29	-22	6
Timor-Leste	8	0	0	8	0	44	-44	0

Saudi Arabia. (1) 3-2 (0).........Palestine
Saudi Arabia. (5) 7-0 (0)..... Timor-Leste
Malaysia .... (0) 1-2 (0).. Saudi Arabia
  Match awarded 3-0 to Saudi Arabia
Saudi Arabia. (1) 2-1 (1)................ UAE
Palestine .... (0) 0-0 (0).. Saudi Arabia
Timor-Leste .... (0) 0-10(4).. Saudi Arabia
Saudi Arabia. (0) 2-0 (0).........Malaysia

UAE............... (0) 1-1 (1).. Saudi Arabia

Group B	P	W	D	L	F	A	GD	P
Japan	10	6	2	2	17	7	10	20
Saudi Arabia	10	6	1	3	17	10	7	19
Australia	10	5	4	1	16	11	5	19
UAE	10	4	1	5	10	13	-3	13
Iraq	10	3	2	5	11	12	-1	11
Thailand	10	0	2	8	6	24	-18	2

Saudi Arabia. (0) 1-0 (0)......... Thailand

Iraq .... (1) 1-2 (0).. Saudi Arabia
Saudi Arabia. (1) 2-2 (1).........Australia
Saudi Arabia. (0) 3-0 (0)................. UAE
Japan............ (1) 2-1 (0).. Saudi Arabia
Thailand......... (0) 0-3 (1).. Saudi Arabia
Saudi Arabia. (0) 1-0 (0).................Iraq
Australia .... (2) 3-2 (2).. Saudi Arabia
UAE............... (0) 2-1 (1).. Saudi Arabia
Saudi Arabia. (0) 1-0 (0).............Japan

Full qualifying results 228-241

Saudi Arabia celebrate the 1-0 win over Japan that sealed their first finals appearance since 2006

Pos	Players used in qualifying	Club	Career Age	P	G	Qualification P	G	🟦	⬛
GK	Khaled Sharahili	Al-Ra'ed	31	10	-	8	-	-	-
GK	Abdullah Al-Mayoof	Al-Hilal	31	5	-	2	-	-	-
GK	Yasser Al-Mosailem	Al-Ahli	34	31	-	7	-	1	-
GK	Mohammed Al Owais	Al-Ahli	26	5	-	1	-	-	-
DEF	Mohammed Al-Fatil	Al-Ahli	26	7	-	1	-	-	-
DEF	Mohammed Al-Burayk	Al-Ahli	25	7	1	2	-	-	-
DEF	Mohammed Qassem	Al-Ittihad	23	5	-	1	-	-	-
DEF	Osama Hawsawi	Al-Hilal	34	128	7	17	1	2	1
DEF	Motaz Hawsawi	Al-Ahli	26	14	-	4	-	-	-
DEF	Omar Hawsawi	Al-Nassr	32	36	3	13	1	-	-
DEF	Yasser Al-Shahrani	Al-Hilal	26	31	-	11	-	-	-
DEF	Abdullah Al Zoari	Al-Hilal	30	57	1	10	-	-	-
DEF	Yassen Hamza	Al-Ittihad	27	5	-	3	-	-	-
DEF	Hassan Muath Fallatah	Al-Shabab	32	66	4	8	-	2	-
DEF	Mansour Al-Harbi	Al-Ahli	30	36	1	8	-	-	-
MID	Abdulmalek Al-Khaibri	Al-Shabab	32	34	-	17	-	2	-
MID	Abdulaziz Al-Jebreen	Al-Nassr	28	4	-	3	-	-	-
MID	Taisir Al-Jassam	Al-Ahli	33	126	18	18	6	1	-
MID	Shaye Ali Sharahili	Al-Qadsiah	28	4	-	1	-	-	-
MID	Salman Al Faraj	Al-Hilal	28	36	2	17	1	1	-
MID	Salem Al Dawsari	Villarreal	26	28	4	2	1	1	-
MID	Abdullah Otayf	Al-Hilal	25	12	1	2	-	-	-
MID	Abdulmajeed A-Ruwali	Al-Taawoun	31	11	2	3	-	-	-
MID	Waleed Bakshween	Al-Ahli	28	16	-	1	-	1	-
MID	Nawaf Al Abed	Al-Hilal	28	43	8	13	5	2	-
MID	Abdulfattah Asiri	Al-Ahli	24	11	-	2	-	-	-
MID	Yahya Al Shehri	Leganes	27	52	5	18	5	-	-
MID	Hussain Al-Mogahwi	Al-Ahli	30	15	2	3	-	-	-
ATT	Fahad Al Muwallad	Levante	23	41	10	12	4	1	-
ATT	Mohammad Al-Sahlawi	Al-Nassr	31	36	28	14	16	1	-
ATT	Mukhtar Fallatah	Al-Hilal	30	13	2	2	-	-	-
ATT	Naif Hazazi	Unattached	29	56	14	8	1	-	-
ATT	Nasser Al-Shamrani	Al-Shabab	34	78	19	5	1	1	-
ATT	Salman Al-Moasher	Al-Ahli	29	24	2	10	1	-	-
ATT	Muhannad Assiri	Al-Ahli	31	4	-	1	-	-	-

SAUDI ARABIA

Correct scores

	Competitive	Friendly
1-0	4	-
2-0	1	2
2-1	3	1
3-0*	4	-
3-1	-	-
3-2	2	-
4-0	-	1
4-1	1	-
4-2	-	-
4-3	-	-
0-0	2	1
1-1	2	3
2-2	1	-
3-3	-	-
4-4	-	-
0-1	1	1
0-2	1	1
1-2	3	-
0-3	-	1
1-3	1	-
2-3	1	1
0-4	-	1
1-4	-	1
2-4	-	-
3-4	-	-
Other	2	1

Since Brazil 2014

Half-time/full-time double results

Win/Win	8	28%	Win 1st half	10	34%
Draw/Win	8	28%	Win 2nd half	13	45%
Lose/Win	1	3%	Win both halves	4	14%
Win/Draw	2	7%	Goal both halves	10	34%
Draw/Draw	3	10%			
Lose/Draw	0	0%	**Overall**		
Win/Lose	0	0%	● Win	59%	
Draw/Lose	5	17%	● Draw	17%	
Lose/Lose	2	7%	● Lose	24%	

Overall: W17, D5, L7 in 29 competitive games since Brazil 2014

Under & over goals

22 (76%) **Over 1.5** 7 (24%)
✓ ✗

18 (62%) **Over 2.5** 11 (38%)
✓ ✗

8 (28%) **Over 3.5** 21 (72%)
✓ ✗

6 (21%) **Over 4.5** 23 (79%)
✓ ✗

Both teams to score

14 (48%) **Both score** 15 (52%)
✓ ✗

6 (21%) **& win** 23 (79%)
✓ ✗

5 (17%) **& lose** 24 (83%)
✓ ✗

In 29 competitive games since Brazil 2014

Clean sheets

13 (45%) **Clean sheets** 16 (55%)
✓ ✗

11 (38%) **Win to nil** 18 (62%)
✓ ✗

4 (14%) **Fail to score** 25 (86%)
✓ ✗

2 (7%) **Lose to nil** 27 (93%)
✓ ✗

When they score

● For ● Against

Total match goals by half

25 (71%) **1st half** 10 (29%)
F A

35 (66%) **2nd half** 18 (34%)
F A

	0-9	10-18	19-27	28-36	37-45	46-54	55-63	64-72	73-81	82-90
For	3	2	9	6	5	8	2	3	9	13
Against	2	4	1	1	2	4	4	4	5	1

Goals for & against by half

25 (42%) **For** 35 (58%)
1st 2nd

10 (36%) **Against** 18 (64%)
1st 2nd

Saudi Arabia score first

They win	13	72%
They draw	3	17%
They lose	2	11%

Saudi Arabia concede first

They win	4	44%
They draw	0	0%
They lose	5	56%

In 29 competitive games since Brazil 2014

Mohammad Al-Sahlawi scores against Malaysia – nearly all of his goals came early in qualifying

Top scorers in qualifying

	P	G	1st	AT	%	Sau 3-2 Pse	Sau 7-0 Tls	Mys 0-3 Sau*	Sau 2-1 UAE	Pse 0-0 Sau	Tls 0-10 Sau	Sau 2-0 Mys	UAE 1-1 Sau	Sau 1-0 Tha	Irq 1-2 Sau	Sau 2-2 Aus	Sau 3-0 UAE	Jpn 2-1 Sau	Tha 0-3 Sau	Sau 1-0 Irq	Aus 3-2 Sau	UAE 2-1 Sau	Sau 1-0 Jpn
Mohammad Al-Sahlawi	14	16	3	8	36	2	3	1	2	-	5	1	-					-	1	5	1	-	5
Taisir Al-Jassim	18	6	2	6	13	5	1	1	-	-	1	1	1	-	-	1	5	5	-	-	-	-	-
Nawaf Al Abed	13	5	2	4	11	5		5	5	5			1	2	-	1	-	5	5		1	-	
Yahya Al Shehri	18	5	3	5	11	1	1	-	-	-	1	-	-	5	5	1	5	-	1	5	5	-	
Fahad Al Muwallad	12	4	2	4	9	1	5			1	5	5	5	5	5	1	5					5	1
Salem Al Dawsari	2	1	0	1	2															1	5		
Nasser Al Shamrani	5	1	0	1	2								5	1	5		5		5				
Naif Hazazi	8	1	0	1	2			5	5	1		-	5	5	5		5						
Salman Al Moasher	10	1	0	1	2	5	5	5		5	5	5				1	5	5					
Omar Hawsawi	13	1	0	1	2	-							-	-	-	-	5	-	1	-	-	-	-
Osama Hawsawi	17	1	0	1	2	-	-	-	-	1	-	-	-	-	-	-	-	-	-	-	-	-	5
Salman Al Faraj	17	1	0	1	2	1	-	-	-	-	5	5	-	-	-	-	-	-	5	-	-	-	-

*Match v Malaysia abandoned after 87 minutes (crowd trouble) with Saudi Arabia leading 2-1. Match awarded to Saudi Arabia 3-0

G goals scored, **1st** first match goal (own goals don't count) **AT** goals at any time (ie. number of scoring appearances), **P** penalties, **%** percentage of total team goals scored by each player. Russia 2018 qualifying only. Game-by-game stats show goals scored, 1st goals are in red, dash did not score, ⊂ substituted on, ↺ substituted off, blank did not play

Bookings in World Cup qualifying

Played 18 **Cards** (16Y, 1YR) ▯▯▯▯▯▯▯▯▯▯▯▯▯▯▯▯ ◨   **Avg make-up** (▯10 ■25) 10.3

Profile

The most successful African side with seven Africa Cup of Nations triumphs, Egypt have been far less prolific outside their home continent. They have made just two World Cup appearances, the first in 1934 and the most recent 28 years ago at Italia 90. Target number one is to win a World Cup game for the first time.

How they qualified

A campaign which started with a humiliating defeat to Chad eventually finished in triumph with Mohamed Salah's penalty sending the nation wild in a 2-1 win over Congo.

The manager

Much-travelled Argentinian Hector Cuper was appointed in 2015 and led Egypt to the final of the 2017 Afcon. Despite that there have been calls for Cuper to be sacked due to his negative tactics.

The squad

Cuper's gameplan is simple enough – defend with 11 men and attack with one, knowing full well that that one is superstar Salah.

Three 1-0 wins and a 0-0 draw took Egypt to the semi-finals of the last Afcon and they needed a penalty shootout success over Burkina Faso before Cameroon defeated them in the final so don't expect any fireworks from the Pharaohs.

Salah scored five and assisted two of Egypt's seven goals in their qualifying group prior to being rested for the final fixture, while at Afcon the winger scored twice and assisted two of their five goals.

The problem is few outside of Salah can make an impact, and whoever is selected on the other flank – either Trezeguet or Ramadan Sobhi – will be asked to add defensive cover for ageing left-back Mohamed Abdel-Shafy.

Talk of ageing brings us to 45-year-old goalkeeper Essam El-Hadary, who has more than 150 caps and will become the oldest

Factfile

FA founded 1921
www efa.com.eg
Head coach Hector Cuper
Date qualified October 8, 2017

Strengths

☑ Salah will always give them a chance on the counter
☑ Defend well

Weaknesses

☒ The lack of a decent centre forward option is clear for all to see
☒ No plan B should anything happen to Salah

Star rating ★☆☆☆☆

Fixtures

1 June 15, 1pm v Uruguay, Yekaterinburg
2 June 19, 7pm v Russia, Saint Petersburg
3 June 25, 3pm v Saudi Arabia, Volgograd

Base Grozny
Total distance 5,700 miles

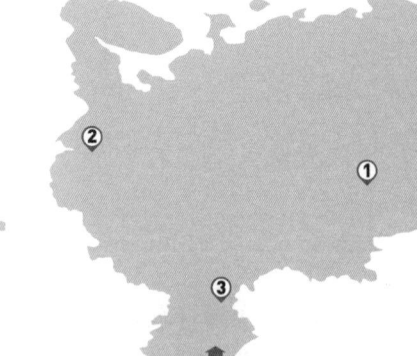

Shikabala can add spark if he makes the final squad

player to ever feature in the World Cup. The veteran stopper gets decent protection from injury-hit centre-back Ramy Rabia and partner Ahmed Hegazi, while midfield is all about solidity and little creativity.

Key man

Salah. The Liverpool flyer is arguably the most important individual to any nation competing this summer. He has proved his quality in Serie A for Roma and Fiorentina before doing likewise in the Premier League.

Rising star

Sobhi has much to live up to after being labelled the Egyptian Messi. Showboater Sobhi has not matched the hype yet but before leaving Egypt for Stoke, he did cause a fracas after becoming renowned for antagonising opponents by standing on the ball.

Wildcard

Shikabala ended a three-year exile from the national team with a goal in the final qualifier against Ghana when Cuper gave fringe players an opportunity, and he kept his place for the March friendlies. This enigmatic character is just the type who could add some much-needed creativity to Egypt's play.

The 32-year-old has a long list of disciplinary issues and is by no means certain to make the final 23-man cut, but it would be some story if he did, having retired from international football in 2010 after suffering racial abuse in a league match.

Prospects

Could be considered value to qualify at the expense of Russia in Group A.

How to back them

Under 2.5 goals in Egypt's matches looks a stick-on and if you are happy to back favourites Salah should land their top-scorer honours. He did just that at Afcon and in World Cup qualifying.

World Cup record		Group stage(s)						Knockout rounds					
		P	W	D	L	F	A	P	W	D	L	F	A
Uruguay 1930	Did not enter	-	-	-	-	-	-	-	-	-	-	-	-
Italy 1934	First round	-	-	-	-	-	-	1	0	0	1	2	4
France 1938	Withdrew	-	-	-	-	-	-	-	-	-	-	-	-
Brazil 1950	Did not enter	-	-	-	-	-	-	-	-	-	-	-	-
Switzerland 1954	Did not qualify	-	-	-	-	-	-	-	-	-	-	-	-
Sweden 1958	Withdrew	-	-	-	-	-	-	-	-	-	-	-	-
Chile 1962	Withdrew	-	-	-	-	-	-	-	-	-	-	-	-
England 1966	Withdrew	-	-	-	-	-	-	-	-	-	-	-	-
Mexico 1970	Did not enter	-	-	-	-	-	-	-	-	-	-	-	-
Germany 1974	Did not qualify	-	-	-	-	-	-	-	-	-	-	-	-
Argentina 1978	Did not qualify	-	-	-	-	-	-	-	-	-	-	-	-
Spain 1982	Did not qualify	-	-	-	-	-	-	-	-	-	-	-	-
Mexico 1986	Did not qualify	-	-	-	-	-	-	-	-	-	-	-	-
Italy 1990	Group stage	3	0	2	1	1	2	-	-	-	-	-	-
USA 1994	Did not qualify	-	-	-	-	-	-	-	-	-	-	-	-
France 1998	Did not qualify	-	-	-	-	-	-	-	-	-	-	-	-
Korea/Japan 2002	Did not qualify	-	-	-	-	-	-	-	-	-	-	-	-
Germany 2006	Did not qualify	-	-	-	-	-	-	-	-	-	-	-	-
South Africa 2010	Did not qualify	-	-	-	-	-	-	-	-	-	-	-	-
Brazil 2014	Did not qualify	-	-	-	-	-	-	-	-	-	-	-	-
Totals		3	0	2	1	1	2	1	0	0	1	2	4

Continental championships

Africa Cup of Nations
Winners (7) 1957, 1959, 1986, 1998, 2006, 2008, 2010

How they qualified

Round 2
Chad .... (0) 1-0 (0) .... Egypt
Egypt .... (4) 4-0 (0) .... Chad
Egypt won 4-1 on aggregate

Round 3

Group E	P	W	D	L	F	A	GD	P
Egypt	6	4	1	1	8	4	4	13
Uganda	6	2	3	1	3	2	1	9
Ghana	6	1	4	1	7	5	2	7
Congo	6	0	2	4	5	12	-7	2

Congo .... (1) 1-2 (1) .... Egypt
Egypt .... (1) 2-0 (0) .... Ghana
Uganda .... (0) 1-0 (0) .... Egypt
Egypt .... (1) 1-0 (0) .... Uganda
Egypt .... (0) 2-1 (0) .... Congo
Ghana .... (0) 1-1 (0) .... Egypt

▶▶ Full qualifying results on
pages 228-241

Egypt lost 1-0 to England at Italia 90

Photo by Albert Cooper/Metropix

World Cup head-to-heads							
Egypt v	P	W	D	L	F	A	Latest
England	1	0	0	1	0	1	1990

GROUP A

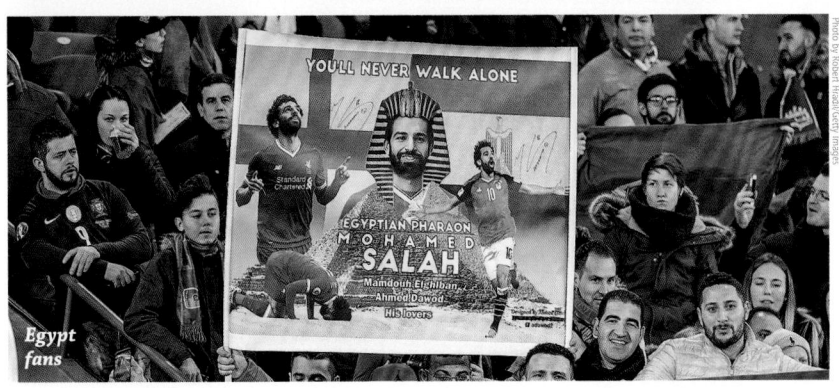

Egypt
fans

Players used in qualifying		Career			Qualification				
Pos		Club	Age	P	G	P	G	⬜	◼
GK	Sherif Ekramy	Al-Ahly	34	22	-	1	-	1	-
GK	Ahmed El-Shenawy	Zamalek	27	27	-	2	-	-	-
GK	Essam El Hadary	Al-Taawon	45	156	-	5	-	-	-
DEF	Ahmed Dowidar	Smouha	30	9	-	1	-	-	-
DEF	Ahmed Hegazy	West Brom	27	42	1	6	-	1	-
DEF	Ali Gabr	West Brom	29	18	1	3	-	-	-
DEF	Omar Gaber	Los Angeles	26	21	-	3	-	-	-
DEF	Saad Samir	Al-Ahly	29	10	-	3	-	-	-
DEF	Sabry Raheel	Al-Ahly	30	6	-	2	-	-	-
DEF	Ahmed Elmohamady	Aston Villa	30	81	1	2	-	-	-
DEF	Islam Gamal	Zamalek	29	2	-	1	-	-	-
DEF	Karim Hafez	Lens	22	5	-	1	-	1	-
DEF	Mohamed A-Shafy	Al-Fateh	32	48	1	5	-	-	-
DEF	Ramy Rabia	Al-Ahly	25	22	3	4	-	-	-
MID	Ahmed Fathi	Al-Ahly	33	127	3	4	-	-	-
MID	Abdallah El Said	Al-Ahly	32	35	6	6	3	-	-
MID	Kahraba	Al-Ittihad	24	19	3	3	-	-	-
MID	Moamen Zakaria	Al-Ahli	30	12	-	3	-	-	-
MID	Mostafa Fathi	Al-Taawon	24	8	-	1	-	-	-
MID	Tarek Hamed	Zamalek	29	21	-	6	-	1	-
MID	Amr Warda	Atromitos	24	14	-	3	-	-	-
MID	Hossam Ghaly	Al-Ahly	36	73	3	2	-	-	-
MID	Trezeguet	Kasimpasa	23	23	2	6	-	-	-
MID	Shikabala	Al-Raed	32	28	1	1	1	-	-
MID	Mohamed Elneny	Arsenal	25	61	5	8	1	1	-
MID	Ramadan Sobhi	Stoke	21	20	1	6	-	-	-
MID	Saleh Gomaa	Al-Faisaly	24	14	-	3	-	-	-
MID	Sam Morsy	Wigan	26	3	-	1	-	-	-
ATT	Amr Gamal	HJK Helsinki	26	19	3	5	-	-	-
ATT	Amr Marei	ES-Sahel	26	2	-	1	-	-	-
ATT	Koka	Braga	25	10	3	5	2	-	-
ATT	Basem Morsy	Zamalek	26	10	7	3	-	1	-
ATT	Mohamed Salah	Liverpool	26	57	35	5	5	1	-

Correct scores

	Competitive	Friendly
1-0	5	4
2-0	4	3
2-1	2	1
3-0	1	2
3-1	-	-
3-2	-	-
4-0	1	-
4-1	-	-
4-2	-	-
4-3	-	-
0-0	1	-
1-1	3	1
2-2	-	-
3-3	-	-
4-4	-	-
0-1	5	2
0-2	1	-
1-2	2	1
0-3	-	-
1-3	-	-
2-3	-	-
0-4	-	-
1-4	-	-
2-4	-	-
3-4	-	-
Other	-	-

Since Brazil 2014

Half-time/full-time double results

Win/Win	5	20%	Win 1st half	7	28%
Draw/Win	8	32%	Win 2nd half	10	40%
Lose/Win	0	0%	Win both halves	2	8%
Win/Draw	0	0%	Goal both halves	3	12%
Draw/Draw	4	16%			
Lose/Draw	0	0%	**Overall**		
Win/Lose	2	8%	● Win	52%	
Draw/Lose	3	12%	● Draw	16%	
Lose/Lose	3	12%	● Lose	32%	

Overall: W13, D4, L8 in 25 competitive games since Brazil 2014

Under & over goals

14 (56%)	Over 1.5	11 (44%)
✓		✗
6 (24%)	Over 2.5	19 (76%)
✓		✗
1 (4%)	Over 3.5	24 (96%)
✓		✗
0 (0%)	Over 4.5	25 (100%)
✓		✗

Both teams to score

7 (28%)	Both score	18 (72%)
✓		✗
2 (8%)	& win	23 (92%)
✓		✗
2 (8%)	& lose	23 (92%)
✓		✗

In 25 competitive games since Brazil 2014

Clean sheets

12 (48%)	Clean sheets	13 (52%)
✓		✗
11 (44%)	Win to nil	14 (56%)
✓		✗

7 (28%)	Fail to score	18 (72%)
✓		✗
6 (24%)	Lose to nil	19 (76%)
✓		✗

When they score

● For ● Against

Total match goals by half

11 (69%) **1st half** 5 (31%)
F ███████ A

18 (62%) **2nd half** 11 (38%)
F ███████ A

2	3	1	1	4	1	8	4	0	5

0-9 10-18 19-27 28-36 37-45 46-54 55-63 64-72 73-81 82-90

1	1	2	0	1	3	2	1	3	2

Goals for & against by half

11 (38%) **For** 18 (62%)
1st ███████ 2nd

5 (31%) **Against** 11 (69%)
1st ███████ 2nd

Egypt score first

They win	12		75%
They draw	2		13%
They lose	2		13%

Egypt concede first

They win	1		13%
They draw	1		13%
They lose	6		75%

In 25 competitive games since Brazil 2014

Mo Salah has enjoyed a great season with Liverpool

Top scorers in qualifying

	P	G	1st	AT	%	Tcd 1-0 Egy	Egy 4-0 Tcd	Cog 1-2 Egy	Egy 2-0 Gha	Uga 1-0 Egy	Egy 1-0 Uga	Egy 2-1 Cog	Gha 1-1 Egy
Mohamed Salah	5	5	3	4	42			1	1	-	1	2	
Abdalla El Said	6	3	0	3	25	1	1	↳1	-		↺		↳
Koka	5	2	0	1	17	-	↳2	↳			↳	↺	
Shikabala	1	1	1	1	8								↳1
Mohamed Elneny	8	1	1	1	8	-	1	-	-	-	-	-	-

G goals scored, **1st** first match goal (own goals don't count) **AT** goals at any time (ie. number of scoring appearances), **P** penalties, **%** percentage of total team goals scored by each player. Russia 2018 qualifying only. Game-by-game stats show goals scored, 1st goals are in red, dash did not score, ↳ substituted on, ↺ substituted off, blank did not play

Bookings in World Cup qualifying

Played 8 **Cards** (7Y) ▢▢▢▢▢▢▢   **Avg make-up** (▢10 ■25) 8.8

URUGUAY

GROUP A

Profile

Uruguay were available at 50-1 before the draw but they have halved in price with some bookmakers after landing a plum spot in Group A and there is no doubt the three-time semi-finalists and double winners have the potential to go deep.

How they qualified

"It's the toughest competition I've ever had and no one is giving us a title or a medal," said manager Oscar Tabarez after Uruguay finished second behind Brazil to avoid the intercontinental playoff for the first time this century.

Edinson Cavani finished as South America's top goalscorer with ten goals, although Uruguay took only two points in their four matches against Conmebol heavyweights Brazil and Argentina.

The manager

Tabarez, a 71-year-old former school teacher, led Uruguay at Italia 90 first time around and has been at the helm since 2006 in this current spell. El Maestro designed the Uruguayan football centre to help build a clear pathway from the junior ranks to the senior team and a squad bond is key despite the presence of Luis Suarez and Cavani.

He told Blizzard magazine: "I don't coach stars, I coach people. If I want to see stars I look in the sky."

The squad

Uruguay are likely to use a 4-4-2 formation which makes sense as it plays to the strengths of the potentially devastating forward pairing of Cavani and Suarez, who are quite rightly considered two of the world's hottest marksman.

The deadly duo can win matches on their own but Uruguay are also solid at centre-back thanks to the all-Atletico Madrid pairing of Diego Godin and Jose Maria Gimenez, while goalkeeper Fernando Muslera and full-backs Alvaro Pereira and Maxi Pereira

Factfile

FA founded 1900

www auf.org.uy

Head coach Oscar Tabarez

Date qualified October 10, 2017

Strengths

☑ The front two of Suarez and Cavani will always give Uruguay a chance

☑ Experienced in most areas without being over the hill

Weaknesses

☒ Could Tabarez be too loyal to his midfield stalwarts?

☒ Their 20 goals conceded was the most of any automatic qualifier in South America

Star rating ★★★☆☆

Fixtures

1 June 15, 1pm v Egypt, Yekaterinburg

2 June 20, 4pm v Saudi Arabia, Rostov-on-Don

3 June 25, 3pm v Russia, Samara

Base Nizhny Novgorod

Total distance 3,250 miles

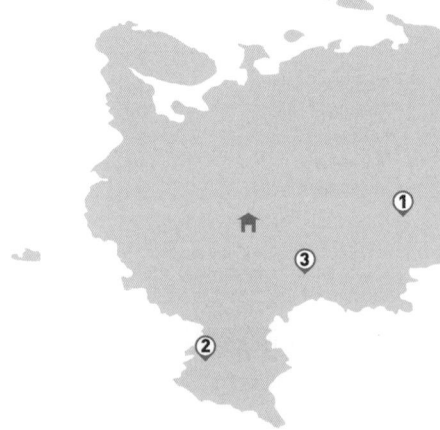

World class: Luis Suarez

possess over 300 caps between them.

The goalkeeper, defence and forward line almost picks itself but there is a midfield revolution developing with 30-somethings Egidio Arevalo Rios, Alvaro Gonzalez, Cristian Rodriguez and Carlos Sanchez coming under increasing pressure from a talented new generation.

Federico Valverde (on loan at Deportivo from Real Madrid), Rodrigo Bentancur (Juventus), Matias Vecino (Inter) and Nahitan Nandez (Boca Juniors) have impressed for the national youth teams constructed so well by Tabarez. Sampdoria's Lucas Torreira is another blossoming midfielder to keep tabs on.

Key man

Suarez, who is likely to be on penalties, just edges Cavani but both are proven goalscorers at international level and in multiple European leagues.

Rising star

Valverde, nicknamed Pajarito, the Little Bird, was voted the second best player at the 2017 Under-20 World Cup and has been described by Suarez as a "phenomenon." The central midfielder, who links play excellently, scored on his debut against Paraguay in September 2017.

Wildcard

A tall, left-footed dribbling winger who cuts in from the right, Gaston Pereiro is another young gun coming through in Europe, this time with PSV. Pereiro says he styles his game on Robin van Persie but his first love is Alvaro Recoba, so much so he has a tattoo of El Chino.

Prospects

This is the last-chance saloon for Tabarez and probably also Suarez, Cavani, Godin et al in terms of World Cup glory. There is a perfect mix of youth and experience and Uruguay should be filed under dangerous dark horses.

How to back them

If the each-way outright bet is too risky then just take them to top a soft Group A.

URUGUAY

World Cup record		Group stage(s)						Knockout rounds					
		P	W	D	L	F	A	P	W	D	L	F	A
Uruguay 1930	● Winners	2	2	0	0	5	0	2	2	0	0	10	3
Italy 1934	Did not enter	-	-	-	-	-	-	-	-	-	-	-	-
France 1938	Did not enter	-	-	-	-	-	-	-	-	-	-	-	-
Brazil 1950	● Winners	4	3	1	0	15	5	-	-	-	-	-	-
Switzerland 1954	Fourth place	2	2	0	0	9	0	3	1	1	1	7	7
Sweden 1958	Did not qualify	-	-	-	-	-	-	-	-	-	-	-	-
Chile 1962	Group stage	3	1	0	2	4	6	-	-	-	-	-	-
England 1966	Quarter-finals	3	1	2	0	2	1	1	0	0	1	0	4
Mexico 1970	Fourth place	3	1	1	1	2	1	3	0	1	2	1	4
Germany 1974	Group stage	3	0	1	2	1	6	-	-	-	-	-	-
Argentina 1978	Did not qualify	-	-	-	-	-	-	-	-	-	-	-	-
Spain 1982	Did not qualify	-	-	-	-	-	-	-	-	-	-	-	-
Mexico 1986	Round of 16	3	0	2	1	2	7	1	0	0	1	0	1
Italy 1990	Round of 16	3	1	1	1	2	3	1	0	0	1	0	2
USA 1994	Did not qualify	-	-	-	-	-	-	-	-	-	-	-	-
France 1998	Did not qualify	-	-	-	-	-	-	-	-	-	-	-	-
Korea/Japan 2002	Group stage	3	0	2	1	4	5	-	-	-	-	-	-
Germany 2006	Did not qualify	-	-	-	-	-	-	-	-	-	-	-	-
South Africa 2010	Fourth place	3	2	1	0	4	0	4	1	1	2	7	8
Brazil 2014	Round of 16	3	2	0	1	4	4	1	0	0	1	0	2
Totals		35	15	11	9	54	38	16	4	3	9	25	31

Continental championships (best perfomance)

Copa America	Winners (15)	1916, 1917, 1920, 1923, 1924, 1926, 1935, 1942, 1956, 1959, 1967, 1983, 1987, 1995, 2011

World Cup head-to-heads

Uruguay v	P	W	D	L	F	A	Latest
Argentina	2	1	0	1	4	3	1986
Belgium	1	0	0	1	1	3	1990
Brazil	2	1	0	1	3	4	1970
Colombia	2	1	0	1	2	3	2014
Costa Rica	1	0	0	1	1	3	2014
Croatia	2	1	0	1	7	4	1962
Denmark	2	0	0	2	2	8	2002
England	3	2	1	0	6	3	2014
France	3	1	2	0	2	1	2010
Germany	4	0	1	3	3	9	2010
Mexico	2	1	1	0	1	0	2010
Peru	1	1	0	0	1	0	1930
Russia	2	0	1	1	1	2	1970
Senegal	1	0	1	0	3	3	2002
Serbia	2	1	0	1	7	4	1962
South Korea	2	2	0	0	3	1	2010
Spain	2	0	2	0	2	2	1990
Sweden	3	1	0	2	3	6	1974

90 mins only, includes games against Yugoslavia, West Germany and USSR

Germany are Uruguay's most frequent World Cup opponents, with four meetings since 1966

Players used in qualifying

Pos	Player	Club	Age	Career P	Career G	Qualification P	Qualification G		
GK	Fernando Muslera	Galatasaray	31	96	-	17	-	2	-
GK	Martin Silva	Vasco da Gama	35	11	-	1	-	-	-
DEF	Alvaro Pereira	Cerro Porteno	32	83	7	9	1	2	-
DEF	Diego Godin	Atl Madrid	32	116	8	16	3	3	-
DEF	Gaston Silva	Independiente	24	17	-	10	-	-	-
DEF	Jorge Fucile	Nacional	33	49	-	4	-	2	-
DEF	Jose Gimenez	Atl Madrid	23	41	4	9	-	3	-
DEF	Martin Caceres	Lazio	31	75	4	8	3	-	-
DEF	Mathias Corujo	Penarol	32	22	1	9	-	3	-
DEF	Mauricio Victorino	Cerro Porteno	35	24	-	2	-	-	-
DEF	Maxi Pereira	Porto	34	124	3	11	-	3	-
DEF	Sebastian Coates	Sporting	27	30	1	9	1	1	-
MID	Diego Laxalt	Genoa	25	5	-	2	-	-	-
MID	Alvaro Gonzalez	Nacional	33	71	3	9	-	2	-
MID	Camilo Mayada	River Place	27	7	-	1	-	-	-
MID	Carlos Sanchez	Monterrey	33	34	1	15	1	-	-
MID	Cristian Rodriguez	Penarol	32	103	11	13	2	1	-
MID	Egidio Arevalo Rios	Unattached	36	90	-	12	-	1	-
MID	Federico Valverde	Deportivo	19	4	1	3	1	-	-
MID	Gaston Ramirez	Sampdoria	27	43	-	4	-	2	-
MID	Giorgian De Arrascaeta	Cruzeiro	24	13	1	3	-	-	-
MID	Matias Vecino	Inter	26	21	1	12	-	1	-
MID	Nahitan Nandez	Boca Juniors	22	11	-	5	-	2	-
MID	Nicolas Lodeiro	Seattle	29	53	4	8	1	3	-
MID	Rodrigo Bentancur	Juventus	20	6	-	2	-	-	-
ATT	Urreta	Monterrey	28	4	-	1	-	1	1
ATT	Abel Hernandez	Hull	27	29	11	5	-	1	-
ATT	Cristhian Stuani	Girona	31	40	5	9	-	-	-
ATT	Diego Rolan	Malaga	25	25	4	8	2	1	-
ATT	Edinson Cavani	Paris St-G.	31	100	42	15	10	2	-
ATT	Luis Suarez	Barcelona	31	97	50	13	5	2	-
ATT	Michael Santos	Sp. Gijon	25	2	-	1	-	-	-

How they qualified

	P	W	D	L	F	A	GD	P
Brazil	18	12	5	1	41	11	30	41
Uruguay	18	9	4	5	32	20	12	31
Argentina	18	7	7	4	19	16	3	28
Colombia	18	7	6	5	21	19	2	27
Peru	18	7	5	6	27	26	1	26
Chile	18	8	2	8	26	27	-1	26
Paraguay	18	7	3	8	19	25	-6	24
Ecuador	18	6	2	10	26	29	-3	20
Bolivia	18	4	2	12	16	38	-22	14
Venezuela	18	2	6	10	19	35	-16	12

Bolivia........... (0) 0-2 (1)........Uruguay
Uruguay........ (1) 3-0 (0)........Colombia

This is the fourth World Cup for Uruguay coach Oscar Tabarez

Ecuador.......... (1) 2-1 (0).........Uruguay
Uruguay........ (1) 3-0 (0)................Chile
Brazil............. (2) 2-2 (1)........Uruguay
Uruguay........ (0) 1-0 (0)............... Peru
Argentina ..... (1) 1-0 (0).........Uruguay
Uruguay........ (3) 4-0 (0).........Paraguay
Uruguay........ (1) 3-0 (0).......Venezuela
Colombia ...... (1) 2-2 (1)........Uruguay
Uruguay........ (2) 2-1 (1)..........Ecuador
Chile.............. (1) 3-1 (1)........Uruguay
Uruguay........ (1) 1-4 (1)..............Brazil
Peru.............. (1) 2-1 (1)........Uruguay
Uruguay........ (0) 0-0 (0)......Argentina
Paraguay........ (0) 1-2 (0)........Uruguay
Venezuela ...... (0) 0-0 (0)........Uruguay
Uruguay........ (2) 4-2 (1)............ Bolivia

URUGUAY

Correct scores

	Competitive	Friendly
1-0	2	4
2-0	1	2
2-1	2	1
3-0	4	1
3-1	-	1
3-2	-	-
4-0	1	-
4-1	-	-
4-2	1	-
4-3	-	-
0-0	2	1
1-1	1	1
2-2	2	-
3-3	-	1
4-4	-	-
0-1	4	1
0-2	-	-
1-2	2	1
0-3	-	1
1-3	2	1
2-3	-	-
0-4	-	-
1-4	1	-
2-4	-	-
3-4	-	-
Other	-	1

Since Brazil 2014

Half-time/full-time double results

Win/Win	8	32%	Win 1st half	8	32%
Draw/Win	3	12%	Win 2nd half	11	44%
Lose/Win	0	0%	Win both halves	7	28%
Win/Draw	0	0%	Goal both halves	9	36%
Draw/Draw	4	16%			
Lose/Draw	1	4%	Overall		
Win/Lose	0	0%	● Win	44%	
Draw/Lose	5	20%	● Draw	20%	
Lose/Lose	4	16%	● Lose	36%	

Overall: W11, D5, L9 in 25 competitive games since Brazil 2014

Under & over goals

17 (68%)	Over 1.5	8 (32%)
✓		✗
15 (60%)	Over 2.5	10 (40%)
✓		✗
7 (28%)	Over 3.5	18 (72%)
✓		✗
2 (8%)	Over 4.5	23 (92%)
✓		✗

Both teams to score

11 (44%)	Both score	14 (56%)
✓		✗
3 (12%)	& win	22 (88%)
✓		✗
5 (20%)	& lose	20 (80%)
✓		✗

In 25 competitive games since Brazil 2014

Clean sheets

10 (40%)	Clean sheets	15 (60%)
✓		✗
8 (32%)	Win to nil	17 (68%)
✓		✗

6 (24%)	Fail to score	19 (76%)
✓		✗
4 (16%)	Lose to nil	21 (84%)
✓		✗

When they score

● For ● Against

Total match goals by half

1	4	3	5	5	7	2	3	6	2

18 (58%)	1st half	13 (42%)
F		A

20 (59%)	2nd half	14 (41%)
F		A

0-9 10-18 19-27 28-36 37-45 46-54 55-63 64-72 73-81 82-90

Goals for & against by half

18 (47%)	For	20 (53%)
1st		2nd

13 (48%)	Against	14 (52%)
1st		2nd

2	1	4	2	4	1	4	0	4	5

Uruguay score first

They win	10		71%
They draw	1		7%
They lose	3		21%

Uruguay concede first

They win	1		11%
They draw	2		22%
They lose	6		67%

In 25 competitive games since Brazil 2014

Edinson Cavani scored almost a third of Uruguay's goals in South American qualifying

Top scorers in qualifying

	P	G	1st	AT	%	Bol 0-2 Ury	Ury 3-0 Col	Ecu 2-1 Ury	Ury 3-0 Chl	Bra 2-2 Ury	Ury 1-0 Per	Arg 1-0 Ury	Ury 4-0 Pry	Ury 3-0 Ven	Col 2-2 Ury	Ury 2-1 Ecu	Chl 3-1 Ury	Ury 1-4 Bra	Per 2-1 Ury	Ury 0-0 Arg	Pry 1-2 Ury	Ven 0-0 Ury	Ury 4-2 Bol
Edinson Cavani	15	10	4	8	31	1	-	1	1	-	·2	2	-		1	1	-	-	-	-			1
Luis Suarez	13	5	0	4	16				1	-	-	·1	-	1	-	-				↩	↩	-	2
Martin Caceres	8	3	2	3	9	1	↩	-	·1											-	-	-	1
Diego Godin	16	3	2	3	9	1	1	-	1	-	-	-	-	-	-	-	-	-	-	-	-	-	-
Diego Rolan	8	2	0	2	6	↳	1	↳	↩			↳	↳					·1		↩			
Cristian Rodriguez	13	2	0	2	6	↩				↩	↩	↩	1	↩	·1		-		↩		↩	↩	↩
Federico Valverde	3	1	1	1	3																1	↩	↩
Abel Hernandez	5	1	0	1	3	↩	·1	↩				↳						↳					
Nicolas Lodeiro	8	1	1	1	3	↳	↳	↳	↩				↩		·1			↳					↩
Sebastian Coates	9	1	1	1	3		-	-	-	-				-	-	1	-	-					
Alvaro Pereira	9	1	0	1	3	-	-	↩	·1	-	-			↳	↳	↳							
Carlos Sanchez	15	1	1	1	3	↩	↩	-	-	↳	↳	↩	-	-	↩	↩	↩	↩	·1			↳	

G goals scored, **1st** first match goal (own goals don't count) **AT** goals at any time (ie. number of scoring appearances), **P** penalties, **%** percentage of total team goals scored by each player. Russia 2018 qualifying only. Game-by-game stats show goals scored, 1st goals are in red, dash did not score, ↳ substituted on, ↩ substituted off, blank did not play

Bookings in World Cup qualifying

Played 18

Cards (37Y, 1YR)

Avg make-up (□10 ■25) 21.9

European champions look value for early flight home

Winning the European Championship is not a reliable form guide for a successful World Cup and that could spell trouble for Portugal, who are in a trickier group than the odds suggest, *writes Mark Langdon*.

Spain won the World Cup between their European Championship triumphs of 2008 and 2012 with a truly exceptional squad but it is worth remembering that La Roja crashed out at the first hurdle when trying to back up the effort of 2014.

France went the same way in 2002 after winning Euro 2000, while 2004 champions Greece and 1992 victors Denmark did not even qualify for the next World Cups.

Holland, champions in 1988, did not win a World Cup match at Italia 90 and Germany were below their usual standards in 1998 after finishing as Europe's elite in 1996. They squeezed past Mexico with two late last-16 goals before a crushing 3-0 loss to Croatia.

Portugal were not exceptional champions, failing to beat Hungary, Iceland and Austria in the group phase, needing penalties to see off Poland and extra-time against France and Croatia while the semi-final success over Wales came against suspension-ravaged outsiders.

Spain are the class act in Group B,

with the disaster of Brazil making it easier for new coach Julen Lopetegui to cull those ageing stars who were passengers four years ago.

If Spain justify their odds-on status and beat Portugal in the first round of Group B fixtures the pressure will increase on their Iberian rivals to such an extent that manager Fernando Santos may be unable to adopt the dour tactics which proved so successful two years ago.

And picking up sufficient points won't be easy given that Morocco did not concede a goal in their World Cup qualifying group and Iran have grown into Asia's strongest side.

Even Cristiano Ronaldo could have trouble filling his boots against such defensively sound opponents in what may easily be the lowest-scoring group.

Iran also have the X-Factor of Portuguese boss Carlos Queiroz calling the shots.

Queiroz developed a bond with Ronaldo during their time at Manchester United and may know enough weaknesses to devise a plan to stifle Portugal's main offensive threat. If Ronaldo is nullified Portugal are in big trouble.

European champions have a disappointing World Cup record

Recommendation

★☆☆☆☆ **Portugal not to qualify**

Group-stage performances since France 98

	Pot	P	W	Q	1998 Group	Pos	2002 Group	Pos	2006 Group	Pos	2010 Group	Pos	2014 Group	Pos
Portugal	1	4	1	2	-	-	D	3	D	1	G	2	G	3
Spain	2	5	3	3	D	3	B	1	H	1	H	1	B	3
Iran	3	3	0	0	F	3	-	-	D	4	-	-	F	4
Morocco	4	1	0	0	A	3	-	-	-	-	-	-	-	-

To win Group B
Win only

	Bet365	BtBrt	Betfair	Btfrd	Btwy	Boyle	Coral	Hills	Lads	P Power	Sky	188
Spain	1-2	8-15	8-15	4-7	8-15	4-7	1-2	4-9	8-15	1-2	1-2	9-20
Portugal	2	15-8	9-5	15-8	15-8	15-8	2	2	15-8	7-4	2	19-10
Morocco	16	16	14	14	16	14	14	16	16	14	16	16
Iran	33	28	33	28	25	28	25	25	20	33	20	30

Morocco v Iran
4pm, Friday June 15, ITV

	Bet365	BtBrt	Betfair	Btfrd	Btwy	Boyle	Coral	Hills	Lads	P Power	Sky	188
Morocco	5-4	5-4	5-4	5-4	13-10	5-4	13-10	6-5	13-10	11-10	5-4	9-7
Draw	19-10	15-8	9-4	2	2	9-5	15-8	21-10	15-8	11-5	2	11-5
Iran	13-5	23-10	12-5	12-5	23-10	23-10	9-4	11-5	9-4	13-5	5-2	23-10

Portugal v Spain
7pm, Friday June 15, BBC

	Bet365	BtBrt	Betfair	Btfrd	Btwy	Boyle	Coral	Hills	Lads	P Power	Sky	188
Spain	10-11	17-20	10-11	9-10	17-20	20-23	17-20	10-11	17-20	19-20	17-20	13-14
Draw	5-2	9-4	12-5	23-10	12-5	21-10	11-5	9-4	11-5	21-10	12-5	5-2
Portugal	3	3	10-3	16-5	16-5	3	16-5	3	16-5	16-5	10-3	58-19

Portugal v Morocco
1pm, Wednesday June 20, BBC

	Bet365	BtBrt	Betfair	Btfrd	Btwy	Boyle	Coral	Hills	Lads	P Power	Sky	188
Portugal	8-13	1-2	4-7	8-15	1-2	1-2	1-2	1-2	1-2	1-2	8-15	8-15
Draw	13-5	13-5	14-5	11-4	3	5-2	13-5	3	13-5	13-5	14-5	58-19
Morocco	5	11-2	11-2	11-2	11-2	11-2	6	5	6	5	6	28-5

Iran v Spain
7pm, Wednesday June 20, ITV

	Bet365	BtBrt	Betfair	Btfrd	Btwy	Boyle	Coral	Hills	Lads	P Power	Sky	188
Spain	2-11	1-6	2-9	2-11	2-11	1-6	2-11	1-6	2-11	1-6	1-5	1-5
Draw	5	9-2	5	11-2	5-1	9-2	5	11-2	5	9-2	19-4	27-5
Iran	18	14	13	14	16	12	18	14	18	11	16	31-2

Iran v Portugal
7pm, Monday June 25, BBC

	Bet365	BetBright	Betfair	Betfred	Betway	Boyle	Hills	P Power	Sky Bet
Portugal	4-11	1-3	4-11	4-11	1-3	1-3	2-5	3-10	1-3
Draw	15-4	10-3	18-5	7-2	10-3	16-5	16-5	10-3	4
Iran	15-2	15-2	17-2	8	15-2	15-2	8	15-2	8

Spain v Morocco
7pm, Monday June 25, BBC

	Bet365	BetBright	Betfair	Betfred	Betway	Boyle	Hills	P Power	Sky Bet
Spain	4-11	1-3	4-11	4-11	4-11	1-3	2-7	3-10	4-11
Draw	15-4	7-2	15-4	18-5	10-3	16-5	4	7-2	4
Morocco	15-2	7	9	15-2	13-2	7	10	8	13-2

Prices correct March 28 2018

Profile

The surprise European champions are top seeds but they have a patchy World Cup record. Portugal reached the semis in 1966 and 2006 but they have been knocked out at the group stage in three of their six World Cup campaigns.

How they qualified

The fight for automatic qualification went down to the wire but Portugal came out on top against Switzerland in the final round of fixtures. Cristiano Ronaldo (15) and strike partner Andre Silva (nine) combined for 24 of Portugal's 32 goals in a soft qualifying section.

The manager

Fernando Santos is a cautious coach with oodles of experience having managed Portugal's big three – Porto, Benfica and Sporting – on top of several spells in Greek football. The success under his leadership of two years ago has been compared to the boring style of Greece's shock European Championship success in 2004.

The squad

Santos is a creature of habit so don't expect him to venture far from his Euro 2016 success with a solid 4-4-2 formation in which only a few spots are up for grabs.

Nani was Ronaldo's partner in France but the emergence of Andre Silva is an upgrade, while Bernardo Silva, who missed the Euros through injury, should force his way into a wide position.

William Carvalho and Joao Moutinho are likely starting central midfielders and there are plenty of options for the other midfield slot, including Andre Gomes, Joao Mario, Gelson Martins, Ricardo Quaresma and Goncalo Guedes.

Santos has a reliable keeper in Rui Patricio and is well-stocked at fullback, where Cedric and Raphael Guerreiro are first choice.

However, there is a problem at the

Factfile

FA founded 1914
www fpf.pt
Head coach Fernando Santos
Date qualified October 10, 2017

Strengths

- ☑ Ronaldo is one of the all-time greats
- ☑ Well-organised side who will give little away

Weaknesses

- ☒ There is no disguising the issue of ageing centre-backs
- ☒ One-dimensional approach can stifle their gifted midfielders

Star rating ★★★☆☆

Fixtures

1 June 15, 7pm v Spain, Sochi
2 June 20, 1pm v Morocco, Luzhniki Stadium, Moscow
3 June 25, 7pm v Iran, Saransk

Base Moscow
Total distance 2,350 miles

GROUP B

Goncalo Guedes is tipped as a future Ballon d'Or winner

heart of the defence where centre-back warriors Pepe, Jose Fonte and Bruno Alves bring a combined age of 105.

Portugal were able to defend deep, protect their lack of pace and find a way to win with Ronaldo at the Euros, but it is asking a lot two years on.

Key man

Captain Ronaldo has won the Ballon d'Or five times, finished as top scorer in the Champions League every season from 2013 to 2017 and took on the role of touchline cheerleader following his injury in the Euro 2016 final.

Rising star

Such has been Guedes's impact on loan at Valencia from Paris Saint-Germain that Spanish-based journalist Graham Hunter believes the winger is capable of following in Eusebio, Luis Figo and Ronaldo's footsteps by becoming a Ballon d'Or winner.

Wildcard

Santos is not known for taking risks but he may need to gamble on a centre-back. Ruben Dias, seen as a future Benfica captain and already signed up by super-agent Jorge Mendes, was selected for the March friendlies before suffering an injury.

Prospects

They are suited to knockout football with their safety-first approach and Ronaldo up front makes for a dangerous combination.

However, it will be a bad tournament should Portugal come out on top and they could be value for an early departure.

How to back them

Portugal drew six of seven games at Euro 2016, including all three group-stage matches against Hungary, Iceland and Austria. The Santos approach won't change and there could be profit in backing the stalemate blind.

World Cup record

World Cup record		Group stage(s)						Knockout rounds					
		P	W	D	L	F	A	P	W	D	L	F	A
Uruguay 1930	Did not enter	-	-	-	-	-	-	-	-	-	-	-	-
Italy 1934	Did not qualify	-	-	-	-	-	-	-	-	-	-	-	-
France 1938	Did not qualify	-	-	-	-	-	-	-	-	-	-	-	-
Brazil 1950	Did not qualify	-	-	-	-	-	-	-	-	-	-	-	-
Switzerland 1954	Did not qualify	-	-	-	-	-	-	-	-	-	-	-	-
Sweden 1958	Did not qualify	-	-	-	-	-	-	-	-	-	-	-	-
Chile 1962	Did not qualify	-	-	-	-	-	-	-	-	-	-	-	-
England 1966	Third place	3	3	0	0	9	2	3	2	0	1	8	6
Mexico 1970	Did not qualify	-	-	-	-	-	-	-	-	-	-	-	-
Germany 1974	Did not qualify	-	-	-	-	-	-	-	-	-	-	-	-
Argentina 1978	Did not qualify	-	-	-	-	-	-	-	-	-	-	-	-
Spain 1982	Did not qualify	-	-	-	-	-	-	-	-	-	-	-	-
Mexico 1986	Group stage	3	1	0	2	2	4	-	-	-	-	-	-
Italy 1990	Did not qualify	-	-	-	-	-	-	-	-	-	-	-	-
USA 1994	Did not qualify	-	-	-	-	-	-	-	-	-	-	-	-
France 1998	Did not qualify	-	-	-	-	-	-	-	-	-	-	-	-
Korea/Japan 2002	Group stage	3	1	0	2	6	4	-	-	-	-	-	-
Germany 2006	Fourth place	3	3	0	0	5	1	4	1	1	2	2	4
South Africa 2010	Round of 16	3	1	2	0	7	0	1	0	0	1	0	1
Brazil 2014	Group stage	3	1	1	1	4	7	-	-	-	-	-	-
Totals		18	10	3	5	33	18	8	3	1	4	10	11

Continental championships (best perfomance)

Uefa European Championship	Winners (1)	2016

World Cup head-to-heads

Portugal v	P	W	D	L	F	A	Latest	Portugal v	P	W	D	L	F	A	Latest
Brazil	2	1	1	0	3	1	2010	Morocco	1	0	0	1	1	3	1986
England	3	1	1	1	2	2	2006	Poland	2	1	0	1	4	1	2002
France	1	0	0	1	0	1	2006	Russia	1	1	0	0	2	1	1966
Germany	2	0	0	2	1	7	2014	South Korea	1	0	0	1	0	1	2002
Iran	1	1	0	0	2	0	2006	Spain	1	0	0	1	0	1	2010
Mexico	1	1	0	0	2	1	2006								

90 mins only, includes games against USSR

How they qualified

Group B	P	W	D	L	F	A	GD	P
Portugal	10	9	0	1	32	4	28	27
Switzerland	10	9	0	1	23	7	16	27
Hungary	10	4	1	5	14	14	0	13
Faroe Islands	10	2	3	5	4	16	-12	9
Latvia	10	2	1	7	7	18	-11	7
Andorra	10	1	1	8	2	23	-21	4

Nine-goal Andre Silva

Switzerland .. (2) 2-0 (0) .... Portugal
Portugal .... (3) 6-0 (0) .... Andorra
Faroe Islands .. (0) 0-6 (3) .... Portugal
Portugal .... (1) 4-1 (0) .... Latvia

Portugal .... (2) 3-0 (0) .... Hungary
Latvia .... (0) 0-3 (1) .... Portugal
Portugal .... (2) 5-1 (1) ... Faroe Islands

Hungary .... (0) 0-1 (0) .... Portugal
Andorra .... (0) 0-2 (0) .... Portugal
Portugal .... (1) 2-0 (0) .... Switzerland

Portugal celebrate
victory at Euro 2016

Photo by Lars Baron/Getty Images

Players used in qualifying		Career			Qualification			
Pos	Club	Age	P	G	P	G		■
GK Rui Patricio	Sporting	30	68	-	10	-	-	-
DEF Eliseu	Benfica	34	29	1	4	-	1	-
DEF Joao Cancelo	Inter	24	7	3	3	2	-	-
DEF Semedo	Barcelona	24	8	-	2	-	-	-
DEF Pepe	Besiktas	35	92	5	8	-	2	-
DEF Bruno Alves	Rangers	36	95	11	3	1	-	-
DEF Cedric Soares	Southampton	26	26	1	6	-	1	-
DEF Fabio Coentrao	Sporting	30	52	5	1	-	-	-
DEF Jose Fonte	Dalian Yifang	34	28	-	8	-	1	-
DEF Luis Neto	Fenerbahce	30	18	-	1	-	-	-
DEF Antunes	Getafe	31	13	1	3	-	-	-
DEF Raphael Guerreiro	B Dortmund	24	21	2	5	-	-	-
MID Adrien Silva	Leicester	29	21	1	1	-	1	-
MID Andre Gomes	Barcelona	24	28	-	7	-	1	-
MID Pizzi	Benfica	28	9	2	1	-	-	-
MID Bernardo Silva	Man City	23	22	2	7	-	-	-
MID Danilo Pereira	Porto	26	27	1	3	-	-	-
MID Joao Mario	West Ham	25	33	1	9	-	-	-
MID Gelson Martins	Sporting	23	17	-	6	-	1	-
MID Joao Moutinho	Monaco	31	107	7	8	1	-	-
MID Renato Sanches	Swansea	20	13	1	1	-	-	-
MID Ricardo Quaresma	Besiktas	34	74	9	9	-	1	-
MID William Carvalho	Sporting	26	40	2	8	2	-	-
ATT Andre Silva	Milan	22	20	11	10	9	-	-
ATT Eder	Lokomotiv Moscow	30	33	4	2	-	-	-
ATT Nelson Oliveira	Norwich	26	17	2	1	1	-	-
ATT Cristiano Ronaldo	Real Madrid	33	149	81	9	15	1	-
ATT Goncalo Guedes	Valencia	21	7	1	1	-	-	-
ATT Nani	Lazio	31	112	24	3	-	-	-

Correct scores

	Competitive	Friendly
1-0	6	2
2-0	3	1
2-1	2	2
3-0	2	2
3-1	-	-
3-2	1	-
4-0	1	1
4-1	1	-
4-2	-	-
4-3	-	-
0-0	4	-
1-1	3	1
2-2	1	-
3-3	1	-
4-4	-	-
0-1	1	4
0-2	1	1
1-2	-	1
0-3	-	1
1-3	-	-
2-3	-	1
0-4	-	-
1-4	-	-
2-4	-	-
3-4	-	-
Other	3	2

Since Brazil 2014

Half-time/full-time double results

Win/Win	11	37%	Win 1st half	12	40%
Draw/Win	8	27%	Win 2nd half	16	53%
Lose/Win	0	0%	Win both halves	8	27%
Win/Draw	1	3%	Goal both halves	13	43%
Draw/Draw	8	27%			
Lose/Draw	0	0%	Overall		
Win/Lose	0	0%	● Win	63%	
Draw/Lose	1	3%	● Draw	30%	
Lose/Lose	1	3%	● Lose	7%	

Overall: W19, D9, L2 in 30 competitive games since Brazil 2014

Under & over goals

19 (63%)	Over 1.5	11 (37%)
✓		✗
12 (40%)	Over 2.5	18 (60%)
✓		✗
8 (27%)	Over 3.5	22 (73%)
✓		✗
6 (20%)	Over 4.5	24 (80%)
✓		✗

Both teams to score

10 (33%)	Both score	20 (67%)
✓		✗
5 (17%)	& win	25 (83%)
✓		✗
0 (0%)	& lose	30 (100%)
✓		✗

In 30 competitive games since Brazil 2014

Clean sheets

18 (60%)	Clean sheets	12 (40%)
✓		✗
14 (47%)	Win to nil	16 (53%)
✓		✗
6 (20%)	Fail to score	24 (80%)
✓		✗
2 (7%)	Lose to nil	28 (93%)
✓		✗

When they score

● For ● Against

Total match goals by half

23 (77%)	1st half	7 (23%)
F		A

35 (78%)	2nd half	10 (22%)
F		A

5	2	1	9	6	5	8	8	2	12
0-9	10-18	19-27	28-36	37-45	46-54	55-63	64-72	73-81	82-90
1	1	2	1	2	4	2	3	0	1

Goals for & against by half

23 (40%)	For	35 (60%)
1st		2nd

7 (41%)	Against	10 (59%)
1st		2nd

Portugal score first

They win	18		90%
They draw	2		10%
They lose	0		0%

Portugal concede first

They win	1		17%
They draw	3		50%
They lose	2		33%

In 30 competitive games since Brazil 2014

Cristiano Ronaldo heads the second of his 15 qualifying goals
Photo by David Ramos/Getty Images

Top scorers in qualifying

	P	G	1st	AT	%	Sui 2-0 Prt	Prt 6-0 And	Fro 0-6 Prt	Prt 4-1 Lva	Prt 3-0 Hun	Lva 0-3 Prt	Prt 5-1 Fro	Hun 0-1 Prt	And 0-2 Prt	Prt 2-0 Sui
Cristiano Ronaldo	9	15	5	7	47	4	1	2	2	2	3	-		ᶜ1	-
Andre Silva	10	9	4	7	28	↳	1	3	-	⁻1	⁻1	↳	⁻1	⁻1	⁻1
Joao Cancelo	3	2	0	2	6	1	1	-							
William Carvalho	8	2	0	2	6	↳		-	1	-		1		↳	-
Nelson Oliveira	1	1	0	1	3						ᶜ1				
Bruno Alves	3	1	0	1	3					1		-		-	
Joao Moutinho	8	1	0	1	3	↳	-	ᶜ1		↳	-		↳	-	-

G goals scored, **1st** first match goal (own goals don't count) **AT** goals at any time (ie. number of scoring appearances), **P** penalties, **%** percentage of total team goals scored by each player. Russia 2018 qualifying only. Game-by-game stats show goals scored, 1st goals are in red, dash did not score, ↳ substituted on, ↩ substituted off, blank did not play

Bookings in World Cup qualifying

Played 10 **Cards** (10Y) ☐☐☐☐☐☐☐☐☐☐   **Avg make-up** (☐10 ■25) 10

Profile

What goes up must come down. Spain's glorious clean sweep of international football could never last and the World Cup win of 2010 sandwiched between European Championship success stories of 2008 and 2012 was a tough act to follow.

La Roja were sent packing at the group stage four years ago but many believe Spain are back in business.

How they qualified

A cruise. The only dropped points came in a 1-1 draw in Italy when Spain were much the better side. They proved that in the return fixture – a 3-0 thrashing of the Azzurri in Madrid was the best performance by any European side in qualifying.

The manager

Julen Lopetegui flopped at club level with Porto but had great success with the Spanish youth teams, nurturing many of the talents who have progressed to the senior side, with a style based around possession football.

He is a flexible coach who has tried a back three for Plan B at the World Cup plus the use of a false nine as well as a more traditional centre forward.

The squad

Lopetegui has a deep squad and will have sleepless nights wondering which talents to leave at home, but most of the starting positions are already locked down and goalkeeper David de Gea is the undisputed number one.

Fitness permitting it will be a combined Barcelona and Real Madrid defensive wall of Dani Carvajal, Sergio Ramos, Gerard Pique and Jordi Alba with Sergio Busquets sitting just in front of those in the preferred formation of 4-1-4-1.

David Silva, Isco and Andres Iniesta will be three of those in the quartet behind the solo striker and Lopetegui will have to choose between Koke, Saul Niguez and Thiago Alcantara as the fourth midfielder,

Factfile

FA founded 1913
www rfef.es
Head coach Julen Lopetegui
Date qualified October 6, 2017

Strengths

- ☑ World-class players in most positions
- ☑ Will keep possession beautifully as ever, but now also have attacking punch

Weaknesses

- ☒ Will the political unrest spill over to the football team?
- ☒ Lack of dynamism in the first-choice midfield

Star rating ★★★★☆

Fixtures

1 June 15, 7pm v Portugal, Sochi
2 June 20, 7pm v Iran, Kazan
3 June 25, 7pm v Morocco, Kaliningrad

Base Krasnodar
Total distance 4,100 miles

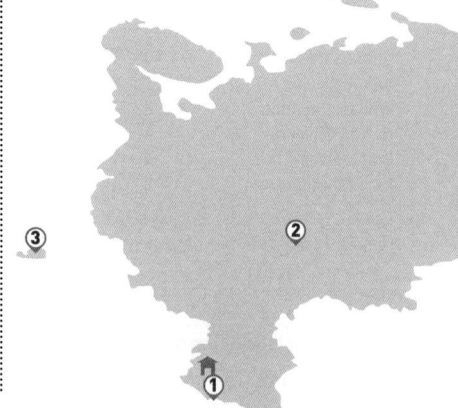

Spain's qualifying campaign was almost flawless, with a 3-0 win over Italy a standout performance

although Marcos Asensio would be another option if width is required.

Diego Costa is favourite for the striking role ahead of Rodrigo and Alvaro Morata in a star-studded side.

Key man

As captain, Ramos has a huge part to play in off-field matters given the political problems in Spain. Centre-back partner Pique is among those pushing for a Catalan independence vote and the two don't get on but Ramos needs to make sure the squad pulls together.

Rising star

"The best left foot since Lionel Messi," was how Zinedine Zidane described Asensio, who has scored important and sensational goals for Real Madrid since signing from Mallorca.

Asensio was named in the team of the tournament at last summer's European U21 Championship.

Wildcard

Lopetegui stunned many when he recalled David Villa, Spain's record goalscorer, for qualifiers against Italy and Liechtenstein for the first time since the 2014 World Cup.

The coach says he will not close the door on anyone. He travelled to New York to watch Villa in the MLS and told Marca newspaper: "What he can contribute is what he has always been able to – quality, intuition and a will and desire to compete that will put him at the service of the team."

Prospects

The market predicts a semi-final clash with Germany that would not be far short of a 50-50 and Spain have enough elite players to win the World Cup.

How to back them

Spain look lively contenders and pairing them with France and Brazil in the name-the-finalists market could be the best value.

World Cup record		Group stage(s)						Knockout rounds					
		P	W	D	L	F	A	P	W	D	L	F	A
Uruguay 1930	Did not enter	-	-	-	-	-	-	-	-	-	-	-	-
Italy 1934	Quarter-finals	-	-	-	-	-	-	3	1	1	1	4	3
France 1938	Withdrew	-	-	-	-	-	-	-	-	-	-	-	-
Brazil 1950	Fourth place	6	3	1	2	10	12	-	-	-	-	-	-
Switzerland 1954	Did not qualify	-	-	-	-	-	-	-	-	-	-	-	-
Sweden 1958	Did not qualify	-	-	-	-	-	-	-	-	-	-	-	-
Chile 1962	Group stage	3	1	0	2	2	3	-	-	-	-	-	-
England 1966	Group stage	3	1	0	2	4	5	-	-	-	-	-	-
Mexico 1970	Did not qualify	-	-	-	-	-	-	-	-	-	-	-	-
Germany 1974	Did not qualify	-	-	-	-	-	-	-	-	-	-	-	-
Argentina 1978	Group stage	3	1	1	1	2	2	-	-	-	-	-	-
Spain 1982	2nd group stage	5	1	2	2	4	5	-	-	-	-	-	-
Mexico 1986	Quarter-finals	3	2	0	1	5	2	2	1	1	0	6	2
Italy 1990	Round of 16	3	2	1	0	5	2	1	0	1	0	1	1
USA 1994	Quarter finals	3	1	2	0	6	4	2	1	0	1	4	2
France 1998	Group stage	3	1	1	1	8	4	-	-	-	-	-	-
Korea/Japan 2002	Quarter-finals	3	3	0	0	9	4	2	0	2	0	1	1
Germany 2006	Round of 16	3	3	0	0	8	1	1	0	0	1	1	3
South Africa 2010	● Winners	3	2	0	1	4	2	4	3	1	0	3	0
Brazil 2014	Group stage	3	1	0	2	4	7	-	-	-	-	-	-
Totals		44	22	8	14	71	53	15	6	6	3	20	12

Continental championships (best perfomance)

Uefa European Championship	Winners (3)	1964, 2008, 2012

World Cup head-to-heads

Spain v	P	W	D	L	F	A	Latest
Argentina	1	0	0	1	1	2	1966
Australia	1	1	0	0	3	0	2014
Belgium	2	1	1	0	3	2	1990
Brazil	5	1	1	3	5	10	1986
Croatia	2	1	1	0	3	2	1990
Denmark	1	1	0	0	5	1	1986
England	2	1	1	0	1	0	1982
France	1	0	0	1	1	3	2006
Germany	4	1	1	2	4	5	2010
Mexico	1	1	0	0	1	0	1962
Nigeria	1	0	0	1	2	3	1998
Portugal	1	1	0	0	1	0	2010
Saudi Arabia	1	1	0	0	1	0	2006
Serbia	2	1	1	0	3	2	1990
South Korea	3	1	2	0	5	3	2002
Sweden	2	1	0	1	2	3	1978
Switzerland	3	2	0	1	5	2	2010
Tunisia	1	1	0	0	3	1	2006
Uruguay	2	0	2	0	2	2	1990

90 mins only, includes games against Yugoslavia and West Germany

David Villa got the only goal when Spain beat Group B rivals Portugal at South Africa 2010

How they qualified

Group G	P	W	D	L	F	A	GD	P
Spain	**10**	**9**	**1**	**0**	**36**	**3**	**33**	**28**
Italy	10	7	2	1	21	8	13	23
Albania	10	4	1	5	10	13	-3	13
Israel	10	4	0	6	10	15	-5	12
Macedonia	10	3	2	5	15	15	0	11
Liechtenstein	10	0	0	10	1	39	-38	0

Julen Lopetegui

Spain .... (1) 8-0 (0)... Liechtenstein
Italy............... (0) 1-1 (0)................**Spain**
Albania .... (0) 0-2 (0)................**Spain**
Spain .... (1) 4-0 (0)...... Macedonia
Spain .... (2) 4-1 (0)............... Israel   Spain .... (2) 3-0 (0)................ Italy   Spain .... (3) 3-0 (0)..........Albania
Macedonia ..... (0) 1-2 (2)................**Spain**   Liechtenstein . (0) 0-8 (4)..............**Spain**   Israel............. (0) 0-1 (0)..............**Spain**

Players used in qualifying

Pos		Club	Age	P	G	P	G	☐	■
				Career		**Qualification**			
GK	David de Gea	Man Utd	27	27	-	9	-	-	-
GK	Pepe Reina	Napoli	35	36	-	1	-	-	-
DEF	Alvaro Odriozola	Sociedad	22	2	-	1	-	-	-
DEF	Nacho	Real Madrid	28	15	-	5	-	-	-
DEF	Cesar Azpilicueta	Chelsea	28	21	-	1	-	-	-
DEF	Daniel Carvajal	Real Madrid	26	15	-	5	-	-	-
DEF	Gerard Pique	Barcelona	31	96	5	8	-	2	-
DEF	Inigo Martinez	Ath Bilbao	27	4	-	1	-	-	-
DEF	Jordi Alba	Barcelona	29	60	8	6	-	1	-
DEF	Marc Bartra	Betis	27	13	-	1	-	-	-
DEF	Nacho Monreal	Arsenal	32	21	1	4	1	-	-
DEF	Sergio Ramos	Real Madrid	32	151	13	9	1	1	-
MID	Vitolo	Atl Madrid	28	12	4	5	4	1	-
MID	Isco	Real Madrid	26	27	10	8	5	-	-
MID	Koke	Atl Madrid	26	38	-	8	-	-	-
MID	Andres Iniesta	Barcelona	34	125	13	6	-	-	-
MID	Asier Illarramendi	Sociedad	28	3	1	1	1	-	-
MID	David Silva	Man City	32	119	35	9	5	2	-
MID	Jonathan Viera	Beijing Guoan	28	1	-	1	-	-	-
MID	Marco Asensio	Real Madrid	22	10	-	4	-	-	-
MID	Saul	Atl Madrid	23	9	-	3	-	-	-
MID	Sergi Busquets	Barcelona	29	102	2	9	-	2	-
MID	Sergi Roberto	Barcelona	26	3	1	1	1	-	-
MID	Thiago Alcantara	B Munich	27	27	2	8	1	1	-
MID	Jose Callejon	Napoli	31	5	-	2	-	-	-
MID	Nolito	Sevilla	31	16	6	2	1	-	-
ATT	Pedro	Chelsea	30	65	17	3	-	-	-
ATT	Alvaro Morata	Chelsea	25	23	13	5	5	-	-
ATT	Aritz Aduriz	Ath Bilbao	37	13	2	3	1	-	-
ATT	David Villa	New York City	36	98	59	1	-	-	-
ATT	Diego Costa	Atl Madrid	29	18	7	5	5	1	-
ATT	Gerard Deulofeu	Watford	24	4	1	1	-	-	-
ATT	Iago Aspas	Celta Vigo	30	8	4	3	2	-	-
ATT	Rodrigo	Valencia	27	4	2	1	-	-	-

GROUP B (side tab)

Correct scores

	Competitive	Friendly
1-0	6	-
2-0	2	3
2-1	1	1
3-0	4	-
3-1	-	1
3-2	-	-
4-0	3	-
4-1	1	-
4-2	-	-
4-3	-	-
0-0	-	1
1-1	1	2
2-2	-	2
3-3	-	1
4-4	-	-
0-1	-	3
0-2	1	1
1-2	2	-
0-3	-	-
1-3	-	-
2-3	-	-
0-4	-	-
1-4	-	-
2-4	-	-
3-4	-	-
Other	3	3

Since Brazil 2014

Half-time/full-time double results

Win/Win	17	71%
Draw/Win	3	13%
Lose/Win	0	0%
Win/Draw	0	0%
Draw/Draw	1	4%
Lose/Draw	0	0%
Win/Lose	0	0%
Draw/Lose	1	4%
Lose/Lose	2	8%

Win 1st half	17	71%
Win 2nd half	13	54%
Win both halves	10	42%
Goal both halves	10	42%

Overall
- Win 83%
- Draw 4%
- Lose 13%

Overall: W20, D1, L3 in 24 competitive games since Brazil 2014

Under & over goals

18 (75%)	Over 1.5	6 (25%)	✓ ✗
14 (58%)	Over 2.5	10 (42%)	✓ ✗
7 (29%)	Over 3.5	17 (71%)	✓ ✗
4 (17%)	Over 4.5	20 (83%)	✓ ✗

Both teams to score

6 (25%)	Both score	18 (75%)	✓ ✗
3 (13%)	& win	21 (87%)	✓ ✗
2 (8%)	& lose	22 (92%)	✓ ✗

In 24 competitive games since Brazil 2014

Clean sheets

18 (75%)	Clean sheets	6 (25%)	✓ ✗
18 (75%)	Win to nil	6 (25%)	✓ ✗

1 (4%)	Fail to score	23 (96%)	✓ ✗
1 (4%)	Lose to nil	23 (96%)	✓ ✗

When they score

● For ● Against

Total match goals by half

32 (89%)	1st half	4 (11%)
F		A

32 (84%)	2nd half	6 (16%)
F		A

Goals for & against by half

32 (50%)	For	32 (50%)
1st		2nd

4 (40%)	Against	6 (60%)
1st		2nd

For (top row): 4, 10, 6, 4, 8, 5, 9, 3, 3, 12
Time bands: 0-9, 10-18, 19-27, 28-36, 37-45, 46-54, 55-63, 64-72, 73-81, 82-90
Against (bottom row): 0, 1, 0, 2, 1, 0, 0, 1, 1, 4

Spain score first

They win	20	91%
They draw	1	5%
They lose	1	5%

Spain concede first

They win	0	0%
They draw	0	0%
They lose	2	100%

In 24 competitive games since Brazil 2014

Isco scored five in qualifying

Photo by Denis Doyle/Getty Images

Top scorers in qualifying

	P	G	1st	AT	%	Esp 8-0 Lie	Ita 1-1 Esp	Alb 0-2 Esp	Esp 4-0 Mkd	Esp 4-1 Isr	Mkd 1-2 Esp	Esp 3-0 Ita	Lie 0-8 Esp	Esp 3-0 Alb	Isr 0-1 Esp
Diego Costa	5	5	2	4	14	2	↺	1		1	1				
Alvaro Morata	5	5	0	3	14	2	↳		↺			1	2		
Isco	8	5	1	4	14			↳	↳	1	-	2	1	1	↳
David Silva	9	5	2	4	14	2	-	-	-	1	1	-	1	↺	
Vitolo	5	4	2	4	11	1	1	↺	1	1					
Iago Aspas	3	2	0	1	6						↳		2		↳
Rodrigo	1	1	1	1	3									1	
Illarramendi	1	1	1	1	3										1
Sergi Roberto	1	1	0	1	3	1									
Nolito	2	1	0	1	3	↳		1							
Aduriz	3	1	0	1	3					1				↳	↳
Nacho Monreal	4	1	0	1	3				-	1			-		-
Thiago Alcantara	8	1	0	1	3	↺	↳	-	-		↺	↳	-	1	
Sergio Ramos	9	1	1	1	3	-	-	↺		-	-	-	1	-	↳

G goals scored, **1st** first match goal (own goals don't count) **AT** goals at any time (ie. number of scoring appearances), **P** penalties, **%** percentage of total team goals scored by each player. Russia 2018 qualifying only. Game-by-game stats show goals scored, 1st goals are in red, dash did not score, ↳ substituted on, ↺ substituted off, blank did not play.

Bookings in World Cup qualifying

Played 10 **Cards** (11Y) ▯▯▯▯▯▯▯▯▯▯▯   **Avg make-up** (▯10 ■25) 11

Profile

In 1986 Morocco became the first African side to reach the knockout phase of a World Cup but this will be their first appearance in a finals for 20 years.

The Atlas Lions are underachievers on the international stage with only one Africa Cup of Nations title – and that was in 1976.

How they qualified

They were in a competitive section with Ivory Coast, Mali and Gabon but Morocco were the only side in the final round of African qualifying not to concede a goal as they finished in style with a 2-0 success away to the Elephants.

The manager

The suave Herve Renard is a demigod of African football after leading Zambia (2012) and Ivory Coast (2015) to Afcon glory, although he was unable to land the hat-trick for injury-hit Morocco last year following an unfortunate quarter-final exit against Egypt.

The squad

Most of Morocco's squad ply their trade in decent leagues and the strength of their side has increased in recent years after they secured the services of a number of European-born players who held dual nationality – Ajax's Hakim Ziyech caused a particular stir in Holland.

"How stupid can you be to choose Morocco if you are in contention for the Dutch national team?" asked Marco van Basten, although he is the one now looking the fool.

It was not all plain sailing for Ziyech, one of the Eredivisie's star men, who had a bust-up with Renard after an Africa Cup of Nations snub and said he would never play for the coach again before the two patched up their differences.

Ziyech is the biggest creative force for the Atlas Lions even though he is usually asked to play wider at international level with Younes Belhanda, Mbark Boussoufa

Captain Medhi Benatia applauds the fans after the recent friendly against Serbia
Photo by Dave Winter/Icon Sport via Getty Images

and Karim El Ahmadi forming the central midfield in a 4-3-3 formation.

The inconsistent but gifted Sofiane Boufal may have to be content with a place on the bench as Morocco are blessed with midfield talent, although that has not spread to the central striking role.

Late bloomer Khalid Boutaib, who scored 20 goals in Ligue 2 last season to earn a move to Turkish top-flight side Yeni Malatyaspor, may be the answer after Morocco's attempts to add Spanish international Munir El Haddadi were thwarted by Fifa.

Another issue was left-back but Real Madrid's right-footed Achraf Hakimi has filled in excellently for a defence in which Juventus's Medhi Benatia excels.

Key man

Captain Benatia is a strong centre-back with plenty of experience in a career which has seen him play for Roma, Bayern Munich and Juve.

Rising star

Amine Harit, born and raised in France and capped by Les Bleus at youth level, has chosen to represent Morocco. He can play in a variety of attacking midfield positions.

Wildcard

Ayoub El Kaabi scored nine goals in the Total African Nations Championship, an event for home-based African players won by hosts Morocco in February.

Prospects

Morocco may go out early but only because of their tough group. They are a decent team who are better than the odds suggest.

How to back them

The current 3-4 offered about at least one team failing to score against Iran on June 15 will surely go off much shorter given the defensive capabilities of both sides as well as so much being at stake.

World Cup record

World Cup record		Group stage(s)						Knockout rounds					
		P	W	D	L	F	A	P	W	D	L	F	A
Uruguay 1930	Did not enter	-	-	-	-	-	-	-	-	-	-	-	-
Italy 1934	Did not enter	-	-	-	-	-	-	-	-	-	-	-	-
France 1938	Did not enter	-	-	-	-	-	-	-	-	-	-	-	-
Brazil 1950	Did not enter	-	-	-	-	-	-	-	-	-	-	-	-
Switzerland 1954	Did not enter	-	-	-	-	-	-	-	-	-	-	-	-
Sweden 1958	Did not enter	-	-	-	-	-	-	-	-	-	-	-	-
Chile 1962	Did not qualify	-	-	-	-	-	-	-	-	-	-	-	-
England 1966	Withdrew	-	-	-	-	-	-	-	-	-	-	-	-
Mexico 1970	Group stage	3	0	1	2	2	6	-	-	-	-	-	-
Germany 1974	Did not qualify	-	-	-	-	-	-	-	-	-	-	-	-
Argentina 1978	Did not qualify	-	-	-	-	-	-	-	-	-	-	-	-
Spain 1982	Did not qualify	-	-	-	-	-	-	-	-	-	-	-	-
Mexico 1986	Round of 16	3	1	2	0	3	1	1	0	0	1	0	1
Italy 1990	Did not qualify	-	-	-	-	-	-	-	-	-	-	-	-
USA 1994	Group stage	3	0	0	3	2	5	-	-	-	-	-	-
France 1998	Group stage	3	1	1	1	5	5	-	-	-	-	-	-
Korea/Japan 2002	Did not qualify	-	-	-	-	-	-	-	-	-	-	-	-
Germany 2006	Did not qualify	-	-	-	-	-	-	-	-	-	-	-	-
South Africa 2010	Did not qualify	-	-	-	-	-	-	-	-	-	-	-	-
Brazil 2014	Did not qualify	-	-	-	-	-	-	-	-	-	-	-	-
Totals		12	2	4	6	12	17	1	0	0	1	0	1

Continental championships (best perfomance)

Africa Cup of nations	Winners (1)	1976

World Cup head-to-heads

Morocco v	P	W	D	L	F	A	Latest
Belgium	1	0	0	1	0	1	1994
Brazil	1	0	0	1	0	3	1998
England	1	0	1	0	0	0	1986
Germany	2	0	0	2	1	3	1986
Peru	1	0	0	1	0	3	1970
Poland	1	0	1	0	0	0	1986
Portugal	1	1	0	0	3	1	1986
Saudi Arabia	1	0	0	1	1	2	1994

90 mins only, includes games against West Germany

Morocco lost 1-0 to Belgium at USA 94

Photo by Beate Mueller/Bongarts/Getty Images

How they qualified

Round 2
Morocco........ (1) 2-0 (0)........Eq Guinea
Eq Guinea ...... (1) 1-0 (0)......... Morocco
    Morocco won 2-1 on aggregate

▶▶ Full qualifying results on pages 228-241

Round 2

Group C	P	W	D	L	F	A	GD	P
Morocco	6	3	3	0	11	0	11	12
Ivory Coast	6	2	2	2	7	5	2	8
Gabon	6	1	3	2	2	7	-5	6
Mali	6	0	4	2	1	9	-8	4

Gabon............ (0) 0-0 (0).......... Morocco
Morocco........ (0) 0-0 (0)...... Ivory Coast
Morocco........ (2) 6-0 (0)........ .... Mali
Mali................ (0) 0-0 (0)......... Morocco
Morocco........ (1) 3-0 (0).............Gabon
Ivory Coast..... (0) 0-2 (2)......... Morocco

Players used in qualifying		Career			Qualification				
Pos		Club	Age	P	G	P	G	□	■
GK	Munir	Numancia	29	25	-	8	-	-	-
DEF	Badr Banoun	R Casablanca	24	7	-	1	-	-	-
DEF	Zou Feddal	Real Betis	28	14	-	2	-	2	-
DEF	Abderrahim Achchakir	FAR Rabat	31	16	-	2	-	-	-
DEF	Achraf Hakimi	Real Madrid	19	7	1	4	1	-	-
DEF	Achraf Lazaar	Benevento	26	18	-	3	-	1	-
DEF	Adil Karrouchy	R Casablanca	35	5	-	1	-	1	1
DEF	Fouad Chafik	Dijon	31	10	-	2	-	1	-
DEF	Hamza Mendyl	Lille	20	11	-	2	-	-	-
DEF	Issam El Adoua	Al Dhafra	31	34	2	2	-	-	-
DEF	Manuel da Costa	Istanbul Buyuk.	32	25	1	2	-	-	-
DEF	Mehdi Benatia	Juventus	31	53	2	7	1	1	-
DEF	Romain Saiss	Wolves	28	23	1	6	-	2	-
MID	Abdelaziz Barrada	Al Nasr	28	28	4	1	-	-	-
MID	Adnane Tighadouini	FC Twente	25	1	-	1	-	-	-
MID	Amine Harit	Schalke	20	3	-	1	-	-	-
MID	Brahim Nakach	W Casablanca	36	6	-	1	-	-	-
MID	Faycal Fajr	Getafe	29	21	2	4	1	-	-
MID	Hakim Ziyech	Ajax	25	15	8	6	2	-	-
MID	Ismail El Haddad	W Casablanca	27	10	2	1	-	-	-
MID	Karim El Ahmadi	Feyenoord	33	48	1	5	-	1	-
MID	Marwane Saadane	Rizespor	26	6	1	1	-	-	-
MID	Moubarak Boussoufa	Al Jazira	33	54	6	6	-	1	-
MID	Mehdi C-Gonzalez	St. Liege	28	20	1	2	-	-	-
MID	Nabil Dirar	Fenerbahce	32	34	3	4	1	1	-
MID	Omar El Kaddouri	PAOK Salonika	27	27	5	2	-	1	-
MID	Sofiane Boufal	Southampton	24	6	-	1	-	-	-
MID	Sofyan Amrabat	Feyenoord	21	4	-	1	-	-	-
MID	Younes Belhanda	Galatasaray	28	42	3	5	-	2	-
MID	Youssef Ait Bennasser	Caen	21	11	-	2	-	-	-
MID	Oussama Tannane	St-Etienne	24	9	2	4	-	-	-
ATT	Mimoun Mahi	FC Groningen	24	2	1	1	1	-	-
ATT	Achraf Bencharki	Al-Hilal	23	6	1	1	-	-	-
ATT	Aziz Bouhaddouz	St Pauli	31	12	3	1	-	-	-
ATT	Khalid Boutaib	Malatyaspor	31	15	7	4	4	1	-
ATT	Nordin Amrabat	Leganes	31	40	4	6	-	-	-
ATT	Rachid Alioui	Nimes	25	8	2	2	-	-	-
ATT	Yacine Bammou	Nantes	26	7	1	2	1	-	-
ATT	Youssef El Arabi	Al-Duhail	31	41	15	3	1	-	-
ATT	Youssef En-Nesyri	Malaga	20	15	1	2	-	-	-

Correct scores

	Competitive	Friendly
1-0	3	2
2-0	4	3
2-1	-	3
3-0	2	2
3-1	1	1
3-2	-	-
4-0	-	2
4-1	-	-
4-2	-	-
4-3	-	-
0-0	3	2
1-1	1	1
2-2	-	-
3-3	-	-
4-4	-	-
0-1	4	3
0-2	-	-
1-2	-	2
0-3	-	-
1-3	-	-
2-3	-	-
0-4	-	-
1-4	-	-
2-4	-	-
3-4	-	-
Other	1	1

Since Brazil 2014

Half-time/full-time double results

Win/Win	7	37%	Win 1st half	8	42%
Draw/Win	4	21%	Win 2nd half	8	42%
Lose/Win	0	0%	Win both halves	4	21%
Win/Draw	1	5%	Goal both halves	4	21%
Draw/Draw	3	16%			
Lose/Draw	0	0%	Overall		
Win/Lose	0	0%	● Win	58%	
Draw/Lose	2	11%	● Draw	21%	
Lose/Lose	2	11%	● Lose	21%	

Overall: W11, D4, L4 in 19 competitive games since Brazil 2014

Under & over goals

9 (47%)	Over 1.5	10 (53%)
4 (21%)	Over 2.5	15 (79%)
2 (11%)	Over 3.5	17 (89%)
1 (5%)	Over 4.5	18 (95%)

Both teams to score

2 (11%)	Both score	17 (89%)
1 (5%)	& win	18 (95%)
0 (0%)	& lose	19 (100%)

In 19 competitive games since Brazil 2014

Clean sheets

13 (68%)	Clean sheets	6 (32%)
10 (53%)	Win to nil	9 (47%)
7 (37%)	Fail to score	12 (63%)
4 (21%)	Lose to nil	15 (79%)

When they score

● For ● Against

Total match goals by half

13 (81%)	1st half	3 (19%)
F		A

14 (82%)	2nd half	3 (18%)
F		A

	0	1	5	4	3	2	4	5	0	3
	0-9	10-18	19-27	28-36	37-45	46-54	55-63	64-72	73-81	82-90
	1	1	0	1	0	0	1	0	0	2

Goals for & against by half

13 (48%)	For	14 (52%)
1st		2nd

3 (50%)	Against	3 (50%)
1st		2nd

Morocco score first

They win	10	91%
They draw	1	9%
They lose	0	0%

Morocco concede first

They win	1	20%
They draw	0	0%
They lose	4	80%

In 19 competitive games since Brazil 2014

Khalid Boutaib, Morocco's top scorer in qualifying

Top scorers in qualifying

	P	G	1st	AT	%	Mar 2-0 Gnq	Gnq 1-0 Mar	Gab 0-0 Mar	Mar 0-0 Civ	Mar 6-0 Mli	Mli 0-0 Mar	Mar 3-0 Gab	Civ 0-2 Mar
Khalid Boutaib	4	4	1	2	31					↶1	-	↶3	↺
Hakim Ziyech	6	2	1	1	15	-	↳			2	↺	-	↺
Mimoun Mahi	1	1	0	1	8					↶1			
Yacine Bammou	2	1	0	1	8	↶1	-						
Youssef El-Arabi	3	1	1	1	8	↶1	↺	↺					
Nabil Dirar	4	1	1	1	8					-	-	-	1
Faycal Fajr	4	1	0	1	8		↺			↶1	↺		↳
Achraf Hakimi	4	1	0	1	8					1	-	-	-
Mehdi Benatia	7	1	0	1	8	-	-		-	-	-	↺	1

G goals scored, **1st** first match goal (own goals don't count) **AT** goals at any time (ie. number of scoring appearances), **P** penalties, **%** percentage of total team goals scored by each player. Russia 2018 qualifying only. Game-by-game stats show goals scored, 1st goals are in red, dash did not score, ↳ substituted on, ↺ substituted off, blank did not play

Bookings in World Cup qualifying

Played 8 **Cards** (15Y, 1R) ⬜⬜⬜⬜⬜⬜⬜⬜⬜⬜⬜⬜⬜⬜⬜ ⬛   **Avg make-up** (⬜10 ⬛25) 21.9

IRAN

Profile

Iran have won only one World Cup match, albeit a pretty special victory against USA, but they are now considered by many to be Asia's strongest side in Russia.

How they qualified

Only Brazil booked their spot before Iran, who made it with two matches to spare. They went 12 matches without conceding at one stage, keeping nine consecutive clean sheets in the final qualifying round.

The manager

Former Manchester United assistant Carlos Queiroz has been in charge of Team Melli since 2011 and has also managed, among others, Real Madrid and Portugal. Defence is his priority.

The squad

Queiroz is delighted with the depth of his squad and has plans to rotate during the finals after they ran out of steam four years ago in the final fixture, a 3-1 defeat to Bosnia, following a respectable 0-0 draw with Nigeria and a heartbreaking late 1-0 loss to Argentina.

Iran are likely to use a 4-2-3-1 formation and counter-attack is set to be their main weapon. AZ Alkmaar's speedy winger Alireza Jahanbakhsh is a major threat and golden boy striker Sardar Azmoun leads the line expertly.

Reza Ghoochannejhad is the reserve striking option, although the forwards are unlikely to get much help from an organised midfield who are more interested in making sure the defence is well protected.

Key man

"I am sure I will be playing for a top European club in the near future," said Azmoun after claiming he turned down a move to Liverpool. A transfer to Lazio also fell through and he eventually returned to former club Rubin from Rostov.

The Real Madrid fan, who just missed

Factfile

FA founded 1920

www ffiri.ir

Head coach Carlos Queiroz

Date qualified June 12, 2017

Strengths

☑ Well-drilled defence has a clean sheet mentality

☑ Azmoun and Jahanbakhsh carry a counter-attacking threat

Weaknesses

☒ Queiroz has gone public in his anger at Iran's World Cup preparations

☒ Tactics unlikely to work should they concede the opening goal

Star rating ★★☆☆☆

Fixtures

1 June 15, 4pm v Morocco, Saint Petersburg

2 June 20, 7pm v Spain, Kazan

3 June 25, 7pm v Portugal, Saransk

Base Moscow

Total distance 2,300 miles

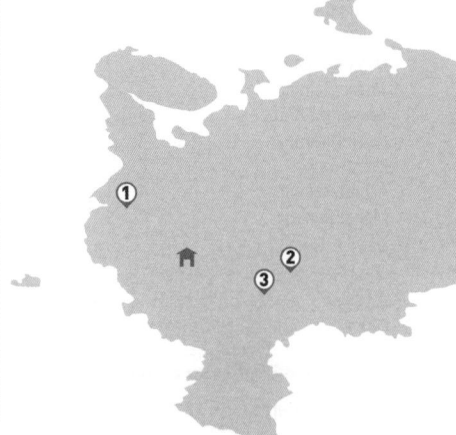

Carlos Queiroz and his side are flying high
Photo by Amin M. Jamali/Getty Images

out on selection as a youngster for the 2014 World Cup, has a strong all-round game and was hailed as "world-class" by the usually conservative Queiroz.

Rising star

Central midfielder Saeid Ezatolahi is banned for the Morocco clash after a disgraceful raking of studs down the head of the floored South Korean Min-Jae Kim and he could well be missed in the opener.

Ezatolahi made his club debut at the age of 16 and earned a move to Atletico Madrid before seeking greater first-team opportunities in Russia.

Wildcard

Masoud Shojaei would ordinarily make Iran's best 11 but the midfielder ignored a ban imposed by the Iranian government forbidding sportsmen from competing against Israelis.

Shojaei and team-mate Ehsan Hajsafi

played for their former club Panionios in the Europa League against Maccabi Tel Aviv and both wore wristbands with the Iranian flag.

Iran's deputy sports minister Mohammad Reza Davarzani said: "It is certain that Masoud Shojaei and Ehsan Hajsafi will never be invited to join the national football team because they violated the red line."

Both returned in March after seven months on the sidelines but will they be picked for the World Cup?

Prospects

Asia's best side have been given a tough draw but Iran can still pick up points.

How to back them

Azmoun takes up plenty of the book in the top Iranian goalscorer so try Jahanbakhsh at fancy odds. The AZ Alkmaar flyer has already bettered last season's ten-goal Eredivisie tally and has easily outperformed Azmoun at club level this season.

IRAN

World Cup record		Group stage(s)						Knockout rounds					
		P	W	D	L	F	A	P	W	D	L	F	A
Uruguay 1930	Did not enter	-	-	-	-	-	-	-	-	-	-	-	-
Italy 1934	Did not enter	-	-	-	-	-	-	-	-	-	-	-	-
France 1938	Did not enter	-	-	-	-	-	-	-	-	-	-	-	-
Brazil 1950	Did not enter	-	-	-	-	-	-	-	-	-	-	-	-
Switzerland 1954	Did not enter	-	-	-	-	-	-	-	-	-	-	-	-
Sweden 1958	Did not enter	-	-	-	-	-	-	-	-	-	-	-	-
Chile 1962	Did not enter	-	-	-	-	-	-	-	-	-	-	-	-
England 1966	Did not enter	-	-	-	-	-	-	-	-	-	-	-	-
Mexico 1970	Did not enter	-	-	-	-	-	-	-	-	-	-	-	-
Germany 1974	Did not qualify	-	-	-	-	-	-	-	-	-	-	-	-
Argentina 1978	Group stage	3	0	1	2	2	8	-	-	-	-	-	-
Spain 1982	Withdrew	-	-	-	-	-	-	-	-	-	-	-	-
Mexico 1986	Excluded	-	-	-	-	-	-	-	-	-	-	-	-
Italy 1990	Did not qualify	-	-	-	-	-	-	-	-	-	-	-	-
USA 1994	Did not qualify	-	-	-	-	-	-	-	-	-	-	-	-
France 1998	Group stage	3	1	0	2	2	4	-	-	-	-	-	-
Korea/Japan 2002	Did not qualify	-	-	-	-	-	-	-	-	-	-	-	-
Germany 2006	Group stage	3	0	1	2	2	6	-	-	-	-	-	-
South Africa 2010	Did not qualify	-	-	-	-	-	-	-	-	-	-	-	-
Brazil 2014	Group stage	3	0	1	2	1	4	-	-	-	-	-	-
Totals		12	1	3	8	7	22	0	0	0	0	0	0

Continental championships (best perfomance)

AFC Asian Cup	Winners (3)	1968, 1972, 1976

World Cup head-to-heads

Deco and Ronaldo got the goals when Iran lost 2-0 to Group B rivals Portugal at Germany 2006

Iran v	P	W	D	L	F	A	Latest	Iran v	P	W	D	L	F	A	Latest
Argentina	1	0	0	1	0	1	2014	Nigeria	1	0	1	0	0	0	2014
Croatia	1	0	0	1	0	1	1998	Peru	1	0	0	1	1	4	1978
Germany	1	0	0	1	2	2	1998	Portugal	1	0	0	1	0	2	2006
Mexico	1	0	0	1	1	3	2006	Serbia	1	0	0	1	0	1	1998

90 mins only, includes games against Yugoslavia

Players used in qualifying · Career · Qualification

Pos		Club	Age	P	G	P	G	☐	■
GK	Alireza Beiranvand	Persepolis	25	20	-	12	-	1	1
GK	Alireza Haghighi	Sundsvall	30	23	-	4	-	-	-
GK	Mohammad Mazaheri	Zob Ahan	29	3	-	1	-	-	-
GK	Sosha Makani	Sanat Naft	31	5	-	1	-	-	-
DEF	Ramin Rezaeian	Oostende	28	26	2	14	1	1	-
DEF	Ezzatollah Pourghaz	Sepahan	31	8	-	4	-	-	-
DEF	Jalal Hosseini	Persepolis	36	112	8	11	2	-	-
DEF	Hossein Kanaanizadega	Saipa	24	3	-	1	-	-	-
DEF	Khosro Heydari	Esteghlal	34	56	-	3	-	-	-
DEF	Mehdi Torabi	Saipa	23	14	3	7	1	-	-
DEF	Milad Mohammadi	Akhmat	24	16	-	10	-	1	-
DEF	Mohammad Ansari	Persepolis	26	3	-	2	-	-	-
DEF	Morteza Pouraliganji	Al-Sadd	26	25	2	13	1	2	-
DEF	Pejman Montazeri	Esteghlal	34	46	1	10	-	1	-
DEF	Rouzbeh Cheshmi	Esteghlal	24	7	-	2	-	-	-
DEF	Vouria Ghafouri	Esteghlal	30	20	-	5	-	-	-
DEF	Ehsan Hajsafi	Olympiakos	28	85	6	13	2	1	-
MID	Ali Karimi	Sepahan	24	9	-	3	-	-	-
MID	Andranik Teymourian	Gostaresh	35	100	9	9	1	-	-
MID	Ashkan Dejagah	Nottm Forest	31	44	8	12	2	3	-
MID	Dariush Shojaeian	Esteghlal	25	3	-	1	-	-	-
MID	Kamal Kamyabinia	Persepolis	29	4	1	2	1	-	-
MID	Masoud Shojaei	AEK Athens	34	72	8	7	1	1	-
MID	Omid Alishah	Teraktor Sazi	25	2	-	2	-	-	-
MID	Omid Ebrahimi	Esteghlal	30	28	-	10	-	2	-
MID	Saeid Ezatolahi	Amkar Perm	21	24	1	13	1	1	1
MID	Vahid Amiri	Persepolis	30	32	1	17	-	2	-
MID	Alireza Jahanbakhsh	AZ Alkmaar	24	36	4	14	2	1	-
ATT	Karim Ansarifard	Olympiakos	28	59	16	6	1	-	-
ATT	Kaveh Rezaei	Charleroi	25	9	1	3	-	-	-
ATT	Mehdi Taremi	Al-Gharafa	25	24	12	16	8	4	-
ATT	Reza Ghoochanneijhad	Heerenveen	30	40	17	9	1	-	-
ATT	Sardar Azmoun	Rubin	23	32	23	14	11	3	-

How they qualified

Round 2

Group D	P	W	D	L	F	A	GD	P
Iran	8	6	2	0	26	3	23	20
Oman	8	4	2	2	11	7	4	14
Turkmenistan	8	4	1	3	10	11	-1	13
Guam	8	2	1	5	3	16	-13	7
India	8	1	0	7	5	18	-13	3

Turkmenistan . (1) 1-1 (1)................**Iran**
Iran............... (4) 6-0 (0)..............Guam
India.............. (0) 0-3 (1)................**Iran**
Oman.............. (0) 1-1 (0)................**Iran**
Iran............... (1) 3-1 (0)...Turkmenistan

Guam .... (0) 0-6 (2)................**Iran**
Iran................ (1) 4-0 (0)...............India
Iran............... (2) 2-0 (0)..............Oman

Round 3

Group A	P	W	D	L	F	A	GD	P
Iran	10	6	4	0	10	2	8	22
South Korea	10	4	3	3	11	10	1	15
Syria	10	3	4	3	9	8	1	13
Uzbekistan	10	4	1	5	6	7	-1	13
China	10	3	3	4	8	10	-2	12
Qatar	10	2	1	7	8	15	-7	7

Iran.............. (0) 2-0 (0) ....Qatar

China.............. (0) 0-0 (0)................**Iran**
Uzbekistan...... (0) 0-1 (1)................**Iran**
Iran............... (1) 1-0 (0)...**South Korea**
Syria............... (0) 0-0 (0)................**Iran**
Qatar.............. (0) 0-1 (0)................**Iran**
Iran............... (0) 1-0 (0)...............China
Iran............... (1) 2-0 (0)...... Uzbekistan
South Korea.. (0) 0-0 (0)................**Iran**
Iran............... (1) 2-2 (1)...............Syria

▶▶ Full qualifying results on pages 228-241

IRAN

Correct scores

	Competitive	Friendly
1-0	6	4
2-0	4	2
2-1	-	3
3-0	1	-
3-1	1	1
3-2	-	-
4-0	1	1
4-1	-	-
4-2	-	-
4-3	-	-
0-0	3	-
1-1	3	2
2-2	1	-
3-3	-	-
4-4	-	-
0-1	-	2
0-2	-	-
1-2	-	-
0-3	-	-
1-3	-	1
2-3	-	-
0-4	-	-
1-4	-	-
2-4	-	-
3-4	-	-
Other	2	1

Since Brazil 2014

Half-time/full-time double results

Win/Win	10	45%
Draw/Win	5	23%
Lose/Win	0	0%
Win/Draw	1	5%
Draw/Draw	6	27%
Lose/Draw	0	0%
Win/Lose	0	0%
Draw/Lose	0	0%
Lose/Lose	0	0%

Win 1st half	11	50%
Win 2nd half	12	55%
Win both halves	7	32%
Goal both halves	8	36%

Overall
- ● Win 68%
- ● Draw 32%
- ● Lose 0%

Overall: W15, D7, L0 in 22 competitive games since Brazil 2014

Under & over goals

13 (59%)	Over 1.5	9 (41%)
6 (27%)	Over 2.5	16 (73%)
5 (23%)	Over 3.5	17 (77%)
2 (9%)	Over 4.5	20 (91%)

Both teams to score

5 (23%)	Both score	17 (77%)
1 (5%)	& win	21 (95%)
0 (0%)	& lose	22 (100%)

In 22 competitive games since Brazil 2014

Clean sheets

17 (77%)	Clean sheets	5 (23%)
14 (64%)	Win to nil	8 (36%)

3 (14%)	Fail to score	19 (86%)
0 (0%)	Lose to nil	22 (100%)

When they score

● For ● Against

Total match goals by half

18 (90%)	1st half	2 (10%)
23 (85%)	2nd half	4 (15%)

F ━━━ A

2	3	5	5	3	8	2	6	1	6
			0-9	10-18	19-27	28-36	37-45	46-54	55-63	64-72	73-81	82-90
0	1	0	0	1	1	2	0	0	1

Goals for & against by half

18 (44%)	For	23 (56%)
1st		2nd

2 (33%)	Against	4 (67%)
1st		2nd

Iran score first

They win	15	88%
They draw	2	12%
They lose	0	0%

Iran concede first

They win	0	0%
They draw	2	100%
They lose	0	0%

In 22 competitive games since Brazil 2014

Sardar Azmoun topped the scoring charts in qualifying

Photo by Amin M. Jamali/Getty Images

Top scorers in qualifying

	P	G	1st	AT	%	Tkm 1-1 Irn	Irn 6-0 Gum	Ind 0-3 Irn	Omn 1-1 Irn	Irn 3-1 Tkm	Gum 0-6 Irn	Irn 4-0 Ind	Irn 2-0 Omn	Irn 2-0 Qat	Chn 0-0 Irn	Uzb 0-1 Irn	Irn 1-0 Kor	Syr 0-0 Irn	Qat 0-1 Irn	Irn 1-0 Chn	Irn 2-0 Uzb	Kor 0-0 Irn	Irn 2-2 Syr
Sardar Azmoun	14	11	5	8	31	1	2	1	↻			1	2	↻	-	↳	1		↳	↳	1		2
Mehdi Taremi	16	8	3	6	22	↳	2	1	↻	2	↳	↳	↳		↳	↳	1	1	1	↳	↳	↳	-
Jalal Hosseini	11	2	1	2	6	-	-	1		↳	-	-	↳	1	-	-		-			-		
Ashkan Dejagah	12	2	1	2	6	1	-	-	1	↳	-	↳		-	↳					↳	↳		
Ehsan Hajsafi	13	2	1	1	6	-	-	-	-	-	2	↳	-	-			-		-				
Alireza Jahanbakhsh	14	2	0	2	6			↳	↳	1	↳	1	-	↳	↳	-	↳	↳	↳	-	↳		
Kamal Kamyabinia	2	1	0	1	3			↳	1														
Karim Ansarifard	6	1	0	1	3				1	↳	↳	↳			-	↳							
Masoud Shojaei	7	1	0	1	3	↳			1			↳	↳		↳	-	↳						
Mehdi Torabi	7	1	0	1	3	↳	1		↳	-	↳		↳		↳								
Reza Ghoochannejhad	9	1	1	1	3	↳			↳			1	↳	↳		↳		↳	↳	↳			
Andranik Teymourian	9	1	0	1	3	-	-	1	-		-			-	-	↳	↳						
Morteza Pouraliganji	13	1	1	1	3		↳		1	-	-												
Saeid Ezatolahi	13	1	0	1	3		↳		1	-	-	-	-	-	-	-	-			↳	-	-	
Ramin Rezaeian	14	1	0	1	3		↳			-	1	-	-	-	-	-	-	-			-		

G goals scored, **1st** first match goal (own goals don't count) **AT** goals at any time (ie. number of scoring appearances), **P** penalties, **%** percentage of total team goals scored by each player. Russia 2018 qualifying only. Game-by-game stats show goals scored, 1st goals are in red, dash did not score, ↳ substituted on, ↻ substituted off, blank did not play

Bookings in World Cup qualifying

Played 18

Cards (24Y, 2R)

Avg make-up (☐10 ◼25) 16.1

GROUP C

Back a European one-two in the group of fun

If Group B is for boring then Group C may be for celebration, *writes Mark Langdon*. The four nations are capable of providing goals and entertainment, and it could finish with a European one-two.

France were relatively unimpressive qualifiers and did not always click at Euro 2016 when they finished as runners-up at home, but few teams in Russia can match them for ability.

Antoine Griezmann was voted as the best player at the last European Championship and also finished as the tournament's top goalscorer. He has come alive in the second half of the domestic campaign for Atletico and a big World Cup looks on the cards.

It's not all about Griezmann. Special teenager Kylian Mbappe is capable of making a major splash in attack and there is emerging talent throughout the squad.

It could be argued that there is actually too much talent for Didier Deschamps to keep them all happy, although at least if he does rotate it is quality being replaced by quality. That quality should see Les Bleus top a gung-ho group which also contains Denmark, Peru and Australia.

Denmark's gang of youngsters improved throughout qualifying which bodes well for their chances of creating a splash.

The 4-0 thrashing of Poland was exceptional as was the 5-1 playoff success in Ireland, with Christian Eriksen the catalyst in both performances.

Captain Simon Kjaer is part of a Sevilla side who reached the latter stages of the Champions League, Andreas Christensen has been receiving high praise from club boss Antonio Conte at Chelsea and Denmark also have a variety of options in attack.

Peru are highly reliant on Paolo Guerrero for goals and used every trick in the book to see off a jet-lagged New Zealand in their playoff match to book their spot in the finals. They were the only South American qualifier to ship more than 20 goals in the group, conceding 26 times.

Australia also needed a playoff to reach Russia, overcoming Honduras, and they will hope that recently appointed coach Bert van Marwijk is able to make a difference.

The Socceroos were found out defensively in Asian qualifying and during last year's Confederations Cup. It was the same story at the last World Cup when Australia conceded nine times in three games.

Photo by Lars Baron/Getty Images

Expect the likes of Antoine Griezmann to bring the fun in Group C

Recommendation

★☆☆☆☆ **France-Denmark straight forecast**

Group-stage performances since France 98

	Pot	P	W	Q	1998 Group	Pos	2002 Group	Pos	2006 Group	Pos	2010 Group	Pos	2014 Group	Pos
France	1	5	2	3	**C**	**1**	A	4	G	2	A	4	**E**	**1**
Peru	2	0	0	0	-	-	-	-	-	-	-	-	-	-
Denmark	3	3	1	2	C	2	**A**	**1**	-	-	E	3	-	-
Australia	4	3	0	1	-	-	-	-	F	2	D	3	B	4

To win Group C
Win only

	Bet365	BtBrt	Betfair	Btfrd	Btwy	Boyle	Coral	Hills	Lads	P Power	Sky	188
France	**1-3**	3-10	1-4	**1-3**	**1-3**	3-10	**1-3**	1-5	3-10	1-4	2-7	7-25
Denmark	9-2	9-2	9-2	7-2	9-2	9-2	9-2	**6**	9-2	9-2	9-2	4
Peru	**10**	**10**	17-2	**10**	17-2	**10**	8	9	9	17-2	**10**	**10**
Australia	14	18	**25**	20	16	20	16	20	16	**25**	16	16

France v Australia
11am, Saturday June 16, BBC

	Bet365	BtBrt	Betfair	Btfrd	Btwy	Boyle	Coral	Hills	Lads	P Power	Sky	188
France	2-11	2-11	**1-4**	1-5	2-9	1-5	1-5	2-11	1-5	1-5	2-9	2-9
Draw	**11-2**	9-2	5	5	19-4	4	9-2	5	9-2	5	9-2	5
Australia	14	12	10	14	12	12	**18**	14	**18**	11	14	14

Peru v Denmark
5pm, Saturday June 16, BBC

	Bet365	BtBrt	Betfair	Btfrd	Btwy	Boyle	Coral	Hills	Lads	P Power	Sky	188
Denmark	11-10	21-20	**5-4**	11-10	11-10	21-20	21-20	Evs	21-20	11-10	23-20	9-8
Draw	9-4	21-10	11-5	9-4	23-10	21-10	21-10	12-5	21-10	11-5	9-4	**5-2**
Peru	**13-5**	12-5	5-2	5-2	**13-5**	12-5	**13-5**	5-2	**13-5**	5-2	5-2	40-17

Denmark v Australia
1pm, Thursday June 21, ITV

	Bet365	BtBrt	Betfair	Btfrd	Btwy	Boyle	Coral	Hills	Lads	P Power	Sky	188
Denmark	**17-20**	4-5	3-4	3-4	4-5	8-11	4-5	3-4	4-5	8-11	3-4	13-16
Draw	12-5	23-10	5-2	5-2	12-5	11-5	9-4	5-2	9-4	23-10	5-2	**45-17**
Australia	10-3	10-3	**4**	18-5	7-2	7-2	18-5	17-5	18-5	7-2	19-5	17-5

France v Peru
4pm, Thursday June 21, ITV

	Bet365	BtBrt	Betfair	Btfrd	Btwy	Boyle	Coral	Hills	Lads	P Power	Sky	188
France	4-11	3-10	**2-5**	4-11	1-3	3-10	1-3	1-3	1-3	1-3	4-11	4-11
Draw	7-2	7-2	7-2	18-5	15-4	10-3	7-2	19-5	7-2	16-5	18-5	**75-19**
Peru	8	15-2	**17-2**	8	8	8	**17-2**	7	**17-2**	15-2	**17-2**	38-5

Australia v Peru
3pm, Tuesday June 26, ITV

	Bet365	BetBright	Betfair	Betfred	Betway	Boyle	Hills	P Power	Sky Bet
Peru	**6-5**	11-10	**6-5**	23-20	23-20	11-10	11-10	11-10	**6-5**
Draw	**23-10**	21-10	9-4	11-5	11-5	2	21-10	21-10	11-5
Australia	23-10	9-4	5-2	12-5	21-10	23-10	**11-4**	23-10	12-5

Denmark v France
3pm, Tuesday June 26, ITV

	Bet365	BetBright	Betfair	Betfred	Betway	Boyle	Hills	P Power	Sky Bet
France	**8-13**	4-7	6-10	3-5	**8-13**	4-7	6-10	8-15	**8-13**
Draw	11-4	5-2	**14-5**	11-4	13-5	23-10	11-4	13-5	11-4
Denmark	9-2	9-2	**11-2**	9-2	4	9-2	5	5	9-2

Prices correct March 28 2018

Profile

France fluffed their lines on home soil in the 2016 European Championship, losing the final to Portugal, and their recent World Cup record is inconsistent to say the least. Winners in 1998 and runners-up in 2006, Les Bleus have also suffered embarrassing group-stage eliminations in 2002 and 2010 before a quarter-final exit four years ago.

How they qualified

As unimpressive group winners with only 18 goals scored in their ten matches and some shocking results, none more so than a 0-0 draw at home to Luxembourg. Hugo Lloris's mistake saw them lose in Sweden and France also drew 0-0 in Belarus.

The manager

World Cup winning captain Didier Deschamps has been at the helm since 2012 and is signed up until after the next Euros. There are question marks over his ability to pick the right side after some bizarre choices down the years.

The squad

With a squad dripping in talent, from skipper Lloris right through to a star-studded forward line, Deschamps could select a B team that would be the envy of most at the World Cup.

Right-back is potentially the only area of weakness as Djibril Sidibe of Monaco is not at the level of former team-mate Benjamin Mendy on the left. Mendy's injury-hit season is a concern but Paris Saint-Germain's Layvin Kurzawa is an adequate understudy.

Raphael Varane, Samuel Umtiti and Laurent Koscielny will fight for two centre-back berths, while midfielders Paul Pogba and N'Golo Kante are virtual certainties in a likely 4-4-2 formation.

Blaise Matuidi, Adrien Rabiot and the versatile Corentin Tolisso are in reserve and there is even more competition for places on the flanks with Ousmane Dembele, Thomas Lemar, Dimitri Payet, Florian Thauvin, Anthony Martial and Kingsley

Factfile

FA founded 1919

www fff.fr

Head coach Didier Deschamps

Date qualified October 10, 2017

Strengths

- ☑ They ooze class and have superb depth across the squad
- ☑ Scored the most goals (13) at Euro 2016

Weaknesses

- ☒ Deschamps sometimes makes bold – or rather foolish – selections
- ☒ Can everyone be kept happy with so many stars wanting to start?

Star rating ★ ★ ★ ★ ★

Fixtures

1 June 16, 11am v Australia, Kazan

2 June 21, 4pm v Peru, Yekaterinburg

3 June 26, 3pm v Denmark, Luzhniki Stadium, Moscow

Base Moscow

Total distance 2,650 miles

N'Golo Kante's defensive work is crucial for France

Coman just some of those in the hunt.

Kylian Mbappe has also been used in a wider role which allows Deschamps to accommodate firm favourite Olivier Giroud alongside Euro 2016 Golden Boot winner Antoine Griezmann. Nabil Fekir and Alexandre Lacazette are fighting just to get into the squad.

Key man

There are bigger stars in the squad but arguably none more important than Kante. The Chelsea anchor will have to get through bundles of defensive work alongside Pogba, who loves the freedom to get forward and sometimes loses discipline off the ball.

Rising star

Magnifique Mbappe will become the world's most expensive teenager when his loan deal to PSG from Monaco is made permanent.

Wildcard

"As long as Didier Deschamps is coach I will have no chance of returning to the French team."

Those were the words of Karim Benzema, who was ditched before the Euros due to his bizarre role in a blackmail plot involving Mathieu Valbuena so, with the Real Madrid man a non-runner, the door could open for Wissam Ben Yedder. The Sevilla striker showed his appetite for the big occasion with a brace away to Manchester United in the Champions League last 16.

Prospects

They have been given a peach of a draw and possess the obvious talent to win the competition. A cosy group followed by a knockout path which the market suggests will be Croatia and Portugal before the semi-finals means the last four has to be a bare minimum target.

How to back them

France are perfect to perm in the name the finalists market.

World Cup record

		Group stage(s) P	W	D	L	F	A	Knockout rounds P	W	D	L	F	A
Uruguay 1930	Group stage	3	1	0	2	4	3	-	-	-	-	-	-
Italy 1934	First round	-	-	-	-	-	-	1	0	1	0	1	1
France 1938	Quarter-finals	-	-	-	-	-	-	2	1	0	1	4	4
Brazil 1950	Withdrew	-	-	-	-	-	-	-	-	-	-	-	-
Switzerland 1954	Group stage	2	1	0	1	3	3	-	-	-	-	-	-
Sweden 1958	Third place	3	2	0	1	11	7	3	2	0	1	12	8
Chile 1962	Did not qualify	-	-	-	-	-	-	-	-	-	-	-	-
England 1966	Group stage	3	0	1	2	2	5	-	-	-	-	-	-
Mexico 1970	Did not qualify	-	-	-	-	-	-	-	-	-	-	-	-
Germany 1974	Did not qualify	-	-	-	-	-	-	-	-	-	-	-	-
Argentina 1978	Group stage	3	1	0	2	5	5	-	-	-	-	-	-
Spain 1982	Fourth place	5	3	1	1	11	6	2	0	1	1	3	4
Mexico 1986	Third place	3	2	1	0	5	1	4	1	2	1	5	5
Italy 1990	Did not qualify	-	-	-	-	-	-	-	-	-	-	-	-
USA 1994	Did not qualify	-	-	-	-	-	-	-	-	-	-	-	-
France 1998	● Winners	3	3	0	0	9	1	4	2	2	0	5	1
Korea/Japan 2002	Group stage	3	0	1	2	0	3	-	-	-	-	-	-
Germany 2006	Finalists	3	1	2	0	3	1	4	3	1	0	6	2
South Africa 2010	Group stage	3	0	1	2	1	4	-	-	-	-	-	-
Brazil 2014	Quarter-finals	3	2	1	0	8	2	2	1	0	1	2	1
Totals		37	16	8	13	62	41	22	10	7	5	38	26

Continental championships (best perfomance)

Uefa European Championship	Winners (2)	1984, 2000

World Cup head-to-heads

France v	P	W	D	L	F	A	Latest	France v	P	W	D	L	F	A	Latest
Argentina	2	0	0	2	1	3	1978	Portugal	1	1	0	0	1	0	2006
Belgium	2	1	1	0	5	3	1986	Russia	1	0	1	0	1	1	1986
Brazil	4	2	1	1	7	6	2006	Saudi Arabia	1	1	0	0	4	0	1998
Croatia	3	1	0	2	4	5	1998	Senegal	1	0	0	1	0	1	2002
Denmark	2	1	0	1	2	3	2002	Serbia	2	0	0	2	2	4	1958
England	2	0	0	2	1	5	1982	South Korea	1	0	1	0	1	1	2006
Germany	4	1	1	2	7	7	2014	Spain	1	1	0	0	3	1	2006
Mexico	4	2	1	1	8	6	2010	Switzerland	2	1	1	0	5	2	2014
Nigeria	1	1	0	0	2	0	2014	Uruguay	3	0	2	1	1	2	2010
Poland	1	0	0	1	2	3	1982								

90 mins only, includes games against USSR, West Germany and Yugoslavia

How they qualified

Group A	P	W	D	L	F	A	GD	P
France	10	7	2	1	18	6	12	23
Sweden	10	6	1	3	26	9	17	19
Holland	10	6	1	3	21	12	9	19
Bulgaria	10	4	1	5	14	19	-5	13
Luxembourg	10	1	3	6	8	26	-18	6
Belarus	10	1	2	7	6	21	-15	5

France boss Didier Deschamps

Belarus.......... (0) 0-0 (0)............France
France .... (3) 4-1 (1)............Bulgaria
Holland .... (0) 0-1 (1)............France
France .... (0) 2-1 (0)............Sweden
Luxembourg... (1) 1-3 (2)............France
Sweden .... (1) 2-1 (1)............France
France .... (1) 4-0 (0)............Holland
France .... (0) 0-0 (0).... Luxembourg
Bulgaria .... (0) 0-1 (1)............France
France .... (2) 2-1 (1)............ Belarus

The French team celebrate after beating world champions Germany to reach the final of Euro 2016

Pos	Players used in qualifying	Club	Age	P	G	P	G		
GK	Hugo Lloris	Tottenham	31	96	-	9	-	1	-
GK	Steve Mandanda	Marseille	33	26	-	1	-	-	-
DEF	Bacary Sagna	Benevento	35	65	-	1	-	-	-
DEF	Benjamin Mendy	Man City	23	4	-	2	-	-	-
DEF	Christophe Jallet	Nice	34	16	1	1	-	-	-
DEF	Djibril Sidibe	Monaco	25	15	1	10	-	1	-
DEF	Laurent Koscielny	Arsenal	32	51	1	8	-	-	-
DEF	Layvin Kurzawa	Paris St-Germain	25	11	1	5	-	1	-
DEF	Lucas Digne	Barcelona	24	21	-	2	-	-	-
DEF	Patrice Evra	West Ham	37	81	-	1	-	-	-
DEF	Raphael Varane	Real Madrid	25	41	2	7	-	-	-
DEF	Samuel Umtiti	Barcelona	24	16	1	5	-	-	-
MID	Adrien Rabiot	Paris St-Germain	23	6	-	2	-	-	-
MID	Blaise Matuidi	Juventus	31	64	9	7	1	1	-
MID	Corentin Tolisso	Bayern Munich	23	6	-	2	-	-	-
MID	Dimitri Payet	Marseille	31	37	8	8	2	-	-
MID	Moussa Sissoko	Tottenham	28	53	2	6	-	-	-
MID	N'Golo Kante	Chelsea	27	22	1	7	-	-	-
MID	Paul Pogba	Man Utd	25	51	9	7	2	4	-
MID	Thomas Lemar	Monaco	22	10	3	4	2	-	-
MID	Ousmane Dembele	Barcelona	21	9	1	2	-	-	-
MID	Kingsley Coman	Bayern Munich	22	15	1	3	-	-	-
ATT	Alexandre Lacazette	Arsenal	27	16	3	3	-	1	-
ATT	Andre-Pierre Gignac	Tigres	32	36	7	2	-	-	-
ATT	Anthony Martial	Man Utd	22	18	1	2	-	-	-
ATT	Antoine Griezmann	Atletico Madrid	27	51	19	10	4	1	-
ATT	Kevin Gameiro	Atletico Madrid	31	13	3	3	2	-	-
ATT	Kylian Mbappe	Paris St-Germain	19	12	3	6	1	-	-
ATT	Nabil Fekir	Lyon	24	10	1	3	-	-	-
ATT	Olivier Giroud	Chelsea	31	71	30	8	4	1	-

Correct scores

	Competitive	Friendly
1-0	2	3
2-0	2	3
2-1	4	3
3-0	-	2
3-1	1	2
3-2	-	3
4-0	1	1
4-1	1	-
4-2	-	1
4-3	-	-
0-0	4	1
1-1	-	2
2-2	-	1
3-3	-	-
4-4	-	-
0-1	-	1
0-2	-	2
1-2	1	-
0-3	-	-
1-3	-	1
2-3	-	1
0-4	-	-
1-4	-	-
2-4	-	-
3-4	-	1
Other	1	1

Since Brazil 2014

Half-time/full-time double results

Win/Win	8	47%	Win 1st half	8	47%
Draw/Win	3	18%	Win 2nd half	8	47%
Lose/Win	1	6%	Win both halves	4	24%
Win/Draw	0	0%	Goal both halves	5	29%
Draw/Draw	4	24%			
Lose/Draw	0	0%	**Overall**		
Win/Lose	0	0%	● Win	71%	
Draw/Lose	1	6%	● Draw	24%	
Lose/Lose	0	0%	● Lose	6%	

Overall: W12, D4, L1 in 17 competitive games since Brazil 2014

Under & over goals

11 (65%)	Over 1.5	6 (35%)	
9 (53%)	Over 2.5	8 (47%)	
4 (24%)	Over 3.5	13 (76%)	
2 (12%)	Over 4.5	15 (88%)	

Both teams to score

8 (47%)	Both score	9 (53%)	
7 (41%)	& win	10 (59%)	
1 (6%)	& lose	16 (94%)	

In 17 competitive games since Brazil 2014

Clean sheets

9 (53%)	Clean sheets	8 (47%)	
5 (29%)	Win to nil	12 (71%)	

4 (24%)	Fail to score	13 (76%)	
0 (0%)	Lose to nil	17 (100%)	

When they score

● For ● Against

Total match goals by half

16 (76%)	1st half	5 (24%)	
F			A
15 (75%)	2nd half	5 (25%)	
F			A

	1	2	4	3	6	0	6	2	2	5
	0-9	10-18	19-27	28-36	37-45	46-54	55-63	64-72	73-81	82-90
	2	0	0	1	2	1	1	1	0	2

Goals for & against by half

16 (52%)	For	15 (48%)	
1st			2nd
5 (50%)	Against	5 (50%)	
1st			2nd

France score first

They win	9		90%
They draw	0		0%
They lose	1		10%

France concede first

They win	3		100%
They draw	0		0%
They lose	0		0%

In 17 competitive games since Brazil 2014

Antoine Griezmann was top scorer at Euro 2016 with six goals

Top scorers in qualifying

	P	G	1st	AT	%	Blr 0-0 Fra	Fra 4-1 Bgr	Nld 0-1 Fra	Fra 2-1 Swe	Lux 1-3 Fra	Swe 2-1 Fra	Fra 4-0 Nld	Fra 0-0 Lux	Bgr 0-1 Fra	Fra 2-1 Blr
Olivier Giroud	8	4	2	3	22	↺			-	2	1	↺	↺	↪	1
Antoine Griezmann	10	4	2	4	22	-	1	↺	↺	1	↺	1	↺	-	1
Kevin Gameiro	3	2	0	1	11	↪	2	↺							
Thomas Lemar	4	2	0	1	11							↪	2	-	↺
Paul Pogba	7	2	1	2	11	-	-	1	1			-	-	-	
Dimitri Payet	8	2	0	2	11	↪	1	↺	1	↺	↺			↪	↪
Kylian Mbappe	6	1	0	1	6					↪	↪	1	↺	↺	↪
Blaise Matuidi	7	1	1	1	6	-	-	-	↺					1	-

G goals scored, **1st** first match goal (own goals don't count) **AT** goals at any time (ie. number of scoring appearances), **P** penalties, **%** percentage of total team goals scored by each player. Russia 2018 qualifying only. Game-by-game stats show goals scored, 1st goals are in red, dash did not score, ↪ substituted on, ↺ substituted off, blank did not play

Bookings in World Cup qualifying

Played 10 **Cards** (11Y) ⬜⬜⬜⬜⬜⬜⬜⬜⬜⬜⬜ **Avg make-up** (☐10 ■25) 11

AUSTRALIA

GROUP C

Profile

No team travelled further to book their World Cup spot than playoff kings Australia, who flew over 150,000 miles on a journey that started in Kyrgyzstan and finished with a win over Honduras. But now the real hard work starts for the Socceroos.

Australia have won only two of their 13 World Cup matches and are long odds-on for a third straight group-stage exit.

How they qualified

The Socceroos were easy winners of their first Asian group, claiming 21 points from a possible 24 in a section where Jordan were their nearest challengers, but things got a whole lot trickier in the final campaign when they finished third behind Japan and Saudi Arabia.

While Australia lost only once, four draws held them back, although they deservedly came through two nerve-jangling playoff ties against Syria and Honduras.

The manager

Ange Postecoglou walked away after the Honduras triumph to be replaced by Bert van Marwijk. The Dutchman led his nation to the 2010 World Cup final and was also in charge of Saudi Arabia for their successful World Cup qualifying campaign.

The squad

Postecoglou was an attack-minded manager who preferred a 3-4-2-1 formation but Van Marwijk changed to a 4-2-3-1 formation for his first game in charge, a 4-1 loss to Norway.

Brighton's Mat Ryan is the undisputed goalkeeper, with Bailey Wright, Matthew Jurman and Trent Sainsbury among the defensive options.

Sainsbury signed for Inter last year but, like a number of his international teammates, failed to get sufficient playing time in a top European league.

Bursaspor's left-sided Aziz Behich is an exception to that rule along with

Factfile

FA founded 1961
www footballaustralia.com.au
Head coach Bert van Marwijk
Date qualified November 15, 2017

....

Strengths
☑ Midfield has decent experience
☑ Van Marwijk has reached a World Cup final as a coach

Weaknesses
☒ The coach has not had long to work with the players
☒ Often found out defensively, with no World Cup clean sheet since 1974

....

Star rating ★☆☆☆☆

....

Fixtures
1 June 16, 11am v France, Kazan
2 June 21, 1pm v Denmark, Samara
3 June 26, 3pm v Peru, Sochi

Base Kazan
Total distance 2,250 miles

FOOTBALL
FEDERATION
AUSTRALIA

Australia celebrate victory in their playoff against Honduras

midfielders Aaron Mooy, Mile Jedinak, Massimo Luongo, Jackson Irvine and Tom Rogic, who are well known to British football fans and help control a relatively strong area for the Socceroos.

Hertha Berlin winger Mathew Leckie is capable of attacking thrusts but there are hardly any strikers of note to such an extent that experienced 38-year-old warrior Tim Cahill still leads the line.

Key man

Mooy failed to make it at Manchester City – in fairness he was never given a chance – but he has found a more suitable level at Huddersfield. The midfielder has a solid all-round game.

Rising star

Awer Mabil left Adelaide United for an A-League record fee when he departed for Midtjylland, although he has really started to shine on loan for Pacos in Portugal.

The rapid Kenyan-born winger, whose father was a soldier and killed in the civil war, spent his early years in a refugee camp before moving to Australia.

Wildcard

The Aussies need a goalscorer and Jamie McClaren scores goals, or at least he did in the A-League, with 37 in two full seasons with Brisbane Roar. However, a move to Darmstadt did not work out and he is now trying his luck with Hibs.

Prospects

Unlikely to get out of the group.

How to back them

Australia deserve to be favourites to finish bottom but they did score in their three Confederations Cup matches against Germany, Cameroon and Chile last summer, so consider overs and both teams to score bets.

Group C | Australia 77

AUSTRALIA

World Cup record		Group stage(s)						Knockout rounds					
		P	W	D	L	F	A	P	W	D	L	F	A
Uruguay 1930	Did not enter	-	-	-	-	-	-	-	-	-	-	-	-
Italy 1934	Did not enter	-	-	-	-	-	-	-	-	-	-	-	-
France 1938	Did not enter	-	-	-	-	-	-	-	-	-	-	-	-
Brazil 1950	Did not enter	-	-	-	-	-	-	-	-	-	-	-	-
Switzerland 1954	Did not enter	-	-	-	-	-	-	-	-	-	-	-	-
Sweden 1958	Did not enter	-	-	-	-	-	-	-	-	-	-	-	-
Chile 1962	Did not enter	-	-	-	-	-	-	-	-	-	-	-	-
England 1966	Did not qualify	-	-	-	-	-	-	-	-	-	-	-	-
Mexico 1970	Did not qualify	-	-	-	-	-	-	-	-	-	-	-	-
Germany 1974	1st group stage	3	0	1	2	0	5	-	-	-	-	-	-
Argentina 1978	Did not qualify	-	-	-	-	-	-	-	-	-	-	-	-
Spain 1982	Did not qualify	-	-	-	-	-	-	-	-	-	-	-	-
Mexico 1986	Did not qualify	-	-	-	-	-	-	-	-	-	-	-	-
Italy 1990	Did not qualify	-	-	-	-	-	-	-	-	-	-	-	-
USA 1994	Did not qualify	-	-	-	-	-	-	-	-	-	-	-	-
France 1998	Did not qualify	-	-	-	-	-	-	-	-	-	-	-	-
Korea/Japan 2002	Did not qualify	-	-	-	-	-	-	-	-	-	-	-	-
Germany 2006	Round of 16	3	1	1	1	5	5	1	0	0	1	0	1
South Africa 2010	Group stage	3	1	1	1	3	6	-	-	-	-	-	-
Brazil 2014	Group stage	3	0	0	3	3	9	-	-	-	-	-	-
Totals		12	2	3	7	11	25	1	0	0	1	0	1

Continental championships (best perfomance)

AFC Asian Cup   Winners (1)   2015

Australia also played in the OFC Nations Cup between 1980 and 2004, winning in 1980, 1996, 2000 and 2004

World Cup head-to-heads

Australia v	P	W	D	L	F	A	Latest		Australia v	P	W	D	L	F	A	Latest
Brazil	1	0	0	1	0	2	2006		Japan	1	1	0	0	3	1	2006
Croatia	1	0	1	0	2	2	2006		Serbia	1	1	0	0	2	1	2010
Germany	2	0	0	2	0	7	2010		Spain	1	0	0	1	0	3	2014

90 mins only, includes games against West Germany

How they qualified

Round 2

Group B	P	W	D	L	F	A	GD	P
Australia	8	7	0	1	29	4	25	21
Jordan	8	5	1	2	21	7	14	16
Kyrgyzstan	8	4	2	2	10	8	2	14
Tajikistan	8	1	2	5	9	20	-11	5
Bangladesh	8	0	1	7	2	32	-30	1

Kyrgyzstan ..... (0) 1-2 (1).....**Australia**
Australia .... (4) 5-0 (0).....Bangladesh
Tajikistan .... (0) 0-3 (0)..............**Australia**
Jordan .... (0) 2-0 (0)..............**Australia**
Australia .... (1) 3-0 (0)........Kyrgyzstan
Bangladesh .... (0) 0-4 (4).........**Australia**
Australia .... (2) 7-0 (0)........ Tajikistan

Australia ...... (3) 5-1 (0)............. Jordan

Round 3

Group B	P	W	D	L	F	A	GD	P
Japan	10	6	2	2	17	7	10	20
Saudi Arabia	10	6	1	3	17	10	7	19
Australia	10	5	4	1	16	11	5	19
UAE	10	4	1	5	10	13	-3	13
Iraq	10	3	2	5	11	12	-1	11
Thailand	10	0	2	8	6	24	-18	2

Australia .... (0) 2-0 (0)..............Iraq
UAE .... (0) 0-1 (0)..........**Australia**
Saudi Arabia . (1) 2-2 (1)..........**Australia**
Australia .... (0) 1-1 (1)............Japan
Thailand.......... (1) 2-2 (1)........**Australia**
Iraq .... (0) 1-1 (1)........**Australia**
Australia .... (1) 2-0 (0).................UAE
Australia .... (2) 3-2 (2)... Saudi Arabia
Japan............. (1) 2-0 (0).........**Australia**
Australia .... (0) 2-1 (0)........ Thailand

Round 4

Syria .... (0) 1-1 (1).........**Australia**
Australia .... (1) 2-1 (1)................. Syria
AET – 1-1 after 90 minutes
Australia won 3-2 on aggregate

Intercontinental playoffs

Honduras .... (0) 0-0 (0).........**Australia**
Australia ...... (0) 3-1 (0)........Honduras
Australia won 3-1 on aggregate

Players used in qualifying		Career			Qualification			
Pos		Club	Age	P	G	P	G	☐	■
GK	Adam Federici	Bournemouth	33	16	-	5	-	-	-
GK	Mathew Ryan	Brighton	26	42	-	16	-	-	-
GK	Mitchell Langerak	Nagoya Grampus	29	8	-	1	-	-	-
DEF	Alex Gersbach	Lens	21	4	-	1	-	-	-
DEF	Alex Wilkinson	Sydney FC	33	16	-	2	-	1	-
DEF	Aziz Behich	Bursaspor	27	21	2	5	-	-	-
DEF	Bailey Wright	Bristol City	25	22	1	12	-	3	-
DEF	Brad Smith	Bournemouth	24	18	-	12	-	1	-
DEF	Ivan Franjic	Brisbane Roar	30	20	-	1	-	-	-
DEF	James Meredith	Millwall	30	2	-	2	-	-	-
DEF	Joshua Risdon	Western Sydney	25	6	-	4	-	2	-
DEF	Matthew Jurman	Suwon Bluewings	28	4	-	4	-	2	-
DEF	Matthew Spiranovic	Unattached	29	35	-	9	-	1	-
DEF	Milos Degenek	Yokohama F-M	24	17	-	9	-	1	-
DEF	Ryan McGowan	Bradford	28	20	-	6	-	1	-
DEF	Tarek Elrich	Adelaide Utd	31	3	-	2	-	-	-
DEF	Trent Sainsbury	Grasshoppers	26	33	3	16	1	3	-
DEF	Mark Milligan	Al-Ahli	32	66	6	18	2	5	-
DEF	Jason Davidson	Olimpija	26	22	1	4	0	0	-
MID	Aaron Mooy	Huddersfield	27	32	5	19	2	3	-
MID	Chris Ikonomidis	Western Sydney	23	6	-	2	-	-	-
MID	Jackson Irvine	Hull	25	17	2	9	1	1	-
MID	James Troisi	Melbourne Vic	29	37	5	9	-	-	-
MID	Massimo Luongo	QPR	25	33	5	16	3	2	-
MID	Matt McKay	Brisbane Roar	35	59	2	3	-	-	-
MID	Mile Jedinak	Aston Villa	33	75	18	13	10	1	-
MID	Mustafa Amini	Aarhus	24	2	-	2	-	-	-
MID	Tom Rogic	Celtic	25	35	6	18	5	2	-
MID	Tommy Oar	Apoel Nicosia	26	28	2	4	1	-	-
MID	Nikita Rukavytsya	Maccabi Haifa	30	18	1	3	-	-	-
ATT	Apostolos Giannou	AEK Larnaca	28	5	-	3	-	-	-
ATT	Robbie Kruse	Bochum	29	62	5	15	1	1	-
ATT	Jamie Maclaren	Hibernian	24	5	-	2	-	-	-
ATT	Matthew Leckie	Hertha Berlin	27	50	6	19	4	4	-
ATT	Nathan Burns	Wellington	30	23	3	10	3	-	-
ATT	Tim Cahill	Millwall	38	105	50	16	11	1	-
ATT	Tomi Juric	Luzurn	26	34	8	16	5	1	-

AUSTRALIA

Correct scores

	Competitive	Friendly
1-0	1	1
2-0	4	-
2-1	2	-
3-0	2	-
3-1	1	-
3-2	1	1
4-0	2	-
4-1	1	-
4-2	-	-
4-3	-	-
0-0	1	3
1-1	7	-
2-2	2	1
3-3	-	-
4-4	-	-
0-1	1	1
0-2	2	1
1-2	-	3
0-3	-	-
1-3	-	-
2-3	1	-
0-4	-	1
1-4	-	1
2-4	-	-
3-4	-	-
Other	3	-

Since Brazil 2014

Half-time/full-time double results

Win/Win	10	32%	Win 1st half	14	45%
Draw/Win	7	23%	Win 2nd half	16	52%
Lose/Win	0	0%	Win both halves	7	23%
Win/Draw	4	13%	Goal both halves	12	39%
Draw/Draw	4	13%			
Lose/Draw	2	6%	**Overall**		
Win/Lose	0	0%	● Win	55%	
Draw/Lose	1	3%	● Draw	32%	
Lose/Lose	3	10%	● Lose	13%	

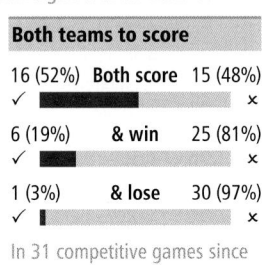

Overall: W17, D10, L4 in 31 competitive games since Brazil 2014

Under & over goals

28 (90%) **Over 1.5** 3 (10%) ✓ ✗

15 (48%) **Over 2.5** 16 (52%) ✓ ✗

11 (35%) **Over 3.5** 20 (65%) ✓ ✗

6 (19%) **Over 4.5** 25 (81%) ✓ ✗

Both teams to score

16 (52%) **Both score** 15 (48%) ✓ ✗

6 (19%) **& win** 25 (81%) ✓ ✗

1 (3%) **& lose** 30 (97%) ✓ ✗

In 31 competitive games since Brazil 2014

Clean sheets

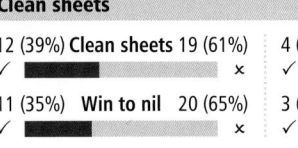

12 (39%) **Clean sheets** 19 (61%) ✓ ✗

11 (35%) **Win to nil** 20 (65%) ✓ ✗

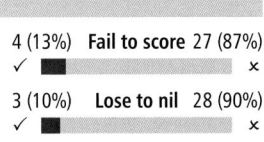

4 (13%) **Fail to score** 27 (87%) ✓ ✗

3 (10%) **Lose to nil** 28 (90%) ✓ ✗

When they score

● For ● Against

Total match goals by half

33 (73%) **1st half** 12 (27%)
F | A

34 (71%) **2nd half** 14 (29%)
F | A

Goals for & against by half

33 (49%) **For** 34 (51%)
1st | 2nd

12 (46%) **Against** 14 (54%)
1st | 2nd

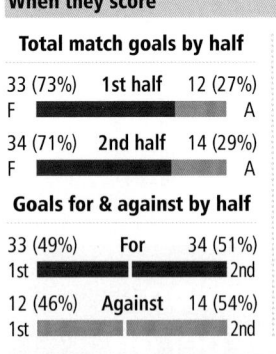

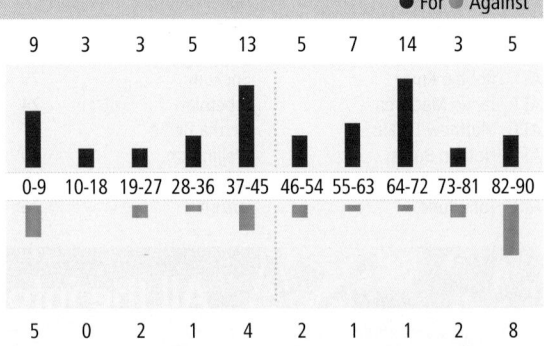

9	3	3	5	13	5	7	14	3	5
0-9	10-18	19-27	28-36	37-45	46-54	55-63	64-72	73-81	82-90
5	0	2	1	4	2	1	1	2	8

Australia score first

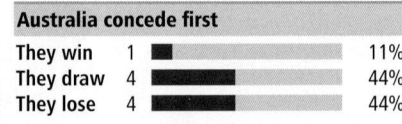

They win	16	76%
They draw	5	24%
They lose	0	0%

In 31 competitive games since Brazil 2014

Australia concede first

They win	1	11%
They draw	4	44%
They lose	4	44%

Tim Cahill and Mile Jedinak scored more than 40 per cent of Australia's goals during qualifying

Top scorers in qualifying

	P	G	1st	AT	%
Tim Cahill	16	11	3	6	22
Mile Jedinak	13	10	4	7	20
Tom Rogic	18	5	0	4	10
Tomi Juric	16	5	2	4	10
Matthew Leckie	19	4	2	4	8
Nathan Burns	10	3	0	2	6
Massimo Luongo	16	3	2	3	6
Mark Milligan	18	2	1	2	4
Aaron Mooy	19	2	0	2	4
Trent Sainsbury	16	1	0	1	2
Robbie Kruse	15	1	1	1	2
Tommy Oar	4	1	0	1	2
Jackson Irvine	9	1	1	1	2

G goals scored, **1st** first match goal (own goals don't count) **AT** goals at any time (ie. number of scoring appearances), **P** penalties, **%** percentage of total team goals scored by each player. Russia 2018 qualifying only. Game-by-game stats show goals scored, 1st goals are in red, dash did not score, ↰ substituted on, ↺ substituted off, blank did not play

Bookings in World Cup qualifying

Played 22 **Cards** (36Y) ☐☐☐☐☐☐☐☐☐☐☐☐☐☐☐☐☐☐☐☐☐☐☐☐☐☐☐☐☐☐☐☐☐☐☐☐
Avg make-up (☐10 ■25) 16.4

PERU

GROUP C

Profile

Peru tend to do well in the Copa America, with semi-final appearances in 2011 and 2015, but it has been 36 years since their last World Cup outing.

Despite their long absence from the finals, Peru were ranked tenth by Fifa at the time of the draw which made them the second highest-placed team in pot two.

How they qualified

A controversial decision to award Peru three points for a defeat in Bolivia because the hosts had briefly fielded an ineligible player proved pivotal as they edged out rivals Chile for fifth spot on goal difference.

Peru finished their Conmebol campaign strongly with only one loss – against Brazil – in their last eight games before a comfortable playoff success against New Zealand.

The manager

Argentinian Ricardo Gareca was not a universally popular appointment, not least as it was his goal which helped to deny Peru a spot at the 1986 World Cup. However, the doubters have been won over by a possession-based approach that was Peru's tradition in a bygone era.

The squad

Gareca is likely to go with a 4-2-3-1 formation and the weakness comes in defence – Peru conceded 26 goals in the Conmebol group. No other South American qualifier shipped more than 20.

Peru's goalkeeper Pedro Gallese plays for a lowly Mexican club (Veracruz) and the defenders in front of him are all based in Mexico or South America. Flamengo left-back Miguel Trauco is arguably the best of those and Alberto Rodriguez is seen as the leader.

There's greater pedigree further forward with Watford winger Andre Carrillo on the right and Danish-based Edison Flores an attractive option in the left. Sao Paulo playmaker Christian Cueva makes the

Factfile

FA founded 1922
www fpf.com.pe
Head coach Ricardo Gareca
Date qualified November 15, 2017

Strengths

☑ Excellent spirit and keep the ball well in midfield
☑ Scored five more goals than Argentina in qualifying

Weaknesses

☒ They don't look like keeping opponents out
☒ Peru could be out before facing Australia last up

Star rating ★★☆☆☆

Fixtures

1 June 16, 5pm v Denmark, Saransk
2 June 21, 4 pm v France, Yekaterinburg
3 June 26, 3pm v Australia, Sochi

Base Moscow
Total distance 4,100 miles

Edison Flores

team tick in the middle with Feyenoord's Renato Tapia and Orlando's Yoshimar Yotun sitting in front of the defence.

Paolo Guerrero is the main source of goals and Jefferson Farfan can chip in too.

Key man

Guerrero is regarded as Peru's best current player and the fact he can play in the tournament after having a drugs ban reduced from one year to six months is huge.

The 34-year-old, formerly of Bayern Munich and Hamburg, says the cocaine metabolite found in his urine was from coca tea.

Rising star

Edison Flores matched Guerrero's five goals in qualifying and is not held back by his nickname of El Orejas – Big Ears. Flores spends much of his spare time watching the great Peruvian side of the 1970s.

Wildcard

Yordy Reyna, a quick, versatile forward with decent close control, moved to the renowned Red Bull ownership as a youngster, first at Salzburg before a loan to Leipzig. Reyna flopped in Europe but has since shown decent form in the MLS for Vancouver, although the 24-year-old was front-page news in Peru after being questioned by police following the death of a female teenage volleyball player.

Prospects

They should be a good side to watch but unfortunately for neutrals they look set to play only three games in Russia.

How to back them

Two clean sheets in 18 qualifiers (excluding the 3-0 win awarded to them in Bolivia) suggest they could struggle against France and Denmark. Expect both teams to score when they face Australia on June 26.

PERU

World Cup record

World Cup record		Group stage(s)						Knockout rounds					
		P	W	D	L	F	A	P	W	D	L	F	A
Uruguay 1930	Group stage	2	0	0	2	1	4	-	-	-	-	-	-
Italy 1934	Withdrew	-	-	-	-	-	-	-	-	-	-	-	-
France 1938	Did not enter	-	-	-	-	-	-	-	-	-	-	-	-
Brazil 1950	Withdrew	-	-	-	-	-	-	-	-	-	-	-	-
Switzerland 1954	Withdrew	-	-	-	-	-	-	-	-	-	-	-	-
Sweden 1958	Did not qualify	-	-	-	-	-	-	-	-	-	-	-	-
Chile 1962	Did not qualify	-	-	-	-	-	-	-	-	-	-	-	-
England 1966	Did not qualify	-	-	-	-	-	-	-	-	-	-	-	-
Mexico 1970	Quarterfinals	3	2	0	1	7	5	1	0	0	1	2	4
Germany 1974	Did not qualify	-	-	-	-	-	-	-	-	-	-	-	-
Argentina 1978	2nd group stage	6	2	1	3	7	12	-	-	-	-	-	-
Spain 1982	1st group stage	3	0	2	1	2	6	-	-	-	-	-	-
Mexico 1986	Did not qualify	-	-	-	-	-	-	-	-	-	-	-	-
Italy 1990	Did not qualify	-	-	-	-	-	-	-	-	-	-	-	-
USA 1994	Did not qualify	-	-	-	-	-	-	-	-	-	-	-	-
France 1998	Did not qualify	-	-	-	-	-	-	-	-	-	-	-	-
Korea/Japan 2002	Did not qualify	-	-	-	-	-	-	-	-	-	-	-	-
Germany 2006	Did not qualify	-	-	-	-	-	-	-	-	-	-	-	-
South Africa 2010	Did not qualify	-	-	-	-	-	-	-	-	-	-	-	-
Brazil 2014	Did not qualify	-	-	-	-	-	-	-	-	-	-	-	-
Totals		14	4	3	7	17	27	1	0	0	1	2	4

Continental championships (best perfomance)

Copa America	Winners (2)	1939, 1975

World Cup head-to-heads

Peru v	P	W	D	L	F	A	Latest
Argentina	1	0	0	1	0	6	1978
Brazil	2	0	0	2	2	7	1978
Germany	1	0	0	1	1	3	1970
Iran	1	1	0	0	4	1	1978
Morocco	1	1	0	0	3	0	1970
Poland	2	0	0	2	1	6	1982
Uruguay	1	0	0	1	0	1	1930

90 mins only, includes games against West Germany

Photo by Monte Fresco/Mirrorpix

Peru need a hero like 70s star Teofilo Cubillas

How they qualified

	P	W	D	L	F	A	GD	P
Brazil	18	12	5	1	41	11	30	41
Uruguay	18	9	4	5	32	20	12	31
Argentina	18	7	7	4	19	16	3	28
Colombia	18	7	6	5	21	19	2	27
Peru	18	7	5	6	27	26	1	26
Chile	18	8	2	8	26	27	-1	26
Paraguay	18	7	3	8	19	25	-6	24
Ecuador	18	6	2	10	26	29	-3	20
Bolivia	18	4	2	12	16	38	-22	14
Venezuela	18	2	6	10	19	35	-16	12

Colombia ...... (1) 2-0 (0) .... Peru
Peru .... (2) 3-4 (3) .... Chile
Peru .... (1) 1-0 (0) .... Paraguay
Brazil .... (1) 3-0 (0) .... Peru
Peru .... (0) 2-2 (1) .... Venezuela
Uruguay .... (0) 1-0 (0) .... Peru
Bolivia .... (1) 2-0 (0) .... Peru
Match awarded 3-0 to Peru
Peru .... (1) 2-1 (1) .... Ecuador
Peru .... (0) 2-2 (1) .... Argentina
Chile .... (1) 2-1 (0) .... Peru
Paraguay .... (1) 1-4 (0) .... Peru

Peru .... (0) 0-2 (0) .... Brazil
Venezuela ...... (2) 2-2 (0) .... Peru
Peru .... (1) 2-1 (1) .... Uruguay
Peru .... (0) 2-1 (0) .... Bolivia
Ecuador .... (0) 1-2 (0) .... Peru
Argentina ...... (0) 0-0 (0) .... Peru
Peru .... (0) 1-1 (0) .... Colombia

Intercontinental playoffs
New Zealand.. (0) 0-0 (0) .... Peru
Peru .... (1) 2-0 (0) ... New Zealand
Peru won 2-0 on aggregate

Players used in qualifying			Career		Qualification			
Pos		**Club**	**Age**	**P**	**G**	**P**	**G**	□ ∎

Pos	Name	Club	Age	P	G	P	G	□	∎
GK	Carlos Caceda	Deportivo Municipal	26	6	-	2	-	1	-
GK	Diego Penny	FBC Melgar	34	17	-	2	-	-	-
GK	Pedro Gallese	Veracruz	28	37	-	16	-	2	-
DEF	Alberto Rodriguez	Junior	34	73	-	13	-	-	-
DEF	Aldo Corzo	Universitario	29	24	-	12	-	2	-
DEF	Carlos Ascues	Alianza Lima	25	21	5	6	-	1	-
DEF	Carlos Zambrano	Dynamo Kiev	28	43	4	5	-	2	-
DEF	Christian Ramos	Veracruz	29	67	3	14	2	4	1
DEF	Jair Cespedes	Sporting Cristal	34	9	-	2	-	-	-
DEF	Luis Abram	Velez Sarsfield	22	4	-	2	-	-	-
DEF	Luis Advincula	Lobos BUAP	28	63	-	9	-	3	-
DEF	Miguel Araujo	Alianza Lima	23	7	-	4	-	-	-
DEF	Miguel Trauco	Flamengo	25	24	-	13	-	3	-
DEF	Nilson Loyola	FBC Melgar	23	3	-	2	-	1	-
DEF	Renzo Revoredo	Sporting Cristal	32	23	-	1	-	-	-
DEF	Adan Balbin	Universitario	31	16	-	1	-	-	-
DEF	Anderson Santamaria	Puebla	26	4	-	1	-	-	-
DEF	Adrian Zela	Deportivo Municipal	29	1	-	1	-	-	-
DEF	Juan Vargas	Universitario	34	62	4	1	-	-	-
MID	Renato Tapia	Feyenoord	22	29	3	16	1	5	-
MID	Yoshimar Yotun	Orlando City	28	71	2	15	-	3	-
MID	Carlos Lobaton	Sporting Cristal	38	49	1	7	-	1	-
MID	Cesar Ortiz	Sport Huancayo	34	1	-	1	-	-	-
MID	Christian Cueva	Sao Paulo	26	43	7	18	4	2	1
MID	Christofer Gonzales	Sport Rosario	25	6	1	2	-	-	-
MID	Cristian Benavente	Charleroi	24	16	2	2	-	-	-
MID	Joel Sanchez	Queretaro	29	13	-	3	-	-	-
MID	Josepmir Ballon	Sporting Cristal	29	49	-	5	-	2	-
MID	Paolo Hurtado	V Guimaraes	27	31	3	7	1	2	-
MID	Pedro Aquino	Lobos BUAP	23	11	-	8	-	2	-
MID	Sergio Pena	Granada	22	5	-	3	-	-	-
MID	Wilder Cartagena	Veracruz	23	2	-	2	-	-	-
MID	Andre Carrillo	Watford	27	44	4	11	1	3	-
ATT	Jefferson Farfan	Lokomotiv Moscow	33	81	24	8	4	2	-
ATT	Yordy Reyna	Vancouver Whitecaps	24	17	2	5	-	-	-
ATT	Luiz Da Silva	Argentinos Juniors	21	6	1	2	-	-	-
ATT	Andy Polo	Portland Timbers	24	15	1	9	-	-	-
ATT	Claudio Pizarro	Cologne	39	85	20	4	-	1	-
ATT	Edison Flores	Aalborg	24	27	9	14	5	1	-
ATT	Irven Avila	Lobos BUAP	27	13	-	2	-	-	-
ATT	Paolo Guerrero	Flamengo	34	87	33	17	5	3	-
ATT	Raul Ruidiaz	Morelia	27	29	4	12	1	-	-

PERU

Correct scores

	Competitive	Friendly
1-0	4	2
2-0	2	3
2-1	4	1
3-0*	1	1
3-1	1	3
3-2	-	-
4-0	-	1
4-1	1	-
4-2	-	-
4-3	-	-
0-0	4	-
1-1	1	2
2-2	4	-
3-3	-	-
4-4	-	-
0-1	1	1
0-2	2	-
1-2	3	2
0-3	1	1
1-3	-	-
2-3	-	-
0-4	-	-
1-4	-	-
2-4	-	-
3-4	1	-
Other	-	-

Since Brazil 2014

Half-time/full-time double results

Win/Win	3	10%	Win 1st half	4	13%
Draw/Win	8	27%	Win 2nd half	13	43%
Lose/Win	1	3%	Win both halves	1	3%
Win/Draw	1	3%	Goal both halves	5	17%
Draw/Draw	5	17%			
Lose/Draw	3	10%	Overall		
Win/Lose	0	0%	● Win	40%	
Draw/Lose	3	10%	● Draw	30%	
Lose/Lose	6	20%	● Lose	30%	

Overall: W12, D9, L9 in 30 competitive games since Brazil 2014

Under & over goals

21 (70%)	Over 1.5	9 (30%)
✓		✗
15 (50%)	Over 2.5	15 (50%)
✓		✗
7 (23%)	Over 3.5	23 (77%)
✓		✗
2 (7%)	Over 4.5	28 (93%)
✓		✗

Both teams to score

15 (50%)	Both score	15 (50%)
✓		✗
6 (20%)	& win	24 (80%)
✓		✗
4 (13%)	& lose	26 (87%)
✓		✗

In 30 competitive games since Brazil 2014

Clean sheets

10 (33%)	Clean sheets	20 (67%)
✓		✗
6 (20%)	Win to nil	24 (80%)
✓		✗
9 (30%)	Fail to score	21 (70%)
✓		✗
5 (17%)	Lose to nil	25 (83%)
✓		✗

When they score

● For ● Against

Total match goals by half

11 (39%)	1st half	17 (61%)
F		A
27 (60%)	2nd half	18 (40%)
F		A

Goals for & against by half

11 (29%)	For	27 (71%)
1st		2nd
17 (49%)	Against	18 (51%)
1st		2nd

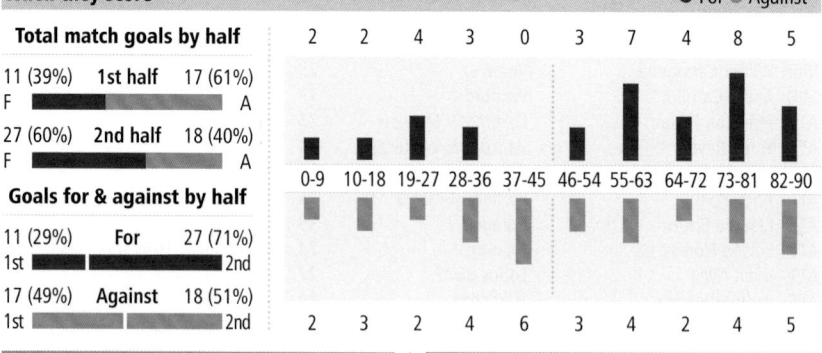

	2	2	4	3	0	3	7	4	8	5
	0-9	10-18	19-27	28-36	37-45	46-54	55-63	64-72	73-81	82-90
	2	3	2	4	6	3	4	2	4	5

Peru score first

They win	10	83%
They draw	1	8%
They lose	1	8%

Peru concede first

They win	2	14%
They draw	4	29%
They lose	8	57%

In 30 competitive games since Brazil 2014

GROUP C

Paolo Guerrero is available for Peru

Top scorers in qualifying

	P	G	1st	AT	%
Edison Flores	14	5	2	5	17
Paolo Guerrero	17	5	0	5	17
Jefferson Farfan	8	4	2	3	14
Christian Cueva	18	4	1	4	14
Christian Ramos	14	2	0	2	7
Paolo Hurtado	7	1	0	1	3
Andre Carrillo	11	1	0	1	3
Raul Ruidiaz	12	1	0	1	3
Renato Tapia	16	1	0	1	3

Game-by-game columns (left to right): Col 2-0 Per, Per 3-4 Chl, Per 1-0 Pry, Bra 3-0 Per, Per 2-2 Ven, Ury 1-0 Per, Bol 2-0 Per, Per 2-1 Ecu, Per 2-2 Arg, Chl 2-1 Per, Pry 1-4 Per, Per 0-2 Bra, Ven 2-2 Per, Per 2-1 Ury, Per 2-1 Bol, Ecu 1-2 Per, Arg 0-0 Per, Per 1-1 Col, Nzl 0-0 Per, Per 2-0 Nzl*

*Bolovia's 2-0 win over Peru was forfeited after Bolivia fielded an ineligible player. Match awarded 3-0 to Peru

G goals scored, **1st** first match goal (own goals don't count) **AT** goals at any time (ie. number of scoring appearances), **P** penalties, **%** percentage of total team goals scored by each player. Russia 2018 qualifying only. Game-by-game stats show goals scored, 1st goals are in red, dash did not score, ↳ substituted on, ↻ substituted off, blank did not play

Bookings in World Cup qualifying

Played 20

Cards (46Y, 1YR, 1R)

Avg make-up (□10 ■25) 25.5

Profile

Denmark have a decent 50 per cent win ratio at the World Cup with eight wins from their 16 previous matches.

The current crop lack the class of the Danish dynamite era of the 1980s but the European champions of 1992 are a dangerous side with the ability to shock.

How they qualified

It looked like being another World Cup watched from the sofa after a shocking start in which they lost to Poland and Montenegro and drew with Romania in the opening five rounds.

However, four straight wins, including a 4-0 demolition job on table-toppers Poland, put them in the playoffs where a Christian Eriksen masterclass helped the Danes to a 5-1 success over Ireland.

The manager

Any prospective Danish managers have had to be patient as Morten Olsen remained in situ for more than 15 years. But after he failed to lead the team to Euro 2016, Norwegian Age Hareide was handed the gig.

The squad

Hareide mainly used a variation of 4-3-3 in qualifying but the emergence of centre-backs Andreas Christensen of Chelsea and former Borussia Monchengladbach teammate Jannick Vestergaard could see Denmark switch to a three-man defence, a tactic which worked beautifully in Dublin.

If they go with a back three expect Christensen, who could also be used at right-back, to be selected with Andreas Bjelland and Sevilla's Simon Kjaer.

Goalkeeper Kasper Schmeichel is nailed-on to start and there is quality in central midfield where Thomas Delaney of Werder Bremen competes with Ajax's Lasse Schone and veteran William Kvist for two spots alongside key playmaker Eriksen.

Nicolai Jorgensen's 21 goals helped Feyenoord to win the Eredivisie in

Factfile

FA founded 1889

www dbu.dk

Head coach Age Hareide

Date qualified November 14, 2017

Strengths

☑ Eriksen is an elite performer

☑ Christensen's emergence strengthens the defence

Weaknesses

☒ First-choice full-backs are below the standard elsewhere

☒ Would struggle should anything happen to Eriksen

Star rating ★★★☆☆

Fixtures

1 June 16, 5pm v Peru, Saransk

2 June 21, 1pm v Australia, Samara

3 June 26, 3pm v France, Luzhniki Stadium, Moscow

Base Anapa

Total distance 4,650 miles

Denmark playmaker
Christian Eriksen

2016-17 and he should edge out Nicklas Bendtner. Yussuf Poulsen of Leipzig and Andreas Cornelius are coming through, although the pick of the younger forward talents is Pione Sisto.

Key man

Eriksen is everything to Denmark and if he plays well, so do the Danes. The Tottenham man scored 11 times in qualifying while also creating havoc with his eye for a pass and wicked set-piece delivery.

Only Robert Lewandowski and Cristiano Ronaldo scored more, which is going some considering how selfless he is in possession.

Rising star

Sisto has done the business for Celta Vigo and will be used wide if Denmark play with a back four and as a more central forward should they play a 3-4-1-2 shape. He is a dangerous dribbler in either position and his box of tricks brings an X-factor to the Danes.

Wildcard

This time last year Kasper Dolberg was one of the hottest properties in European football as his goals helped Ajax to reach the Europa League final but an anonymous performance in that showpiece occasion seems to have totally ruined his confidence.

At Ajax he was being spoken about as the next Marco van Basten, but the 20-year-old son of two former professional handball players had to wait until October to open his account for this season.

Prospects

Unlikely to go all the way but Denmark are better than their dismissive odds suggest.

How to back them

The Danes are potentially a big price to reach the quarter-finals, but for those looking for something safer they should qualify and look a cracking bet to overcome Australia on June 21.

World Cup record

World Cup record	Group stage(s)	P	W	D	L	F	A	P	W	D	L	F	A
Uruguay 1930	Did not enter	-	-	-	-	-	-	-	-	-	-	-	-
Italy 1934	Did not enter	-	-	-	-	-	-	-	-	-	-	-	-
France 1938	Did not enter	-	-	-	-	-	-	-	-	-	-	-	-
Brazil 1950	Did not enter	-	-	-	-	-	-	-	-	-	-	-	-
Switzerland 1954	Did not enter	-	-	-	-	-	-	-	-	-	-	-	-
Sweden 1958	Did not qualify	-	-	-	-	-	-	-	-	-	-	-	-
Chile 1962	Did not enter	-	-	-	-	-	-	-	-	-	-	-	-
England 1966	Did not qualify	-	-	-	-	-	-	-	-	-	-	-	-
Mexico 1970	Did not qualify	-	-	-	-	-	-	-	-	-	-	-	-
Germany 1974	Did not qualify	-	-	-	-	-	-	-	-	-	-	-	-
Argentina 1978	Did not qualify	-	-	-	-	-	-	-	-	-	-	-	-
Spain 1982	Did not qualify	-	-	-	-	-	-	-	-	-	-	-	-
Mexico 1986	Round of 16	3	3	0	0	9	1	1	0	0	1	1	5
Italy 1990	Did not qualify	-	-	-	-	-	-	-	-	-	-	-	-
USA 1994	Did not qualify	-	-	-	-	-	-	-	-	-	-	-	-
France 1998	Quarter-finals	3	1	1	1	3	3	2	1	0	1	6	4
Korea/Japan 2002	Round of 16	3	2	1	0	5	2	1	0	0	1	0	3
Germany 2006	Did not qualify	-	-	-	-	-	-	-	-	-	-	-	-
South Africa 2010	Group stage	3	1	0	2	3	6	-	-	-	-	-	-
Brazil 2014	Did not qualify	-	-	-	-	-	-	-	-	-	-	-	-
Totals		12	7	2	3	20	12	4	1	0	3	7	12

Continental championships (best perfomance)

Uefa European Championship	Winners (1)	1992

World Cup head-to-heads

Denmark v	P	W	D	L	F	A	Latest
Brazil	1	0	0	1	2	3	1998
England	1	0	0	1	0	3	2002
France	2	1	0	1	3	2	2002
Germany	1	1	0	0	2	0	1986
Japan	1	0	0	1	1	3	2010
Nigeria	1	1	0	0	4	1	1998
Saudi Arabia	1	1	0	0	1	0	1998
Senegal	1	0	1	0	1	1	2002
Spain	1	0	0	1	1	5	1986
Uruguay	2	2	0	0	8	2	2002

90 mins only, includes games against West Germany

Dennis Rommedahl scored first when the Danes ended France's World Cup defence in 2002

How they qualified

Group E	P	W	D	L	F	A	GD	P
Poland	10	8	1	1	28	14	14	25
Denmark	10	6	2	2	20	8	12	20
Montenegro	10	5	1	4	20	12	8	16
Romania	10	3	4	3	12	10	2	13
Armenia	10	2	1	7	10	26-16	7	
Kazakhstan	10	0	3	7	6	26-20	3	

Denmark........ (1) 1-0 (0)..........Armenia
Poland.......... (2) 3-2 (0)........Denmark
Denmark........ (0) 0-1 (1).... Montenegro
Denmark........ (2) 4-1 (1).....Kazakhstan
Romania........ (0) 0-0 (0).........Denmark
Kazakhstan .... (0) 1-3 (1)........Denmark
Denmark........ (2) 4-0 (0)............ Poland
Armenia .... (1) 1-4 (2)........Denmark

Montenegro... (0) 0-1 (1)........Denmark
Denmark........ (0) 1-1 (0)......... Romania

Playoffs

Denmark........ (0) 0-0 (0)..Rep of Ireland
Rep of Ireland (1) 1-5 (2)........Denmark
Denmark won 5-1 on aggregate

GROUP C

Players used in qualifying		Career			Qualification				
Pos		**Club**	**Age**	**P**	**G**	**P**	**G**	**▢**	**■**
GK	Frederik Ronnow	Brondby	25	6	-	3	-	-	-
GK	Kasper Schmeichel	Leicester	31	33	-	9	-	1	-
DEF	Andreas Bjelland	Brentford	29	28	2	6	-	-	-
DEF	Andreas Christensen	Chelsea	22	13	1	6	1	-	-
DEF	Henrik Dalsgaard	Brentford	28	9	-	5	-	1	-
DEF	Jannik Vestergaard	Mgladbach	25	15	1	4	-	-	-
DEF	Jens Stryger Larsen	Udinese	27	11	1	6	-	-	-
DEF	Mathias Jorgensen	Huddersfield	28	12	-	2	-	-	-
DEF	Peter Ankersen	FC Copenhagen	27	21	1	7	1	1	-
DEF	Riza Durmisi	Real Betis	24	23	-	8	-	-	-
DEF	Simon Kjaer	Sevilla	29	76	3	12	-	1	-
MID	Christian Eriksen	Tottenham	26	77	21	12	11	1	-
MID	Lasse Schone	Ajax	32	34	3	4	-	-	-
MID	Lukas Lerager	Bordeaux	24	3	-	1	-	-	-
MID	Mike Jensen	Rosenborg	30	6	-	1	-	-	-
MID	Pierre Hojbjerg	Southampton	22	21	1	3	-	-	-
MID	Thomas Delaney	Werder Bremen	26	25	4	12	4	1	-
MID	William Kvist	FC Copenhagen	33	78	2	11	-	-	-
MID	Pione Sisto	Celta Vigo	23	12	1	8	-	-	-
ATT	Andreas Cornelius	Atalanta	25	18	4	8	2	3	-
ATT	Kasper Dolberg	Ajax	20	4	1	3	1	-	-
ATT	Martin Braithwaite	Bordeaux	27	18	1	2	-	-	-
ATT	Nicklas Bendtner	Rosenborg	30	81	30	5	1	-	-
ATT	Nicolai Jorgensen	Feyenoord	27	29	8	9	2	1	-
ATT	Viktor Fischer	FC Copenhagen	24	17	3	4	-	1	-
ATT	Yussuf Poulsen	RB Leipzig	24	26	3	9	1	1	-

Photo by Catherine Ivill/Getty Images

Pione Sisto adds creativity to the Danish attack

Correct scores

	Competitive	Friendly
1-0	2	1
2-0	1	-
2-1	1	2
3-0	-	-
3-1	2	-
3-2	-	1
4-0	2	-
4-1	2	-
4-2	-	-
4-3	-	-
0-0	4	1
1-1	2	2
2-2	2	-
3-3	-	-
4-4	-	-
0-1	3	1
0-2	-	2
1-2	1	2
0-3	-	-
1-3	-	-
2-3	1	-
0-4	-	-
1-4	-	-
2-4	-	-
3-4	-	-
Other	1	1

Since Brazil 2014

Half-time/full-time double results

Win/Win	9	38%	Win 1st half	10	42%
Draw/Win	1	4%	Win 2nd half	12	50%
Lose/Win	1	4%	Win both halves	7	29%
Win/Draw	1	4%	Goal both halves	7	29%
Draw/Draw	5	21%			
Lose/Draw	2	8%	Overall		
Win/Lose	0	0%	● Win	46%	
Draw/Lose	2	8%	● Draw	33%	
Lose/Lose	3	13%	● Lose	21%	

Overall: W11, D8, L5 in 24 competitive games since Brazil 2014

Under & over goals

15 (63%)	Over 1.5	9 (37%)
12 (50%)	Over 2.5	12 (50%)
10 (42%)	Over 3.5	14 (58%)
4 (17%)	Over 4.5	20 (83%)

Both teams to score

12 (50%)	Both score	12 (50%)
6 (25%)	& win	18 (75%)
2 (8%)	& lose	22 (92%)

In 24 competitive games since Brazil 2014

Clean sheets

9 (38%)	Clean sheets	15 (62%)
5 (21%)	Win to nil	19 (79%)

7 (29%)	Fail to score	17 (71%)
3 (13%)	Lose to nil	21 (87%)

When they score

● For ● Against

Total match goals by half

15 (60%)	1st half	10 (40%)
F		A

27 (73%)	2nd half	10 (27%)
F		A

Goals for & against by half

15 (36%)	For	27 (64%)
1st		2nd

10 (50%)	Against	10 (50%)
1st		2nd

	0	6	2	4	3	2	5	3	10	7
For										
Against	0-9	10-18	19-27	28-36	37-45	46-54	55-63	64-72	73-81	82-90
	3	1	2	2	2	4	0	1	2	3

Denmark score first

They win	7		78%
They draw	2		22%
They lose	0		0%

In 24 competitive games since Brazil 2014

Denmark concede first

They win	4		36%
They draw	2		18%
They lose	5		45%

Thomas Delaney celebrates scoring Denmark's opener against Poland

Top scorers in qualifying

	P	G	1st	AT	%	Dnk 1-0 Arm	Pol 3-2 Dnk	Dnk 0-1 Mne	Dnk 4-1 Kaz	Rou 0-0 Dnk	Kaz 1-3 Dnk	Dnk 4-0 Pol	Arm 1-4 Dnk	Mne 0-1 Dnk	Dnk 1-1 Rou	Dnk 0-0 Irl	Irl 1-5 Dnk
Christian Eriksen	12	11	3	8	44	1	-	-	2	-	1	1	1	1	1	-	3
Thomas Delaney	12	4	1	2	16	↪	↪	-	-	-	-	↪1	3	-	-	-	-
Andreas Cornelius	8	2	1	2	8			↪	↪1	-		↪1	↩	↩		↩	↪
Nicolai Jorgensen	9	2	1	2	8	↩	↩	↪	-		1	↪1	-			-	↩
Kasper Dolberg	3	1	0	1	4				↪		◁1				↪		
Nicklas Bendtner	5	1	0	1	4								↪		↪	↩	↪	◁1
Andreas Christensen	6	1	0	1	4	-	-	-		-	-					-	1
Peter Ankersen	7	1	0	1	4	-	-	-	1	-						-	↩
Yussuf Poulsen	9	1	0	1	4	↪	◁1	-	-		↩				-	↩	↩

G goals scored, **1st** first match goal (own goals don't count) **AT** goals at any time (ie. number of scoring appearances), **P** penalties, **%** percentage of total team goals scored by each player. Russia 2018 qualifying only. Game-by-game stats show goals scored, 1st goals are in red, dash did not score, ↪ substituted on, ↩ substituted off, blank did not play

Bookings in World Cup qualifying

Played 12 **Cards** (12Y) ▯▯▯▯▯▯▯▯▯▯▯▯   **Avg make-up** (▯10 ▮25) 10

Note: Denmark's World Cup kit had not been released when we went to press

GROUP D

Take Croatia to pip Argentina to the post

Croatia upset the odds to top their group at Euro 2016 by beating Spain to first spot and they could topple favourites Argentina in World Cup Group D, *writes Mark Langdon*.

This bet is all about potential rather than what Croatia have achieved in recent years – they were knocked out of the European Championship by Portugal at the last-16 stage and followed up by only just squeezing into this tournament after finishing second in qualifying to Iceland.

However, when the pressure was on Croatia produced, winning away in Ukraine before trouncing Greece in the playoffs, and it is possible that improvement will continue under coach Zlatko Dalic, who replaced Ante Cacic before the trip to Kiev.

There are problems behind the scenes and while Luka Modric's name has been dragged through the mud for off-field issues, this is a team with serious ability if they show up.

Modric, Ivan Rakitic, Mateo Kovacic and Mario Mandzukic are playing at the highest level with clubs such as Real Madrid, Barcelona and Juventus. That's without mentioning Ivan Perisic, Inter teammate Marcelo Brozovic and Milan's Nikola Kalinic.

Croatia may not be able to match Argentina for individual brilliance but they might be a better unit.

Sergio Aguero, Paulo Dybala, Gonzalo Higuain and many more are fighting to partner Lionel Messi in Argentina's attack but defensively there is nowhere near the same kind of ability.

Argentina won all three group-stage matches at Brazil 2014, but only just. They beat Bosnia, Iran and Nigeria all by one goal and face a nervy opener against an Iceland side who just love the chance to take down more illustrious countries.

Iceland can make that fixture awkward for Jorge Sampaoli's men who, inexcusably for a team with their ability, nearly failed to book their place in Russia.

If Argentina can provide the platform for Messi to deliver his magic they will progress but there has been enough evidence throughout his international career – one which is still without a senior title – to suggest the Barcelona superstar may not get that opportunity.

Nigeria may be the value for bottom spot, if only because Iceland are a consistent team whereas the superior Super Eagles are more erratic.

Photo by Shaun Botterill/Getty Images

With the likes of Ivan Rakitic, Croatia have some real ability in their ranks

Recommendation

⭐☆☆☆☆ **Croatia to win Group D**

Group-stage performances since France 98

	Pot	P	W	Q	1998 Group	Pos	2002 Group	Pos	2006 Group	Pos	2010 Group	Pos	2014 Group	Pos
Argentina	1	5	4	4	H	1	F	3	C	1	B	1	F	1
Croatia	2	4	0	1	H	2	G	3	F	3	-	-	A	3
Iceland	3	0	0	0	-	-	-	-	-	-	-	-	-	-
Nigeria	4	4	1	2	D	1	F	4	-	-	B	4	F	2

To win Group D
Win only

	Bet365	BtBrt	Betfair	Btfrd	Btwy	Boyle	Coral	Hills	Lads	P Power	Sky	188
Argentina	8-13	4-7	**4-6**	4-7	8-13	**4-6**	8-15	**4-6**	4-7	**4-6**	1-2	11-20
Croatia	9-4	5-2	9-4	5-2	5-2	9-4	**11-4**	7-4	5-2	2	**11-4**	23-10
Nigeria	**10**	**10**	7	**10**	9	9	9	9	**10**	7	**10**	**10**
Iceland	12	12	11	10	10	12	11	**14**	10	11	12	10

Argentina v Iceland
2pm, Saturday June 16, ITV

	Bet365	BtBrt	Betfair	Btfrd	Btwy	Boyle	Coral	Hills	Lads	P Power	Sky	188
Argentina	4-11	1-3	**40-85**	4-11	7-20	1-3	1-3	3-10	1-3	4-11	4-11	6-17
Draw	7-2	16-5	16-5	10-3	10-3	3	13-4	18-5	13-4	7-2	10-3	**37-10**
Iceland	8	8	7	17-2	9	15-2	**10**	9	**10**	15-2	**10**	9

Croatia v Nigeria
8pm, Saturday June 16, ITV

	Bet365	BtBrt	Betfair	Btfrd	Btwy	Boyle	Coral	Hills	Lads	P Power	Sky	188
Croatia	17-20	5-6	**19-20**	17-20	17-20	5-6	20-23	5-6	20-23	**19-20**	17-20	7-8
Draw	12-5	9-4	23-10	23-10	12-5	21-10	11-5	12-5	11-5	11-5	12-5	**28-11**
Nigeria	10-3	3	16-5	10-3	16-5	3	13-4	16-5	13-4	3	**7-2**	16-5

Argentina v Croatia
7pm, Thursday June 21, BBC

	Bet365	BtBrt	Betfair	Btfrd	Btwy	Boyle	Coral	Hills	Lads	P Power	Sky	188
Argentina	4-5	4-5	**10-11**	4-5	4-5	3-4	3-4	4-5	3-4	5-6	4-5	13-16
Draw	5-2	23-10	23-10	12-5	12-5	9-4	23-10	5-2	23-10	21-10	5-2	**27-10**
Croatia	7-2	10-3	7-2	7-2	7-2	10-3	**15-4**	16-5	**15-4**	16-5	18-5	57-17

Nigeria v Iceland
4pm, Friday June 22, BBC

	Bet365	BtBrt	Betfair	Btfrd	Btwy	Boyle	Coral	Hills	Lads	P Power	Sky	188
Iceland	8-5	6-4	**9-5**	8-5	6-4	6-4	31-20	6-4	31-20	13-8	13-8	19-12
Nigeria	**2**	7-4	9-5	9-5	15-8	17-10	9-5	7-4	9-5	13-8	9-5	9-5
Draw	19-10	2	21-10	21-10	21-10	2	19-10	11-5	19-10	15-8	21-10	**23-10**

Iceland v Croatia
7pm, Tuesday June 26, BBC

	Bet365	BetBright	Betfair	Betfred	Betway	Boyle	Hills	P Power	Sky Bet
Croatia	5-6	5-6	3-4	5-6	17-20	4-5	**10-11**	4-6	4-5
Draw	5-2	9-4	**13-5**	12-5	11-5	11-5	11-5	12-5	5-2
Iceland	10-3	3	**4**	10-3	3	16-5	10-3	7-2	7-2

Nigeria v Argentina
7pm, Tuesday June 26, BBC

	Bet365	BetBright	Betfair	Betfred	Betway	Boyle	Hills	P Power	Sky Bet
Argentina	1-2	4-9	**8-13**	1-2	9-20	4-9	4-9	8-15	1-2
Draw	3	14-5	14-5	3	3	14-5	**10-3**	13-5	3
Nigeria	**6**	11-2	5	11-2	5	5	**6**	9-2	11-2

Prices correct March 28 2018

ARGENTINA

Profile

Argentina are one of the most glamorous names in the tournament but they have often flattered to deceive, earning a reputation as chokers.

The 2014 runners-up last lifted the World Cup in 1986, and, astonishingly, they are winless in the Copa America since 1993 after suffering defeat in four of the last five finals of the competition.

How they qualified

By the skin of their teeth, and there was the very real prospect of a World Cup without Lionel Messi until he scored a hat-trick in Ecuador on the final night to seal qualification.

Argentina used three managers and scored 19 goals in 18 games – the same as rock-bottom Venezuela.

The manager

Jorge Sampaoli, who won the Copa America as manager of Chile in 2015, is often seen as a disciple of Marcelo Bielsa but claims he prefers to take the bits from many philosophies. "When there are ten religions and you only follow one, you miss out on the other nine," he said.

The squad

Sampaoli is an attack-minded manager, which is just as well because the pool of players to choose from, led by skipper Messi, is top-heavy with forward talent and finding the right partners for him will be key.

Such is the striking depth that not all of Gonzalo Higuain, Paulo Dybala and Mauro Icardi are likely to join Messi and Sergio Aguero in Russia. And a spot must also be found somewhere in the team for Angel Di Maria.

In an ideal world Sampaoli would line up with a 3-4-3 formation, although his preferred back three of Javier Mascherano, Nicolas Otamendi and Gabriel Mercado isn't necessarily suited to that shape. There is also a lack of suitable wing-backs.

Factfile

FA founded 1893
www afa.org.ar
Head coach Jorge Sampaoli
Date qualified October 10, 2017

Strengths

☑ Magical Messi can win matches on his own
☑ Huge amount of depth to the attacking department

Weaknesses

☒ Too many similar players in many areas
☒ Lack of options at centre-back, wing-back, goalkeeper and central midfield

Star rating ★★★☆☆

Fixtures

1 June 16, 2pm v Iceland, Otkrytie Arena, Moscow
2 June 21, 7pm v Croatia, Nizhny Novgorod
3 June 26, 7pm v Nigeria, Saint Petersburg

Base Moscow
Total distance 1,300 miles

GROUP D

Lionel Messi has won it all with Barcelona but it's been a case of so near, yet so far with Argentina

Manchester United reserve keeper Sergio Romero is the undisputed number one for his country and the equilibrium in midfield, where Lucas Biglia and Ever Banega are among the options, is far from perfect.

Key man

Five-time Ballon d'Or winner Messi, who was voted the best player at the last World Cup, briefly quit the national team following their Copa America defeat on penalties to Chile in 2016.

It's just as well Messi returned as he was the only Argentinian to score in their last six Conmebol qualifiers.

Rising star

Lautaro Martinez, nicknamed The Bull, has been in rampaging scoring form for Racing this season and is said to be signing for Inter.

Wildcard

The delightful Dybala would walk into most international squads but Argentina don't possess a normal squad. "It is complicated for Dybala to get used to our system," said Sampaoli of the ace Juventus forward after leaving him and Icardi out of the March friendlies.

Prospects

Messi will turn 31 during the tournament so it's probably now or never for him and there could be more heartbreak in store. Given their forward threats, Argentina will always have a chance but there does not appear to be any balance to the side.

How to back them

If there is to be a huge first-round casualty it could be Argentina, who won't find it easy against Iceland, Croatia and Nigeria.

Consider getting with the outsiders on the match handicap as even in the last World Cup, none of Argentina's wins were by more than one goal.

ARGENTINA

GROUP D

World Cup record		Group stage(s)						Knockout rounds					
		P	W	D	L	F	A	P	W	D	L	F	A
Uruguay 1930	Finalists	3	3	0	0	10	4	2	1	0	1	8	5
Italy 1934	First round	-	-	-	-	-	-	1	0	0	1	2	3
France 1938	Withdrew	-	-	-	-	-	-	-	-	-	-	-	-
Brazil 1950	Withdrew	-	-	-	-	-	-	-	-	-	-	-	-
Switzerland 1954	Withdrew	-	-	-	-	-	-	-	-	-	-	-	-
Sweden 1958	Group stage	3	1	0	2	5	10	-	-	-	-	-	-
Chile 1962	Group stage	3	1	1	1	2	3	-	-	-	-	-	-
England 1966	Quarter-finals	3	2	1	0	4	1	1	0	0	1	0	1
Mexico 1970	Did not qualify	-	-	-	-	-	-	-	-	-	-	-	-
Germany 1974	2nd group stage	6	1	2	3	9	12	-	-	-	-	-	-
Argentina 1978	● Winners	6	4	1	1	12	3	1	0	1	0	1	1
Spain 1982	2nd group stage	5	2	0	3	8	7	-	-	-	-	-	-
Mexico 1986	● Winners	3	2	1	0	6	2	4	4	0	0	8	3
Italy 1990	Runners-up	3	1	1	1	3	2	4	1	2	1	2	2
USA 1994	Round of 16	3	2	0	1	6	3	1	0	0	1	2	3
France 1998	Quarter-finals	3	3	0	0	7	0	2	0	1	1	3	4
Korea/Japan 2002	Group stage	3	1	1	1	2	2	-	-	-	-	-	-
Germany 2006	Quarter-finals	3	2	1	0	8	1	2	0	2	0	2	2
South Africa 2010	Quarter-finals	3	3	0	0	7	1	2	1	0	1	3	5
Brazil 2014	Finalists	3	3	0	0	6	3	4	1	3	0	1	0
Totals		53	31	9	13	95	54	24	8	9	7	32	29

Continental championships (best perfomance)

Copa America	Winners (14)	1921, 1925, 1927, 1929, 1937, 1941, 1945, 1946, 1947, 1955, 1957, 1959, 1991, 1993

World Cup head-to-heads

Argentina v	P	W	D	L	F	A	Latest	Argentina v	P	W	D	L	F	A	Latest
Belgium	3	2	0	1	3	1	2014	Peru	1	1	0	0	6	0	1978
Brazil	4	1	1	2	3	5	1990	Poland	2	1	0	1	4	3	1978
Croatia	2	1	1	0	1	0	1998	Russia	1	1	0	0	2	0	1990
England	5	1	1	3	5	8	2002	Serbia	2	1	1	0	6	0	2006
France	2	2	0	0	3	1	1978	South Korea	2	2	0	0	7	2	2010
Germany	7	1	3	3	5	11	2014	Spain	1	1	0	0	2	1	1966
Iran	1	1	0	0	1	0	2014	Sweden	2	0	1	1	3	4	2002
Japan	1	1	0	0	1	0	1998	Switzerland	2	1	0	1	2	0	2014
Mexico	3	2	1	0	10	5	2010	Uruguay	2	1	0	1	3	4	1986
Nigeria	4	4	0	0	7	3	2014								

90 mins only, includes games against Yugoslavia, Serbia & Montenegro, USSR and West Germany

How they qualified

Top five	P	W	D	L	F	A	GD	P
Brazil	18	12	5	1	41	11	30	41
Uruguay	18	9	4	5	32	20	12	31
Argentina	18	7	7	4	19	16	3	28
Colombia	18	7	6	5	21	19	2	27
Peru	18	7	5	6	27	26	1	26

Argentina ..... (0) 0-2 (0)........... Ecuador
Paraguay......... (0) 0-0 (0)......Argentina
Argentina ..... (1) 1-1 (0)..............Brazil
Colombia ...... (0) 0-1 (1)........Argentina
Chile.............. (1) 1-2 (2)........Argentina
Argentina ..... (2) 2-0 (0)............. Bolivia
Argentina ..... (1) 1-0 (0).........Uruguay
Venezuela ...... (1) 2-2 (0)........Argentina
Peru............... (0) 2-2 (1)........Argentina

Argentina ..... (0) 0-1 (1)........ Paraguay
Brazil .... (2) 3-0 (0)......Argentina
Argentina ..... (2) 3-0 (0)......Colombia
Argentina ..... (1) 1-0 (0)............. Chile
Bolivia............ (1) 2-0 (0)........Argentina
Uruguay ..... (0) 0-0 (0)........Argentina
Argentina ..... (0) 1-1 (0)......Venezuela
Argentina ..... (0) 0-0 (0)............... Peru
Ecuador........ (1) 1-3 (2)........Argentina

▶▶ Full qualifying results 228-241

Players used in qualifying		Career			In qualifying			
Pos		Club	Age	P	G	P	G		
GK	Sergio Romero	Man Utd	31	94	-	18	-	1	-
DEF	Emmanuel Mas	Boca Juniors	29	8	-	6	-	1	-
DEF	Ezequiel Garay	Valencia	31	32	-	1	-	-	-
DEF	Facundo Roncaglia	Celta Vigo	31	14	-	4	-	2	-
DEF	Federico Fazio	Roma	31	8	1	3	-	-	-
DEF	Gabriel Mercado	Sevilla	31	19	3	9	2	2	-
DEF	Gino Peruzzi	Nacional	26	5	-	1	-	-	-
DEF	Javier Mascherano	Hebei CFFC	34	141	3	15	-	5	-
DEF	Javier Pinola	River Plate	35	2	-	1	-	-	-
DEF	Marcos Rojo	Man Utd	28	56	2	9	-	1	-
DEF	Martin Demichelis	Retired	37	51	2	2	-	-	-
DEF	Mateo Musacchio	Milan	27	6	-	3	-	-	-
DEF	Matias Caruzzo	San Lorenzo	33	6	-	1	-	-	-
DEF	Nicolas Otamendi	Man City	30	53	4	15	1	7	-
DEF	Pablo Zabaleta	West Ham	33	58	-	5	-	2	-
DEF	Ramiro Funes Mori	Everton	27	19	1	10	1	6	-
MID	Alejandro Gomez	Atalanta	30	4	1	1	-	-	-
MID	Angel Di Maria	Paris St-Germain	30	93	19	18	2	1	-
MID	Augusto Fernandez	Beijing Renhe	32	16	1	2	-	-	-
MID	Eduardo Salvio	Benfica	28	8	-	1	-	-	-
MID	Emiliano Rigoni	Zenit	25	2	-	1	-	-	-
MID	Enzo Perez	River Plate	32	23	1	6	-	-	-
MID	Erik Lamela	Tottenham	26	23	3	3	-	-	-
MID	Ever Banega	Sevilla	29	61	7	12	-	3	-
MID	Fernando Gago	Boca Juniors	32	61	-	1	-	-	-
MID	Guido Pizarro	Sevilla	28	3	-	3	-	-	-
MID	Javier Pastore	Paris St-Germain	28	29	2	4	-	1	-
MID	Joaquin Correa	Sevilla	23	3	1	1	-	-	-
MID	Leandro Paredes	Zenit	23	3	1	1	-	-	-
MID	Lucas Biglia	Milan	32	57	1	13	1	4	-
MID	Marcos Acuna	Sporting Lisbon	26	9	-	6	-	2	-
MID	Matias Kranevitter	Zenit	25	9	-	3	-	-	-
MID	Nicolas Gaitan	Dalian Yifang	30	19	2	5	-	-	-
ATT	Angel Correa	Atletico Madrid	23	8	1	6	-	-	-
ATT	Carlos Tevez	Boca Juniors	34	76	13	2	-	1	-
ATT	Dario Benedetto	Boca Juniors	28	4	-	3	-	-	-
ATT	Ezequiel Lavezzi	Hebei CFFC	33	51	9	5	1	2	-
ATT	Gonzalo Higuain	Juventus	30	71	32	9	1	2	-
ATT	Lautaro Acosta	Lanus	30	2	-	2	-	1	-
ATT	Lionel Messi	Barcelona	30	123	61	10	7	-	-
ATT	Lucas Alario	Bayer Leverkusen	25	3	1	2	-	-	-
ATT	Lucas Pratto	River Plate	30	5	2	5	2	1	-
ATT	Mauro Icardi	Inter	25	4	-	3	-	-	-
ATT	Paulo Dybala	Juventus	24	12	-	8	-	3	1
ATT	Sergio Aguero	Man City	30	84	36	8	-	1	-

ARGENTINA

Correct scores

	Competitive	Friendly
1-0	5	3
2-0	1	2
2-1	2	3
3-0	2	-
3-1	1	-
3-2	-	-
4-0	1	-
4-1	1	-
4-2	-	1
4-3	-	-
0-0	6	-
1-1	2	-
2-2	3	1
3-3	-	-
4-4	-	-
0-1	1	1
0-2	2	1
1-2	-	-
0-3	1	-
1-3	-	-
2-3	-	-
0-4	-	-
1-4	-	-
2-4	-	1
3-4	-	-
Other	2	5

Since Brazil 2014

Half-time/full-time double results

Win/Win	13	43%	Win 1st half	16	53%
Draw/Win	2	7%	Win 2nd half	9	30%
Lose/Win	0	0%	Win both halves	6	20%
Win/Draw	3	10%	Goal both halves	7	23%
Draw/Draw	7	23%			
Lose/Draw	1	3%	Overall		
Win/Lose	0	0%	● Win	50%	
Draw/Lose	1	3%	● Draw	37%	
Lose/Lose	3	10%	● Lose	13%	

Overall: W15, D11, L4 in 30 competitive games since Brazil 2014

Under & over goals

18 (60%) **Over 1.5** 12 (40%) ✓ ✗

13 (43%) **Over 2.5** 17 (57%) ✓ ✗

8 (27%) **Over 3.5** 22 (73%) ✓ ✗

3 (10%) **Over 4.5** 27 (90%) ✓ ✗

Both teams to score

10 (33%) **Both score** 20 (67%) ✓ ✗

4 (13%) **& win** 26 (87%) ✓ ✗

0 (0%) **& lose** 30 (100%) ✓ ✗

In 30 competitive games since Brazil 2014

Clean sheets

16 (53%) **Clean sheets** 14 (47%) ✓ ✗

10 (33%) **Win to nil** 20 (67%) ✓ ✗

10 (33%) **Fail to score** 20 (67%) ✓ ✗

4 (13%) **Lose to nil** 26 (87%) ✓ ✗

When they score

● For ● Against

Total match goals by half

26 (76%) **1st half** 8 (24%)
F A

21 (62%) **2nd half** 13 (38%)
F A

Goals for & against by half

26 (55%) **For** 21 (45%)
1st 2nd

8 (38%) **Against** 13 (62%)
1st 2nd

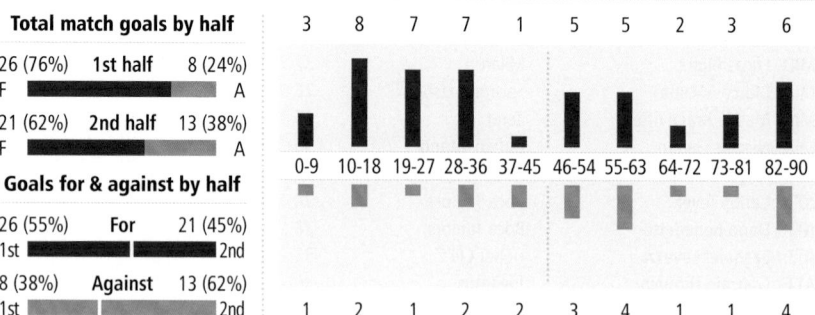

3	8	7	7	1	5	5	2	3	6
0-9	10-18	19-27	28-36	37-45	46-54	55-63	64-72	73-81	82-90
1	2	1	2	2	3	4	1	1	4

Argentina score first

They win	13	81%
They draw	3	19%
They lose	0	0%

Argentina concede first

They win	2	25%
They draw	2	25%
They lose	4	50%

In 30 competitive games since Brazil 2014

Lionel Messi played in just over half of Argentina's qualifiers and scored over a third of their goals

Photo by Robert Cianflone/Getty Images

Top scorers in qualifying

	P	G	1st	AT	%	Arg 0-2 Ecu	Pry 0-0 Arg	Arg 1-1 Bra	Col 0-1 Arg	Chi 1-2 Arg	Arg 2-0 Bol	Arg 1-0 Ury	Ven 2-2 Arg	Per 2-2 Arg	Arg 0-1 Pry	Bra 3-0 Arg	Arg 3-0 Col	Arg 1-0 Chi	Bol 2-0 Arg	Ury 0-0 Arg	Arg 1-1 Ven	Arg 0-0 Per	Ecu 1-3 Arg
Lionel Messi	10	7	3	5	37					-	1	1			-	1	1			-	-	-	3
Lucas Pratto	5	2	0	2	11						↩	1		↪	1	-							
Gabriel Mercado	9	2	1	2	11						↪	1	1				-	↪					
Angel Di Maria	18	2	0	2	11	-	-	-	-	↪	↩	↩	-	-	↩	1	-	-	↩	1	↩	↩	↩
Ezequiel Lavezzi	5	1	1	1	5	↪	↪	1	↪	↪													
Gonzalo Higuain	9	1	0	1	5						↩	↩	↪	↩		1	-	-	↩	-			
Ramiro Funes Mori	10	1	1	1	5		-	-	-	-		-	-	1	-		-	-	↩				
Lucas Biglia	13	1	1	1	5	-		-	1	-		-	↩				-	-	-	-			
Nicolas Otamendi	15	1	0	1	5	-		-	-	-		-	1				-	-	-	-			

G goals scored, **1st** first match goal (own goals don't count) **AT** goals at any time (ie. number of scoring appearances), **P** penalties, **%** percentage of total team goals scored by each player. Russia 2018 qualifying only. Game-by-game stats show goals scored, 1st goals are in red, dash did not score, ↪ substituted on, ↩ substituted off, blank did not play

Bookings in World Cup qualifying

Played 18

Cards (49Y, 1YR)

Avg make-up (□10 ■25) 28.6

ICELAND

GROUP D

Profile

Iceland will become the smallest country ever to play in the World Cup and their population of 340,000 is around a tenth of any other nation competing in Russia. However, Iceland showed size isn't everything with a quarter-final run at Euro 2016.

How they qualified

No European group winner qualified having scored fewer goals than Iceland's 16, although it is worth bearing in mind that their section was the only one to house four Euro 2016 participants as Croatia, Ukraine and Turkey helped to form an ultra-competitive pool.

The manager

Critics of Iceland's direct style suggest watching them is like pulling teeth and that's quite apt with qualified dentist Heimir Hallgrimsson in charge.

Hallgrimsson, who was still practising dentistry when assistant to Lars Lagerback in France two years ago, said: "We know what we are good at, we know our strengths. We play the way that suits us."

The squad

In an ideal world Hallgrimsson would maintain the 4-4-2 formation he used at the Euros but an injury to Kolbeinn Sigthorsson means a 4-2-3-1 shape is more probable.

However, the pattern of play from two years ago remains, as do most of the players, and the limited pool to select from has fostered a club-like team spirit. The vast majority of those who started the Euros are set for major roles once more.

One of the few changes could come at left-back where Bristol City's Hordur Magnusson is pushing Ari Skulason.

Wide players Birkir Bjarnason and Johann Berg Gudmundsson work tirelessly and long-throw expert Aron Gunnarsson sits just in front of the back four.

A switch to 4-2-3-1 would see Gylfi

Factfile

FA founded 1947
www ksi.is
Head coach Heimir Hallgrimsson
Date qualified October 9, 2017

Strengths

☑ A major threat from set-pieces
☑ Team spirit is spot on

Weaknesses

☒ Lack individual quality outside of injury doubt Sigurdsson
☒ There won't be any shock factor for opponents this time

Star rating ★★☆☆☆

Fixtures

1 June 16, 2pm v Argentina, Otkrytie Arena, Moscow
2 June 22, 4pm v Nigeria, Volgograd
3 June 26, 7pm v Croatia, Rostov-on-Don

Base Gelendzhik
Total distance 2,800 miles

Iceland showed at Euro 2016 – to England's cost – that they should not be underestimated

Sigurdsson, fitness permitting, shift from partnering Gunnarsson and move further forward, closer to either Alfred Finnbogason or Jon Dadi Bodvarsson as the lone striker.

Key man

Everton signed Sigurdsson from Swansea for £45m but his contribution to this Icelandic side is almost priceless.

He finished as their top scorer in qualifying and Siggy's superb set-piece delivery is a major weapon so there was understandable widespread panic when it was reported a knee injury could keep him out of the finals.

Rising star

Under-21 captain Albert Gudmundsson was given permission by club side PSV Eindhoven to miss their winter training camp in Orlando to push his World Cup claims outside of official Fifa international dates in January.

The winger, who can play on either flank, was promoted to PSV's senior squad after impressing for their B side.

Wildcard

Sigthorsson suffered a serious knee injury in August 2016 and was sidelined until returning for Nantes reserves in March. He would obviously be a risky squad pick but only Eidur Gudjohnsen has scored more international goals for the Nordic nation.

Prospects

Don't underestimate Iceland – just ask England about their ability to shock – and facing Argentina first up is perfect. However, they will need the South Americans and Croatia to underperform to qualify.

How to back them

Some bookies have them as rank outsiders for Group D which feels a little harsh. Consider backing a third-place finish.

ICELAND

World Cup record

World Cup record		Group stage(s)						Knockout rounds					
		P	W	D	L	F	A	P	W	D	L	F	A
Uruguay 1930	Did not enter	-	-	-	-	-	-	-	-	-	-	-	-
Italy 1934	Did not enter	-	-	-	-	-	-	-	-	-	-	-	-
France 1938	Did not enter	-	-	-	-	-	-	-	-	-	-	-	-
Brazil 1950	Did not enter	-	-	-	-	-	-	-	-	-	-	-	-
Switzerland 1954	Entry not accepted	-	-	-	-	-	-	-	-	-	-	-	-
Sweden 1958	Did not qualify	-	-	-	-	-	-	-	-	-	-	-	-
Chile 1962	Did not enter	-	-	-	-	-	-	-	-	-	-	-	-
England 1966	Did not enter	-	-	-	-	-	-	-	-	-	-	-	-
Mexico 1970	Did not enter	-	-	-	-	-	-	-	-	-	-	-	-
Germany 1974	Did not qualify	-	-	-	-	-	-	-	-	-	-	-	-
Argentina 1978	Did not qualify	-	-	-	-	-	-	-	-	-	-	-	-
Spain 1982	Did not qualify	-	-	-	-	-	-	-	-	-	-	-	-
Mexico 1986	Did not qualify	-	-	-	-	-	-	-	-	-	-	-	-
Italy 1990	Did not qualify	-	-	-	-	-	-	-	-	-	-	-	-
USA 1994	Did not qualify	-	-	-	-	-	-	-	-	-	-	-	-
France 1998	Did not qualify	-	-	-	-	-	-	-	-	-	-	-	-
Korea/Japan 2002	Did not qualify	-	-	-	-	-	-	-	-	-	-	-	-
Germany 2006	Did not qualify	-	-	-	-	-	-	-	-	-	-	-	-
South Africa 2010	Did not qualify	-	-	-	-	-	-	-	-	-	-	-	-
Brazil 2014	Did not qualify	-	-	-	-	-	-	-	-	-	-	-	-
Totals		0	0	0	0	0	0	0	0	0	0	0	0

Continental championships (best perfomance)

Uefa European Championship   Quarter-finals (1)   2016

How they qualified

Group I	P	W	D	L	F	A	GD	P
Iceland	10	7	1	2	16	7	9	22
Croatia	10	6	2	2	15	4	11	20
Ukraine	10	5	2	3	13	9	4	17
Turkey	10	4	3	3	14	13	1	15
Finland	10	2	3	5	9	13	-4	9
Kosovo	10	0	1	9	3	24	-21	1

Ukraine .... (1) 1-1 (1)............Iceland
Iceland .... (1) 3-2 (2)............ Finland
Iceland .... (2) 2-0 (0)............Turkey
Croatia .... (1) 2-0 (0)............Iceland
Kosovo .... (0) 1-2 (2)............Iceland
Iceland .... (0) 1-0 (0)............Croatia
Finland........... (1) 1-0 (0)............Iceland
Iceland .... (0) 2-0 (0)............Ukraine
Turkey .... (0) 0-3 (2)............Iceland
Iceland .... (1) 2-0 (0)............Kosovo

Hordur Magnusson scored the only goal when Iceland beat Group D rivals Croatia in Reykjavik during qualifying

Photo by Ian Walton/Getty Images

Heimir Hallgrimsson, Iceland's most famous dentist, is all smiles

Players used in qualifying		Career			Qualification			
Pos		**Club**	**Age**	**P**	**G**	**P**	**G**	
GK	Ogmundur Kristinsson	Excelsior	28	15	-	1	-	-	-
GK	Hannes Halldorsson	Randers	34	48	-	9	-	-	-
DEF	Ari Skulason	Lokeren	30	54	-	5	-	-	-
DEF	Birkir Saevarsson	Valur	33	78	1	10	-	-	-
DEF	Hordur Magnusson	Bristol City	25	14	2	8	1	-	-
DEF	Kari Arnason	Aberdeen	35	65	4	9	2	1	-
DEF	Ragnar Sigurdsson	Rostov	31	75	3	10	1	1	-
DEF	Sverrir Ingason	Rostov	24	18	3	4	-	-	-
MID	Arnor Ingvi Traustason	Malmo	25	18	5	3	-	-	-
MID	Aron Gunnarsson	Cardiff	29	77	2	9	-	3	-
MID	Birkir Bjarnason	Aston Villa	30	65	9	9	1	1	-
MID	Emil Hallfredsson	Udinese	33	62	1	6	-	2	-
MID	Gylfi Sigurdsson	Everton	28	55	18	10	4	1	-
MID	Johann Gudmundsson	Burnley	27	65	7	9	2	1	-
MID	Olafur Ingi Skulason	Karabukspor	35	35	1	3	-	1	-
MID	Runar Sigurjonsson	St Gallen	27	15	1	1	-	-	-
MID	Rurik Gislason	Sandhausen	30	45	3	3	-	2	1
MID	Theodor Bjarnason	Elazigspor	31	40	-	3	-	2	-
ATT	Alfred Finnbogason	Augsburg	29	45	11	8	3	1	-
ATT	Bjorn Sigurdarson	Rostov	27	11	1	6	1	-	-
ATT	Jon Dadi Bodvarsson	Reading	26	36	2	8	-	-	-
ATT	Vidar Kjartansson	Maccabi Tel Aviv	28	17	2	4	-	-	-

ICELAND

Correct scores

	Competitive	Friendly
1-0	2	2
2-0	4	2
2-1	4	1
3-0	4	-
3-1	-	-
3-2	1	1
4-0	-	1
4-1	-	1
4-2	-	-
4-3	-	-
0-0	1	-
1-1	3	3
2-2	1	-
3-3	-	-
4-4	-	-
0-1	2	2
0-2	1	-
1-2	1	3
0-3	-	1
1-3	-	3
2-3	-	2
0-4	-	-
1-4	-	-
2-4	-	1
3-4	-	-
Other	1	-

Since Brazil 2014

Half-time/full-time double results

Win/Win	9	36%
Draw/Win	5	20%
Lose/Win	1	4%
Win/Draw	2	8%
Draw/Draw	2	8%
Lose/Draw	1	4%
Win/Lose	0	0%
Draw/Lose	2	8%
Lose/Lose	3	12%

Win 1st half	11	44%
Win 2nd half	12	48%
Win both halves	4	16%
Goal both halves	6	24%

Overall
- Win 60%
- Draw 20%
- Lose 20%

Overall: W15, D5, L5 in 25 competitive games since Brazil 2014

Under & over goals

20 (80%)	Over 1.5	5 (20%)
✓		×
12 (48%)	Over 2.5	13 (52%)
✓		×
3 (12%)	Over 3.5	22 (88%)
✓		×
2 (8%)	Over 4.5	23 (92%)
✓		×

Both teams to score

11 (44%)	Both score	14 (56%)
✓		×
5 (20%)	& win	20 (80%)
✓		×
2 (8%)	& lose	23 (92%)
✓		×

In 25 competitive games since Brazil 2014

Clean sheets

11 (44%)	Clean sheets	14 (56%)
✓		×
10 (40%)	Win to nil	15 (60%)
✓		×

4 (16%)	Fail to score	21 (84%)
✓		×
3 (12%)	Lose to nil	22 (88%)
✓		×

When they score

● For ● Against

Total match goals by half

21 (64%)	1st half	12 (36%)
F		A
20 (67%)	2nd half	10 (33%)
F		A

Goals for & against by half

21 (51%)	For	20 (49%)
1st		2nd
12 (55%)	Against	10 (45%)
1st		2nd

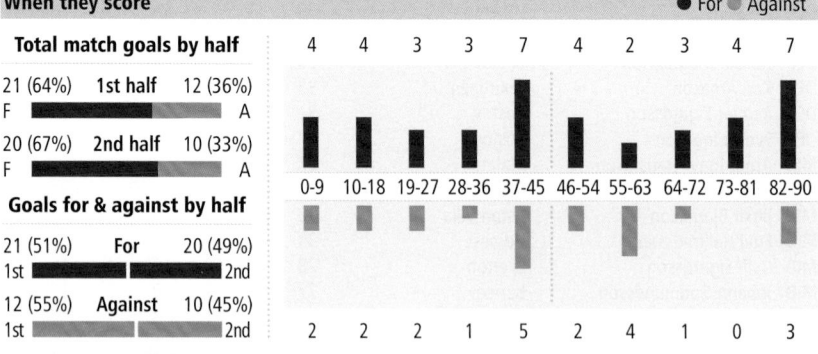

	0-9	10-18	19-27	28-36	37-45	46-54	55-63	64-72	73-81	82-90
For	4	4	3	3	7	4	2	3	4	7
Against	2	2	2	1	5	2	4	1	0	3

Iceland score first

They win	12	75%
They draw	3	19%
They lose	1	6%

Iceland concede first

They win	3	38%
They draw	1	13%
They lose	4	50%

In 25 competitive games since Brazil 2014

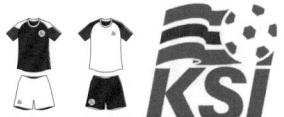

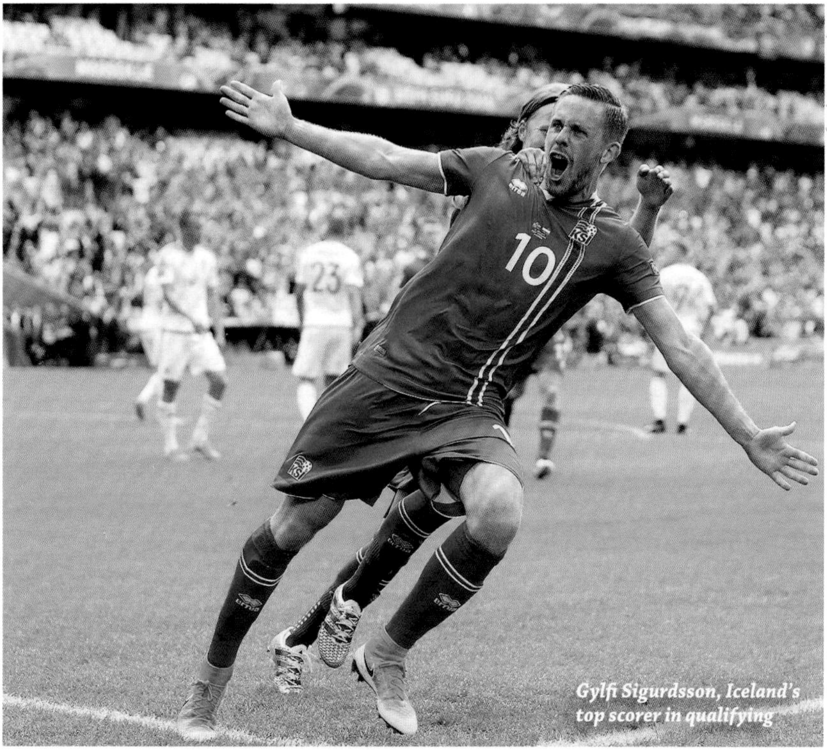

Gylfi Sigurdsson, Iceland's top scorer in qualifying

Photo by Lars Baron/Getty Images

Top scorers in qualifying

	P	G	1st	AT	%	Ukr 1-1 Isl	Isl 3-2 Fin	Isl 2-0 Tur	Hrv 2-0 Isl	Kos 1-2 Isl	Isl 1-0 Hrv	Fin 1-0 Isl	Isl 2-0 Ukr	Tur 0-3 Isl	Isl 2-0 Kos
Gylfi Sigurdsson	10	4	2	3	25	-	-	-	-	1	-	-	↩2	-	1
Alfred Finnbogason	8	3	2	3	19	1	1	↩1			↩	↩	↪	↩	↪
Kari Arnason	9	2	0	2	13	-	1	-	-	-	-	-		1	-
Johann Gudmundsson	9	2	1	2	13	↩	-	-	-		-	-	-	↩1	1
Bjorn Sigurdarson	6	1	1	1	6		↩	↪		↩1	↪	↪	↪		
Birkir Bjarnason	9	1	0	1	6	↩	-	-	-		↩	-	-	1	-
Hordur Magnusson	8	1	1	1	6	↪		↪	-		1	-	-	-	-
Ragnar Sigurdsson	10	1	0	1	6	-	1	-	-	-	↩	-	-	-	-

G goals scored, **1st** first match goal (own goals don't count) **AT** goals at any time (ie. number of scoring appearances), **P** penalties, **%** percentage of total team goals scored by each player. Russia 2018 qualifying only. Game-by-game stats show goals scored, 1st goals are in red, dash did not score, ↪ substituted on, ↩ substituted off, blank did not play

Bookings in World Cup qualifying

Played 10 **Cards** (16Y, 1YR) □□□□□□□□□□□□□□□□ ◪ **Avg make-up** (□10 ■25) 18.5

CROATIA

Profile

Croatia's first World Cup resulted in a glorious third-place finish at France 98 but it has been a sorry story of failure since with three further bids for glory ending at the group stage. This Croatia side has the talent to go well – but we have heard that before.

How they qualified

Croatia were in cruise control after claiming 13 points from the opening five matches before a 1-0 defeat in Iceland derailed them. They also lost by the same score in Turkey and a 1-1 home draw with Finland meant Croatia had to win in Ukraine just to make the playoffs.

A 2-0 success in Kiev was followed by an excellent 4-1 aggregate success over Greece.

The manager

Zlatko Dalic replaced the sacked Ante Cacic for the trip to Ukraine and has since signed a permanent contract.

Dalic, who has little European coaching pedigree but has a greater reputation for his work with sides in the Gulf, is seen as a puppet for those in power.

The squad

Central midfield is where the magic is for Croatia. Luka Modric pulls the strings and the Real Madrid star gets help from Bernabeu buddy Mateo Kovacic and Barcelona's Ivan Rakitic. Milan Badelj is another option and the versatile Marcelo Brozovic is more likely to start wide.

Brozovic's Inter teammate Ivan Perisic offers an excellent threat down the left, while Juventus striker Mario Mandzukic is likely to lead the line with Nikola Kalinic and Andrej Kramaric in reserve. The midfield and forward line has the potential to be special.

However, there are question marks in defence and over whether Dalic is the man to bring unity to the infighting which has led to their passionate fanbase becoming disconnected because of off-

Factfile

FA founded 1912
www hns-cff.hr
Head coach Zlatko Dalic
Date qualified November 12, 2017

Strengths
- ☑ Their midfield is one of the best in the competition
- ☑ Most of their players ply their trade at huge European clubs

Weaknesses
- ☒ There are issues at centre-back and left-back
- ☒ Coach needs to prove himself at this level

Star rating ★★★☆☆

Fixtures
1 June 16, 8pm v Nigeria, Kaliningrad
2 June 21, 7pm v Argentina, Nizhny Novgorod
3 June 26, 7pm v Iceland, Rostov-on-Don

Base Saint Petersburg
Total distance 4,050 miles

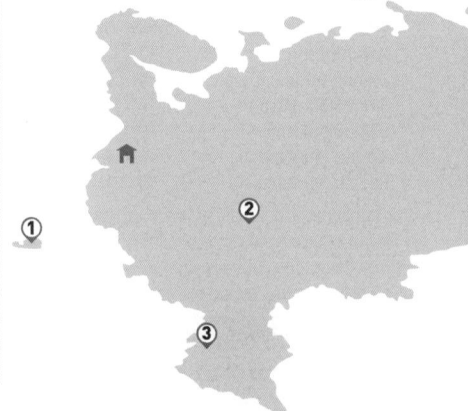

Real Madrid man Luka Modric is the star of one of the best midfields at the tournament

field issues involving federation chiefs such as one-time legend Davor Suker.

Monaco's Danijel Subasic remains the regular goalkeeper and Sime Vrsaljko is a fine right-back, although left-backs Josip Pivaric or Ivan Strinic are rated less highly. Dalic also needs to find the perfect partner for Besiktas centre-back Domagoj Vida. Vedran Corluka or Dejan Lovren will fill that particular void.

Key man

Modric has been a master at Real Madrid for years, helping them to land back-to-back Champions League titles, although he has angered many in his homeland for his close links to Zdravko Mamic, who critics claim holds too much influence in Croatian football.

Modric insists his "conscience is clear" following perjury charges after being suspected of changing his testimony during a court trial involving Mamic.

Rising star

Marko Pjaca, a versatile player who can play in all of the advanced midfield positions, headed to Schalke on loan in January from Juventus to regain fitness following a serious injury. His favourite player is Ronaldinho.

Wildcard

Tin Jedvaj is capable of filling in as a full-back or at centre-back but has suffered injury problems at Bayer Leverkusen.

Prospects

Croatia could win it or go out in the first round. They are in a tough group but should be seen as dangerous tournament outsiders.

How to back them

Croatia's flaky mentality makes them difficult to trust but an each-way outright punt could be of interest because they are capable of out-performing their odds.

CROATIA

World Cup record		Group stage(s)						Knockout rounds					
		P	W	D	L	F	A	P	W	D	L	F	A
Uruguay 1930	Semi-finals	2	2	0	0	6	1	1	0	0	1	1	6
Italy 1934	Did not qualify	-	-	-	-	-	-	-	-	-	-	-	-
France 1938	Did not qualify	-	-	-	-	-	-	-	-	-	-	-	-
Brazil 1950	Group stage	3	2	0	1	7	3	-	-	-	-	-	-
Switzerland 1954	Quarter-finals	2	1	1	0	2	1	1	0	0	1	0	2
Sweden 1958	Quarter-finals	3	1	2	0	7	6	1	0	0	1	0	1
Chile 1962	Fourth place	3	2	0	1	8	3	3	1	0	2	2	4
England 1966	Did not qualify	-	-	-	-	-	-	-	-	-	-	-	-
Mexico 1970	Did not qualify	-	-	-	-	-	-	-	-	-	-	-	-
Germany 1974	2nd group stage	6	1	2	3	12	7	-	-	-	-	-	-
Argentina 1978	Did not qualify	-	-	-	-	-	-	-	-	-	-	-	-
Spain 1982	Group stage	3	1	1	1	2	2	-	-	-	-	-	-
Mexico 1986	Did not qualify	-	-	-	-	-	-	-	-	-	-	-	-
Italy 1990	Quarter-finals	3	2	0	1	6	5	2	0	2	0	1	1
USA 1994	Did not enter	-	-	-	-	-	-	-	-	-	-	-	-
France 1998	Third place	3	2	0	1	4	2	4	3	0	1	7	3
Korea/Japan 2002	Group stage	3	1	0	2	2	3	-	-	-	-	-	-
Germany 2006	Group stage	3	0	2	1	2	3	-	-	-	-	-	-
South Africa 2010	Did not qualify	-	-	-	-	-	-	-	-	-	-	-	-
Brazil 2014	Group stage	3	1	0	2	6	6	-	-	-	-	-	-
Totals		37	16	8	13	64	42	12	4	2	6	11	17

Competed as part of Yugoslavia until 1992

Continental championships (best perfomance)

Uefa European Championship	Quarter-finals (2)	1996, 2008

Also beaten finalists as part of Yugoslavia 1960 & 1968

World Cup head-to-heads

Croatia v	P	W	D	L	F	A	Latest	Croatia v	P	W	D	L	F	A	Latest
Argentina	2	0	1	1	0	1	1998	Mexico	3	1	0	2	5	5	2014
Australia	1	0	1	0	2	2	2006	Poland	1	0	0	1	1	2	1974
Brazil	6	1	2	3	4	8	2014	Russia	1	0	0	1	0	2	1962
Colombia	2	2	0	0	6	0	1990	Spain	2	0	1	1	2	3	1990
France	3	2	0	1	5	4	1998	Sweden	1	0	0	1	1	2	1974
Germany	7	2	1	4	7	11	1998	Switzerland	1	1	0	0	3	0	1950
Iran	1	1	0	0	1	0	1998	Uruguay	2	1	0	1	4	7	1962
Japan	2	1	1	0	1	0	2006								

90 mins only. Includes games played as part of Yugoslavia and games against West Germany and USSR

How they qualified

Group I	P	W	D	L	F	A	GD	P
Iceland	10	7	1	2	16	7	9	22
Croatia	10	6	2	2	15	4	11	20
Ukraine	10	5	2	3	13	9	4	17
Turkey	10	4	3	3	14	13	1	15
Finland	10	2	3	5	9	13	-4	9
Kosovo	10	0	1	9	3	24	-21	1

Croatia .... (1) 1-1 (1) .... Turkey
Kosovo .... (0) 0-6 (3) .... Croatia
Finland .... (0) 0-1 (1) .... Croatia
Croatia .... (1) 2-0 (0) .... Iceland
Croatia .... (1) 1-0 (0) .... Ukraine
Iceland .... (0) 1-0 (0) .... Croatia
Croatia .... (0) 1-0 (0) .... Kosovo
Match suspended – completed on Sep 3

Turkey .... (0) 1-0 (0) .... Croatia
Croatia .... (0) 1-1 (0) .... Finland
Ukraine .... (0) 0-2 (0) .... Croatia

Playoffs
Croatia .... (3) 4-1 (1) .... Greece
Greece........... (0) 0-0 (0) .... Croatia
Croatia won 4-1 on aggregate

Croatian players pose ahead of their 4-1 win in the first leg of their playoff against Greece

Players used in qualifying		Career			Qualification			
Pos		Club	Age	P	G	P	G		
GK	Danijel Subasic	Monaco	33	36	-	10	-	-	-
GK	Lovre Kalinic	Gent	28	10	-	2	-	-	-
DEF	Dejan Lovren	Liverpool	28	37	2	6	-	-	-
DEF	Domagoj Vida	Besiktas	29	57	2	12	1	1	-
DEF	Ivan Strinic	Sampdoria	30	42	-	3	-	-	-
DEF	Josip Pivaric	Dynamo Kiev	29	19	-	9	-	1	-
DEF	Matej Mitrovic	Club Brugge	25	9	1	6	1	-	-
DEF	Sime Vrsaljko	Atletico Madrid	26	34	-	10	-	1	-
DEF	Tin Jedvaj	Bayer Leverkusen	22	10	-	2	-	-	-
DEF	Vedran Corluka	Lokomotiv Moscow	32	97	4	3	-	-	-
MID	Ivan Perisic	Inter	29	64	17	11	2	1	1
MID	Ivan Rakitic	Barcelona	30	90	14	8	1	-	-
MID	Luka Modric	Real Madrid	32	104	12	10	1	-	-
MID	Marcelo Brozovic	Inter	25	33	6	11	2	1	-
MID	Mario Pasalic	Spartak Moscow	23	6	-	3	-	-	-
MID	Marko Pjaca	Schalke	23	15	1	1	-	-	-
MID	Marko Rog	Napoli	22	12	-	5	-	1	-
MID	Mateo Kovacic	Real Madrid	24	39	1	7	-	-	-
MID	Milan Badelj	Fiorentina	29	36	1	9	-	2	-
MID	Nikola Vlasic	Everton	20	2	-	1	-	-	-
ATT	Andrej Kramaric	Hoffenheim	26	29	8	11	3	-	-
ATT	Ante Rebic	Eintracht Frankfurt	24	14	1	2	-	-	-
ATT	Duje Cop	Standard Liege	28	13	2	4	-	-	-
ATT	Ivan Santini	Caen	29	2	-	1	-	-	-
ATT	Mario Mandzukic	Juventus	32	82	30	11	5	-	-
ATT	Nikola Kalinic	Milan	30	41	15	9	3	1	-

CROATIA

Correct scores

	Competitive	Friendly
1-0	6	2
2-0	3	2
2-1	1	1
3-0	1	1
3-1	-	1
3-2	-	-
4-0	-	1
4-1	1	-
4-2	-	-
4-3	-	-
0-0	3	-
1-1	4	3
2-2	1	-
3-3	-	-
4-4	-	-
0-1	2	-
0-2	1	1
1-2	-	1
0-3	-	1
1-3	-	-
2-3	-	-
0-4	-	-
1-4	-	-
2-4	-	-
3-4	-	-
Other	3	1

Since Brazil 2014

Half-time/full-time double results

Win/Win	11	42%	Win 1st half	12	46%
Draw/Win	4	15%	Win 2nd half	10	38%
Lose/Win	0	0%	Win both halves	6	23%
Win/Draw	1	4%	Goal both halves	8	31%
Draw/Draw	7	27%			
Lose/Draw	0	0%	**Overall**		
Win/Lose	0	0%	● Win	58%	
Draw/Lose	3	12%	● Draw	31%	
Lose/Lose	0	0%	● Lose	12%	

Overall: W15, D8, L3 in 26 competitive games since Brazil 2014

Under & over goals

15 (58%) ✓	**Over 1.5**	11 (42%) ✗
7 (27%) ✓	**Over 2.5**	19 (73%) ✗
5 (19%) ✓	**Over 3.5**	21 (81%) ✗
4 (15%) ✓	**Over 4.5**	22 (85%) ✗

Both teams to score

8 (31%) ✓	**Both score**	18 (69%) ✗
3 (12%) ✓	**& win**	23 (88%) ✗
0 (0%) ✓	**& lose**	26 (100%) ✗

In 26 competitive games since Brazil 2014

Clean sheets

15 (58%) ✓	**Clean sheets**	11 (42%) ✗
12 (46%) ✓	**Win to nil**	14 (54%) ✗

6 (23%) ✓	**Fail to score**	20 (77%) ✗
3 (12%) ✓	**Lose to nil**	23 (88%) ✗

When they score

● For ● Against

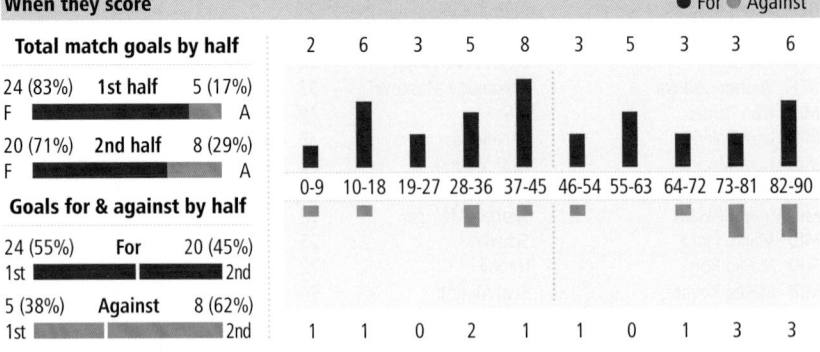

Total match goals by half

24 (83%) F	**1st half**	5 (17%) A
20 (71%) F	**2nd half**	8 (29%) A

Goals for & against by half

24 (55%) 1st	**For**	20 (45%) 2nd
5 (38%) 1st	**Against**	8 (62%) 2nd

	0-9	10-18	19-27	28-36	37-45	46-54	55-63	64-72	73-81	82-90
For	2	6	3	5	8	3	5	3	3	6
Against	1	1	0	2	1	1	0	1	3	3

Croatia score first

They win	14		78%
They draw	4		22%
They lose	0		0%

Croatia concede first

They win	1		20%
They draw	1		20%
They lose	3		60%

In 26 competitive games since Brazil 2014

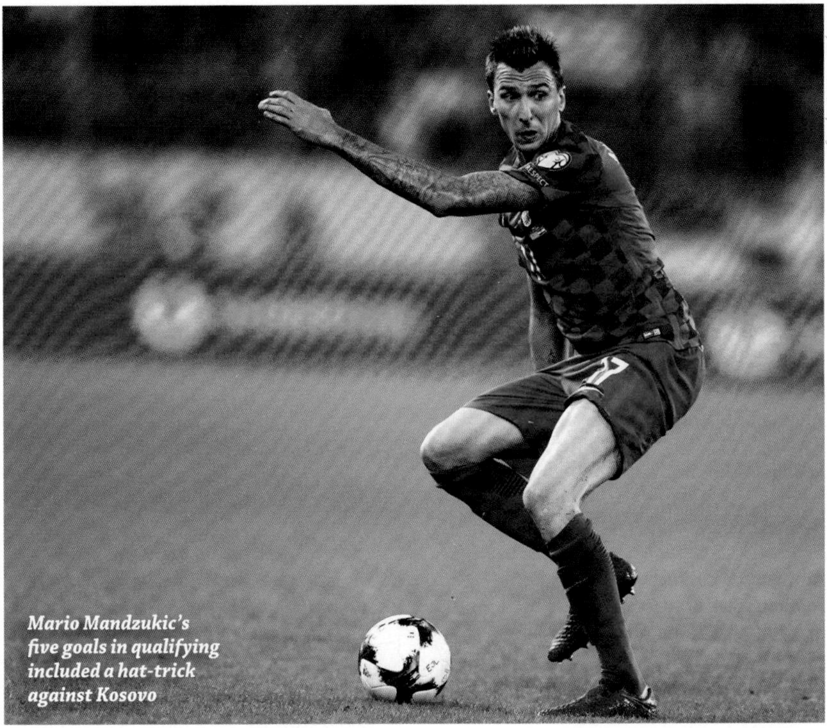

Mario Mandzukic's five goals in qualifying included a hat-trick against Kosovo

Top scorers in qualifying

	P	G	1st	AT	%	Hrv 1-1 Tur	Kos 0-6 Hrv	Fin 0-1 Hrv	Hrv 2-0 Isl	Hrv 1-0 Ukr	Isl 1-0 Hrv	Hrv 1-0 Kos	Tur 1-0 Hrv	Hrv 1-1 Fin	Ukr 0-2 Hrv	Hrv 4-1 Grc	Grc 0-0 Hrv
Mario Mandzukic	11	5	3	3	26	↺	3	1	↺	-	↺	-	↳	1	↺		-
Nikola Kalinic	9	3	1	3	16	↳	1	↳		1	↺	↳	↺			1	↺
Andrej Kramaric	11	3	1	2	16	↳	↺	↺	↳	↳		↳	↳	↺	2	1	↳
Marcelo Brozovic	11	2	1	1	11	↳	-	↺	2	↺	↳	↺	-	↺		-	-
Matej Mitrovic	6	1	0	1	5		1	-		-				-	-		↳
Ivan Rakitic	8	1	1	1	5	1		↺	↺		↺		-	-	-	-	-
Luca Modric	10	1	1	1	5	-		↳		-	-	-	-	-	-	1	↺
Ivan Perisic	11	2	0	2	11	-	1	-	-	-	-	-	-	-	-	1	↺
Domagoj Vida	12	1	1	1	5	-	-	-	-	-	-	1	-	-	-	-	-

G goals scored, **1st** first match goal (own goals don't count) **AT** goals at any time (ie. number of scoring appearances), **P** penalties, **%** percentage of total team goals scored by each player. Russia 2018 qualifying only. Game-by-game stats show goals scored, 1st goals are in red, dash did not score, ↳ substituted on, ↺ substituted off, blank did not play

Bookings in World Cup qualifying

Played 12 **Cards** (9Y, 1R) ⬜⬜⬜⬜⬜⬜⬜⬜⬜ ⬛   **Avg make-up** (⬜10 ⬛25) 9.6

NIGERIA

GROUP D

Profile

Nigeria has nearly double the population of any other African country but the Super Eagles have flattered to deceive in the World Cup.

They have never been beyond the last 16 in five previous attempts and have won only one of their last 12 World Cup matches.

How they qualified

Drawn in a tough group alongside Zambia, Cameroon and Algeria, Nigeria nonetheless strolled to top spot.

Their only 'defeat' came away to Algeria but the final score was 1-1 and the Super Eagles were handed a 3-0 loss by Fifa for fielding a suspended player.

The manager

Experienced German Gernot Rohr has brought discipline back to Nigerian football after predecessor Sunday Oliseh quit following administrative failings.

"This is the first time since I started playing for the senior team that everything is in a binding agreement," said skipper John Obi Mikel after an agreement was reached in November for World Cup bonuses.

The squad

Rohr's squad lacks the type of player neutrals have previously enjoyed watching, such as Okocha, George or Kanu, but they they remain expansive as shown by their 4-2 win over Argentina in November.

Width was a key strength during qualifying – Victor Moses is influential and the speedy Moses Simon offers a threat on the left, although Alex Iwobi could be shifted wide should he miss out centrally.

Kelechi Iheanacho is arguably the best of many choices for the main striking role – Ahmed Musa, Odion Ighalo and 2017 Belgian Golden Boot winner Henry Onyekuru are other options.

Mikel is a mainstay of the midfield and should form a solid base alongside

Factfile

FA founded 1945
www thenff.com
Head coach Gernot Rohr
Date qualified October 7, 2017

Strengths

☑ Pace and trickery in wide attacking positions
☑ Depth to their central striking options

Weaknesses

☒ The goalkeeping position is one of major concern
☒ Terrible draw in the group of death

Star rating ★★☆☆☆

Fixtures

1 June 16, 8pm v Croatia, Kaliningrad
2 June 22, 4pm v Iceland, Volgograd
3 June 26, 7pm v Argentina, Saint Petersburg

Base Essentuki
Total distance 5,600 miles

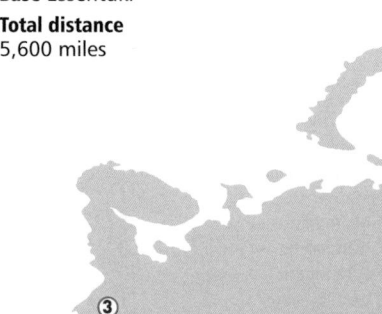

Victor Moses in action at Brazil 2014

Leicester's impressive Wilfred Ndidi and Ogenyi Onazi of Trabzonspor.

Leon Balogun and William Troost-Ekong built-up a solid understanding at the back during qualifying, while full-backs Ola Aina and Brian Idowu recently registered to play for the Super Eagles.

Defence is still a weakness and with goalkeeper Carl Ikeme fighting leukemia, locally based Ikechukwu Ezenwa or teenager Francis Uzoho, who features in Spain's third tier, could wear the gloves.

Key man

Moses has found a permanent home at Chelsea, albeit as a wing-back, and he seems to relish the opportunity to play further forward for his country where he does not have the same defensive responsibilities.

Rising star

This season has not gone well for Iwobi at Arsenal but he is not the first youngster to go stale under Arsene Wenger. A talented dribbler with an eye for a defence-splitting pass, Iwobi can certainly make an impact for Nigeria.

Wildcard

Cap centurion Vincent Enyeama has retired from international football but there have been calls for him to return in goal following Ikeme's illness.

Rohr says he won't pick the 35-year-old but he is arguably their best option.

Prospects

The Super Eagles are capable of an upset but their group is the toughest of the lot and they could be on the first plane home.

How to back them

Moses top-scored in qualifying with three goals and can do so again. He looks sure to start every match and notched a penalty in the 1-0 win over Poland in March.

NIGERIA

World Cup record		Group stage(s)						Knockout rounds					
		P	W	D	L	F	A	P	W	D	L	F	A
Uruguay 1930	Did not enter	-	-	-	-	-	-	-	-	-	-	-	-
Italy 1934	Did not enter	-	-	-	-	-	-	-	-	-	-	-	-
France 1938	Did not enter	-	-	-	-	-	-	-	-	-	-	-	-
Brazil 1950	Did not enter	-	-	-	-	-	-	-	-	-	-	-	-
Switzerland 1954	Did not enter	-	-	-	-	-	-	-	-	-	-	-	-
Sweden 1958	Did not enter	-	-	-	-	-	-	-	-	-	-	-	-
Chile 1962	Did not qualify	-	-	-	-	-	-	-	-	-	-	-	-
England 1966	Withdrew	-	-	-	-	-	-	-	-	-	-	-	-
Mexico 1970	Did not qualify	-	-	-	-	-	-	-	-	-	-	-	-
Germany 1974	Did not qualify	-	-	-	-	-	-	-	-	-	-	-	-
Argentina 1978	Did not qualify	-	-	-	-	-	-	-	-	-	-	-	-
Spain 1982	Did not qualify	-	-	-	-	-	-	-	-	-	-	-	-
Mexico 1986	Did not qualify	-	-	-	-	-	-	-	-	-	-	-	-
Italy 1990	Did not qualify	-	-	-	-	-	-	-	-	-	-	-	-
USA 1994	Round of 16	3	2	0	1	6	2	1	0	1	0	1	1
France 1998	Round of 16	3	2	0	1	5	5	1	0	0	1	1	4
Korea/Japan 2002	Group stage	3	0	1	2	1	3	-	-	-	-	-	-
Germany 2006	Did not qualify	-	-	-	-	-	-	-	-	-	-	-	-
South Africa 2010	Group stage	3	0	1	2	3	5	-	-	-	-	-	-
Brazil 2014	Round of 16	3	1	1	1	3	3	1	0	0	1	0	2
Totals		15	5	3	7	18	18	3	0	1	2	2	7

Continental championships (best perfomance)

Africa Cup of Nations	Winners (3)	1980, 1994, 2013

World Cup head-to-heads

Nigeria have played Group D rivals Argentina four times at the World Cup – they lost 3-2 in 2014

Nigeria v	P	W	D	L	F	A	Latest	Nigeria v	P	W	D	L	F	A	Latest
Argentina	4	0	0	4	3	7	2014	Iran	1	0	1	0	0	0	2014
Denmark	1	0	0	1	1	4	1998	South Korea	1	0	1	0	2	2	2010
England	1	0	1	0	0	0	2002	Spain	1	1	0	0	3	2	1998
France	1	0	0	1	0	2	2014	Sweden	1	0	0	1	1	2	2002

90 mins only

Players used in qualifying		Career			Qualification			
Pos		Club	Age	P	G	P	G	□	■
GK	Carl Ikeme	Wolves	32	10	-	3	-	-	-
GK	Daniel Akpeyi	Chippa United	31	6	-	1	-	-	-
GK	Ikechukwu Ezenwa	Sunshine	29	5	-	4	-	-	-
DEF	Ola Aina	Hull	21	4	-	2	-	-	-
DEF	Austin Oboroakpo	Abia Warriors	25	1	-	1	-	-	-
DEF	Chima Uche Akas	Kalmar	24	5	-	1	-	-	-
DEF	Efe Ambrose	Hibernian	29	51	4	2	1	1	-
DEF	Elderson Echiejile	Sivasspor	30	59	3	7	-	-	-
DEF	Godfrey Oboabona	Al-Ahli	27	48	1	1	-	1	-
DEF	Kenneth Omeruo	Kasimpasa	24	37	-	2	-	-	-
DEF	Leon Balogun	Mainz	29	16	-	5	-	1	-
DEF	William Troost-Ekong	Bursaspor	24	18	-	6	-	-	-
MID	Rabiu Ibrahim	Slovan Bratislava	27	4	-	1	-	-	-
MID	Shehu Abdullahi	Bursaspor	25	19	-	6	-	1	-
MID	Alex Iwobi	Arsenal	22	15	4	4	2	-	-
MID	Anderson Esiti	Gent	24	2	-	1	-	-	-
MID	Oghenekaro Etebo	Las Palmas	22	9	1	3	-	1	-
MID	John Obi Mikel	Tianjin Teda	31	84	6	6	2	1	-
MID	John Ogu	H Beer Sheva	30	17	2	1	1	1	-
MID	Mikel Agu	Bursaspor	25	4	-	3	-	1	-
MID	Ogenyi Onazi	Trabzonspor	25	49	1	7	-	1	-
MID	Onyinye Ndidi	Leicester	21	15	-	6	-	-	-
MID	Paul Onobi	Abia Warriors	25	1	-	1	-	1	-
MID	Victor Moses	Chelsea	27	34	11	4	3	1	-
ATT	Suleiman Abdullahi	E Braunschweig	21	2	-	2	-	1	-
ATT	Ahmed Musa	CSKA Moscow	25	68	11	6	-	-	-
ATT	Anthony Nwakaeme	H Beer Sheva	29	1	-	1	-	-	-
ATT	Brown Ideye	Malaga	29	28	6	1	-	-	-
ATT	Henry Onyekuru	Anderlecht	21	1	-	1	-	-	-
ATT	Ezekiel Bassey	Paykan	21	1	-	1	-	-	-
ATT	Kelechi Iheanacho	Leicester	21	14	7	6	2	-	-
ATT	Moses Simon	Gent	22	19	4	6	2	-	-
ATT	Obafemi Martins	Shanghai Shenhua	33	42	18	2	-	-	-
ATT	Odion Ighalo	Changchun Yatai	29	17	4	5	1	1	-
ATT	Sylvester Igboun	Ufa	27	6	-	2	-	1	-

How they qualified

Round 2
Swaziland ...... (0) 0-0 (0) ....**Nigeria**
Nigeria .... (0) 2-0 (0) .... Swaziland
Nigeria won 2-0 on aggregate

Round 3

Group B	P	W	D	L	F	A	GD	P
Nigeria	6	4	1	1	11	6	5	13
Zambia	6	2	2	2	8	7	1	8
Cameroon	6	1	4	1	7	9	-2	7
Algeria	6	1	1	4	6	10	-4	4

Zambia .... (0) 1-2 (2) ....**Nigeria**
Nigeria .... (2) 3-1 (0) ....Algeria
Nigeria .... (2) 4-0 (0) ....Cameroon
Cameroon ...... (0) 1-1 (1) ....**Nigeria**
Nigeria .... (0) 1-0 (0) .... Zambia
Algeria .... (0) 1-1 (0) ....**Nigeria**
Match awarded 3-0 to Algeria

Under Gernot Rohr, right,
Nigeria booked their place in
Russia with a game to spare

NIGERIA

Correct scores

	Competitive	Friendly
1-0	2	2
2-0	2	2
2-1	1	-
3-0	-	2
3-1	2	1
3-2	-	-
4-0	1	-
4-1	-	-
4-2	-	1
4-3	-	-
0-0	3	-
1-1	2	2
2-2	1	-
3-3	-	-
4-4	-	-
0-1	2	2
0-2	1	2
1-2	-	-
0-3	1*	-
1-3	-	-
2-3	1	-
0-4	-	-
1-4	-	-
2-4	-	-
3-4	-	-
Other	-	-

Since Brazil 2014

Half-time/full-time double results

Win/Win	3	16%	Win 1st half	4	21%
Draw/Win	5	26%	Win 2nd half	7	37%
Lose/Win	0	0%	Win both halves	1	5%
Win/Draw	1	5%	Goal both halves	3	16%
Draw/Draw	5	26%			
Lose/Draw	1	5%	Overall		
Win/Lose	0	0%	● Win	42%	
Draw/Lose	2	11%	● Draw	37%	
Lose/Lose	2	11%	● Lose	21%	

Overall: W8, D7, L4 in 19 competitive games since Brazil 2014

Under & over goals

12 (63%)	**Over 1.5**	7 (37%)
✓		✗
6 (32%)	**Over 2.5**	13 (68%)
✓		✗
5 (26%)	**Over 3.5**	14 (74%)
✓		✗
1 (5%)	**Over 4.5**	18 (95%)
✓		✗

Both teams to score

8 (42%)	**Both score**	11 (58%)
✓		✗
3 (16%)	**& win**	16 (84%)
✓		✗
1 (5%)	**& lose**	18 (95%)
✓		✗

In 19 competitive games since Brazil 2014

Clean sheets

8 (42%)	**Clean sheets**	11 (58%)
✓		✗
5 (26%)	**Win to nil**	14 (74%)
✓		✗

6 (32%)	**Fail to score**	13 (68%)
✓		✗
3 (16%)	**Lose to nil**	16 (84%)
✓		✗

When they score

● For ● Against

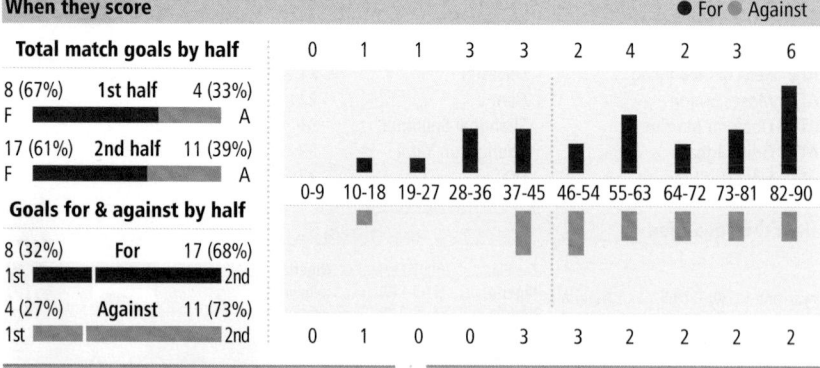

Total match goals by half

8 (67%)	**1st half**	4 (33%)
F		A

17 (61%)	**2nd half**	11 (39%)
F		A

	0	1	1	3	3	2	4	2	3	6
	0-9	10-18	19-27	28-36	37-45	46-54	55-63	64-72	73-81	82-90

Goals for & against by half

8 (32%)	**For**	17 (68%)
1st		2nd

4 (27%)	**Against**	11 (73%)
1st		2nd

| | 0 | 1 | 0 | 0 | 3 | 3 | 2 | 2 | 2 | 2 |

Nigeria score first

They win	8	67%
They draw	3	25%
They lose	1	8%

Nigeria concede first

They win	0	0%
They draw	1	25%
They lose	3	75%

In 19 competitive games since Brazil 2014

Alex Iwobi scored twice for the Super Eagles in November's 4-2 friendly win over Argentina

Photo by Oleg Nikishin Getty Images

Top scorers in qualifying

	P	G	1st	AT	%	Swz 0-0 Nga	Nga 2-0 Swz	Zmb 1-2 Nga	Nga 3-1 Alg	Nga 4-0 Cmr	Cmr 1-1 Nga	Nga 1-0 Zmb	Alg 1-1* Nga
Victor Moses	4	3	1	2	21					2	↺1	-	-
Alex Iwobi	4	2	2	2	14				1	↺		↺1	↺
Moses Simon	6	2	2	2	14	-	1	↺		-	1	↺	
Kelechi Iheanacho	6	2	0	2	14	↳	1	-	↺1	↳			-
John Obi Mikel	6	2	0	2	14	↺		-	↺1	↺1		↺	
John Ogu	1	1	1	1	7								1
Efe Ambrose	2	1	0	1	7	-	1						
Odion Ighalo	5	1	1	1	7	-	-			↺1	↺	-	

*Nigeria's 1-1 draw with Algeria was forfeited after Nigeria fielded an ineligible player. Match awarded 3-0 to Algeria

G goals scored, **1st** first match goal (own goals don't count) **AT** goals at any time (ie. number of scoring appearances), **P** penalties, **%** percentage of total team goals scored by each player. Russia 2018 qualifying only. Game-by-game stats show goals scored, 1st goals are in red, dash did not score, ↳ substituted on, ↺ substituted off, blank did not play

Bookings in World Cup qualifying

Played 8 **Cards** (14Y) ▯▯▯▯▯▯▯▯▯▯▯▯▯▯ **Avg make-up** (▯10 ■25) 17.5

Switzerland set to struggle to reach knockout phase

Brazil are usually seen as World Cup bankers in the opening phase, and rightly so having topped every group since finishing second to Austria in 1978, *writes Mark Langdon*.

The fact that Tite, injuries permitting – and Neymar's recent problems will have sent a nation into panic – knows his best team should help the South Americans hit the ground running with the boss appearing to have come close to naming his side for the opener against Switzerland in Rostov.

Neymar, Philippe Coutinho and Gabriel Jesus should get the job done with the minimum of fuss and if Tite wants to make changes he can do so by turning to somebody like Roberto Firmino.

The real battle comes for the second qualification spot and that's where the majority of betting focus will be. The pick of the prices could be Switzerland not to qualify.

Switzerland's major problem is a lack of goals, a point proven at the European Championship two years ago when they scored just three times in four matches and never more than once.

The only game they won was 1-0 against Albania, who were reduced to ten men in the first half, and in qualifying for this World Cup it was a struggle in the 1-0 aggregate playoff

success over Northern Ireland.

Switzerland had plenty of the ball but only scored thanks to a controversial penalty awarded by referee Ovidiu Hategan. The Romanian reckons the reason he has been dropped from the World Cup is because of his woeful decision to blow for a handball on Corry Evans.

Serbia, their main qualification rivals, could benefit from facing Brazil in the last group match should Tite's odds-on favourites have the group sewn up by that point and, in what looks a true pick 'em choice, the value could be in choosing the outsiders.

New coach Mladen Krstajic is promising a more attack-minded approach after a dull qualifying campaign under sacked boss Slavoljub Muslin and that should suit a Serbian side blessed with the brilliance of Lazio's barnstorming midfielder Sergej Milinkovic-Savic.

Costa Rica could also play their part after reaching the quarter-finals in Brazil four years ago. Their ultra-defensive approach may particularly upset a Swiss side missing an attacking spark and the race for second looks less obvious than the betting suggests.

The Swiss may be on an early flight home

Recommendation

★☆☆☆☆ **Switzerland not to qualify**

Group-stage performances since France 98

	Pot	P	W	Q	1998 Group	Pos	2002 Group	Pos	2006 Group	Pos	2010 Group	Pos	2014 Group	Pos
Brazil	1	5	5	5	A	1	C	1	F	1	G	1	A	1
Switzerland	2	3	1	2	-	-	-	-	G	1	H	3	E	2
Costa Rica	3	3	1	1	-	-	C	3	A	4			D	1
Serbia	4	1	0	0	-	-	-	-	-	-	D	4	-	-

To win Group E
Win only

	Bet365	BtBrt	Betfair	Btfrd	Btwy	Boyle	Coral	Hills	Lads	P Power	Sky	188
Brazil	2-7	2-7	3-10	**1-3**	1-5	3-10	2-7	2-9	1-4	3-10	2-7	27-100
Switzerland	6	6	5	11-2	**7**	6	6	6	13-2	5	11-2	11-2
Serbia	8	13-2	13-2	7	**9**	8	7	**9**	7	13-2	15-2	15-2
Costa Rica	18	18	16	12	**20**	16	18	16	**20**	16	16	16

Costa Rica v Serbia
1pm, Sunday June 17, ITV

	Bet365	BtBrt	Betfair	Btfrd	Btwy	Boyle	Coral	Hills	Lads	P Power	Sky	188
Serbia	Evs	10-11	**11-10**	19-20	19-20	10-11	19-20	17-20	19-20	19-20	Evs	66-67
Draw	11-5	21-10	11-5	9-4	9-4	21-10	21-10	23-10	21-10	11-5	21-10	**40-17**
Costa Rica	3	14-5	14-5	3	3	14-5	3	**16-5**	3	3	**16-5**	3

Brazil v Switzerland
7pm, Sunday June 17, ITV

	Bet365	BtBrt	Betfair	Btfrd	Btwy	Boyle	Coral	Hills	Lads	P Power	Sky	188
Brazil	1-3	1-3	**4-11**	**4-11**	**4-11**	1-3	1-3	1-3	1-3	**4-11**	**4-11**	**4-11**
Draw	**4**	7-2	**4**	18-5	15-4	16-5	7-2	19-5	7-2	7-2	18-5	**4**
Switzerland	8	7	7	8	7	15-2	**17-2**	7	**17-2**	15-2	15-2	38-5

Brazil v Costa Rica
1pm, Friday June 22, ITV

	Bet365	BtBrt	Betfair	Btfrd	Btwy	Boyle	Coral	Hills	Lads	P Power	Sky	188
Brazil	2-9	1-5	**2-7**	2-9	2-9	1-5	2-9	1-5	2-9	1-4	1-4	4-17
Draw	5	9-2	4	9-2	5	4	9-2	5	9-2	7-2	9-2	**51-10**
Costa Rica	**12**	11	**12**	**12**	11	11	**12**	11	**12**	9	**12**	11

Serbia v Switzerland
7pm, Friday June 22, BBC

	Bet365	BtBrt	Betfair	Btfrd	Btwy	Boyle	Coral	Hills	Lads	P Power	Sky	188
Switzerland	8-5	6-4	29-20	8-5	6-4	6-4	31-20	6-4	31-20	13-10	**13-8**	11-7
Serbia	2	7-4	**11-5**	9-5	9-5	17-10	7-4	7-4	7-4	2	9-5	25-14
Draw	19-10	2	21-10	21-10	21-10	2	2	11-5	2	15-8	21-10	**23-10**

Serbia v Brazil
7pm, Wednesday June 27, ITV

	Bet365	BetBright	Betfair	Betfred	Betway	Boyle	Hills	P Power	Sky Bet
Brazil	4-11	4-11	2-5	4-11	4-11	4-11	**4-9**	**4-9**	4-11
Draw	15-4	10-3	15-4	18-5	7-2	16-5	10-3	11-4	**4**
Serbia	**15-2**	13-2	7	7	6	13-2	6	11-2	13-2

Switzerland v Costa Rica
7pm, Wednesday June 27, ITV

	Bet365	BetBright	Betfair	Betfred	Betway	Boyle	Hills	P Power	Sky Bet
Switzerland	4-5	4-5	**10-11**	4-5	3-4	3-4	**10-11**	5-6	4-5
Draw	**5-2**	23-10	12-5	12-5	12-5	11-5	23-10	9-4	12-5
Costa Rica	7-2	16-5	7-2	7-2	16-5	10-3	16-5	16-5	**18-5**

Prices correct March 28 2018

BRAZIL

Profile

Brazil are the World Cup's most successful nation with five tournament successes, but their bid for glory on home soil four years ago ended in humiliation with a 7-1 defeat to Germany.

The Selecao have been busy rebuilding their battered reputation with an Olympic triumph in Rio but it's 60 years since Brazil last lifted the World Cup in Europe.

How they qualified

The World Cup hangover was evident as they managed only two victories in the first six matches but Tite's appointment as coach in June 2016 changed everything.

The Samba Stars suddenly played to a different beat, winning ten and drawing two of their remaining qualifiers by an aggregate 30-3 to become the first country to qualify.

The manager

Replacing Dunga with Tite was a masterstroke and not before time either.

Tite, who was in charge of Corinthians when they became the last South American side to win the Club World Cup in 2012, has got the fans, media and players on side.

The squad

The team almost picks itself and that is bad news for anyone looking to break into the line-up. Roma's Alisson is expected to edge out Ederson in the goalkeeper position and the back four of Dani Alves, Miranda, Marquinhos and Marcelo is virtually set in stone.

Alves and Marcelo love to get forward which places huge emphasis on Casemiro to offer defensive protection from a deep midfield position in a 4-1-4-1 formation. Paulinho and Beijing Guoan's Renato Augusto fill the two other central slots. Fernandinho's form may yet force him past Augusto, but Tite has already hinted at his starting team and Augusto is in for now.

Brazil's front three of Gabriel Jesus flanked by Neymar and Barcelona's record

Factfile

FA founded 1914
www cbf.com.br
Head coach Tite
Date qualified March 28, 2017

Strengths

- ☑ World-class players all over the pitch, particularly in the front three
- ☑ Coach Tite has fostered a great team spirit

Weaknesses

- ☒ Attacking full-backs could be exposed on the counter
- ☒ Lack of creativity in central midfield

Star rating ☆ ☆ ☆ ☆ ☆

Fixtures

1 June 17, 7pm v Switzerland, Rostov-on-Don

2 June 22, 1pm v Costa Rica, Saint Petersburg

3 June 27, 7pm v Serbia, Otkrytie Arena, Moscow

Base Sochi
Total distance 4,600 miles

Neymar in action against Ecuador
Photo by Lucas Uebel/Getty Images

signing Philippe Coutinho is superb.

In terms of reserves Brazil have Ederson, Thiago Silva, Alex Sandro, Filipe Luis, Willian, Roberto Firmino and Douglas Costa, highlighting their strength in depth.

Key man

Neymar scored the winning penalty to secure a long-awaited Olympic gold and is the world's most expensive player.

A nation will pin their hopes on Neymar, but is too much expected of the 25-year-old? 'Neymardependencia' is a word that has entered Brazil's footballing jargon so the panic over the injury he sustained while playing for PSG was real even if he is expected to return in time for the finals.

Rising star

Only Edinson Cavani scored more goals than Gabriel Jesus in Conmebol qualifying and the electric youngster has brought a new dimension to Brazil's play.

Wildcard

Tite has not abandoned Plan B and that gives Diego Souza, who started his career as a defensive midfielder but has moved further forward as he has matured, a chance despite not making the March friendlies.

Diego scored 11 league goals in 2017 to help Sport Recife avoid relegation.

Prospects

The draw is seeded for Brazil to meet Belgium in the quarter-finals and France in the semi-finals – not easy ties, but it's far from the worst draw and they should go close.

How to back them

Germany will presumably top their section so Brazil will have to win Group E to avoid the champions. Expect them to be focused and claim maximum points, particularly as the depth of their squad means Tite will be able to rotate without weakening his side in most positions.

BRAZIL

World Cup record		Group stage(s)						Knockout rounds					
		P	W	D	L	F	A	P	W	D	L	F	A
Uruguay 1930	Group stage	2	1	0	1	5	2	-	-	-	-	-	-
Italy 1934	First round	-	-	-	-	-	-	1	0	0	1	1	3
France 1938	Third place	-	-	-	-	-	-	5	2	2	1	12	10
Brazil 1950	Runners-up	6	4	1	1	22	6	-	-	-	-	-	-
Switzerland 1954	Quarter-finals	2	1	1	0	6	1	1	0	0	1	2	4
Sweden 1958	● Winners	3	2	1	0	5	0	3	3	0	0	11	4
Chile 1962	● Winners	3	2	1	0	4	1	3	3	0	0	10	4
England 1966	Group stage	3	1	0	2	4	6	-	-	-	-	-	-
Mexico 1970	● Winners	3	3	0	0	8	3	3	3	0	0	11	4
Germany 1974	Fourth place	6	3	2	1	6	3	1	0	0	1	0	1
Argentina 1978	Third place	6	3	3	0	8	2	1	1	0	0	2	1
Spain 1982	2nd group stage	5	4	0	1	15	6	-	-	-	-	-	-
Mexico 1986	Quarter-finals	3	3	0	0	5	0	2	1	1	0	5	1
Italy 1990	Round of 16	3	3	0	0	4	1	1	0	0	1	0	1
USA 1994	● Winners	3	2	1	0	6	1	4	3	1	0	5	2
France 1998	Finalists	3	2	0	1	6	3	4	2	1	1	8	7
Korea/Japan 2002	● Winners	3	3	0	0	11	3	4	4	0	0	7	1
Germany 2006	Quarter-finals	3	3	0	0	7	1	2	1	0	1	3	1
South Africa 2010	Quarter-finals	3	2	1	0	5	2	2	1	0	1	4	2
Brazil 2014	Fourth place	3	2	1	0	7	2	4	1	1	2	4	12
Totals		63	44	12	7	134	43	41	25	6	10	85	58

Continental championships (best perfomance)

Copa America	Winners (8)	1919, 1922, 1949, 1989, 1997, 1999, 2004, 2007

World Cup head-to-heads

Brazil v	P	W	D	L	F	A	Latest	Brazil v	P	W	D	L	F	A	Latest
Argentina	4	2	1	1	5	3	1990	Mexico	4	3	1	0	11	0	2014
Australia	1	1	0	0	2	0	2006	Morocco	1	1	0	0	3	0	1998
Belgium	1	1	0	0	2	0	2002	Peru	2	2	0	0	7	2	1978
Colombia	1	1	0	0	2	1	2014	Poland	4	2	1	1	11	6	1986
Costa Rica	2	2	0	0	6	2	2002	Portugal	2	0	1	1	1	3	2010
Croatia	6	3	2	1	8	4	2014	Russia	3	3	0	0	6	1	1994
Denmark	1	1	0	0	3	2	1998	Serbia	4	1	2	1	4	3	1974
England	4	3	1	0	6	2	2002	Spain	5	3	1	1	10	5	1986
France	4	1	1	2	6	7	2006	Sweden	7	5	2	0	21	8	1994
Germany	2	1	0	1	3	7	2014	Switzerland	1	0	1	0	2	2	1950
Japan	1	1	0	0	4	1	2006	Uruguay	2	1	0	1	4	3	1970

90 mins only, includes games against Yugoslavia and USSR

Follow us for the latest
World Cup betting advice

RACING POST sport

Players used in qualifying		Career		Qualification			
Pos	**Club**	**Age**	**P**	**G**	**P**	**G**	□ ■
GK Alisson	Roma	25	24	-	16	-	- -
GK Ederson	Man City	24	1	-	1	-	- -
GK Jefferson	Botafogo	35	22	-	1	-	- -
DEF Fagner	Corinthians	29	4	-	1	-	- -
DEF Filipe Luis	Atletico Madrid	32	31	2	9	2	1 -
DEF Gil	Shandong L.	31	11	-	3	-	- -
DEF Marcelo	Real Madrid	30	52	6	7	1	4 -
DEF Marquinhos	Paris St-Germain	24	24	-	14	-	- -
DEF Miranda	Inter	33	45	2	17	1	1 -
DEF Rodrigo Caio	Sao Paulo	24	4	-	1	-	- -
DEF Alex Sandro	Juventus	27	10	-	2	-	- -
DEF Dani Alves	Paris St-Germain	35	107	7	17	1	3 -
DEF David Luiz	Chelsea	31	57	3	3	-	2 1
DEF Thiago Silva	Paris St-Germain	33	69	5	5	-	- -
MID Casemiro	Real Madrid	26	22	-	7	-	1 -
MID Elias	Atl Mineiro	33	35	-	4	-	- -
MID Fernandinho	Man City	33	42	2	11	-	1 -
MID Giuliano	Fenerbahce	28	14	-	3	-	1 -
MID Kaka	Retired	36	92	29	1	-	- -
MID Lucas Lima	Palmeiras	27	14	2	7	1	1 -
MID Luiz Gustavo	Marseille	30	41	2	6	-	1 -
MID Oscar	Shanghai SIPG	26	48	12	3	-	- -
MID Paulinho	Barcelona	29	48	12	11	6	3 -
MID Renato Augusto	Beijing Guoan	30	28	5	16	3	1 -
ATT Diego Souza	Sao Paulo	32	7	2	2	-	- -
ATT Willian	Chelsea	29	55	8	17	4	- -
ATT Taison	Shakhtar	30	6	1	2	-	- -
ATT Douglas Costa	Juventus	27	23	3	8	2	1 -
ATT Philippe Coutinho	Barcelona	26	34	9	13	4	1 -
ATT Roberto Firmino	Liverpool	26	19	5	6	1	- -
ATT Gabriel Jesus	Man City	21	15	9	10	7	1 -
ATT Hulk	Shanghai SIPG.	31	48	11	3	-	- -
ATT Jonas	Benfica	34	12	3	1	-	- -
ATT Luan	Gremio	25	2	-	1	-	- -
ATT Neymar	Paris St-Germain	26	83	53	14	6	6 -
ATT Ricardo Oliveira	Atl Mineiro	38	16	5	5	2	- -

How they qualified

	P	W	D	L	F	A	GD	P
Brazil	18	12	5	1	41	11	30	41
Uruguay	18	9	4	5	32	20	12	31
Argentina	18	7	7	4	19	16	3	28
Colombia	18	7	6	5	21	19	2	27
Peru	18	7	5	6	27	26	1	26
Chile	18	8	2	8	26	27	-1	26
Paraguay	18	7	3	8	19	25	-6	24
Ecuador	18	6	2	10	26	29	-3	20
Bolivia	18	4	2	12	16	38	-22	14
Venezuela	18	2	6	10	19	35	-16	12

Chile..............(0) 2-0 (0)..............Brazil
Brazil..............(2) 3-1 (0)......Venezuela
Argentina.......(1) 1-1 (0)..............Brazil
Brazil..............(1) 3-0 (0)................Peru
Brazil..............(2) 2-2 (1)......Uruguay
Paraguay........(1) 2-2 (0)..............Brazil
Ecuador..........(0) 0-3 (0)..............Brazil
Brazil..............(1) 2-1 (1)......Colombia
Brazil..............(4) 5-0 (0)..........Bolivia
Venezuela......(0) 0-2 (1)..............Brazil
Brazil..............(2) 3-0 (0).........Argentina

Peru ....(0) 0-2 (0)..............Brazil
Uruguay.........(1) 1-4 (1)..............Brazil
Brazil..............(1) 3-0 (0)........Paraguay
Brazil..............(0) 2-0 (0)..........Ecuador
Colombia ......(0) 1-1 (1)..............Brazil
Bolivia ......(0) 0-0 (0)..............Brazil
Brazil..............(0) 3-0 (0)..............Chile

▶▶ Full qualifying results on pages 228-241

BRAZIL

Correct scores

	Competitive	Friendly
1-0	-	7
2-0	3	3
2-1	3	1
3-0	5	1
3-1	1	2
3-2	-	-
4-0	-	3
4-1	1	1
4-2	-	-
4-3	-	-
0-0	2	1
1-1	3	-
2-2	2	-
3-3	-	-
4-4	-	-
0-1	2	1
0-2	1	-
1-2	-	-
0-3	-	-
1-3	-	-
2-3	-	-
0-4	-	-
1-4	-	-
2-4	-	-
3-4	-	-
Other	2	-

Since Brazil 2014

Half-time/full-time double results

Win/Win	8	32%	Win 1st half	11	44%
Draw/Win	7	28%	Win 2nd half	15	60%
Lose/Win	0	0%	Win both halves	6	24%
Win/Draw	3	12%	Goal both halves	11	44%
Draw/Draw	2	8%			
Lose/Draw	2	8%	Overall		
Win/Lose	0	0%	● Win	60%	
Draw/Lose	2	8%	● Draw	28%	
Lose/Lose	1	4%	● Lose	12%	

Overall: W15, D7, L3 in 25 competitive games since Brazil 2014

Under & over goals

21 (84%) **Over 1.5** 4 (16%) ✓ ✗

14 (56%) **Over 2.5** 11 (44%) ✓ ✗

6 (24%) **Over 3.5** 19 (76%) ✓ ✗

3 (12%) **Over 4.5** 22 (88%) ✓ ✗

Both teams to score

11 (44%) **Both score** 14 (56%) ✓ ✗

6 (24%) **& win** 19 (76%) ✓ ✗

0 (0%) **& lose** 25 (100%) ✓ ✗

In 25 competitive games since Brazil 2014

Clean sheets

11 (44%) **Clean sheets** 14 (56%) ✓ ✗

9 (36%) **Win to nil** 16 (64%) ✓ ✗

5 (20%) **Fail to score** 20 (80%) ✓ ✗

3 (12%) **Lose to nil** 22 (88%) ✓ ✗

When they score

● For ● Against

Total match goals by half		

22 (76%) **1st half** 7 (24%)
F A

31 (76%) **2nd half** 10 (24%)
F A

Goals for & against by half

22 (42%) **For** 31 (58%)
1st 2nd

7 (41%) **Against** 10 (59%)
1st 2nd

	0-9	10-18	19-27	28-36	37-45	46-54	55-63	64-72	73-81	82-90
For	6	3	5	3	5	3	7	4	8	9
Against	2	0	0	4	1	2	1	4	1	2

Brazil score first

They win	13		81%
They draw	3		19%
They lose	0		0%

Brazil concede first

They win	2		29%
They draw	2		29%
They lose	3		43%

In 25 competitive games since Brazil 2014

Only Edinson Cavani scored more in South American qualifying than Gabriel Jesus

Photo by Lucas Uebel/Getty Images

Top scorers in qualifying

	P	G	1st	AT	%	Chl 2-0 Bra	Bra 3-1 Ven	Arg 1-1 Bra	Bra 3-0 Per	Bra 2-2 Ury	Pry 2-2 Bra	Ecu 0-3 Bra	Bra 2-1 Col	Bra 5-0 Bol	Ven 0-2 Bra	Bra 3-0 Arg	Per 0-2 Bra	Ury 1-4 Bra	Bra 3-0 Pry	Bra 2-0 Ecu	Col 1-1 Bra	Bol 0-0 Bra	Bra 3-0 Chl
Gabriel Jesus	10	7	2	5	17							2	↩	↩1	1	↩	↩1				-	↪	-	2
Paulinho	11	6	2	4	15							-	↩	-	1	-	3	-	1	-	↩	1
Neymar	14	6	2	6	15	-	-	-			1	1	↩1		1	-	1	1	-	-	-	↩
Philippe Coutinho	13	4	2	4	10				↪		↪	↪	1	↩	↩1	↩	↩	↩1	↩1	↪	↩	↩
Willian	17	4	2	3	10	-	2	↩	↩	↩	-	↩	↩	↪	↩1	↪	↪	↪	↩	1	↪	↪
Renato Augusto	16	3	0	3	7		↪	1	1	-	-	-	-	-	1	↩	-	↩	↩	-	↩
Ricardo Oliveira	5	2	0	2	5	↪	↩1	↩		↪	↩1												
Douglas Costa	8	2	2	2	5	-	↩	↪	↩1	↩1	-			↪	↪							
Filipe Luis	9	2	0	2	5	-	-	1	-	-		1	-	-		-						
Roberto Firmino	6	1	0	1	2							↩1		↪		↩	↩		↩		↪	
Marcelo	7	1	0	1	2	-						-	-			-		-	1	-		
Lucas Lima	7	1	0	1	2	↪	↪	↩1	↪	↪	↪		↪									
Miranda	17	1	1	1	2	-	-	-	-	-	-	1	-	-	↩	-	-	↩	-	-	-
Dani Alves	17	1	0	1	2	-	-	-	-	-	1	-	-	-	-	-	-	-	-	-	-

G goals scored, **1st** first match goal (own goals don't count) **AT** goals at any time (ie. number of scoring appearances), **P** penalties, **%** percentage of total team goals scored by each player. Russia 2018 qualifying only. Game-by-game stats show goals scored, 1st goals are in red, dash did not score, ↪ substituted on, ↩ substituted off, blank did not play

Bookings in World Cup qualifying

Played 18 ⬜⬜⬜⬜⬜⬜⬜⬜⬜⬜⬜⬜⬜⬜⬜⬜⬜⬜
Cards (29Y, 1YR) ⬜⬜⬜⬜⬜⬜⬜⬜⬜⬜⬜⬜⬜⬜⬜⬛

Avg make-up (⬜10 ⬛25) 17.5

YOUR
ULTIMATE
WORLD CUP
BETTING
COMRADE

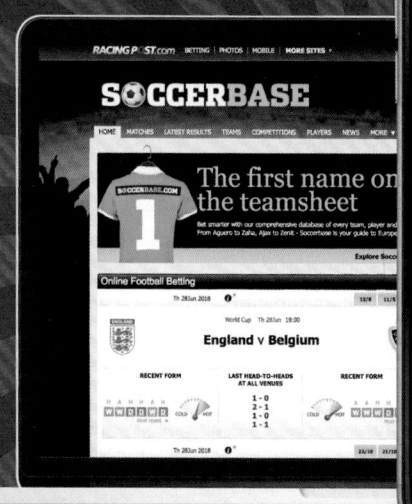

SOCCERBASE.COM

SWITZERLAND

Profile

The Swiss are on a roll in terms of World Cup qualifying – this will be their fourth successive finals – but never have they been beyond the quarter-finals and the last of those appearances was on home soil in 1954.

How they qualified

Switzerland missed out on automatic qualification on goal difference to Portugal despite dropping points just once, as a 2-0 loss away to the table-toppers proved costly.

A controversial penalty saw them overcome Northern Ireland 1-0 in their playoff and, while the spot-kick award was incorrect, Switzerland deservedly qualified.

The manager

The Sarajevo-born Vladimir Petkovic was not first choice when appointed in 2014 but has won over the public. He is said to help integrate the many in the squad who were born elsewhere, or as critics refer to them, papierli-Schweizer – "Swiss on paper only".

The squad

Petkovic appears married to a 4-2-3-1 formation and the biggest concern is who will start up front. Haris Seferovic, who top-scored in qualifying with just four goals, was jeered by his own supporters after missing several chances against Northern Ireland.

Rangy forward Breel Embolo remains their most talented attacker despite injuries, but many doubt the capabilities of Admir Mehmedi and Mario Gavranovic so Benfica's Seferovic may still lead the line come the opener against Brazil.

Steven Zuber and the inconsistent Xherdan Shaqiri offer thrust on the wings and central midfielder Granit Xhaka is one of the first names on the teamsheet. Valon Behrami and Blerim Dzemaili provide experience, although one of those will surely miss out given the emergence of the robust Denis Zakaria at Borussia Monchengladbach.

Factfile

FA founded 1895
www football.ch
Head coach Vladimir Petkovic
Date qualified November 12, 2017

Strengths

☑ Attacking oomph provided by galloping full-backs
☑ A mainly young team who could still improve

Weaknesses

☒ Lack a natural goalscorer
☒ Political problems never seem far away

Star rating ★★☆☆☆

Fixtures

1 June 17, 7pm v Brazil, Rostov-on-Don
2 June 22, 7pm v Serbia, Kaliningrad
3 June 27, 7pm v Costa Rica, Nizhny Novgorod

Base Togliatti
Total distance 4,150 miles

Swiss player of the year 2017, Granit Xhaka

Zakaria's clubmate Yann Sommer is a competent keeper and Serie A-based full-backs Ricardo Rodriguez and captain Stephan Lichtsteiner love to get forward. Lichtsteiner scored three times in qualifying and Rodriguez's penalty saw off Northern Ireland.

Key man
Xhaka has not earned universal praise for his Arsenal performances and he missed a spot-kick in the last-16 loss to Poland at Euro 2016 but the midfielder is clearly respected by supporters, who named him as Switzerland's player of last season.

Rising star
Centre-back has been a weak spot but the Swiss will hope Manuel Akanji can change all that. Following excellent performances for Basel he was snapped up by Borussia Dortmund in January.
Akanji is a ball-playing defender who uses

both feet and his middle name, Obafemi, comes from his dad's admiration of former Nigerian forward Obafemi Martins.

Wildcard
Basel's speedy forward Dimitri Oberlin, who made his debut against Greece in March, is so quick he'd give Usain Bolt a decent race and has been linked with bigger clubs.

Prospects
The Swiss look to be in a battle with Serbia for second spot. They can be dangerous but the last 16 would appear to be the absolute limit.

How to back them
Seferovic looks a vulnerable favourite to top-score for Switzerland, who may not bag many in a tight section. Split stakes on set-piece guru Rodriguez and centre-back Fabian Schar, who has an excellent goalscoring record at international level.

SWITZERLAND

World Cup record	Group stage(s)						Knockout rounds					
	P	W	D	L	F	A	P	W	D	L	F	A
Uruguay 1930	Did not enter	-	-	-	-	-	-	-	-	-	-	-	-
Italy 1934	Quarter-finals	-	-	-	-	-	-	2	1	0	1	5	5
France 1938	Quarter-finals	-	-	-	-	-	-	3	1	1	1	5	5
Brazil 1950	Group stage	3	1	1	1	4	6	-	-	-	-	-	-
Switzerland 1954	Quarter-finals	3	2	0	1	6	4	1	0	0	1	5	7
Sweden 1958	Did not qualify	-	-	-	-	-	-	-	-	-	-	-	-
Chile 1962	Group stage	3	0	0	3	2	8	-	-	-	-	-	-
England 1966	Group stage	3	0	0	3	1	9	-	-	-	-	-	-
Mexico 1970	Did not qualify	-	-	-	-	-	-	-	-	-	-	-	-
Germany 1974	Did not qualify	-	-	-	-	-	-	-	-	-	-	-	-
Argentina 1978	Did not qualify	-	-	-	-	-	-	-	-	-	-	-	-
Spain 1982	Did not qualify	-	-	-	-	-	-	-	-	-	-	-	-
Mexico 1986	Did not qualify	-	-	-	-	-	-	-	-	-	-	-	-
Italy 1990	Did not qualify	-	-	-	-	-	-	-	-	-	-	-	-
USA 1994	Round of 16	3	1	1	1	5	4	1	0	0	1	0	3
France 1998	Did not qualify	-	-	-	-	-	-	-	-	-	-	-	-
Korea/Japan 2002	Did not qualify	-	-	-	-	-	-	-	-	-	-	-	-
Germany 2006	Round of 16	3	2	1	0	4	0	1	0	1	0	0	0
South Africa 2010	Group stage	3	1	1	1	1	1	-	-	-	-	-	-
Brazil 2014	Round of 16	3	2	0	1	7	6	1	0	1	0	0	0
Totals		24	9	4	11	30	38	9	2	3	4	15	20

Continental championships (best perfomance)

Uefa European Championship	Round of 16 (1)	2016

World Cup head-to-heads

Switzerland v	P	W	D	L	F	A	Latest
Argentina	2	0	1	1	0	2	2014
Brazil	1	0	1	0	2	2	1950
Colombia	1	0	0	1	0	2	1994
Croatia	1	0	0	1	0	3	1950
England	1	0	0	1	0	2	1954
France	2	0	1	1	2	5	2014
Germany	4	1	1	2	6	10	1966
Mexico	1	1	0	0	2	1	1950
Serbia	1	0	0	1	0	3	1950
South Korea	1	1	0	0	2	0	2006
Spain	3	1	0	2	2	5	2010

90 mins only, includes games against Yugoslavia and West Germany

Switzerland would most likely face Germany in the last 16 if they finished runners-up in Group E – they last met their neighbours at a World Cup in 1966

How they qualified

Group B	P	W	D	L	F	A	GD	P
Portugal	10	9	0	1	32	4	28	27
Switzerland	10	9	0	1	23	7	16	27
Hungary	10	4	1	5	14	14	0	13
Faroe Islands	10	2	3	5	4	16	-12	9
Latvia	10	2	1	7	7	18	-11	7
Andorra	10	1	1	8	2	23	-21	4

Switzerland .. (2) 2-0 (0)......... Portugal
Hungary .... (0) 2-3 (0).... Switzerland
Andorra.......... (0) 1-2 (1)....Switzerland
Switzerland .. (1) 2-0 (0)... Faroe Islands
Switzerland .. (0) 1-0 (0)............. Latvia
Faroe Islands.. (0) 0-2 (1)....Switzerland
Switzerland .. (1) 3-0 (0).......... Andorra
Latvia............. (0) 0-3 (1).... Switzerland
Switzerland .. (3) 5-2 (0)..........Hungary
Portugal........ (1) 2-0 (0)....Switzerland

The Swiss players pose before the second leg of their playoff against Northern Ireland

Playoffs
N Ireland........ (0) 0-1 (0)....Switzerland
Switzerland .. (0) 0-0 (0)......... N Ireland
Switzerland won 1-0 on aggregate

Players used in qualifying		Career				Qualification			
Pos		**Club**	**Age**	**P**	**G**	**P**	**G**	⬜	⬛
GK	Roman Burki	B Dortmund	27	8	-	1	-	-	-
GK	Yann Sommer	Mgladbach	29	34	-	11	-	-	-
DEF	Fabian Schar	Deportivo	26	37	7	11	1	3	-
DEF	Francois Moubandje	Toulouse	27	16	-	3	-	-	-
DEF	Johan Djourou	Antalyaspor	31	73	2	7	-	-	-
DEF	Manuel Akanji	B Dortmund	22	5	-	4	-	-	-
DEF	Michael Lang	Basel	27	23	2	2	-	1	-
DEF	Nico Elvedi	Mgladbach	21	5	-	2	-	-	-
DEF	Ricardo Rodriguez	Milan	25	51	3	9	3	1	-
DEF	Silvan Widmer	Udinese	25	9	-	1	-	-	-
DEF	Stefan Lichtsteiner	Juventus	34	98	8	11	3	-	-
DEF	Timm Klose	Norwich	30	16	-	1	-	-	-
MID	Blerim Dzemaili	Bologna	32	63	10	9	1	1	-
MID	Denis Zakaria	Mgladbach	21	9	-	7	-	1	-
MID	Fabian Frei	Basel	29	14	3	2	1	-	-
MID	Gelson Fernandes	E Frankfurt	31	66	2	4	-	1	-
MID	Granit Xhaka	Arsenal	25	61	9	11	2	1	1
MID	Remo Freuler	Atalanta	26	9	-	6	-	1	-
MID	Renato Steffen	Wolfsburg	26	5	-	1	-	-	-
MID	Steven Zuber	Hoffenheim	26	10	3	7	2	-	-
MID	Valentin Stocker	Basel	29	36	6	3	1	-	-
MID	Valon Behrami	Udinese	33	77	2	5	-	2	-
MID	Xherdan Shaqiri	Stoke	26	68	20	10	1	-	-
MID	Edimilson Fernandes	West Ham	22	3	-	2	-	-	-
ATT	Admir Mehmedi	Wolfsburg	27	58	7	11	2	1	-
ATT	Breel Embolo	Schalke	21	23	3	7	1	-	-
ATT	Eren Derdiyok	Galatasaray	30	60	11	7	1	-	-
ATT	Haris Seferovic	Benfica	26	49	11	12	4	1	-
ATT	Josip Drmic	Mgladbach	25	27	10	1	1	-	-

SWITZERLAND

Correct scores

	Competitive	Friendly
1-0	4	2
2-0	3	-
2-1	2	2
3-0	3	1
3-1	-	-
3-2	2	-
4-0	2	-
4-1	-	-
4-2	-	-
4-3	-	-
0-0	2	-
1-1	2	1
2-2	-	1
3-3	-	-
4-4	-	-
0-1	1	1
0-2	3	1
1-2	-	1
0-3	-	-
1-3	-	-
2-3	-	1
0-4	-	-
1-4	-	-
2-4	-	-
3-4	-	-
Other	2	1

Since Brazil 2014

Half-time/full-time double results

Win/Win	11	42%	Win 1st half	11	42%
Draw/Win	6	23%	Win 2nd half	16	62%
Lose/Win	1	4%	Win both halves	7	27%
Win/Draw	0	0%	Goal both halves	9	35%
Draw/Draw	2	8%			
Lose/Draw	2	8%	**Overall**		
Win/Lose	0	0%	● Win	69%	
Draw/Lose	3	12%	● Draw	16%	
Lose/Lose	1	4%	● Lose	16%	

Overall: W18, D4, L4 in 26 competitive games since Brazil 2014

Under & over goals

19 (73%)	Over 1.5	7 (27%)	
11 (42%)	Over 2.5	15 (58%)	
6 (23%)	Over 3.5	20 (77%)	
4 (15%)	Over 4.5	22 (85%)	

Both teams to score

7 (27%)	Both score	19 (73%)	
5 (19%)	& win	21 (81%)	
0 (0%)	& lose	26 (100%)	

In 26 competitive games since Brazil 2014

Clean sheets

15 (58%)	Clean sheets	11 (42%)	
13 (50%)	Win to nil	13 (50%)	
6 (23%)	Fail to score	20 (77%)	
4 (15%)	Lose to nil	22 (85%)	

When they score

● For ● Against

Total match goals by half

17 (81%)	1st half	4 (19%)
F		A
34 (72%)	2nd half	13 (28%)
F		A

Goals for & against by half

17 (33%)	For	34 (67%)
1st		2nd
4 (24%)	Against	13 (76%)
1st		2nd

2	4	6	3	2	3	6	8	7	10
0-9	10-18	19-27	28-36	37-45	46-54	55-63	64-72	73-81	82-90
0	1	0	0	3	2	3	3	1	4

Switzerland score first

They win	16		100%
They draw	0		0%
They lose	0		0%

In 26 competitive games since Brazil 2014

Switzerland concede first

They win	2		25%
They draw	2		25%
They lose	4		50%

Top scorers in qualifying

Haris Seferovic
Photo by Alex Grimm/Getty Images

	P	G	1st	AT	%	Sui 2-0 Prt	Hun 2-3 Sui	And 1-2 Sui	Sui 2-0 Fro	Sui 1-0 Lva	Fro 0-2 Sui	Sui 3-0 And	Lva 0-3 Sui	Sui 5-2 Hun	Prt 2-0 Sui	Nir 0-1 Sui	Sui 0-0 Nir
Haris Seferovic	12	4	3	3	17	↩	1	-	↪	↩	↩	2	1	↩	-	↩	↩
Ricardo Rodriguez	9	3	1	3	13	-	1	-	-			-	1			1	-
Stefan Lichtsteiner	11	3	0	3	13	↩	-		1	-		1	↩	1	-	-	-
Steven Zuber	7	2	0	1	8					↪	↪	↩		2	↪	↩	
Granit Xhaka	11	2	2	2	8	-		-	-	-	1	↩	↩	1	-		
Admir Mehmedi	11	2	0	2	8	1	↩	1	-	-	↩	↩	-		↩	↪	↪
Josip Drmic	1	1	1	1	4					1							
Fabian Frei	2	1	0	1	4									1		↪	
Valentin Stocker	3	1	0	1	4		1	↪	↩								
Breel Embolo	7	1	1	1	4	1	-	-						↪	↪	↪	↪
Eren Derdiyok	7	1	1	1	4	↪	↪		1		↪	↪	↪	↪			
Blerim Dzemaili	9	1	0	1	4	↩	-		↩		-		↩	1	↩	↩	↩
Xherdan Shaqiri	10	1	0	1	4	↩	↩		↩			1	1	-	-	-	-
Fabian Schar	11	1	1	1	4	-	-		1	-	-	-		-	-	-	-

G goals scored, **1st** first match goal (own goals don't count) **AT** goals at any time (ie. number of scoring appearances), **P** penalties, **%** percentage of total team goals scored by each player. Russia 2018 qualifying only. Game-by-game stats show goals scored, 1st goals are in red, dash did not score, ↪ substituted on, ↩ substituted off, blank did not play

Bookings in World Cup qualifying

Played 12 **Cards** (14Y, 1YR) ◻◻◻◻◻◻◻◻◻◻◻◻◻◻◼   **Avg make-up** (◻10 ◼25) 13.8

Profile

No team started the last World Cup at a bigger price than 4,000-1 outsiders Costa Rica, who were the talk of the planet after reaching the quarter-finals where they lost to Holland on penalties. Can lightning strike twice?

How they qualified

A 95th-minute equaliser from Kendall Waston against Honduras sealed qualification in the penultimate round of Concacaf qualifying. They did the double over USA and lost just one meaningful fixture, 2-0 in Mexico.

The manager

Oscar Ramirez has carried on the good work of 2014 World Cup manager Jorge Luis Pinto. Ramirez, who will stick with the 5-4-1 formation from four years ago, was in the Costa Rica side who beat Scotland 1-0 at Italia 90.

The squad

A number of faces remain from the last World Cup including Real Madrid goalkeeper Keylor Navas, the hero of that run to the quarter-finals, who is a crucial last line of defence for a side who will look to absorb pressure.

The midfield remains almost untouched as Bryan Ruiz, the great creative spark, has fought his way back into Sporting's squad.

Ruiz and fellow 30-something Christian Bolanos form part of a midfield quartet which also includes Deportivo La Coruna's Celso Borges. Yeltsin Tejeda was a mainstay of the midfield at the last World Cup but finds his place under threat from David Guzman and Randall Azofeifa.

Marco Urena, who plays for new MLS franchise Los Angeles, could edge out injury-hit Joel Campbell in attack but the real collective strength comes in defence.

Celtic's Cristian Gamboa is the right wing-back and three centre-backs will be chosen from Waston, Giancarlo Gonzalez,

Factfile

FA founded 1921

www fedefutbol.com

Head coach Oscar Ramirez

Date qualified October 7, 2017

Strengths

☑ Defensively solid, with a keeper who can make extraordinary stops

☑ A togetherness and unity which is not often found at international level

Weaknesses

☒ Lack of depth in most positions

☒ Creative players are either ageing or hit by injuries

Star rating ★☆☆☆☆

Fixtures

1 June 17, 1pm v Serbia, Samara

2 June 22, 1pm v Brazil, Saint Petersburg

3 June 27, 7pm v Switzerland, Nizhny Novgorod

Base Saint Petersburg

Total distance 2,900 miles

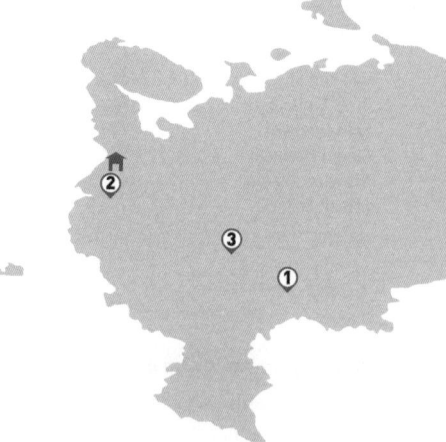

Keylor Navas earned a place in Costa Rican folklore at Brazil 2014
Photo by Lawrence Griffiths/Getty Images

Johnny Acosta and Espanyol's Oscar Duarte, who has returned from an ACL injury which ruled him out of a chunk of qualifying.

Key man

Penalty-saving expert Navas became a national hero at the last World Cup. His performances during the tournament earned him a transfer to Real Madrid, where he has won successive Champions League trophies.

A stadium was named after Navas in his hometown of San Isidro but the name was swiftly changed as local laws prohibit such actions until a person has died.

Rising star

New York City's left wing-back Ronald Matarrita has the potential to be decent. The 23-year-old reportedly turned down interest from Borussia Dortmund and Hamburg to stay in MLS but has since been hit with injury setbacks.

Wildcard

Campbell should still be good for a place in the squad but his selection as a starter is debatable. Clearly a talented performer, as he showed at the last World Cup, the Real Betis man, on loan from Arsenal, has suffered greatly with injury this season.

Prospects

They deserve to be the group outsiders, although whether they are quite as inferior to Switzerland and Serbia as the odds suggest is questionable. Even so, a group-stage exit is the most likely outcome.

How to back them

The Ticos are an under 2.5 goals machine. Four of their five matches at the last World Cup featured no more than two goals (three featured under 1.5) and Costa Rica failed to score in two of their three group-stage matches as guests at the Copa America in 2016.

World Cup record		Group stage(s)						Knockout rounds					
		P	W	D	L	F	A	P	W	D	L	F	A
Uruguay 1930	Did not enter	-	-	-	-	-	-	-	-	-	-	-	-
Italy 1934	Did not enter	-	-	-	-	-	-	-	-	-	-	-	-
France 1938	Did not enter	-	-	-	-	-	-	-	-	-	-	-	-
Brazil 1950	Did not enter	-	-	-	-	-	-	-	-	-	-	-	-
Switzerland 1954	Did not enter	-	-	-	-	-	-	-	-	-	-	-	-
Sweden 1958	Did not qualify	-	-	-	-	-	-	-	-	-	-	-	-
Chile 1962	Did not qualify	-	-	-	-	-	-	-	-	-	-	-	-
England 1966	Did not qualify	-	-	-	-	-	-	-	-	-	-	-	-
Mexico 1970	Did not qualify	-	-	-	-	-	-	-	-	-	-	-	-
Germany 1974	Did not qualify	-	-	-	-	-	-	-	-	-	-	-	-
Argentina 1978	Did not qualify	-	-	-	-	-	-	-	-	-	-	-	-
Spain 1982	Did not qualify	-	-	-	-	-	-	-	-	-	-	-	-
Mexico 1986	Did not qualify	-	-	-	-	-	-	-	-	-	-	-	-
Italy 1990	Round of 16	3	2	0	1	3	2	1	0	0	1	1	4
USA 1994	Did not qualify	-	-	-	-	-	-	-	-	-	-	-	-
France 1998	Did not qualify	-	-	-	-	-	-	-	-	-	-	-	-
Korea/Japan 2002	Group stage	3	1	1	1	5	6	-	-	-	-	-	-
Germany 2006	Group stage	3	0	0	3	3	9	-	-	-	-	-	-
South Africa 2010	Did not qualify	-	-	-	-	-	-	-	-	-	-	-	-
Brazil 2014	Quarter-finals	3	2	1	0	4	1	2	0	2	0	1	1
Totals		12	5	2	5	15	18	3	0	2	1	2	5

Continental championships (best perfomance)

Concacaf Gold Cup	Winners (3)	1963, 1969, 1989

World Cup head-to-heads

Edmilson scored a special goal when Costa Rica lost 5-2 to Brazil at the 2002 World Cup

Costa Rica v	P	W	D	L	F	A	Latest	Costa Rica v	P	W	D	L	F	A	Latest
Brazil	2	0	0	2	2	6	2002	Poland	1	0	0	1	1	2	2006
England	1	0	1	0	0	0	2014	Sweden	1	1	0	0	2	1	1990
Germany	1	0	0	1	2	4	2006	Uruguay	1	1	0	0	3	1	2014

90 mins only

GROUP E

Players used in qualifying

Pos	Player	Club	Age	P	G	P	G	□	■
GK	Esteban Alvarado	Trabzonspor	29	12	-	1	-	-	-
GK	Keylor Navas	Real Madrid	31	78	-	11	-	-	-
GK	Patrick Pemberton	Alajuelense	36	39	-	4	-	2	-
DEF	Allan Miranda	Antigua	31	5	-	1	-	-	-
DEF	Ronald Matarrita	New York City	23	21	2	10	2	1	-
DEF	Cristian Gamboa	Celtic	28	66	3	13	1	4	-
DEF	Francisco Calvo	Minnesota U	25	34	3	7	1	2	-
DEF	Giancarlo Gonzalez	Bologna	30	67	2	9	-	-	1
DEF	Jhonny Acosta	Rionegro	34	66	2	13	1	3	-
DEF	Jose Salvatierra	Alajuelense	28	35	-	3	-	1	-
DEF	Junior Diaz	Herediano	34	80	1	2	-	-	-
DEF	Kendall Waston	Vancouver W	30	25	3	12	2	4	-
DEF	Kenner Gutierrez	Alajuelense	29	9	-	1	-	-	-
DEF	Michael Umana	Cartagines	35	104	1	6	-	1	-
DEF	Oscar Duarte	Espanyol	29	36	2	5	-	-	-
MID	Bryan Oviedo	Sunderland	28	41	1	7	-	2	-
MID	Celso Borges	Deportivo	30	110	20	15	1	-	-
MID	Christian Bolanos	Saprissa	34	80	6	14	4	1	-
MID	David Guzman	Portland Timbers	28	41	-	10	-	2	-
MID	Oscar Granados	Herediano	32	14	-	1	-	-	-
MID	Randall Azofeifa	Herediano	33	56	3	11	1	-	-
MID	Rodney Wallace	New York City	29	28	3	5	-	-	-
MID	Yeltsin Tejeda	Lausanne	26	47	-	2	-	-	-
ATT	Bryan Ruiz	Sporting	32	110	24	15	3	1	-
ATT	Alvaro Saborio	San Carlos	36	110	36	4	-	-	-
ATT	Daniel Colindres	Saprissa	33	12	-	2	-	-	-
ATT	Joel Campbell	Real Betis	25	74	14	12	2	1	-
ATT	Johan Venegas	Saprissa	29	43	8	13	3	-	-
ATT	Marco Urena	Los Angeles	28	59	15	14	4	1	-
ATT	Yendrick Ruiz	Herediano	31	8	-	1	-	-	-

How they qualified

Round 4

Group B	P	W	D	L	F	A	GD	P
Costa Rica	6	5	1	0	11	3	8	16
Panama	6	3	1	2	7	5	2	10
Haiti	6	1	1	4	2	4	-2	4
Jamaica	6	1	1	4	2	10	-8	4

Costa Rica..... (1) 1-0 (0)................Haiti
Panama......... (0) 1-2 (0)...... Costa Rica
Jamaica......... (1) 1-1 (0)...... Costa Rica
Costa Rica..... (2) 3-0 (0)........... Jamaica
Haiti .... (0) 0-1 (0)...... Costa Rica
Costa Rica..... (1) 3-1 (0).......... Panama

Oscar Ramirez, a veteran of Costa Rica's 1990 World Cup team, will employ the safety-first tactics they used under Jorge Luis Pinto in 2014

Round 5

	P	W	D	L	F	A	GD	P
Mexico	10	6	3	1	16	7	9	21
Costa Rica	10	4	4	2	14	8	6	16
Panama	10	3	4	3	9	10	-1	13
Honduras	10	3	4	3	13	19	-6	13
USA	10	3	3	4	17	13	4	12
Trin & Tobago	10	2	0	8	7	19	-12	6

Trin & Tobago (0) 0-2 (0)...... Costa Rica
Costa Rica..... (1) 4-0 (0).................USA
Mexico .... (2) 2-0 (0)...... Costa Rica
Honduras .... (1) 1-1 (0)...... Costa Rica
Costa Rica..... (0) 0-0 (0).......... Panama
Costa Rica..... (2) 2-1 (1)..Trin & Tobago
USA............... (0) 0-2 (0)...... Costa Rica
Costa Rica..... (0) 1-1 (1)...........Mexico
Costa Rica..... (0) 1-1 (0).........Honduras
Panama......... (0) 2-1 (1)...... Costa Rica

Correct scores

	Competitive	Friendly
1-0	4	4
2-0	2	-
2-1	3	1
3-0	4	-
3-1	1	1
3-2	1	-
4-0	1	-
4-1	-	-
4-2	-	-
4-3	-	2
0-0	6	1
1-1	7	-
2-2	2	1
3-3	-	1
4-4	-	-
0-1	1	6
0-2	2	-
1-2	1	2
0-3	-	-
1-3	-	-
2-3	-	-
0-4	1	-
1-4	-	-
2-4	-	-
3-4	-	-
Other	-	1

Since Brazil 2014

Half-time/full-time double results

Win/Win	11	31%	Win 1st half	13	36%
Draw/Win	5	14%	Win 2nd half	16	44%
Lose/Win	0	0%	Win both halves	7	19%
Win/Draw	1	3%	Goal both halves	9	25%
Draw/Draw	10	28%			
Lose/Draw	4	11%	**Overall**		
Win/Lose	1	3%	● Win	44%	
Draw/Lose	2	6%	● Draw	42%	
Lose/Lose	2	6%	● Lose	14%	

Overall: W16, D15, L5 in 36 competitive games since Brazil 2014

Under & over goals

25 (69%) **Over 1.5** 11 (31%) ✓ ✗

14 (39%) **Over 2.5** 22 (61%) ✓ ✗

6 (17%) **Over 3.5** 30 (83%) ✓ ✗

1 (3%) **Over 4.5** 35 (97%) ✓ ✗

Both teams to score

15 (42%) **Both score** 21 (58%) ✓ ✗

5 (14%) **& win** 31 (86%) ✓ ✗

1 (3%) **& lose** 35 (97%) ✓ ✗

In 36 competitive games since Brazil 2014

Clean sheets

17 (47%) **Clean sheets** 19 (53%) ✓ ✗

11 (31%) **Win to nil** 25 (69%) ✓ ✗

10 (28%) **Fail to score** 26 (72%) ✓ ✗

4 (11%) **Lose to nil** 32 (89%) ✓ ✗

When they score

● For ● Against

Total match goals by half

19 (58%) **1st half** 14 (42%)
F A

29 (67%) **2nd half** 14 (33%)
F A

Goals for & against by half

19 (40%) **For** 29 (60%)
1st 2nd

14 (50%) **Against** 14 (50%)
1st 2nd

	0-9	10-18	19-27	28-36	37-45	46-54	55-63	64-72	73-81	82-90
For	4	0	2	6	7	2	4	8	7	8
Against	3	3	2	2	4	3	0	5	1	5

Costa Rica score first

They win	15	88%
They draw	1	6%
They lose	1	6%

Costa Rica concede first

They win	1	8%
They draw	8	62%
They lose	4	31%

In 36 competitive games since Brazil 2014

GROUP E

Marco Urena tied with Christian Bolanos to score four goals in qualifying

Top scorers in qualifying

	P	G	1st	AT	%	Cri 1-0 Hti	Pan 1-2 Cri	Jam 1-1 Cri	Cri 3-0 Jam	Hti 0-1 Cri	Cri 3-1 Pan	Tto 0-2 Cri	Cri 4-0 USA	Mex 2-0 Cri	Hnd 1-1 Cri	Cri 0-0 Pan	Cri 2-1 Tto	USA 0-2 Cri	Cri 1-1 Mex	Cri 1-1 Hnd	Pan 2-1 Cri
Christian Bolanos	14	4	2	3	16	↶	↶	↶	↺	-	2	1	1	↶	↺			↺	↺	↺	
Marco Urena	14	4	2	3	16	↶	↺1	↺	↺	↺		↺		↶	-	↶	↺	2	1	↺	↶
Johan Venegas	13	3	2	3	12	-		↺1	↶	-	↶	↺1	↺		↺	↺	↶	↶	↶	↶	1
Bryan Ruiz	15	3	1	3	12	-	1	-	1	↺		↺	↺	-	-	-	1	-	-	-	↺
Ronald Matarrita	10	2	0	2	8	-	↺	↺	↺	-	↺1	1	1	-	-						↺
Kendall Waston	12	2	0	2	8	-	-	-	-	-		-	-	1	-	↺	-	-	1		
Joel Campbell	12	2	0	1	8	↺	↺	↺	-	↶	↺	↺	↺2	↶	↺	↶	-				
Francisco Calvo	7	1	1	1	4				-	↺		-			1	-	-	-			
Randall Azofeifa	11	1	1	1	4	↶	-	-	↺1	↺	-	↺	↺	↺	↺						↶
Cristian Gamboa	13	1	1	1	4	1	-	-	-	-	-	-	-	-	-	-	-	↺	-	-	
Jhonny Acosta	13	1	0	1	4	-	-	1	-	-	-	-	-	-	-	-	-	-	-	↺	
Celso Borges	15	1	1	1	4	↺		-	1	-	-	-	-	-	-	-	-	-	-	-	-

G goals scored, **1st** first match goal (own goals don't count) **AT** goals at any time (ie. number of scoring appearances), **P** penalties, **%** percentage of total team goals scored by each player. Russia 2018 qualifying only. Game-by-game stats show goals scored, 1st goals are in red, dash did not score, ↶ substituted on, ↺ substituted off, blank did not play

Bookings in World Cup qualifying

Played 16 ⬜⬜⬜⬜⬜⬜⬜⬜⬜⬜⬜⬜⬜⬜⬜⬜

Avg make-up (☐10 ■25) 17.8

Cards (26Y, 1R) ⬜⬜⬜⬜⬜⬜⬜⬜⬜⬜⬜⬜■

Note: Costa Rica's World Cup away kit had not been released when we went to press

Profile

The Fifa Rankings rate Serbia as Europe's weakest side – they were the only country from Uefa who were housed in the bottom set of seeds – but it would be unwise to read too much into those numbers. Serbia are rightly targeting a first knockout appearance since 1998.

How they qualified

Serbia were in a balanced group which included three Euro 2016 qualifiers in Wales, Ireland and Austria but they were always in control, suffering just one defeat, 3-2 away to Austria, when the finish line was in sight and nerves set in.

The manager

Slavoljub Muslin oversaw Serbia's qualification but was sacked shortly afterwards to be replaced by assistant Mladen Krstajic in his first managerial role.

"We parted ways because we don't think alike on how the team should look for the World Cup," said Muslin, who was accused of playing negative football and not selecting enough of the youngsters that helped Serbia to win the Under-20 World Cup in 2015.

The squad

Krstajic has quickly gone about changing the side since picking his first squad in November, bringing in a raft of younger players and switching to a 4-3-3 formation from Muslin's back five.

Among the more drastic moves have been axing Branislav Ivanovic as captain in favour of Aleksandar Kolarov and Eibar's Marko Dimtrovic has been given his opportunity to displace veteran goalkeeper Vladimir Stojkovic.

Krstajic has plenty of talent at his disposal with a nice blend of experienced stalwarts such as Ivanovic, Kolarov, Nemanja Matic, Ljubomir Fejsa and Dusan Tadic to go with this batch of hyped-up young guns in Andrija Zivkovic,

Factfile

FA founded 1919
www fss.rs
Head coach Mladen Krstajic
Date qualified October 9, 2017

Strengths

☑ Nice blend of youth and experience
☑ Midfield is an area where Serbia can dominate opponents

Weaknesses

☒ Not many options beyond Mitrovic to lead the line
☒ Could the inexperienced manager be too gung-ho in his determination to pick youngsters?

Star rating

Fixtures

1 June 17, 1pm v Costa Rica, Samara
2 June 22, 7pm v Switzerland, Kaliningrad
3 June 27, 7pm v Brazil, Otkrytie Arena, Moscow

Base Kaliningrad
Total distance 3,800 miles

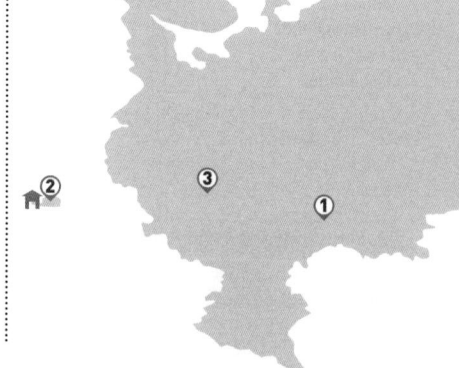

Nemanja Matic holds everything together for Serbia

Mijat Gacinovic, Marko Grujic, Nemanja Maksimovic and Sergej Milinkovic-Savic, who is the pick of the bunch.

There are also players like Adem Ljajic, Matija Nastasic, Luka Milivojevic and Filip Kostic who should be entering their prime, so Krstajic has some nice selection problems.

However, there is little competition at centre forward for six-goal Aleksandar Mitrovic, their top scorer in qualifying.

Key man
Manchester United's midfield holder Matic will be crucial in terms of his big-game temperament and positional play if Serbia become more adventurous.

Rising star
When Milinkovic-Savic leaves Lazio he will cost a fortune and rightly so.

He is a powerful midfielder who has everything in his locker and it was widely reported that Muslin mainly lost his job after continually overlooking Milinkovic-Savic to the dismay of Serbia's supporters.

Krstajic has since said: "Milinkovic-Savic's performances at Lazio and Serbia's 2015 Under-20 World Cup-winning side have shown that he fully deserves to be here."

Wildcard
In 2013 Zivkovic, then 17, became the youngest player ever to represent Serbia and he was the same age when he captained Partizan. The left-footer was a star at youth level for Serbia and has since moved to Benfica.

Prospects
Good enough to reach the knockout stages.

How to back them
A last-16 exit looks on the cards. They are unlikely to topple Brazil and are set to face Germany in the first knockout phase if they take second spot in Group E.

World Cup record		Group stage(s)						Knockout rounds					
		P	W	D	L	F	A	P	W	D	L	F	A
Uruguay 1930	Fourth place	2	2	0	0	6	1	1	0	0	1	1	6
Italy 1934	Did not qualify	-	-	-	-	-	-	-	-	-	-	-	-
France 1938	Did not qualify	-	-	-	-	-	-	-	-	-	-	-	-
Brazil 1950	Group stage	3	2	0	1	7	3	-	-	-	-	-	-
Switzerland 1954	Quarter-finals	2	1	1	0	2	1	1	0	0	1	0	2
Sweden 1958	Quarter-finals	3	1	2	0	7	6	1	0	0	1	0	1
Chile 1962	Fourth place	3	2	0	1	8	3	3	1	0	2	2	4
England 1966	Did not qualify	-	-	-	-	-	-	-	-	-	-	-	-
Mexico 1970	Did not qualify	-	-	-	-	-	-	-	-	-	-	-	-
Germany 1974	2nd group stage	6	1	2	3	12	7	-	-	-	-	-	-
Argentina 1978	Did not qualify	-	-	-	-	-	-	-	-	-	-	-	-
Spain 1982	Group stage	3	1	1	1	2	2	-	-	-	-	-	-
Mexico 1986	Did not qualify	-	-	-	-	-	-	-	-	-	-	-	-
Italy 1990	Quarter-final	3	2	0	1	6	5	2	0	2	0	1	1
USA 1994	Banned	-	-	-	-	-	-	-	-	-	-	-	-
France 1998	Round of 16	3	2	1	0	4	2	1	0	0	1	1	2
Korea/Japan 2002	Did not qualify	-	-	-	-	-	-	-	-	-	-	-	-
Germany 2006	Group stage	3	0	0	3	2	10	-	-	-	-	-	-
South Africa 2010	Group stage	3	1	0	2	2	3	-	-	-	-	-	-
Brazil 2014	Did not qualify	-	-	-	-	-	-	-	-	-	-	-	-
Totals		34	15	7	12	58	43	9	1	2	6	5	16

Competed as part of Yugoslavia until 2003 and as Serbia & Montengro until 2006

Continental championships (best perfomance)

Uefa European Championship   Quarter-finals (1)   2000

Also beaten finalists as part of Yugoslavia 1960 & 1968

World Cup head-to-heads

Serbia v	P	W	D	L	F	A	Latest
Argentina	2	0	1	1	0	6	2006
Australia	1	0	0	1	1	2	2010
Brazil	4	1	2	1	3	4	1974
Colombia	2	2	0	0	6	0	1990
France	2	2	0	0	4	2	1958
Germany	7	2	1	4	5	11	2010
Iran	1	1	0	0	1	0	1998
Mexico	1	1	0	0	4	1	1950
Poland	1	0	0	1	1	2	1974
Russia	1	0	0	1	0	2	1962
Spain	2	0	1	1	2	3	1990
Sweden	1	0	0	1	1	2	1974
Switzerland	1	1	0	0	3	0	1950
Uruguay	2	1	0	1	4	7	1962

90 mins only, includes games played as Yugoslavia and Serbia & Montenegro and against West Germany and USSR

Serbia coach Mladen Krstajic in action for his country against Argentina in the 2006 World Cup

How they qualified

Group D	P	W	D	L	F	A	GD	P
Serbia	10	6	3	1	20	10	10	21
Rep of Ireland	10	5	4	1	12	6	6	19
Wales	10	4	5	1	13	6	7	17
Austria	10	4	3	3	14	12	2	15
Georgia	10	0	5	5	8	14	-6	5
Moldova	10	0	2	8	4	23	-19	2

Serbia............ (0) 2-2 (1)..Rep of Ireland
Moldova........ (0) 0-3 (2)............. Serbia
Serbia............ (2) 3-2 (1)............Austria
Wales.............. (1) 1-1 (0)............. Serbia
Georgia.......... (1) 1-3 (1)............. Serbia
Serbia............ (0) 1-1 (1)............. Wales
Serbia............ (2) 3-0 (0)......... Moldova
Rep of Ireland (0) 0-1 (0)............. Serbia
Austria .... (1) 3-2 (1)............. Serbia
Serbia............ (0) 1-0 (0).......... Georgia

Serbia celebrate the win over Georgia that confirmed their qualification for the finals

Players used in qualifying		Career			Qualification			
Pos		Club	Age	P	G	P	G	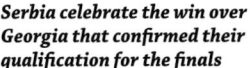
GK	Predrag Rajkovic	M. Tel Aviv	22	7	-	2	-	-	-
GK	Vladimir Stojkovic	Partizan	34	79	-	8	-	3	-
DEF	Aleksandar Kolarov	Roma	32	74	10	8	2	2	-
DEF	Antonio Rukavina	Villarreal	34	45	-	9	-	1	-
DEF	Branislav Ivanovic	Zenit	34	101	12	10	1	-	-
DEF	Dusko Tosic	Besiktas	33	21	1	2	-	-	-
DEF	Filip Mladenovic	Lechia Gdansk	26	5	-	1	-	-	-
DEF	Ivan Obradovic	Anderlecht	29	27	1	2	-	-	-
DEF	Jagos Vukovic	Verona	30	8	-	5	-	1	-
DEF	Matija Nastasic	Schalke	25	27	-	7	-	2	-
DEF	Nikola Maksimovic	Napoli	26	21	-	6	-	1	1
DEF	Stefan Mitrovic	Gent	28	13	-	4	-	1	-
MID	Adem Ljajic	Torino	26	27	5	3	-	-	-
MID	Aleksandr Katai	Chicago Fire	27	6	-	4	-	2	-
MID	Dusan Tadic	Southampton	29	51	13	10	4	1	-
MID	Filip Kostic	Hamburg	25	21	2	9	2	-	-
MID	Ljubomir Fejsa	Benfica	29	23	-	1	-	-	-
MID	Luka Milivojevic	Crystal Palace	27	26	1	9	1	2	-
MID	Mijat Gacinovic	E Frankfurt	23	7	2	3	2	-	-
MID	Nemanja Gudelj	Guangzhou	26	22	1	9	-	-	-
MID	Nemanja Matic	Man Utd	29	38	2	7	1	2	-
MID	Nemanja Radoja	Celta Vigo	25	2	-	1	-	-	-
MID	Zoran Tosic	Partizan	31	76	12	1	-	-	-
ATT	Aleksandar Mitrovic	Fulham	23	35	13	9	6	-	-
ATT	Aleksandar Prijovic	PAOK Salonika	28	8	1	5	1	1	-
ATT	Andrija Pavlovic	FC Copenhagen	24	5	-	2	-	-	-

Correct scores

	Competitive	Friendly
1-0	2	1
2-0	2	3
2-1	-	1
3-0	2	-
3-1	1	1
3-2	1	-
4-0	-	-
4-1	-	1
4-2	-	-
4-3	-	-
0-0	-	1
1-1	3	3
2-2	1	-
3-3	-	-
4-4	-	-
0-1	-	1
0-2	1	1
1-2	2	2
0-3*	1	1
1-3	1	-
2-3	1	-
0-4	-	-
1-4	-	1
2-4	-	-
3-4	-	-
Other	-	-

Since Brazil 2014

Half-time/full-time double results

Win/Win	4	24%	Win 1st half	5	29%
Draw/Win	4	24%	Win 2nd half	10	59%
Lose/Win	0	0%	Win both halves	3	18%
Win/Draw	0	0%	Goal both halves	6	35%
Draw/Draw	1	6%			
Lose/Draw	3	18%	**Overall**		
Win/Lose	1	6%	● Win	47%	
Draw/Lose	1	6%	● Draw	24%	
Lose/Lose	3	18%	● Lose	29%	

Overall: W8, D4, L5 in 17 completed competitive games since Brazil 2014

Under & over goals

15 (88%) **Over 1.5** 2 (12%) ✓ ✗

9 (53%) **Over 2.5** 8 (47%) ✓ ✗

5 (29%) **Over 3.5** 12 (71%) ✓ ✗

2 (12%) **Over 4.5** 15 (88%) ✓ ✗

Both teams to score

10 (59%) **Both score** 7 (41%) ✓ ✗

2 (12%) **& win** 15 (88%) ✓ ✗

4 (24%) **& lose** 13 (76%) ✓ ✗

In 17 completed competitive games since Brazil 2014

Clean sheets

8 (47%) **Clean sheets** 9 (53%) ✓ ✗

8 (47%) **Win to nil** 9 (53%) ✓ ✗

1 (6%) **Fail to score** 16 (94%) ✓ ✗

1 (6%) **Lose to nil** 16 (94%) ✓ ✗

When they score

● For ● Against

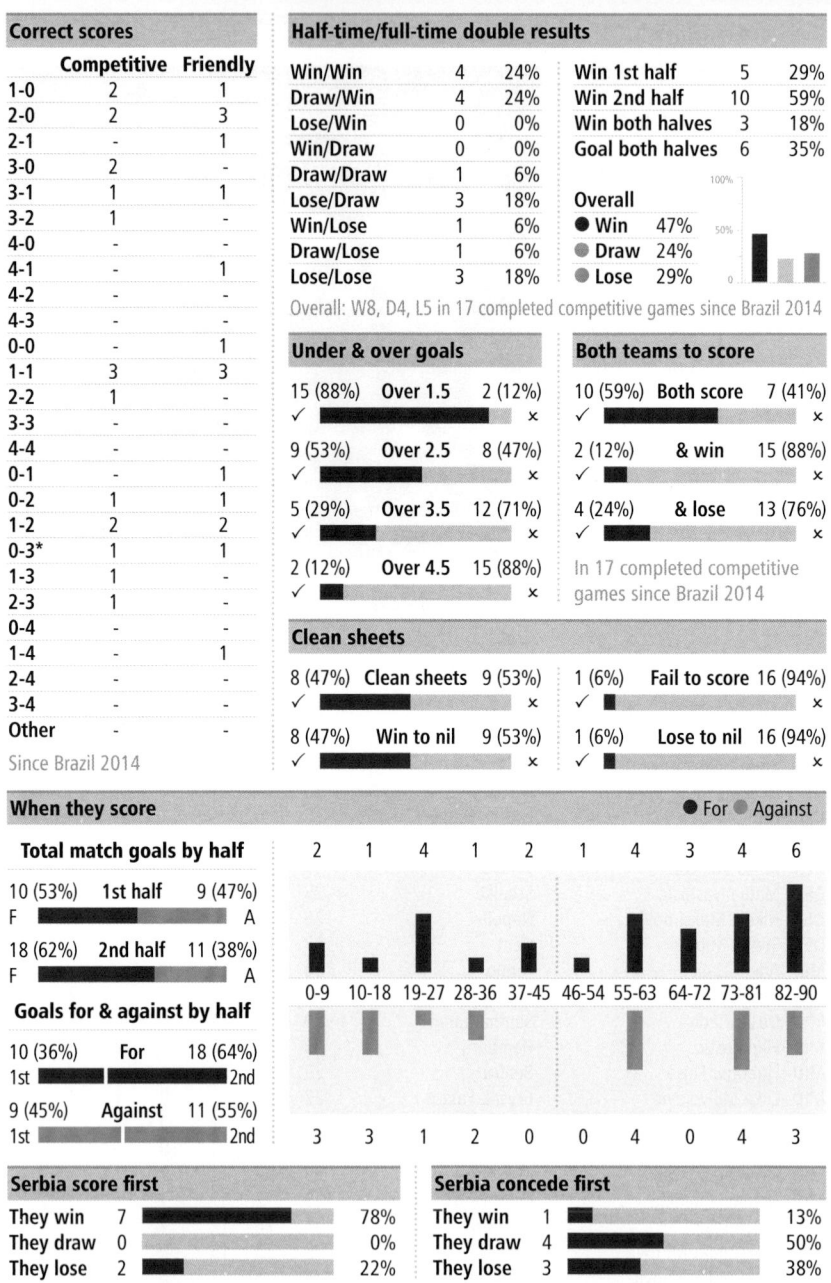

Total match goals by half

10 (53%) **1st half** 9 (47%)
F A

18 (62%) **2nd half** 11 (38%)
F A

2 1 4 1 2 1 4 3 4 6

0-9 10-18 19-27 28-36 37-45 46-54 55-63 64-72 73-81 82-90

Goals for & against by half

10 (36%) **For** 18 (64%)
1st 2nd

9 (45%) **Against** 11 (55%)
1st 2nd

3 3 1 2 0 0 4 0 4 3

Serbia score first

They win	7	78%
They draw	0	0%
They lose	2	22%

Serbia concede first

They win	1	13%
They draw	4	50%
They lose	3	38%

*In 17 completed competitive games since Brazil 2014. A Euro 2016 qualifier v Albania was abandoned after 41 minutes with the score at 0-0. Match awarded to Albania 3-0

GROUP E

Aleksandar Mitrovic was top scorer in qualifying but had to leave Newcastle to get playing time

Top scorers in qualifying

	P	G	1st	AT	%	Srb 2-2 Irl	Mda 0-3 Srb	Srb 3-2 Aut	Wal 1-1 Srb	Geo 1-3 Srb	Srb 1-1 Wal	Srb 3-0 Mda	Irl 0-1 Srb	Aut 3-2 Srb	Srb 1-0 Geo
Aleksandar Mitrovic	9	6	1	5	30	↻		2	1	1	1	1		-	↻
Dusan Tadic	10	4	0	4	20	1	1	1	-	1	-	↻	↻	-	↻
Mijat Gacinovic	3	2	1	2	10					1		1		↻	
Aleksandar Kolarov	8	2	1	2	10		-	-			-	-	1	1	-
Filip Kostic	9	2	1	2	10	1	1	↻	↻	↻	↻	-	↻		↺
Aleksandar Prijovic	5	1	1	1	5						↺	↺	↺	↺	1
Nemanja Matic	7	1	0	1	5					-	-	-	↻	1	-
Luka Milivojevic	9	1	1	1	5	-	-	-	-	-	↻	-		1	↺
Branislav Ivanovic	10	1	0	1	5	-	1	-	-	-	-	-	-	-	-

G goals scored, **1st** first match goal (own goals don't count) **AT** goals at any time (ie. number of scoring appearances), **P** penalties, **%** percentage of total team goals scored by each player. Russia 2018 qualifying only. Game-by-game stats show goals scored, 1st goals are in red, dash did not score, ↺ substituted on, ↻ substituted off, blank did not play

Bookings in World Cup qualifying

Played 10 **Cards** (19Y, 1R) ▯▯▯▯▯▯▯▯▯▯▯▯▯▯▯▯▯▯▯ ▮ **Avg make-up** (▯10 ▮25) 21.5

Seventh time unlucky for Mexico in the last 16

The World Cup draw has thrown up some obvious looking group winners and punters wanting to play multiples can definitely consider Germany alongside Brazil as the safest double, *writes Mark Langdon*.

Joachim Low's side head to Russia as world champions and Confederations Cup winners and this group should be a formality.

Mexico can follow Germany through although, just like in each of the last six World Cups, their race is set to run only to the last 16 with Brazil expected to be waiting for them.

First things first and Mexico must get their noses in front of Sweden and South Korea, a task that is eminently possible for the commanding Concacaf regional top dogs.

Juan Carlos Osorio's free-scoring outfit had a taste of life in Russia in last summer's Confederations Cup where they reached the semi-finals before a 4-1 hammering at the hands of Germany. Mexico had beaten the hosts and New Zealand and deserved a 2-2 draw with European champions Portugal to reach that point.

Young PSV winger Hirving Lozano could be a special player and those kind of attacking talents could separate Mexico from likely second-spot rivals Sweden.

Make no mistake, Sweden can be awkward opponents – just ask Holland and Italy who were dumped out of the qualifiers by the Scandinavians, not to mention France, who lost 2-1 in Stockholm.

But even with the now retired Zlatan Ibrahimovic in their ranks they managed only one goal at Euro 2016, failed to qualify for the last World Cup and were eliminated early at Euro 2012 following defeats by Ukraine, France and England.

The playoff win over Italy will live long in the memory, yet across the two matches they averaged just over 30 per cent possession, forced four shots on target, had another four off target and won one corner.

A deflected goal beat Italy and that kind of luck may well be needed to make the last 16 with Mexico's superior technical players fancied to be the difference in a probable decider between the nations in the final round of fixtures on June 27.

South Korea deserve to be favourites for bottom spot. Heung-Min Son will need to have a storming finals if they are to get involved as, outside of the 2002 World Cup on home soil, Korea usually disappoint at this level.

Last-16 heartbreak for Mexico

Recommendation

★☆☆☆☆ **Mexico last 16 stage of elimination**

Group-stage performances since France 98

	Pot	P	W	Q	1998 Group	Pos	2002 Group	Pos	2006 Group	Pos	2010 Group	Pos	2014 Group	Pos
Germany	1	5	5	5	F	1	E	1	A	1	D	1	G	1
Mexico	2	5	1	5	E	2	G	1	D	2	A	2	A	2
Sweden	3	2	1	2	-	-	F	1	B	2	-	-	-	-
South Korea	4	5	1	2	E	4	D	1	G	3	B	2	H	4

To win Group F

Win only

	Bet365	BtBrt	Betfair	Btfrd	Btwy	Boyle	Coral	Hills	Lads	P Power	Sky	188
Germany	4-11	4-11	1-3	**4-9**	**4-9**	4-11	4-11	2-9	2-5	1-3	4-11	37-100
Mexico	5	5	5	5	9-2	5	**11-2**	**11-2**	5	5	5	5
Sweden	6	13-2	11-2	11-2	6	6	6	**17-2**	6	11-2	13-2	5
S Korea	16	16	16	9	12	**20**	14	**20**	12	17	12	15

Germany v Mexico

4pm, Sunday June 17, BBC

	Bet365	BtBrt	Betfair	Btfrd	Btwy	Boyle	Coral	Hills	Lads	P Power	Sky	188
Germany	1-2	4-9	**4-7**	1-2	1-2	4-9	1-2	4-9	1-2	8-15	1-2	1-2
Draw	3	3	14-5	16-5	3	14-5	29-10	16-5	29-10	11-4	16-5	**38-11**
Mexico	**6**	11-2	11-2	11-2	11-2	5	5	11-2	5	11-2	11-2	26-5

Sweden v South Korea

1pm, Monday June 18, ITV

	Bet365	BtBrt	Betfair	Btfrd	Btwy	Boyle	Coral	Hills	Lads	P Power	Sky	188
Sweden	21-20	11-10	3-4	23-20	23-20	11-10	23-20	11-10	23-20	11-10	23-20	**19-16**
Draw	11-5	2	**14-5**	21-10	11-5	2	21-10	11-5	21-10	11-5	11-5	12-5
S Korea	14-5	12-5	**15-4**	5-2	12-5	12-5	12-5	12-5	12-5	13-5	5-2	23-10

South Korea v Mexico

4pm, Saturday June 23, ITV

	Bet365	BtBrt	Betfair	Btfrd	Btwy	Boyle	Coral	Hills	Lads	P Power	Sky	188
Mexico	**21-20**	19-20	Evs	19-20	Evs	10-11	Evs	Evs	Evs	10-11	Evs	68-67
Draw	9-4	21-10	23-10	9-4	21-10	21-10	21-10	21-10	21-10	11-5	23-10	**5-2**
S Korea	11-4	14-5	3	3	3	11-4	14-5	29-10	14-5	11-4	29-10	11-4

Germany v Sweden

7pm, Saturday June 23, ITV

	Bet365	BtBrt	Betfair	Btfrd	Btwy	Boyle	Coral	Hills	Lads	P Power	Sky	188
Germany	8-15	1-2	**11-20**	1-2	8-15	1-2	1-2	1-2	1-2	1-2	8-15	6-11
Draw	14-5	14-5	3	3	16-5	11-4	29-10	16-5	29-10	11-4	3	**33-10**
Sweden	**11-2**	5	**11-2**	**11-2**	9-2	5	5	24-5	5	5	5	47-10

South Korea v Germany

3pm, Wednesday June 27, BBC

	Bet365	BetBright	Betfair	Betfred	Betway	Boyle	Hills	P Power	Sky Bet
Germany	**2-7**	1-4	1-4	1-4	1-4	2-9	1-4	1-5	**2-7**
Draw	4	4	**5**	9-2	17-4	4	9-2	9-2	4
S Korea	11	9	**12**	10	8	9	11	10	10

Mexico v Sweden

3pm, Wednesday June 27, BBC

	Bet365	BetBright	Betfair	Betfred	Betway	Boyle	Hills	P Power	Sky Bet
Mexico	6-4	7-5	**17-10**	6-4	7-5	11-8	6-4	6-4	11-8
Sweden	15-8	15-8	15-8	19-10	7-4	15-8	2	7-4	**21-10**
Draw	**11-5**	2	2	21-10	21-10	19-10	2	15-8	21-10

Prices correct March 28 2018

GERMANY

Profile

Winning the World Cup is tough but retaining it is even tougher – Brazil were the last side to successfully defend the crown in 1962.

However, world champions Germany won the Confederations Cup with a virtual B side and have reached at least the semi-finals in each of the last six major tournaments.

How they qualified

Germany were the only European team to win all ten matches and Joachim Low's side also equalled the record for goals scored with 43. Germany used 37 different players, the most of any Uefa qualifier.

The manager

Low has been in position since 2006 and has a contract until after the next European Championship. He is a loyal manager who has on occasion put the serenity of the group above talent.

The squad

No coach has bigger issues whittling down his pool of players into just 23, as shown by their Confederations Cup success which came without Manuel Neuer, Mats Hummels, Jerome Boateng, Toni Kroos, Mesut Ozil, Thomas Muller, Ilkay Gundogan, Marco Reus, Mario Gotze, Sami Khedira and Leroy Sane.

Low's default formation is 4-2-3-1 but he has toyed with a back three, which is likely to be plan B for the Euro 2016 semi-finalists.

Neuer wears the gloves, Joshua Kimmich plays at right-back with Mats Hummels and Jerome Boateng as centre-backs. Cologne's Jonas Hector fills the problematic left-back position and is set to be the only non-Bayern Munich performer in the defence.

And here is where things get slightly more tricky with stiff competition for places in midfield. Thomas Muller, who has scored ten World Cup goals, looks favourite on the right. Toni Kroos sitting deep and Mesut Ozil as the playmaker also appear locks in

Factfile

FA founded 1900
www dfb.de
Head coach Joachim Low
Date qualified October 5, 2017

Strengths

☑ Depth of talent will allow seamless rotation
☑ So many goals in the side from midfield as well as from Werner

Weaknesses

☒ Will Low stay loyal to those on the downgrade like Khedira?
☒ History – the last three European World Cup winners have all gone out in the group stage

Star rating ⭐⭐⭐⭐⭐

Fixtures

1 June 17, 4pm v Mexico, Luzhniki Stadium, Moscow
2 June 23, 7 pm v Sweden, Sochi
3 June 27, 3pm v South Korea, Kazan

Base Moscow
Total distance 2,600 miles

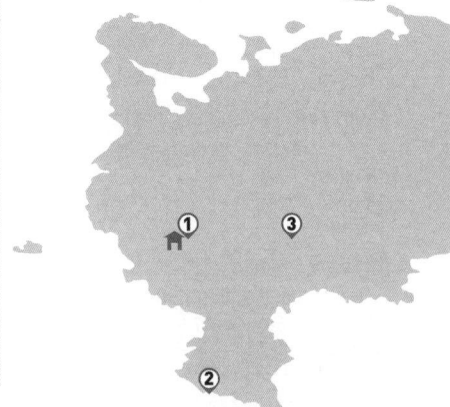

Joachim Low has so much quality to choose from

Photo by Laurence Griffiths/Getty Images

the starting 11. However, Leon Goretzka, Gundogan, Sebastian Rudy and Emre Can are among those putting pressure on Sami Khedira, while on the left it could be any one of Sane, Julian Draxler or Reus.

Low has sometimes fielded a false nine to fit in more midfielders but the emergence of Timo Werner as a genuine striker of great promise is a boost.

Key man

It's about the team rather than the individual so Low is key and must make the right decision on when to ditch the old guard for the young upstarts.

Rising star

Werner showed glimpses of his ability at Stuttgart but his reputation has risen after a controversial move to Leipzig. A quick, mobile frontman in the mould of a young Michael Owen, Werner scored three times at the Confederations Cup to claim the Golden Boot.

Wildcard

Reus has been one of football's unluckiest men after missing the World Cup triumph due to an ankle problem as he watched best friend Gotze score the winning goal. He was also sidelined for Euro 2016 due to injury.

Reus has had another disruptive campaign this season but when fit he is a star for Borussia Dortmund.

Prospects

They are clearly contenders, although that is reflected in their favourites tag.

How to back them

You have to go back to 1986 for the last time Germany or West Germany failed to win their group so Low's men should be bankers for the multiples. Another short-odds bet that should collect is for Germany to reach at least the quarter-finals.

GERMANY

World Cup record

World Cup record		Group stage(s)						Knockout rounds					
		P	W	D	L	F	A	P	W	D	L	F	A
Uruguay 1930	Did not enter	-	-	-	-	-	-	-	-	-	-	-	-
Italy 1934	Third place	-	-	-	-	-	-	4	3	0	1	11	8
France 1938	First round	-	-	-	-	-	-	2	0	1	1	3	5
Brazil 1950	Banned	-	-	-	-	-	-	-	-	-	-	-	-
Switzerland 1954	● Winners	3	2	0	1	14	11	3	3	0	0	11	3
Sweden 1958	Fourth place	3	1	2	0	7	5	3	1	0	2	5	9
Chile 1962	Quarter-finals	3	2	1	0	4	1	1	0	0	1	0	1
England 1966	Finalists	3	2	1	0	7	1	3	2	1	0	8	3
Mexico 1970	Third place	3	3	0	0	10	4	3	1	2	0	4	3
Germany 1974	● Winners	6	5	0	1	11	3	1	1	0	0	2	1
Argentina 1978	2nd group stage	6	1	4	1	10	5	-	-	-	-	-	-
Spain 1982	Finalists	5	3	1	1	8	4	2	0	1	1	2	4
Mexico 1986	Finalists	3	1	1	1	3	4	4	2	1	1	5	3
Italy 1990	● Winners	3	2	1	0	10	3	4	3	1	0	5	2-
USA 1994	Quarter-finals	3	2	1	0	5	3	2	1	0	1	4	4
France 1998	Quarter-finals	3	2	1	0	6	0	2	1	0	1	2	4
Korea/Japan 2002	Finalists	3	2	1	0	11	1	4	3	0	1	3	2
Germany 2006	Third place	3	3	0	0	8	2	4	2	2	0	6	2
South Africa 2010	Third place	3	2	0	1	5	1	4	3	0	1	11	4
Brazil 2014	● Winners	3	2	1	0	7	2	4	2	2	0	8	1
Totals		56	35	15	6	126	52	50	28	11	11	90	59

Competed as Germany 1930-38, East and West Germany 1950-90 (only West Germany's record shown)

Continental championships (best perfomance)

Uefa European Championship	Winners (3)	1972, 1980, 1996

World Cup head-to-heads

Germany v	P	W	D	L	F	A	Latest	Germany v	P	W	D	L	F	A	Latest
Argentina	7	3	3	1	11	5	2014	Peru	1	1	0	0	3	1	1970
Australia	2	2	0	0	7	0	2010	Poland	3	2	1	0	2	0	2006
Belgium	2	2	0	0	8	4	1994	Portugal	2	2	0	0	7	1	2014
Brazil	2	1	0	1	7	3	2014	Russia	1	1	0	0	2	1	1966
Colombia	1	0	1	0	1	1	1990	Saudi Arabia	1	1	0	0	8	0	2002
Costa Rica	1	1	0	0	4	2	2006	Serbia	7	4	1	2	11	5	2010
Croatia	7	4	1	2	11	7	1998	South Korea	2	2	0	0	4	2	2002
Denmark	1	0	0	1	0	2	1986	Spain	4	2	1	1	5	4	2010
England	5	1	4	0	9	6	2010	Sweden	4	3	0	1	9	6	2006
France	4	2	1	1	7	7	2014	Switzerland	4	2	1	1	10	6	1966
Iran	1	1	0	0	2	0	1998	Tunisia	1	0	1	0	0	0	1978
Mexico	3	2	1	0	8	1	1998	Uruguay	4	3	1	0	9	3	2010
Morocco	2	2	0	0	3	1	1986								

90 mins only, includes played as West Germany, and games against Yugoslavia and USSR

Follow us for the latest World Cup betting advice

RACING POST sport

How they qualified

Group C	P	W	D	L	F	A	GD	P
Germany	10	10	0	0	43	4	39	30
N Ireland	10	6	1	3	17	6	11	19
Czech Rep	10	4	3	3	17	10	7	15
Norway	10	4	1	5	17	16	1	13
Azerbaijan	10	3	1	6	10	19	-9	10
San Marino	10	0	0	10	2	51	-49	0

Goals galore v San Marino

Norway .... (0) 0-3 (2) .... **Germany**
Germany .... (1) 3-0 (0) ...... Czech Rep
Germany .... (2) 2-0 (0) ...... N Ireland
San Marino .... (0) 0-8 (3) .... **Germany**

Azerbaijan ...... (1) 1-4 (3) .... **Germany**
Germany .... (4) 7-0 (0) ..... San Marino
Czech Rep ...... (0) 1-2 (1) .... **Germany**

Germany .... (4) 6-0 (0) .... Norway
N Ireland .... (0) 1-3 (2) .... **Germany**
Germany .... (1) 5-1 (1) ...... Azerbaijan

Players used in qualifying

Pos		Club	Age	Career P	G	Qualification P	G	🟨	🟥
GK	Bernd Leno	B Leverkusen	26	6	-	2	-	-	-
GK	Manuel Neuer	B Munich	32	74	-	3	-	-	-
GK	Marc-Andre ter Stegen	Barcelona	26	19	-	5	-	-	-
DEF	Antonio Rudiger	Chelsea	25	23	1	3	1	-	-
DEF	Benedikt Howedes	Juventus	30	44	2	3	-	1	-
DEF	Benjamin Henrichs	B Leverkusen	21	3	-	1	-	-	-
DEF	Jerome Boateng	B Munich	29	70	1	3	-	-	-
DEF	Jonas Hector	Cologne	28	36	3	8	2	-	-
DEF	Joshua Kimmich	B Munich	23	27	3	10	2	-	-
DEF	Marvin Plattenhardt	Hertha Berlin	26	6	-	2	-	-	-
DEF	Mats Hummels	B Munich	29	63	5	8	1	1	-
DEF	Matthias Ginter	Mgladbach	24	17	-	2	-	-	-
DEF	Niklas Sule	B Munich	22	9	-	1	-	-	-
DEF	Shkodran Mustafi	Arsenal	26	20	2	3	1	-	-
MID	Diego Demme	RB Leipzig	26	1	-	1	-	-	-
MID	Emre Can	Liverpool	24	20	1	4	1	-	-
MID	Ilkay Gundogan	Man City	27	24	4	3	-	-	-
MID	Julian Brandt	B Leverkusen	22	14	1	5	1	-	-
MID	Julian Draxler	Paris St-Germain	24	42	6	8	3	-	-
MID	Julian Weigl	B Dortmund	22	5	-	1	-	-	-
MID	Leon Goretzka	Schalke	23	14	6	5	3	-	-
MID	Leroy Sane	Man City	22	11	-	3	-	-	-
MID	Mario Gotze	B Dortmund	26	63	17	4	-	-	-
MID	Max Meyer	Schalke	22	4	1	2	-	-	-
MID	Mesut Ozil	Arsenal	29	89	22	6	1	-	-
MID	Sami Khedira	Juventus	31	73	7	6	2	2	-
MID	Sebastian Rudy	Bayern Munich	28	24	1	3	1	-	-
MID	Serge Gnabry	Hoffenheim	22	2	3	1	3	-	-
MID	Toni Kroos	Real Madrid	28	82	12	7	1	-	-
ATT	Andre Schurrle	B Dortmund	27	57	22	1	2	-	-
ATT	Amin Younes	Ajax	24	5	2	2	1	-	-
ATT	Kevin Volland	B Leverkusen	25	10	1	2	1	-	-
ATT	Lars Stindl	Mgladbach	29	11	4	4	-	-	-
ATT	Mario Gomez	Stuttgart	32	73	31	3	2	-	-
ATT	Sandro Wagner	B Munich	30	8	5	3	5	-	-
ATT	Thomas Muller	B Munich	28	90	38	9	5	1	-
ATT	Timo Werner	RB Leipzig	22	12	7	3	3	-	-

GERMANY

Correct scores

	Competitive	Friendly
1-0	2	2
2-0	3	2
2-1	3	-
3-0	3	-
3-1	3	-
3-2	2	-
4-0	1	-
4-1	2	1
4-2	-	-
4-3	-	-
0-0	1	2
1-1	3	2
2-2	-	2
3-3	-	-
4-4	-	-
0-1	1	1
0-2	2	1
1-2	-	1
0-3	-	-
1-3	-	1
2-3	-	1
0-4	-	-
1-4	-	-
2-4	-	1
3-4	-	-
Other	5	-

Since Brazil 2014

Half-time/full-time double results

Win/Win	20	65%	Win 1st half	20	65%
Draw/Win	4	13%	Win 2nd half	16	52%
Lose/Win	0	0%	Win both halves	12	39%
Win/Draw	0	0%	Goal both halves	18	58%
Draw/Draw	4	13%			
Lose/Draw	0	0%	Overall		
Win/Lose	0	0%	● Win	77%	
Draw/Lose	2	6%	● Draw	13%	
Lose/Lose	1	3%	● Lose	10%	

Overall: W24, D4, L3 in 31 competitive games since Brazil 2014

Under & over goals

27 (87%) **Over 1.5** 4 (13%) ✓ ✗

19 (61%) **Over 2.5** 12 (39%) ✓ ✗

13 (42%) **Over 3.5** 18 (58%) ✓ ✗

9 (29%) **Over 4.5** 22 (71%) ✓ ✗

Both teams to score

14 (45%) **Both score** 17 (55%) ✓ ✗

11 (35%) **& win** 20 (65%) ✓ ✗

0 (0%) **& lose** 31 (100%) ✓ ✗

In 31 competitive games since Brazil 2014

Clean sheets

14 (45%) **Clean sheets** 17 (55%) ✓ ✗

13 (42%) **Win to nil** 18 (58%) ✓ ✗

4 (13%) **Fail to score** 27 (87%) ✓ ✗

3 (10%) **Lose to nil** 28 (90%) ✓ ✗

When they score

● For ● Against

Total match goals by half

44 (85%) **1st half** 8 (15%)
F ■■■■■ A

42 (76%) **2nd half** 13 (24%)
F ■■■■■ A

9	12	6	7	10	10	5	12	7	8
0-9	10-18	19-27	28-36	37-45	46-54	55-63	64-72	73-81	82-90
1	0	0	4	3	2	1	3	3	4

Goals for & against by half

44 (51%) **For** 42 (49%)
1st ■■■■■ 2nd

8 (38%) **Against** 13 (62%)
1st ■■■■■ 2nd

Germany score first

They win	24	92%
They draw	2	8%
They lose	0	0%

In 31 competitive games since Brazil 2014

Germany concede first

They win	0	0%
They draw	1	25%
They lose	3	75%

GROUP F

Timo Werner is one of Germany's rising stars

Top scorers in qualifying

	P	G	1st	AT	%	Nor 0-3 Ger	Ger 3-0 Cze	Ger 2-0 Nir	Smr 0-8 Ger	Aze 1-4 Ger	Ger 7-0 Smr	Cze 1-2 Ger	Ger 6-0 Nor	Nir 1-3 Ger	Ger 5-1 Aze
Sandro Wagner	3	5	0	3	12						3			1	1
Thomas Muller	9	5	2	3	12	2	2	-	-	1	-	⟲	⟲	⟲	
Serge Gnabry	1	3	0	1	7					3					
Timo Werner	3	3	1	2	7							↳	⟲1	⟲2	
Leon Goretzka	5	3	1	2	7					↳	-		⟲1	⟲	2
Julian Draxler	8	3	2	3	7	⟲	⟲	1			↳	⟲1	↳	1	⟲
Andre Schurrle	1	2	1	1	5					2					
Mario Gomez	3	2	0	2	5						⟲1		⟲1		
Sami Khedira	6	2	1	2	5	⟲	-	1	⟲1	-		↳			
Jonas Hector	8	2	0	1	5	-	⟲	⟲	2	-	⟲	-	-		
Joshua Kimmich	10	2	0	2	5	1	-	-	-	-	-	-	-	1	-
Kevin Volland	2	1	0	1	2					↳	⟲1				
Amin Younes	2	1	0	1	2							1			↳
Antonio Rudiger	3	1	0	1	2								↳	-	⟲1
Shkodran Mustafi	3	1	0	1	2				↳		1				⟲
Sebastian Rudy	3	1	1	1	2					↳			⟲	1	
Emre Can	4	1	0	1	2							-	↳	↳	1
Julian Brandt	5	1	0	1	2	↳	↳					1	⟲		-
Mesut Ozil	6	1	1	1	2	-	-	⟲		↳			-	1	
Toni Kroos	7	1	0	1	2	-	⟲1	-		↳			-	-	-
Mats Hummels	8	1	0	1	2	-	-	-	-	-			1	-	

G goals scored, **1st** first match goal (own goals don't count) **AT** goals at any time (ie. number of scoring appearances), **P** penalties, **%** percentage of total team goals scored by each player. Russia 2018 qualifying only. Game-by-game stats show goals scored, 1st goals are in red, dash did not score, ↳ substituted on, ⟲ substituted off, blank did not play

Bookings in World Cup qualifying

Played 10 **Cards** (5Y) ▯▯▯▯▯

Avg make-up (▯10 ▮25) 5

MEXICO

Profile

Mexico will go out of the World Cup in the last 16. How do we know? Because Mexico *always* go out at the last-16 stage.

Since being banned from Italia 90, El Tri have played in six successive World Cups and have been eliminated after four matches in all six of them.

How they qualified

Concacaf qualifying is a long-winded process but it was easy enough for Mexico, who were on cruise control in their first group before comfortably topping the more demanding final hex. Their only defeat came in Honduras when qualification had already been secured.

The manager

Colombian Juan Carlos Osorio is not a universally popular figure. He is seen by some as the leader of chokers who lost their bottle in spectacular style in successive tournaments, first going down 7-0 to Chile at the Copa America Centenario in 2016 and then 4-1 to Germany in the Confederations Cup semi-finals.

The squad

Osorio likes to spread the net wide, using 43 players in his 23 competitive matches in charge (excluding the Gold Cup, where he named an inexperienced squad) and versatility is key for a coach who was previously a 4-3-3 merchant.

In more recent times he has looked at a five-man defence and a double defensive midfield pivot in an attempt to tighten up in preparation for the tougher tests to come.

However, Mexico's strength remains in attack where Javier Hernandez, Raul Jimenez, Oribe Peralta and Hirving Lozano are more than capable of shooting the lights out, while Porto midfielder Hector Herrera impressed at the last World Cup.

Others to catch the eye four years ago include centre-back Hector Moreno, back in Spain with Real Sociedad

Factfile

FA founded 1927
www femexfut.org.mx
Head coach Juan Carlos Osorio
Date qualified September 1, 2017

Strengths

- ☑ A number of players capable of scoring their goals
- ☑ Tactically flexible side who can alter their style to fit their opponents

Weaknesses

- ☒ Soft mentality in big matches
- ☒ Playing group favourites Germany first up is bad news

Star rating ★★☆☆☆

Fixtures

1 June 17, 4pm v Germany, Luzhniki Stadium, Moscow

2 June 23, 4 pm v South Korea, Rostov-on-Don

3 June 27, 3pm v Sweden, Yekaterinburg

Base Moscow
Total distance 2,950 miles

Penalty-box predator Javier Hernandez scores against Portugal at last year's Confederation Cup

after a difficult spell with Roma, and athletic keeper Guillermo Ochoa.

Mexico used the most players at the Confederations Cup (22) and are likely to be one of the more tactically flexible sides in Russia.

Key man

Hernandez has not always nailed down a starting berth for West Ham in 2017-18 , but the former Real Madrid and Manchester United hitman is Mexico's record goalscorer. Nicknamed Chicharito (the Pea) because of his green eyes, Hernandez is not a striker who wants to get involved in the build-up play but is a penalty-box predator.

Rising star

Hirving Lozano has been given the nickname El Chucky because of his resemblance to the doll in horror movie Child's Play and he has been scaring opposition defences all season for PSV Eindhoven. The left winger became the first player in Eredivisie history to score in seven of his first eight matches and is likely to command a big-money transfer fee should he leave after the World Cup.

Wildcard

Can Rafael Marquez join compatriot Antonio Carbajal and German legend Lothar Matthaus in playing in five World Cups? At the time of writing, the veteran captain has been fighting off-field problems after the United States Treasury announced Marquez is one of 22 people being sanctioned for alleged ties to drugs trafficking. He has denied the allegations and returned to club football but that – as well as poor form – may still jeopardise his chance at equalling the record.

Prospects

Same old story for Mexico, who can qualify but will struggle to get to a fifth match.

How to back them

A last-16 elimination for the seventh straight World Cup looks a good bet with Mexico expected to meet Brazil in the first knockout round.

MEXICO

World Cup record		P	W	D	L	F	A	P	W	D	L	F	A
		Group stage(s)						**Knockout rounds**					
Uruguay 1930	Group stage	3	0	0	3	4	13	-	-	-	-	-	-
Italy 1934	Did not qualify	-	-	-	-	-	-	-	-	-	-	-	-
France 1938	Withdrew	-	-	-	-	-	-	-	-	-	-	-	-
Brazil 1950	Group stage	3	0	0	3	2	10	-	-	-	-	-	-
Switzerland 1954	Group stage	2	0	0	2	2	8	-	-	-	-	-	-
Sweden 1958	Group stage	3	0	1	2	1	8	-	-	-	-	-	-
Chile 1962	Group stage	3	1	0	2	3	4	-	-	-	-	-	-
England 1966	Group stage	3	0	2	1	1	3	-	-	-	-	-	-
Mexico 1970	Quarter-finals	3	2	1	0	5	0	1	0	0	1	1	4
Germany 1974	Did not qualify	-	-	-	-	-	-	-	-	-	-	-	-
Argentina 1978	Group stage	3	0	0	3	2	12	-	-	-	-	-	-
Spain 1982	Did not qualify	-	-	-	-	-	-	-	-	-	-	-	-
Mexico 1986	Quarter-finals	3	2	1	0	4	2	2	1	1	0	2	0
Italy 1990	Banned	-	-	-	-	-	-	-	-	-	-	-	-
USA 1994	Round of 16	3	1	1	1	3	3	1	0	1	0	1	1
France 1998	Round of 16	3	1	2	0	7	5	1	0	0	1	1	2
Korea/Japan 2002	Round of 16	3	2	1	0	4	2	1	0	0	1	0	2
Germany 2006	Round of 16	3	1	1	1	4	3	1	0	1	0	1	1
South Africa 2010	Round of 16	3	1	1	1	3	2	1	0	0	1	1	3
Brazil 2014	Round of 16	3	2	1	0	4	1	1	0	0	1	1	2
Totals		44	13	12	19	49	76	9	1	3	5	8	15

Continental championships (best perfomance)

Concacaf Gold Cup   Winners (10)   1965, 1971, 1977, 1993, 1996, 1998, 2003, 2009, 2011, 2015

World Cup head-to-heads

Mexico v	P	W	D	L	F	A	Latest	Mexico v	P	W	D	L	F	A	Latest
Argentina	3	0	1	2	5	10	2010	Portugal	1	0	0	1	1	2	2006
Belgium	3	2	1	0	5	3	1998	Russia	1	0	1	0	0	0	1970
Brazil	4	0	1	3	0	11	2014	Serbia	1	0	0	1	1	4	1950
Croatia	3	2	0	1	5	5	2014	South Korea	1	1	0	0	3	1	1998
England	1	0	0	1	0	2	1966	Spain	1	0	0	1	0	1	1962
France	4	1	1	2	6	8	2010	Sweden	1	0	0	1	0	3	1958
Germany	3	0	1	2	1	8	1998	Switzerland	1	0	1	0	1	2	1950
Iran	1	1	0	0	3	1	2006	Tunisia	1	0	1	0	1	3	1978
Poland	1	0	0	1	1	3	1978	Uruguay	2	0	1	1	0	1	2010

90 mins only, includes games against Yugoslavia, West Germany and USSR

How they qualified

Round 4	P	W	D	L	F	A	GD	P
Mexico	6	5	1	0	13	1	12	16
Honduras	6	2	2	2	6	6	0	8
Canada	6	2	1	3	5	8	-3	7
El Salvador	6	0	2	4	4	13	-9	2

Mexico .... (2) 3-0 (0)...... El Salvador
Honduras .... (0) 0-2 (0)........... Mexico
Canada........... (0) 0-3 (2)........... Mexico
Mexico .... (2) 2-0 (0)........... Canada

El Salvador..... (1) 1-3 (0)...........Mexico
Mexico .... (0) 0-0 (0)........Honduras

Round 5	P	W	D	L	F	A	GD	P
Mexico	10	6	3	1	16	7	9	21
Costa Rica	10	4	4	2	14	8	6	16
Panama	10	3	4	3	9	10	-1	13
Honduras	10	3	4	3	13	19	-6	13
USA	10	3	3	4	17	13	4	12
Trin & Tobago	10	2	0	8	7	19	-12	6

USA .... (0) 1-2 (1)...........Mexico
Panama......... (0) 0-0 (0)...........Mexico
Mexico .... (2) 2-0 (0)...... Costa Rica
Trin & Tobago .. (0) 0-1 (0)...........Mexico
Mexico .... (1) 3-0 (0)........Honduras
Mexico .... (1) 1-1 (1)...............USA
Mexico .... (0) 1-0 (0)....... Panama
Costa Rica..... (0) 1-1 (1)...........Mexico
Mexico .... (0) 3-1 (0)..Trin & Tobago
Honduras .... (1) 3-2 (2)...........Mexico

GROUP F

Players used in qualifying		Career			Qualification			
Pos	Club	Age	P	G	P	G	🟨	🟥
GK Alfredo Talavera	Toluca	35	28	-	5	-	-	-
GK Guillermo Ochoa	Standard Liege	32	92	-	8	-	-	-
GK Jose Corona	Cruz Azul	37	55	-	2	-	-	-
GK Moises Munoz	Puebla	38	19	-	1	-	-	-
DEF Raul Lopez	Pachuca	25	7	-	1	-	-	-
DEF Yasser Corona	Tijuana	30	7	-	1	-	-	-
DEF Carlos Salcedo	E Frankfurt	24	18	-	6	-	2	1
DEF Cesar Montes	Monterrey	21	5	-	2	-	-	-
DEF Diego Reyes	Porto	25	55	1	11	1	2	-
DEF Edson Alvarez	Club America	20	10	1	2	-	1	-
DEF Hector Moreno	Sociedad	30	91	3	13	1	2	-
DEF Hugo Ayala	Tigres	31	40	1	7	-	-	-
DEF Jair Pereira	Guadalajara	31	7	-	1	-	-	-
DEF Jorge Torres	Tigres	30	52	1	1	-	1	-
DEF Luis Fuentes	UNAM	31	1	-	1	-	-	-
DEF Nestor Araujo	Santos Laguna	26	27	3	6	1	2	-
DEF Oswaldo Alanis	Guadalajara	29	21	2	4	1	1	-
DEF Paul Aguilar	Club America	32	55	5	2	-	-	-
DEF Rafael Marquez	Atlas	39	142	17	5	1	-	-
MID Jurgen Damm	Tigres	25	9	1	3	1	1	-
MID Andres Guardado	Real Betis	31	147	25	11	2	-	-
MID Candido Ramirez	Atlas	25	2	-	1	-	-	-
MID Elias Hernandez	Leon	30	23	4	1	-	-	-
MID Hector Herrera	Porto	28	63	5	15	2	2	-
MID Javier Aquino	Tigres	28	51	-	7	-	1	-
MID Jesus Duenas	Tigres	29	23	1	4	-	1	-
MID Jesus Gallardo	UNAM	23	20	-	5	-	1	-
MID Jesus Corona	Porto	25	30	7	10	3	-	-
MID Jesus Molina	Monterrey	30	31	-	5	-	-	-
MID Jonathan dos Santos	LA Galaxy	28	33	-	6	-	1	-
MID Jose Vazquez	Santos Laguna	30	18	-	2	-	-	-
MID Luis Reyes	Atlas	27	8	-	2	-	1	-
MID Marco Fabian	E Frankfurt	28	36	9	4	-	-	-
MID Miguel Layun	Porto	29	61	6	12	1	1	-
MID Orbelin Pineda	Guadalajara	22	15	1	3	-	-	-
MID Rodolfo Pizarro	Guadalajara	24	14	3	1	-	-	-
ATT Angel Sepulveda	Morelia	27	8	2	2	1	-	-
ATT Angel Zaldivar	Guadalajara	24	1	-	1	-	-	-
ATT Carlos Vela	Los Angeles	29	67	18	10	3	1	-
ATT Giovani Dos Santos	LA Galaxy	29	103	18	5	-	-	-
ATT Hirving Lozano	PSV Eindhoven	22	26	7	9	4	-	-
ATT Javier Hernandez	West Ham	30	100	49	11	3	-	-
ATT Oribe Peralta	Club America	34	63	25	5	1	-	-
ATT Raul Jimenez	Benfica	27	62	14	10	2	-	-

Follow us for the latest World Cup betting advice

RACING POST sport

Correct scores

	Competitive	Friendly
1-0	3	11
2-0	5	2
2-1	3	2
3-0	3	2
3-1	5	1
3-2	-	1
4-0	-	-
4-1	-	-
4-2	-	-
4-3	-	-
0-0	6	2
1-1	6	1
2-2	1	2
3-3	1	2
4-4	1	-
0-1	1	1
0-2	-	2
1-2	1	1
0-3	-	-
1-3	-	-
2-3	1	1
0-4	-	-
1-4	1	-
2-4	-	-
3-4	-	-
Other	2	-

Since Brazil 2014

Half-time/full-time double results

Win/Win	13	33%
Draw/Win	5	13%
Lose/Win	2	5%
Win/Draw	2	5%
Draw/Draw	12	30%
Lose/Draw	1	3%
Win/Lose	1	3%
Draw/Lose	1	3%
Lose/Lose	3	8%

Win 1st half	16	40%
Win 2nd half	17	43%
Win both halves	9	23%
Goal both halves	14	35%

Overall
- Win 50%
- Draw 38%
- Lose 13%

Overall: W20, D15, L5 in 40 competitive games since Brazil 2014

Under & over goals

30 (75%) **Over 1.5** 10 (25%) ✓ ✗

19 (48%) **Over 2.5** 21 (52%) ✓ ✗

12 (30%) **Over 3.5** 28 (70%) ✓ ✗

6 (15%) **Over 4.5** 34 (85%) ✓ ✗

Clean sheets

18 (45%) **Clean sheets** 22 (55%) ✓ ✗

12 (30%) **Win to nil** 28 (70%) ✓ ✗

Both teams to score

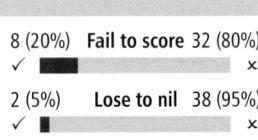

20 (50%) **Both score** 20 (50%) ✓ ✗

8 (20%) **& win** 32 (80%) ✓ ✗

3 (8%) **& lose** 37 (92%) ✓ ✗

In 40 competitive games since Brazil 2014

8 (20%) **Fail to score** 32 (80%) ✓ ✗

2 (5%) **Lose to nil** 38 (95%) ✓ ✗

When they score

● For ● Against

Total match goals by half

31 (66%) **1st half** 16 (34%)
F ▬▬▬ A

37 (61%) **2nd half** 24 (39%)
F ▬▬▬ A

Goals for & against by half

31 (46%) **For** 37 (54%)
1st ▬▬▬ 2nd

16 (40%) **Against** 24 (60%)
1st ▬▬▬ 2nd

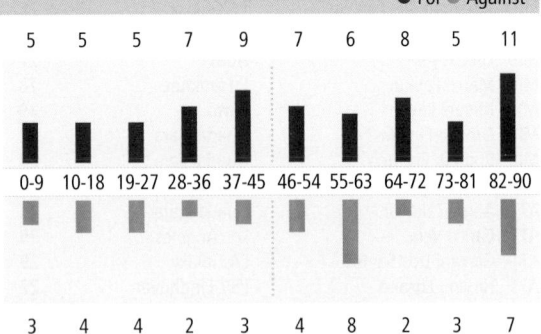

For	5	5	5	7	9	7	6	8	5	11
	0-9	10-18	19-27	28-36	37-45	46-54	55-63	64-72	73-81	82-90
Against	3	4	4	2	3	4	8	2	3	7

Mexico score first

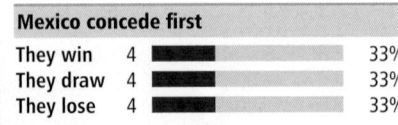

They win	16	73%
They draw	5	23%
They lose	1	5%

In 40 competitive games since Brazil 2014

Mexico concede first

They win	4	33%
They draw	4	33%
They lose	4	33%

Hirving Lozano

Top scorers in qualifying

	P	G	1st	AT	%	Mex 3-0 Slv	Hnd 0-2 Mex	Can 0-3 Mex	Mex 2-0 Can	Slv 1-3 Mex	Mex 0-0 Hnd	USA 1-2 Mex	Pan 0-0 Mex	Mex 2-0 Cri	Tto 0-1 Mex	Mex 3-0 Hnd	Mex 1-1 USA	Mex 1-0 Pan	Cri 1-1 Mex	Mex 3-1 Tto	Hnd 3-2 Mex
Hirving Lozano	9	4	1	4	14		⌐1					⌐	⌐	⌐		⌐1	-	⌐1	-	⌐1	
Jesus Corona	10	3	1	3	10	-	⌐1	1	1			-				ↄ		ↄ	ↄ	-	ↄ
Carlos Vela	10	3	0	3	10	1									ↄ	-	ↄ	-	1	ↄ	ↄ1
Javier Hernandez	11	3	2	3	10	ↄ	ↄ	⌐1	ↄ			-	-	ↄ1	-				-	-	1
Raul Jimenez	10	2	0	2	7	ↄ	ↄ				ↄ	1				-	ↄ	1		ↄ	-
Andres Guardado	11	2	2	2	7	1	-	-	1	-	-	ↄ						-	ↄ	-	ↄ
Hector Herrera	15	2	0	2	7	1	-	-	ↄ	-	-	-	ↄ	-	-	-	-	-	1	-	
Angel Sepulveda	2	1	0	1	3						1	ↄ									
Jurgen Damm	3	1	0	1	3	⌐1									ↄ			ↄ			
Oswaldo Alanis	4	1	1	1	3	-										1	ↄ				ↄ
Oribe Peralta	5	1	1	1	3	ↄ									ↄ	ↄ				ↄ	1
Rafael Marquez	5	1	0	1	3			ↄ		ↄ		1	ↄ	ↄ							
Nestor Araujo	6	1	0	1	3					-				-	1			-		-	
Diego Reyes	11	1	1	1	3		-	-						ↄ	ↄ	⌐1	-	-	-		ↄ
Miguel Layun	12	1	1	1	3	ↄ								-		1				-	-
Hector Moreno	13	1	0	1	3	-	-	-		ↄ	1										-

G goals scored, **1st** first match goal (own goals don't count) **AT** goals at any time (ie. number of scoring appearances), **P** penalties, **%** percentage of total team goals scored by each player. Russia 2018 qualifying only. Game-by-game stats show goals scored, 1st goals are in red, dash did not score, ⌐ substituted on, ↄ substituted off, blank did not play

Bookings in World Cup qualifying

Played 16
Cards (21Y, 1YR)

Avg make-up (□10 ■25) 14.7

SWEDEN

Profile

Sweden have already defied the odds on numerous occasions to reach Russia and they must do so again if they are to make an impact in their first World Cup finals since 2006.

How they qualified

They upset the purists, eliminating Holland on goal difference – helped by an 8-0 win over Luxembourg in the penultimate round of fixtures – before taking out Italy with a shock 1-0 aggregate playoff success.

The Swedes, who also beat France in qualifying, triumphed in the home leg and then grimly held on for a San Siro shutout, labelled the Miracle of Milan.

The manager

Janne Andersson took over following a disappointing Euro 2016 and was always the frontrunner to replace Erik Hamren after leading IFK Norrkoping to the Swedish Allsvenskan in 2015, one year after keeping them in the top flight by a whisker.

It was a remarkable turnaround given that IFK had only four points from the first four matches of their championship campaign.

The squad

Sweden live up to Scandinavian footballing stereotypes – they are a physical, organised, hard-working, robust bunch in a 4-4-2 using a direct style of play where possession is seen as overrated. Since Zlatan Ibrahimovic retired it's more about the team than individuals.

Marcus Berg top-scored in qualifying with eight goals (four against Luxembourg). His partner is likely to be Ola Toivonen, with John Guidetti another option.

Set-pieces will be key and Sweden have two men capable of a precise delivery in midfielders Emil Forsberg and Seb Larsson, while on the right Krasnodar-based Viktor Claesson is one of the leading assist-makers in the Russian Premier League.

However, Sweden's success will depend

Factfile

FA founded 1904
www svenskfotboll.se
Head coach Janne Andersson
Date qualified November 13, 2017

Strengths

☑ Andersson has fostered a club-like spirit
☑ Good under pressure

Weaknesses

☒ Give away cheap possession
☒ Not much depth to the squad

Star rating ★★☆☆☆

Fixtures

1 June 18, 1pm v South Korea, Nizhny Novgorod
2 June 23, 7pm v Germany, Sochi
3 June 27, 3pm v Mexico, Yekaterinburg

Base Gelendzhik
Total distance 4,500 miles

Emil Fosberg's precise delivery means Sweden will be dangerous at set-pieces

on how well they protect goalkeeper Robin Olsen, who injured his shoulder on club duty but is expected to return in April.

Skipper and centre-back Andreas Granqvist will be 33 when the World Cup starts but he was immense in Milan and his partnership with Victor Lindelof, who has had some shaky moments at Manchester United, will be the platform for Sweden.

Key man

Forsberg took the Bundesliga by storm last season with Leipzig, finishing top of the assists charts with 19 in just 30 matches.

Football has always been in Forsberg's DNA – his grandfather played in the Swedish top flight in the 1950s and his dad Leif 'Foppa' Forsberg is a Sundsvall legend.

Rising star

Lindelof has struggled since becoming the most expensive defender in United's history, although his £30.8m fee is an

indication of his previous form with Benfica.

Wildcard

When Ibrahimovic said 'Zlat's all folks' it seemed impossible that he would return and Andersson was furious when talk surfaced of the veteran forward making an international comeback so soon after qualification.

Ibrahimovic is an iconic figure, voted Sweden's second-greatest sportsman behind Bjorn Borg, and if he hits form at LA Galaxy expect the speculation to continue.

Prospects

Sweden's final group fixture against Mexico could be like a playoff game before the knockouts. They are good under pressure but don't appear to have enough talent to progress too far.

How to back them

Group-stage elimination.

SWEDEN

World Cup record		Group stage(s)						Knockout rounds					
		P	W	D	L	F	A	P	W	D	L	F	A
Uruguay 1930	Did not enter	-	-	-	-	-	-	-	-	-	-	-	-
Italy 1934	Quarter-finals	-	-	-	-	-	-	2	1	0	1	4	4
France 1938	Fourth place	-	-	-	-	-	-	3	1	0	2	11	9
Brazil 1950	Third place	5	2	1	2	11	15	-	-	-	-	-	-
Switzerland 1954	Did not qualify	-	-	-	-	-	-	-	-	-	-	-	-
Sweden 1958	Finalists	3	2	1	0	5	1	3	2	0	1	7	6
Chile 1962	Did not qualify	-	-	-	-	-	-	-	-	-	-	-	-
England 1966	Did not qualify	-	-	-	-	-	-	-	-	-	-	-	-
Mexico 1970	Group stage	3	1	1	1	2	2	-	-	-	-	-	-
Germany 1974	2nd group stage	6	2	2	2	7	6	-	-	-	-	-	-
Argentina 1978	1st group stage	3	0	1	2	1	3	-	-	-	-	-	-
Spain 1982	Did not qualify	-	-	-	-	-	-	-	-	-	-	-	-
Mexico 1986	Did not qualify	-	-	-	-	-	-	-	-	-	-	-	-
Italy 1990	Group stage	3	0	0	3	3	6	-	-	-	-	-	-
USA 1994	Third place	3	1	2	0	6	4	4	2	1	1	8	3
France 1998	Did not qualify	-	-	-	-	-	-	-	-	-	-	-	-
Korea/Japan 2002	Round of 16	3	1	2	0	4	3	1	0	1	0	1	1
Germany 2006	Round of 16	3	1	2	0	3	2	1	0	0	1	0	2
South Africa 2010	Did not qualify	-	-	-	-	-	-	-	-	-	-	-	-
Brazil 2014	Did not qualify	-	-	-	-	-	-	-	-	-	-	-	-
Totals		32	10	12	10	42	42	14	6	2	6	31	25

Continental championships (best perfomance)

Uefa European Championship	Semi-finals (1)	1992

World Cup head-to-heads

Sweden v	P	W	D	L	F	A	Latest
Argentina	2	1	1	0	4	3	2002
Brazil	7	0	2	5	8	21	1994
Costa Rica	1	0	0	1	1	2	1990
Croatia	1	1	0	0	2	1	1974
England	2	0	2	0	3	3	2006
Germany	4	1	0	3	6	9	2006
Mexico	1	1	0	0	3	0	1958
Nigeria	1	1	0	0	2	1	2002
Poland	1	0	0	1	0	1	1974
Russia	2	2	0	0	5	1	1994
Saudi Arabia	1	1	0	0	3	1	1994
Senegal	1	0	1	0	1	1	2002
Serbia	1	1	0	0	2	1	1974
Spain	2	1	0	1	3	2	1978
Uruguay	3	2	0	1	6	3	1974

90 mins only, includes games against Yugoslavia, West Germany and USSR

Photo by Ben Radford/Getty Images

Sweden's most recent World Cup match was a 2-0 defeat by Group F rivals Germany in 2006

How they qualified

Isaac Thelin celebrates as Sweden qualify at Italy's expense

Group A	P	W	D	L	F	A	GD	P
France	10	7	2	1	18	6	12	23
Sweden	10	6	1	3	26	9	17	19
Holland	10	6	1	3	21	12	9	19
Bulgaria	10	4	1	5	14	19	-5	13
Luxembourg	10	1	3	6	8	26	-18	6
Belarus	10	1	2	7	6	21	-15	5

Sweden .... (1) 1-1 (0) ....Holland
Luxembourg... (0) 0-1 (0) ....**Sweden**
Sweden .... (2) 3-0 (0) ....Bulgaria
France .... (0) 2-1 (0) ....**Sweden**
Sweden .... (1) 4-0 (0) .... Belarus
Sweden .... (1) 2-1 (1) ....**France**
Bulgaria .... (2) 3-2 (2) ....**Sweden**
Belarus........... (0) 0-4 (3) ....**Sweden**
Sweden .... (3) 8-0 (0) .... Luxembourg
Holland .... (2) 2-0 (0) ....**Sweden**

Playoffs
Sweden .... (0) 1-0 (0) ....Italy
Italy .... (0) 0-0 (0) ....**Sweden**
Sweden won 1-0 on aggregate

Players used in qualifying

Pos		Club	Age	Career P	G	Qualification P	G		
GK	Robin Olsen	FC Copenhagen	28	16	-	12	-	1	-
DEF	Andreas Granqvist	FK Krasnodar	33	70	6	12	3	1	-
DEF	Emil Krafth	Bologna	23	11	-	4	-	1	-
DEF	Filip Helander	Bologna	25	4	-	1	-	-	-
DEF	Ludwig Augustinsson	Werder Bremen	24	14	-	10	-	-	-
DEF	Martin Olsson	Swansea	30	42	5	3	-	1	-
DEF	Mikael Lustig	Celtic	31	64	6	9	3	3	-
DEF	Oscar Wendt	Mgladbach	32	28	-	2	-	-	-
DEF	Pontus Jansson	Leeds	27	14	-	2	-	-	-
DEF	Victor Lindelof	Man Utd	23	19	1	11	1	1	-
MID	Albin Ekdal	Hamburg	28	32	-	7	-	-	-
MID	Alexander Fransson	Lausanne	24	6	-	2	-	-	-
MID	Emil Forsberg	RB Leipzig	26	34	6	12	4	1	-
MID	Gustav Svensson	Seattle	31	11	-	4	-	-	-
MID	Jakob Johansson	AEK Athens	27	14	1	9	1	1	-
MID	Jimmy Durmaz	Toulouse	29	44	3	8	1	1	-
MID	Marcus Rohden	Crotone	27	10	1	2	-	-	-
MID	Oscar Hiljemark	Genoa	25	20	2	5	1	-	-
MID	Sebastian Larsson	Hull	33	98	6	7	-	-	-
MID	Viktor Claesson	FK Krasnodar	26	21	3	8	-	-	-
ATT	Christoffer Nyman	Braunschweig	25	10	1	3	1	2	-
ATT	Emir Kujovic	F Dusseldorf	29	5	1	1	-	-	-
ATT	Isaac Thelin	W Beveren	25	18	2	7	1	1	-
ATT	John Guidetti	Alaves	26	20	1	5	-	-	-
ATT	Marcus Berg	Al-Ain	31	55	18	11	8	1	-
ATT	Ola Toivonen	Toulouse	31	57	13	10	3	2	-
ATT	Samuel Armenteros	Portland Timbers	28	2	1	1	-	-	-

SWEDEN

Correct scores

	Competitive	Friendly
1-0	2	-
2-0	4	3
2-1	2	-
3-0	1	2
3-1	1	1
3-2	-	1
4-0	2	-
4-1	-	-
4-2	-	-
4-3	-	-
0-0	1	2
1-1	5	3
2-2	1	-
3-3	-	-
4-4	-	-
0-1	3	3
0-2	1	-
1-2	1	3
0-3	-	-
1-3	-	-
2-3	1	-
0-4	-	-
1-4	1	-
2-4	-	-
3-4	-	-
Other	1	1

Since Brazil 2014

Half-time/full-time double results

Win/Win	9	33%	Win 1st half	12	44%
Draw/Win	4	15%	Win 2nd half	12	44%
Lose/Win	0	0%	Win both halves	7	26%
Win/Draw	3	11%	Goal both halves	10	37%
Draw/Draw	3	11%			
Lose/Draw	1	4%	**Overall**		
Win/Lose	0	0%	● Win	48%	
Draw/Lose	4	15%	● Draw	26%	
Lose/Lose	3	11%	● Lose	26%	

Overall: W13, D7, L7 in 27 competitive games since Brazil 2014

Under & over goals

21 (78%)	**Over 1.5**	6 (22%)
✓		✗
11 (41%)	**Over 2.5**	16 (59%)
✓		✗
7 (26%)	**Over 3.5**	20 (74%)
✓		✗
3 (11%)	**Over 4.5**	24 (89%)
✓		✗

Both teams to score

12 (44%)	**Both score**	15 (56%)
✓		✗
3 (11%)	**& win**	24 (89%)
✓		✗
3 (11%)	**& lose**	24 (89%)
✓		✗

In 27 competitive games since Brazil 2014

Clean sheets

11 (41%)	**Clean sheets**	16 (59%)
✓		✗
10 (37%)	**Win to nil**	17 (63%)
✓		✗

5 (19%)	**Fail to score**	22 (81%)
✓		✗
4 (15%)	**Lose to nil**	23 (85%)
✓		✗

When they score

● For ● Against

Total match goals by half

23 (70%)	**1st half**	10 (30%)
F		A
24 (63%)	**2nd half**	14 (37%)
F		A

Goals for & against by half

23 (49%)	**For**	24 (51%)
1st		2nd
10 (42%)	**Against**	14 (58%)
1st		2nd

	0-9	10-18	19-27	28-36	37-45	46-54	55-63	64-72	73-81	82-90
For	1	5	4	2	11	8	6	3	3	4
Against	2	3	0	1	4	1	1	3	5	4

Sweden score first

They win	12	75%
They draw	3	19%
They lose	1	6%

Sweden concede first

They win	1	10%
They draw	3	30%
They lose	6	60%

In 27 competitive games since Brazil 2014

Marcus Berg's eight goals included four at home to Luxembourg
Photo by Nils Petter Nilsson/Ombrello/Getty Images

Top scorers in qualifying

	P	G	1st	AT	%	Swe 1-1 Nld	Lux 0-1 Swe	Swe 3-0 Bgr	Fra 2-1 Swe	Swe 4-0 Blr	Swe 2-1 Fra	Bgr 3-2 Swe	Blr 0-4 Swe	Swe 8-0 Lux	Nld 2-0 Swe	Swe 1-0 Ita	Ita 0-0 Swe
Marcus Berg	11	8	1	5	30	1	-	↺		1	↺	1	1	4	-		↺
Emil Forsberg	12	4	3	3	15	-	-	↺	1	2	-	-	1	-	-	-	-
Mikael Lustig	9	3	1	3	11	-	1			-	-	1	-	1	-		
Ola Toivonen	10	3	1	3	11		↪	1	-	↺	1	-		1	↺	-	↺
Andreas Granqvist	12	3	1	2	11	-	-	-	-	-	-	-	1	2	-	-	-
Christoffer Nyman	3	1	0	1	4	↪	↪							1			
Oscar Hiljemark	5	1	0	1	4	-	-	1	↪	-							
Isaac Thelin	7	1	0	1	4				↺	1				↺	↺	↺	↺
Jimmy Durmaz	8	1	0	1	4	↪	↺	-	↺	↺	1	↺	↺				
Jakob Johansson	9	1	1	1	4				-	↺	-	↺	↺	-	-	1	↺
Victor Lindelof	11	1	0	1	4	-	-	1	-		-	-	-	-	-	-	-

G goals scored, **1st** first match goal (own goals don't count) **AT** goals at any time (ie. number of scoring appearances), **P** penalties, **%** percentage of total team goals scored by each player. Russia 2018 qualifying only. Game-by-game stats show goals scored, 1st goals are in red, dash did not score, ↪ substituted on, ↺ substituted off, blank did not play

Bookings in World Cup qualifying

Played 12 **Cards** (18Y) ☐☐☐☐☐☐☐☐☐☐☐☐☐☐☐☐☐☐ **Avg make-up** (☐10 ■25) 15

Profile

South Korea astonishingly reached the semi-finals on home soil under Guus Hiddink in 2002 but that was an exception in an otherwise poor World Cup record.

Excluding those home games, South Korea have played 24 finals matches, winning just twice and qualifying from the group phase only in 2010.

How they qualified

You have to go back to 1982 for the last time South Korea failed to reach the World Cup but they were in danger of missing out, or at least having to go through the playoffs, before eventually edging past Syria.

The Taeguk Warriors were hopeless on their travels in the final round of qualifying, claiming just two points from five matches, and they failed to score on four of those trips.

The manager

It was not a surprise that Uli Stielike was given the boot, more that it was left until a 3-2 defeat in Qatar with two games to go before the German was replaced by his assistant Shin Tae-Yong, who forced South Korea over the qualification line with goalless draws against Iran and Uzbekistan.

Shin will lead the side in Russia despite calls for Hiddink to return and is promising a more attack-minded approach, something that was evident in his relatively successful spell with South Korea's youth teams. Critics claim Shin is a tinkerman and some suggest that his attempts to be too clever tactically could be his downfall.

The squad

Shin has already used 4-2-3-1, 4-4-2, 4-3-3 and 3-4-3 formations since taking over from Stielike, and it could be that the 2010 Asian Champions League-winning coach will be fluid in his planning depending on the opponents.

There are unlikely to be any Europe-based performers in the defensive positions but

Factfile

FA founded 1933

www kfa.or.kr

Head coach Shin Tae-Yong

Date qualified September 5, 2017

Strengths

☑ Son has become a lethal Champions League-level performer

☑ Their final group match is against Germany, who may well have already qualified

Weaknesses

☒ No kind of form outside of South Korea

☒ Is Shin even close to knowing his best starting 11?

Star rating

Fixtures

1 June 18, 1pm v Sweden, Nizhny Novgorod

2 June 23, 4pm v Mexico, Rostov-on-Don

3 June 27, 3pm v Germany, Kazan

Base Saint Petersburg

Total distance 4,550 miles

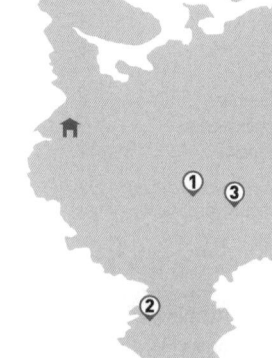

GROUP F

Heung-Min Son provides South Korea's goal threat

there are more obvious qualities further forward, where Swansea's Sung-Yueng Ki is an influential central playmaker alongside Augsburg's Ja-Cheol Koo.

Shin's biggest dilemma is how to get the best from Heung-Min Son. Sonny can be a delight in numerous positions but scored twice in a 2-1 win over Colombia in November as a striker in a 4-4-2.

Key man

If South Korea are to qualify they will need Son to shine bright. He has become a key figure for Tottenham, either on the left flank or as an understudy to Harry Kane, and his speedy dribbles and ability to shoot with either foot make him a dangerous customer.

Rising star

Baker's son Chang-Hoon Kwon has been mustard for Dijon in Ligue 1 this season, cutting in from the right on to his preferred left foot.

In a society which preaches that youngsters should stay in education – much to the annoyance of Stielike – Kwon took the footballing route earlier than most in South Korea and seems to be benefitting from that gamble.

Wildcard

Dong-Gook Lee flopped many moons ago at Middlesbrough but has reached double figures in all nine of his domestic seasons for champions Jeonbuk Motors. He will be 39 by the time of the World Cup but is the most prolific goalscorer in K-League history.

Prospects

An early exit looks likely.

How to back them

Son is their biggest threat by a long way. If Shin builds the side around him he can oblige for favourite backers in the top South Korean goalscorer market.

World Cup record

World Cup record		Group stage(s)						Knockout rounds					
		P	W	D	L	F	A	P	W	D	L	F	A
Uruguay 1930	Did not enter	-	-	-	-	-	-	-	-	-	-	-	-
Italy 1934	Did not enter	-	-	-	-	-	-	-	-	-	-	-	-
France 1938	Did not enter	-	-	-	-	-	-	-	-	-	-	-	-
Brazil 1950	Did not enter	-	-	-	-	-	-	-	-	-	-	-	-
Switzerland 1954	Group stage	2	0	0	2	0	16	-	-	-	-	-	-
Sweden 1958	Entry not accepted	-	-	-	-	-	-	-	-	-	-	-	-
Chile 1962	Did not qualify	-	-	-	-	-	-	-	-	-	-	-	-
England 1966	Did not enter	-	-	-	-	-	-	-	-	-	-	-	-
Mexico 1970	Did not qualify	-	-	-	-	-	-	-	-	-	-	-	-
Germany 1974	Did not qualify	-	-	-	-	-	-	-	-	-	-	-	-
Argentina 1978	Did not qualify	-	-	-	-	-	-	-	-	-	-	-	-
Spain 1982	Did not qualify	-	-	-	-	-	-	-	-	-	-	-	-
Mexico 1986	Group stage	3	0	1	2	4	7	-	-	-	-	-	-
Italy 1990	Group stage	3	0	0	3	1	6	-	-	-	-	-	-
USA 1994	Group stage	3	0	2	1	4	5	-	-	-	-	-	-
France 1998	Group stage	3	0	1	2	2	9	-	-	-	-	-	-
Korea/Japan 2002	Fourth place	3	2	1	0	4	1	4	0	2	2	3	5
Germany 2006	Group stage	3	1	1	1	3	4	-	-	-	-	-	-
South Africa 2010	Round of 16	3	1	1	1	5	6	1	0	0	1	1	2
Brazil 2014	Group stage	3	0	1	2	3	6	-	-	-	-	-	-
Totals		26	4	8	14	26	60	5	0	2	3	4	7

Continental championships (best perfomance)

AFC Asian Cup   Winners (2)   1956, 1960

World Cup head-to-heads

S Korea v	P	W	D	L	F	A	Latest	S Korea v	P	W	D	L	F	A	Latest
Argentina	2	0	0	2	2	7	2010	Poland	1	1	0	0	2	0	2002
Belgium	3	0	1	2	1	4	2014	Portugal	1	1	0	0	1	0	2002
France	1	0	1	0	1	1	2006	Russia	1	0	1	0	1	1	2014
Germany	2	0	0	2	2	4	2002	Spain	3	0	2	1	3	5	2002
Mexico	1	0	0	1	1	3	1998	Switzerland	1	0	0	1	0	2	2006
Nigeria	1	0	1	0	2	2	2010	Uruguay	2	0	0	2	1	3	2010

90 mins only

How they qualified

Round 2

Group G	P	W	D	L	F	A	GD	P
South Korea	8	8	0	0	27	0	27	24
Lebanon	8	3	2	3	12	6	6	11
Kuwait	8	3	1	4	12	10	2	10
Myanmar	8	2	2	4	9	21	-12	8
Laos	8	1	1	6	29	-23	4

Myanmar........ (0) 0-2 (1)... **South Korea**
South Korea (3) 8-0 (0)................Laos
Lebanon........ (0) 0-3 (2)... **South Korea**
Kuwait .... (0) 0-1 (1)... **South Korea**

South Korea (2) 4-0 (0)........ Myanmar
Laos .... (0) 0-5 (4)... **South Korea**
South Korea (0) 1-0 (0).......... Lebanon
South Korea.... P-P ....Kuwait
   Match awarded 3-0 to South Korea

Round 3

Group A	P	W	D	L	F	A	GD	P
Iran	10	6	4	0	10	2	8	22
South Korea	10	4	3	3	11	10	1	15
Syria	10	3	4	3	9	8	1	13
Uzbekistan	10	4	1	5	6	7	-1	13
China	10	3	3	4	8	10	-2	12
Qatar	10	2	1	7	8	15	-7	7

South Korea.. (1) 3-2 (0).............. China
Syria .... (0) 0-0 (0)... **South Korea**
South Korea.. (1) 3-2 (2).............. Qatar
Iran................. (1) 1-0 (0)... **South Korea**
South Korea.. (0) 2-1 (1)...... Uzbekistan
China............... (1) 1-0 (0)... **South Korea**
South Korea.. (1) 1-0 (0)................ Syria
Qatar............... (1) 3-2 (0)... **South Korea**
South Korea.. (0) 0-0 (0)................ Iran
Uzbekistan..... (0) 0-0 (0)... **South Korea**

▶▶ Full qualifying results on
pages 228-241

Players used in qualifying		Career			Qualification				
Pos	Club	Age	P	G	P	G	□	■	
GK Sung-Ryong Jung	Kawasaki F	33	67	-	1	-	-	-	
GK Jin-Hyeon Kim	Cerezo Osaka	30	14	-	1	-	-	-	
GK Seung-Gyu Kim	Vissel Kobe	27	31	-	10	-	-	-	
GK Sun-Tae Kwoun	Kashima Antlers	33	6	-	5	-	1	-	
DEF Chul-Soon Choi	Jeonbuk Motors	31	11	-	3	-	2	-	
DEF Jeong-Ho Hong	Jeonbuk Motors	28	43	2	5	1	1	1	
DEF Hyun-Soo Jang	FC Tokyo	26	49	3	16	2	1	-	
DEF Dong-Ho Jeong	Ulsan Hyundai	27	5	-	1	-	-	-	
DEF Chang-Soo Kim	Ulsan Hyundai	32	26	-	3	-	-	-	
DEF Jin-Su Kim	Jeonbuk Motors	26	35	-	9	-	-	-	
DEF Ju-Young Kim	Hebei CFFC	29	10	-	1	-	-	-	
DEF Ki-Hee Kim	Seattle	28	23	-	6	-	-	-	
DEF Min-Woo Kim	Sangju Sangmu	28	16	1	1	-	-	-	
DEF Young-Gwon Kim	Guangzhou Ev	28	50	2	8	-	3	-	
DEF Yo-Han Ko	FC Seoul	29	18	-	1	-	-	-	
DEF Tae-Hwi Kwak	FC Seoul	36	59	5	9	-	-	-	
DEF Yong Lee	Jeonbuk Motors	31	24	-	2	-	-	-	
DEF Jae-Suk Oh	Gamba Osaka	28	4	-	3	-	2	-	
DEF Joo-Ho Park	Ulsan Hyundai	31	34	-	3	-	-	-	
DEF Chang-Woo Lim	Al-Wahda	26	6	-	1	-	-	-	
DEF Young-Sun Yun	Sangju Sangmu	29	4	-	1	-	-	-	
DEF Chul Hong	Suwon Bluewings	27	14	-	4	-	-	-	
DEF Min-Jae Kim	Jeonbuk Motors	21	7	-	2	-	-	-	
MID Il-Su Hwang	Ulsan Hyundai	30	4	-	1	-	-	-	
MID Sung-Yueng Ki	Swansea	29	101	10	14	4	1	-	
MID Bo-Kyung Kim	Kashiwa Reysol	28	37	4	2	-	-	-	
MID Chung-Yong Lee	Crystal Palace	29	79	8	8	2	-	-	
MID Kook-Young Han	Gangwon	28	41	-	9	-	1	-	
MID Yong-Joon Heo	Jeonnam Dragons	25	1	-	1	-	-	-	
MID Dong-Won Ji	Augsburg	27	48	11	9	1	2	-	
MID Woo-Young Jung	Vissel Kobe	28	26	1	8	-	2	-	
MID Myong-Jin Koh	Al-Rayyan	30	5	-	2	-	-	-	
MID Jae-Sung Lee	Jeonbuk Motors	25	31	5	12	3	-	-	
MID Tae-Hee Nam	Al-Duhail	26	38	4	8	2	-	-	
MID Ki-Hun Yeom	Suwon Bluewings	35	56	5	2	-	-	-	
MID Ja-Cheol Koo	Augsburg	29	66	19	13	4	2	-	
ATT Heung-Min Son	Tottenham	25	64	20	12	7	2	-	
ATT Ui-Jo Hwang	Gamba Osaka	25	11	1	5	-	-	-	
ATT Shin-Wook Kim	Jeonbuk Motors	30	45	10	5	-	1	-	
ATT Chang-Hoon Kwon	Dijon	23	15	4	6	3	-	-	
ATT Dong-Gook Lee	Jeonbuk Motors	39	107	33	2	-	-	-	
ATT Jeong-Hyeop Lee	Shonan Bellmare	26	20	5	5	1	-	-	
ATT Keun-Ho Lee	Gangwon	33	86	19	2	-	-	-	
ATT Yong-Jae Lee	Fagiano Okayama	26	4	1	1	-	-	-	
ATT Hee-Chan Hwang	RB Salzburg	22	11	2	7	1	-	-	
ATT Jun-Suk Hyun	Troyes	26	11	4	7	2	2	-	

Correct scores

	Competitive	Friendly
1-0	7	5
2-0	3	3
2-1	1	2
3-0	1	2
3-1	-	1
3-2	2	-
4-0	1	-
4-1	1	-
4-2	-	-
4-3	-	-
0-0	5	1
1-1	2	2
2-2	1	1
3-3	-	-
4-4	-	-
0-1	2	2
0-2	-	-
1-2	-	1
0-3	-	-
1-3	-	2
2-3	1	1
0-4	-	-
1-4	-	-
2-4	-	1
3-4	-	-
Other	2	1

Since Brazil 2014

Half-time/full-time double results

Win/Win	14	48%	Win 1st half	15	52%
Draw/Win	2	7%	Win 2nd half	13	45%
Lose/Win	2	7%	Win both halves	8	28%
Win/Draw	1	3%	Goal both halves	10	34%
Draw/Draw	6	21%			
Lose/Draw	1	3%	**Overall**		
Win/Lose	0	0%	● Win	62%	
Draw/Lose	0	0%	● Draw	28%	
Lose/Lose	3	10%	● Lose	10%	

Overall: W18, D8, L3 in 29 competitive games since Brazil 2014

Under & over goals

15 (52%) **Over 1.5** 14 (48%)
✓ ✗

10 (34%) **Over 2.5** 19 (66%)
✓ ✗

8 (28%) **Over 3.5** 21 (72%)
✓ ✗

6 (21%) **Over 4.5** 23 (79%)
✓ ✗

Both teams to score

8 (28%) **Both score** 21 (72%)
✓ ✗

4 (14%) **& win** 25 (86%)
✓ ✗

1 (3%) **& lose** 28 (97%)
✓ ✗

In 29 competitive games since Brazil 2014

Clean sheets

19 (66%) **Clean sheets** 10 (34%)
✓ ✗

14 (48%) **Win to nil** 15 (52%)
✓ ✗

7 (24%) **Fail to score** 22 (76%)
✓ ✗

2 (7%) **Lose to nil** 27 (93%)
✓ ✗

When they score

● For ● Against

Total match goals by half

27 (73%) **1st half** 10 (27%)
F A

24 (83%) **2nd half** 5 (17%)
F A

2	7	7	8	3	1	7	7	2	7
0-9	10-18	19-27	28-36	37-45	46-54	55-63	64-72	73-81	82-90
2	1	3	1	3	1	0	0	4	0

Goals for & against by half

27 (53%) **For** 24 (47%)
1st 2nd

10 (67%) **Against** 5 (33%)
1st 2nd

South Korea score first

They win	16	94%
They draw	1	6%
They lose	0	0%

South Korea concede first

They win	2	29%
They draw	2	29%
They lose	3	43%

In 29 competitive games since Brazil 2014

Chang-Hoon Kwon's three goals came in the easier first stage, but he's been red hot for Dijon

Top scorers in qualifying

	P	G	1st	AT	%	Mmr 0-2 Kor	Kor 8-0 Lao	Lbn 0-3 Kor	Kwt 0-1 Kor	Kor 4-0 Mmr	Lao 0-5 Kor	Kor 1-0 Lbn	Kor 3-2 Chn	Syr 0-0 Kor	Kor 3-2 Qat	Irn 1-0 Kor	Kor 2-1 Uzb	Chn 1-0 Kor	Kor 1-0 Syr	Qat 3-2 Kor	Kor 0-0 Irn	Uzb 0-0 Kor
Heung-Min Son	12	7	0	4	20	1	3		↺	2	↺	↷1	-	-	-	-	↺	-	-
Ja-Cheol Koo	13	4	1	4	11		↺	1	↷1		↺	↷1	↺	↺	↺	1	-	↺	-	↺
Sung-Yueng Ki	14	4	2	3	11	-	-	-	-	2	-	-	-	1	-	-	-	-	1
Chang-Hoon Kwon	6	3	0	2	9	2	1			↺				↺					-	↺
Jae-Sung Lee	12	3	2	3	9	1	↷1	↺	↺	↷1	-	↺	↺	↺		↺		-	↺
Jun-Suk Hyun	7	2	0	2	6	↷1	↺	↺	↺	↷1	↺		↺						
Chung-Yong Lee	8	2	2	2	6	↺	↷1	-			↺	-	↷1	-		↺			
Tae-Hee Nam	8	2	0	2	6			↺	↷1	↺	↺				1	↺	-	↺	
Hyun-Soo Jang	16	2	1	2	6	-	-	↷1	-	1		-	-	-	-	-	-	-	-	↺
Jeong-Hyeop Lee	5	1	1	1	3	↺			↷1					↺	↺	↺	
Jeong-Ho Hong	5	1	1	1	3	-					-		-			-	1
Hee-Chan Hwang	7	1	0	1	3			↺	↺			↺	↺	1	↺	-
Dong-Won Ji	9	1	0	1	3	↺	-		-	-	1	-	↺	-		↺

G goals scored, **1st** first match goal (own goals don't count) **AT** goals at any time (ie. number of scoring appearances), **P** penalties, **%** percentage of total team goals scored by each player. Russia 2018 qualifying only. Game-by-game stats show goals scored, 1st goals are in red, dash did not score, ↳ substituted on, ↺ substituted off, blank did not play

Bookings in World Cup qualifying

Played 17

Cards (23Y, 1YR)

Avg make-up (☐10 ■25) 15

Attacking class can make the difference for Belgium

Goal difference is the first criteria used in the World Cup to separate teams level on points and that is one reason why Belgium can overcome England to top spot in Group G, *writes Mark Langdon*.

Something will have to go horribly wrong for the two big European nations to miss out on qualification against Tunisia and Panama and it would not be a big surprise should England take on Belgium in Kaliningrad on June 28 with both sides already through to the last 16.

However, Belgium showed in qualifying with a goal difference of +37 compared to England's +15 that they are far better at putting weaker opponents to the sword and the Red Devils should be in pole position for top spot heading into the final round of games.

Roberto Martinez's lack of tactical nous could hinder Belgium in the knockout rounds but the sheer ability of their forward players makes the Red Devils a dangerous outfit with Romelu Lukaku, Eden Hazard and Kevin De Bruyne in the ranks.

There is also more scope for Martinez to rotate without weakening the team – Dries Mertens and Mousa Dembele, players who would walk into the England starting 11, are not guaranteed to make

Photo by Dean Mouhtaropoulos/Getty Images

Belgium can fill their boots against Group G's weaker sides

Belgium's opener with Panama.

Belgium have a more settled look than England with Gareth Southgate still pondering many positions, except up front where Harry Kane could take the Three Lions a long way almost on his own.

Kane does not always get fantastic service, however, from a side who will offer a counter-attacking threat but lack the creativity to open up the type of packed defences set to be provided by Tunisia and Panama.

On paper Tunisia is a soft start for England but, given they failed to beat Russia, Slovakia and Iceland at Euro 2016, it could be a nervy 90 minutes. England collected one point at the last World Cup and in 2010 failed to beat Algeria and USA.

Buckling under pressure in major tournaments is a concern for England supporters and with any kind of victory likely to be greeted with huge relief, boosting the goal difference will be way down the list of priorities.

Tunisia can pip Panama to third place with the debutants rightly considered wooden spoon favourites.

Recommendation

☆☆☆ ☆☆ **Belgium to win Group G**

Group-stage performances since France 98

	Pot	P	W	Q	1998 Group	Pos	2002 Group	Pos	2006 Group	Pos	2010 Group	Pos	2014 Group	Pos
Belgium	1	3	1	2	E	3	H	2	-	-	-	-	**H**	**1**
England	2	5	1	4	G	2	F	2	**B**	**1**	C	2	D	4
Tunisia	3	3	0	0	G	4	H	4	H	3	-	-	-	-
Panama	4	0	0	0	-	-	-	-	-	-	-	-	-	-

To win Group G
Win only

	Bet365	BtBrt	Betfair	Btfrd	Btwy	Boyle	Coral	Hills	Lads	P Power	Sky	188
Belgium	**5-6**	4-5	3-4	4-5	**5-6**	**5-6**	**5-6**	**5-6**	4-5	8-11	8-11	4-5
England	6-5	6-5	23-20	**5-4**	23-20	6-5	6-5	6-5	**5-4**	6-5	**5-4**	5-4
Tunisia	14	16	**20**	12	16	16	16	14	14	**20**	**20**	10
Panama	**40**	33	25	25	**40**	33	25	20	28	25	33	30

Belgium v Panama
4pm, Monday June 18, BBC

	Bet365	BtBrt	Betfair	Btfrd	Btwy	Boyle	Coral	Hills	Lads	P Power	Sky	188
Belgium	2-11	1-6	**1-4**	2-11	2-11	1-6	2-11	1-6	2-11	1-5	1-5	1-5
Draw	**6**	5	9-2	5	11-2	9-2	5	11-2	5	5	5	28-5
Panama	12	12	15	**16**	14	12	**16**	14	**16**	12	**16**	14

Tunisia v England
7pm, Monday June 18, BBC

	Bet365	BtBrt	Betfair	Btfrd	Btwy	Boyle	Coral	Hills	Lads	P Power	Sky	188
England	1-3	3-10	4-11	1-3	1-3	1-3	3-10	3-10	3-10	**2-5**	4-11	6-17
Draw	**4**	7-2	**4**	19-5	15-4	16-5	18-5	**4**	18-5	10-3	18-5	**4**
Tunisia	8	15-2	15-2	8	8	15-2	**9**	8	**9**	7	17-2	8

Belgium v Tunisia
1pm, Saturday June 23, BBC

	Bet365	BtBrt	Betfair	Btfrd	Btwy	Boyle	Coral	Hills	Lads	P Power	Sky	188
Belgium	3-10	1-4	**4-11**	2-7	2-7	1-4	2-7	1-4	2-7	3-10	3-10	5-18
Draw	4	4	15-4	4	17-4	15-4	4	**9-2**	4	7-2	17-4	**9-2**
Tunisia	9	9	9	10	9	17-2	**11**	9	**11**	15-2	9	10

England v Panama
1pm, Sunday June 24, BBC

	Bet365	BtBrt	Betfair	Btfrd	Btwy	Boyle	Coral	Hills	Lads	P Power	Sky	188
England	1-4	1-5	**3-10**	2-9	1-4	2-9	1-4	2-9	1-4	2-7	1-4	1-4
Draw	9-2	9-2	4	9-2	9-2	4	21-5	9-2	21-5	7-2	9-2	**24-5**
Panama	11	11	13	12	10	11	**14**	11	**14**	11	12	23-2

England v Belgium
7pm, Thursday June 28, ITV

	Bet365	BtBrt	Betfair	Btfrd	Btwy	Boyle	Coral	Hills	Lads	P Power	Sky
Belgium	6-4	7-5	6-4	6-4	7-5	11-8	7-5	**13-8**	7-5	7-5	6-4
England	15-8	7-4	**21-10**	7-4	7-4	7-4	17-10	15-8	17-10	15-8	19-10
Draw	11-5	2	21-10	21-10	21-10	21-10	**9-4**	2	**9-4**	2	21-10

Panama v Tunisia
7pm, Thursday June 28, ITV

	Bet365	BetBright	Betfair	Betfred	Betway	Boyle	Hills	P Power	Sky Bet
Tunisia	13-10	6-5	**7-5**	5-4	23-20	6-5	13-10	13-10	5-4
Draw	**21-10**	2	**21-10**	**21-10**	**21-10**	2	**21-10**	2	**21-10**
Panama	23-10	9-4	11-5	9-4	11-5	21-10	11-5	2	**12-5**

Prices correct March 28 2018

Profile

The history of international football is littered with golden generations who are destined for greatness only to come up short, and Belgium look next in line.

After quarter-final appearances at the last two major tournaments now is the time for the Red Devils to deliver.

How they qualified

Belgium made short work of a comfortable group, becoming the first European nation to qualify.

Along with Germany they broke the record for goals scored with 43, finishing with a goal difference of +37, with their only dropped points coming in a draw with Greece.

The manager

Roberto Martinez was seen to have lucked out to get this gig following his departure from Everton having previously managed Wigan to FA Cup glory and Premier League relegation in the same season.

Martinez teams usually play attractive football but Belgian journalist Kristof Terreur, writing in the Guardian, commented: "The main problem with Martinez is there is still no real defensive organisation."

That will sound familiar to anyone who has seen Martinez's teams but he is still an upgrade on the woeful Marc Wilmots.

The squad

Martinez seems settled on a 3-4-3 or 3-4-2-1 formation which enables Belgium to field many of their wonderful attacking talents. It is possible to select Romelu Lukaku as the central striker with Eden Hazard and Dries Mertens either side in a three, or centrally as a pair behind the Manchester United forward.

Kevin De Bruyne would then play in a central midfield two, probably alongside Axel Witsel, although the Manchester City man could also be selected in a more

Factfile

FA founded 1895

www belgianfootball.be

Head coach Roberto Martinez

Date qualified September 3, 2017

Strengths
- ☑ Goals won't be a problem with so many attacking threats
- ☑ Alderweireld, De Bruyne and Hazard are genuine world-class talents

Weaknesses
- ☒ Martinez's tactical nous is open to debate
- ☒ Unbalanced squad which lacks depth at centre-back and wing-back

Star rating ★★★★☆

Fixtures

1 June 18, 4pm v Panama, Sochi

2 June 23, 1pm v Tunisia, Otkrytie Arena, Moscow

3 June 28, 7pm v England, Kaliningrad

Base Moscow

Total distance 3,050 miles

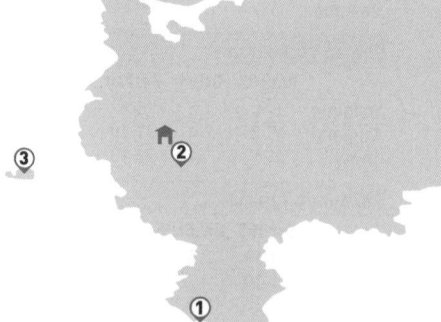

GROUP G

Kevin De Bruyne has enjoyed an outstanding season

advanced role should Mertens' inclusion be seen as one forward too many.

Mousa Dembele, Radja Nainggolan and Marouane Fellaini are also midfield options.

If fit, the back three of Jan Vertonghen, Toby Alderweireld and Vincent Kompany picks itself, while Thomas Meunier and Yannick Carrasco are favourites to fill the wing-back positions despite a lack of action for their clubs. Carrasco has since moved to China from Atletico for money and minutes.

Goalkeeper Thibaut Courtois is the undisputed number one.

Key man

De Bruyne and Hazard are world-class talents and the extent to which Martinez can get them to deliver their club form in Russia could well determine Belgium's fate.

Rising star

Leander Dendoncker, one of the few in Martinez's squad still playing in Belgium,

is likely to be the next cab off the rank.

The tall, adaptable Anderlecht man can play as a defensive midfielder or centre-back, positions where Belgium lack depth.

Wildcard

Nainggolan and Martinez have a rocky relationship and the combustible Roma midfielder briefly quit international football after being dropped from the August 2017 squad. Nainggolan makes the squad stronger but he may put Martinez's man-management skills to the test.

Prospects

An absolute stroll to the quarter-finals where Brazil are likely to be waiting. Belgium are comfortably the best side at double-figure odds and worthy of consideration.

How to back them

Quotes of 4-6 to reach the last eight should be snapped up.

World Cup record

World Cup record		Group stage(s)						Knockout rounds					
		P	W	D	L	F	A	P	W	D	L	F	A
Uruguay 1930	Group stage	2	0	0	2	0	4	-	-	-	-	-	-
Italy 1934	First round	-	-	-	-	-	-	1	0	0	1	2	5
France 1938	First round	-	-	-	-	-	-	1	0	0	1	1	3
Brazil 1950	Withdrew	-	-	-	-	-	-	-	-	-	-	-	-
Switzerland 1954	Group stage	2	0	1	1	4	7	-	-	-	-	-	-
Sweden 1958	Did not qualify	-	-	-	-	-	-	-	-	-	-	-	-
Chile 1962	Did not qualify	-	-	-	-	-	-	-	-	-	-	-	-
England 1966	Did not qualify	-	-	-	-	-	-	-	-	-	-	-	-
Mexico 1970	Group stage	3	1	0	2	4	5	-	-	-	-	-	-
Germany 1974	Did not qualify	-	-	-	-	-	-	-	-	-	-	-	-
Argentina 1978	Did not qualify	-	-	-	-	-	-	-	-	-	-	-	-
Spain 1982	2nd group stage	5	2	1	2	3	5	-	-	-	-	-	-
Mexico 1986	Fourth place	3	1	1	1	5	5	4	0	3	1	5	7
Italy 1990	Round of 16	3	2	0	1	6	3	1	0	1	0	0	0
USA 1994	Round of 16	3	2	0	1	2	1	1	0	0	1	2	3
France 1998	Group stage	3	0	3	0	3	3	-	-	-	-	-	-
Korea/Japan 2002	Round of 16	3	1	2	0	6	5	1	0	0	1	0	2
Germany 2006	Did not qualify	-	-	-	-	-	-	-	-	-	-	-	-
South Africa 2010	Did not qualify	-	-	-	-	-	-	-	-	-	-	-	-
Brazil 2014	Quarter-finals	3	3	0	0	4	1	2	0	1	1	0	1
Totals		30	12	8	10	37	39	11	0	5	6	10	21

Continental championships (best perfomance)

Uefa European Championship	Beaten finalists (1)	1980

World Cup head-to-heads

Belgium v	P	W	D	L	F	A	Latest	Belgium v	P	W	D	L	F	A	Latest
Argentina	3	1	0	2	1	3	2014	Poland	1	0	0	1	0	3	1982
Brazil	1	0	0	1	0	2	2002	Russia	5	2	1	2	7	9	2014
England	2	0	2	0	3	3	1990	Saudi Arabia	1	0	0	1	0	1	1994
France	2	0	1	1	3	5	1986	South Korea	3	2	1	0	4	1	2014
Germany	2	0	0	2	4	8	1994	Spain	2	0	1	1	2	3	1990
Japan	1	0	1	0	2	2	2002	Tunisia	1	0	1	0	1	1	2002
Mexico	3	0	1	2	3	5	1998	Uruguay	1	1	0	0	3	1	1990
Morocco	1	1	0	0	1	0	1994								

90 mins only, includes games against USSR

How they qualified

Group H	P	W	D	L	F	A	GD	P
Belgium	10	9	1	0	43	6	37	28
Greece	10	5	4	1	17	6	11	19
Bosnia-Hz	10	5	2	3	24	13	11	17
Estonia	10	3	2	5	13	19	-6	11
Cyprus	10	3	1	6	9	18	-9	10
Gibraltar	10	0	0	10	3	47	-44	0

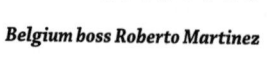

Belgium boss Roberto Martinez

Cyprus............ (0) 0-3 (1)............ **Belgium**
Belgium........ (2) 4-0 (0)........ Bosnia-Hz
Gibraltar......... (0) 0-6 (3).......... **Belgium**
Belgium........ (3) 8-1 (1)............ Estonia
Belgium........ (0) 1-1 (0)............ Greece
Estonia............ (0) 0-2 (1)........... **Belgium**
Belgium........ (6) 9-0 (0)........ Gibraltar
Greece............. (0) 1-2 (0).......... **Belgium**
Bosnia-Hz........ (2) 3-4 (1).......... **Belgium**
Belgium........ (1) 4-0 (0)............ Cyprus

Eden Hazard delivers a corner kick during Belgium's 9-0 qualifying win over Gibraltar

Players used in qualifying		Career			Qualification			
Pos	Club	Age	P	G	P	G	□	■
GK Thibaut Courtois	Chelsea	26	55	-	10	-	-	-
DEF Jan Vertonghen	Tottenham	31	99	8	10	2	-	-
DEF Jordan Lukaku	Lazio	23	8	-	1	-	-	-
DEF Laurent Ciman	Los Angeles	32	19	1	5	-	-	-
DEF Thomas Meunier	Paris St-Germain	26	22	5	8	5	1	-
DEF Thomas Vermaelen	Barcelona	32	66	1	3	-	1	-
DEF Toby Alderweireld	Tottenham	29	74	3	9	1	-	-
DEF Vincent Kompany	Man City	32	76	4	2	-	-	-
MID Axel Witsel	Tianjin Quanjian	29	88	9	8	2	1	1
MID Eden Hazard	Chelsea	27	83	21	8	6	-	-
MID Kevin De Bruyne	Man City	26	59	14	7	-	1	-
MID Leander Dendoncker	Anderlecht	22	4	-	3	-	-	-
MID Marouane Fellaini	Man Utd	30	80	16	6	-	3	-
MID Mousa Dembele	Tottenham	30	74	5	3	-	1	-
MID Nacer Chadli	West Brom	28	42	5	6	1	-	-
MID Radja Nainggolan	Roma	30	30	6	2	-	-	-
MID Steven Defour	Burnley	30	52	2	1	-	-	-
MID Thorgan Hazard	Mgladbach	25	8	1	2	1	-	-
MID Timmy Simons	Club Brugge	41	94	6	1	-	-	-
MID Yannick F-Carrasco	Dalian Yifang	24	23	5	9	3	2	-
MID Youri Tielemans	Monaco	21	8	-	4	-	-	-
ATT Christian Benteke	Crystal Palace	27	33	12	2	3	-	-
ATT Dries Mertens	Napoli	31	66	13	9	5	1	-
ATT Kevin Mirallas	Everton	30	60	10	4	-	-	-
ATT Romelu Lukaku	Man Utd	25	66	33	8	11	1	-
ATT Michy Batshuayi	Bor Dortmund	24	14	6	5	1	1	-

Correct scores

	Competitive	Friendly
1-0	3	1
2-0	1	1
2-1	1	2
3-0	2	-
3-1	2	2
3-2	-	1
4-0	3	1
4-1	1	-
4-2	-	-
4-3	1	1
0-0	1	-
1-1	2	2
2-2	-	-
3-3	-	2
4-4	-	-
0-1	1	-
0-2	1	1
1-2	-	1
0-3	-	-
1-3	1	-
2-3	-	-
0-4	-	-
1-4	-	-
2-4	-	-
3-4	-	-
Other	5	-

Since Brazil 2014

Half-time/full-time double results

Win/Win	13	52%	Win 1st half	13	52%
Draw/Win	5	20%	Win 2nd half	19	76%
Lose/Win	1	4%	Win both halves	12	48%
Win/Draw	0	0%	Goal both halves	13	52%
Draw/Draw	2	8%			
Lose/Draw	1	4%	Overall		
Win/Lose	0	0%	● Win	76%	
Draw/Lose	1	4%	● Draw	12%	
Lose/Lose	2	8%	● Lose	12%	

Overall: W19, D3, L3 in 25 competitive games since Brazil 2014

Under & over goals

20 (80%)	Over 1.5	5 (20%)
16 (64%)	Over 2.5	9 (36%)
13 (52%)	Over 3.5	12 (48%)
7 (28%)	Over 4.5	18 (72%)

Both teams to score

9 (36%)	Both score	16 (64%)
6 (24%)	& win	19 (76%)
1 (4%)	& lose	24 (96%)

In 25 competitive games since Brazil 2014

Clean sheets

14 (56%)	Clean sheets	11 (44%)
13 (52%)	Win to nil	12 (48%)
3 (12%)	Fail to score	22 (88%)
2 (8%)	Lose to nil	23 (92%)

When they score

● For ● Against

Total match goals by half

30 (79%)	1st half	8 (21%)
F		A
46 (85%)	2nd half	8 (15%)
F		A

Goals for & against by half

30 (39%)	For	46 (61%)
1st		2nd
8 (50%)	Against	8 (50%)
1st		2nd

4	7	8	5	6	4	10	12	10	10
0-9	10-18	19-27	28-36	37-45	46-54	55-63	64-72	73-81	82-90
0	1	1	5	1	2	1	0	1	4

Belgium score first

They win	18	95%
They draw	0	0%
They lose	1	5%

Belgium concede first

They win	1	20%
They draw	2	40%
They lose	2	40%

In 25 competitive games since Brazil 2014

Only Lewandowksi and Ronaldo scored more than Romelu Lukaku in European qualifying

Top scorers in qualifying

	P	G	1st	AT	%	Cyp 0-3 Bel	Bel 4-0 Bos	Gib 0-6 Bel	Bel 8-1 Est	Bel 1-1 Grc	Est 0-2 Bel	Bel 9-0 Gib	Grc 1-2 Bel	Bos 3-4 Bel	Bel 4-0 Cyp
Romelu Lukaku	8	11	1	7	26	2	1	-	2	1	-	3	1		1
Eden Hazard	8	6	2	5	14	-	1	1	1			1	↳	-	2
Thomas Meunier	8	5	2	3	12	-	-	-	1			3	-	1	↺
Dries Mertens	9	5	2	4	12		-	1	2	-	1	1	-	↺	↳
Christian Benteke	2	3	1	1	7	↳	3								
Yannick F-Carrasco	9	3	0	3	7	1	-	↺	1	-	-	-	↺	1
Axel Witsel	8	2	0	2	5	-	-	1	↺	-	-	1			-
Jan Vertonghen	10	2	1	2	5	-	-	-	-	-	-	-	1	1	-
Thorgan Hazard	2	1	0	1	2							↳			1
Michy Batshuayi	5	1	0	1	2	↳		↳			↳			1	↺
Nacer Chadli	6	1	0	1	2		↳			-	1		↳	↳	-
Toby Alderweireld	9	1	0	1	2	-	1		-	-	-	-	-	-	-

G goals scored, **1st** first match goal (own goals don't count) **AT** goals at any time (ie. number of scoring appearances), **P** penalties, **%** percentage of total team goals scored by each player. Russia 2018 qualifying only. Game-by-game stats show goals scored, 1st goals are in red, dash did not score, ↳ substituted on, ↺ substituted off, blank did not play

Bookings in World Cup qualifying

Played 10 **Cards** (13Y, 1R) ▯▯▯▯▯▯▯▯▯▯▯▯▯ ▮ **Avg make-up** (▯10 ▮25) 15.5

Profile

A national holiday was declared when Panama won a spot at the World Cup finals for the first time and a country which used to consider football behind more popular sports such as boxing, basketball and baseball has fallen in love with the beautiful game.

How they qualified

It was the most dramatic of finishes of any region as Panama, who had barely been in an automatic qualifying spot throughout the final Concacaf hexagon campaign, suddenly leaped into the top three with two minutes remaining as Roman Torres's goal against Costa Rica combined with USA's surprise loss away to Trinidad & Tobago saw a nation go wild.

Panama won only three of their ten matches and finished with a goal difference of minus one. Their equalising goal against Costa Rica on that dramatic October evening "scored" by Blas Perez was actually a ghost goal that failed to cross the line.

There was sadness too as midfielder Amilcar Henriquez, 33, was killed in April 2017 after being shot outside his home.

The manager

Hernan Dario Gomez has previously led both Colombia (1998), his home nation, and Ecuador (2002) to the World Cup. He claimed he nearly quit management following the 2015 Concacaf Gold Cup semi-final loss to Mexico, a game that included controversial refereeing decisions.

Gomez, nicknamed El Bolillo (The Truncheon), was forced to quit his job as Colombia manager second time around in 2011 after sponsors and politicians demanded his removal once it was revealed he had punched a woman outside a bar.

The squad

Ageing in parts but not short of heart, Panama will hope their determination in a 4-4-2 formation can keep them

Factfile

FA founded 1937
www fepafut.com
Head coach Hernan Dario Gomez
Date qualified October 10, 2017

Strengths

☑ Never-say-die spirit
☑ Coach Gomez gained a win for debutants Ecuador over Croatia in 2002

Weaknesses

☒ General lack of quality and exposure at this level
☒ Could be four years too late for some of their key men

Star rating ★☆☆☆☆

Fixtures

1 June 18, 4pm v Belgium, Sochi
2 June 24, 1pm v England, Nizhny Novgorod
3 June 28, 7pm v Tunisia, Saransk

Base Saransk
Total distance 1,850 miles

Centre-back Roman Torres has a habit of popping up and scoring crucial goals

competitive in the fixtures against Belgium and England before a more winnable contest with Tunisia last up.

Perez, 37 and a stalwart of over 100 caps and nearly as many different club sides, is the definition of a much-travelled journeyman forward who should partner Chilean-based Gabriel Torres in attack, while the midfield is full of grafters with Alberto Quintero the one asked to create.

Midfield anchor Gabriel Gomez, who will be 34 by the time the World Cup starts, organises those around him and won't venture too far away from centre-backs Roman Torres and 37-year-old Felipe Baloy.

Dinamo Bucharest goalie Jaime Penedo is one of the few to ply his trade in Europe.

Key man

Roman Torres is the man for the big occasion. The centre-back scored the goal which earned Panama a World Cup spot – there is talk of naming the stadium after him – and he also notched the winning spot kick in the 2016 MLS Cup to earn

Seattle Sounders their only championship.

Rising star

Fidel Escobar headed to Sporting after catching the eye with his performances at the Under-20 World Cup in 2015, where he scored a late equaliser against Argentina. The centre-back is now with New York Red Bulls.

Wildcard

Winger Ismael Diaz was picked up by Porto in 2015 and initially did some damage for their B side. He has since moved to Spain where he has scored at a decent rate for Deportivo Fabril (Deportivo La Coruna's B team).

Prospects

Bleak.

How to back them

To collect no points – they scored only nine times in ten matches in the final round of qualifying.

World Cup record		Group stage(s)						Knockout rounds					
		P	W	D	L	F	A	P	W	D	L	F	A
Uruguay 1930	Did not enter	-	-	-	-	-	-	-	-	-	-	-	-
Italy 1934	Did not enter	-	-	-	-	-	-	-	-	-	-	-	-
France 1938	Did not enter	-	-	-	-	-	-	-	-	-	-	-	-
Brazil 1950	Did not enter	-	-	-	-	-	-	-	-	-	-	-	-
Switzerland 1954	Did not enter	-	-	-	-	-	-	-	-	-	-	-	-
Sweden 1958	Did not enter	-	-	-	-	-	-	-	-	-	-	-	-
Chile 1962	Did not enter	-	-	-	-	-	-	-	-	-	-	-	-
England 1966	Did not enter	-	-	-	-	-	-	-	-	-	-	-	-
Mexico 1970	Did not enter	-	-	-	-	-	-	-	-	-	-	-	-
Germany 1974	Did not enter	-	-	-	-	-	-	-	-	-	-	-	-
Argentina 1978	Did not qualify	-	-	-	-	-	-	-	-	-	-	-	-
Spain 1982	Did not qualify	-	-	-	-	-	-	-	-	-	-	-	-
Mexico 1986	Did not qualify	-	-	-	-	-	-	-	-	-	-	-	-
Italy 1990	Did not qualify	-	-	-	-	-	-	-	-	-	-	-	-
USA 1994	Did not qualify	-	-	-	-	-	-	-	-	-	-	-	-
France 1998	Did not qualify	-	-	-	-	-	-	-	-	-	-	-	-
Korea/Japan 2002	Did not qualify	-	-	-	-	-	-	-	-	-	-	-	-
Germany 2006	Did not qualify	-	-	-	-	-	-	-	-	-	-	-	-
South Africa 2010	Did not qualify	-	-	-	-	-	-	-	-	-	-	-	-
Brazil 2014	Did not qualify	-	-	-	-	-	-	-	-	-	-	-	-
Totals		0	0	0	0	0	0	0	0	0	0	0	0

Continental championships (best perfomance)

Concacaf Gold Cup	Beaten finalists (2)	2005, 2013

How they qualified

Round 4

Group B	P	W	D	L	F	A	GD	P
Costa Rica	6	5	1	0	11	3	8	16
Panama	6	3	1	2	7	5	2	10
Haiti	6	1	1	4	2	4	-2	4
Jamaica	6	1	1	4	2	10	-8	4

Jamaica.......... (0) 0-2 (1)......... Panama
Panama.......... (0) 1-2 (0)...... Costa Rica
Haiti .... (0) 0-0 (0)............. Panama
Panama.......... (0) 1-0 (0)................Haiti
Panama........ (1) 2-0 (0)........... Jamaica
Costa Rica..... (1) 3-1 (0)......... Panama

Round 5

	P	W	D	L	F	A	GD	P
Mexico	10	6	3	1	16	7	9	21
Costa Rica	10	4	4	2	14	8	6	16
Panama	10	3	4	3	9	10	-1	13
Honduras	10	3	4	3	13	19	-6	13
USA	10	3	3	4	17	13	4	12
Trin & Tobago	10	2	0	8	7	19	-12	6

Honduras .... (0) 0-1 (1)......... Panama
Panama......... (0) 0-0 (0)............Mexico

Trin & Tobago (1) 1-0 (0)......... Panama
Panama.......... (1) 1-1 (1)..................USA
Costa Rica..... (0) 0-0 (0)......... Panama
Panama.......... (1) 2-2 (1).........Honduras

Mexico .... (0) 1-0 (0)......... Panama
Panama......... (1) 3-0 (0).. Trin & Tobago
USA .... (3) 4-0 (0)......... Panama
Panama......... (0) 2-1 (1)...... Costa Rica

After they qualified for their first ever World Cup, Panamanian president Juan Carlos Varela declared a national holiday

Players used in qualifying		Career			Qualification			
Pos	Club	Age	P	G	P	G		
GK Jaime Penedo	Din. Bucharest	36	130	-	12	-	-	-
GK Jose Calderon	Chorrillo	32	29	-	4	-	-	-
DEF Adolfo Machado	Houston	33	74	1	12	-	2	-
DEF Eric Davis	Dunajska Streda	27	37	-	4	-	1	-
DEF Felipe Baloy	Municipal	37	101	3	11	1	3	-
DEF Fidel Escobar	NY Red Bulls	23	21	1	9	1	-	-
DEF Harold Cummings	San Jose	26	51	-	2	-	1	-
DEF Luis Henriquez	Tauro	36	85	2	2	-	-	-
DEF Luis Ovalle	Olimpia	29	24	-	11	-	1	-
DEF Amir Murillo	NY Red Bulls	22	21	2	5	-	2	-
DEF Richard Dixon	Tauro	25	8	-	3	-	-	-
DEF Roberto Chen	Arabe Unido	24	22	-	2	-	-	-
DEF Roderick Miller	Atletico Nacional	26	28	1	4	-	-	-
DEF Roman Torres	Seattle	32	109	10	9	2	3	-
MID Alberto Quintero	Universitario	30	89	5	15	-	1	-
MID Amilcar Henriquez	(Deceased)	34	85	-	8	-	-	-
MID Anibal Godoy	San Jose	28	87	2	14	-	1	-
MID Armando Cooper	Universidad de Chile	30	96	7	14	1	3	-
MID Gabriel Gomez	Bucaramanga	34	142	12	14	1	3	-
MID Jose Gonzalez	Union Comercio	27	9	-	1	-	1	-
MID Manuel Vargas	San Francisco	27	8	-	1	-	-	-
MID Miguel Camargo	USMP	24	18	2	1	-	-	-
MID Ricardo Buitrago	Dep. Municipal	32	27	3	2	-	-	-
MID Valentin Pimentel	Plaza Amador	27	20	1	5	-	3	-
MID Joel Barcenas	Cafetaleros	24	27	-	11	-	1	-
ATT Abdiel Arroyo	Alajuelense	24	33	5	9	2	-	-
ATT Ismael Diaz	Deportivo Fabril	21	9	2	2	-	1	-
ATT Blas Perez	Municipal	37	116	43	13	2	-	-
ATT Gabriel Torres	Huachipato	29	71	14	11	2	-	-
ATT Luis Tejada	Sport Boys	36	104	43	10	2	1	-
ATT Roberto Nurse	Zacatecas	34	20	3	2	-	-	-
ATT Tony Taylor	Ottawa Fury	28	3	-	1	-	-	-

Correct scores

	Competitive	Friendly
1-0	5	2
2-0	3	-
2-1	4	1
3-0	2	-
3-1	-	1
3-2	-	-
4-0	1	1
4-1	-	-
4-2	-	-
4-3	-	-
0-0	4	3
1-1	8	3
2-2	2	-
3-3	-	-
4-4	-	-
0-1	4	6
0-2	-	2
1-2	1	2
0-3	-	1
1-3	1	-
2-3	-	-
0-4	1	1
1-4	-	-
2-4	1	-
3-4	-	-
Other	1	2

Since Brazil 2014

Half-time/full-time double results

Win/Win	9	24%	Win 1st half	12	32%
Draw/Win	5	13%	Win 2nd half	11	29%
Lose/Win	1	3%	Win both halves	5	13%
Win/Draw	3	8%	Goal both halves	8	21%
Draw/Draw	11	29%			
Lose/Draw	0	0%	Overall		
Win/Lose	0	0%	● Win	39%	
Draw/Lose	3	8%	● Draw	37%	
Lose/Lose	6	16%	● Lose	24%	

Overall: W15, D14, L9 in 38 competitive games since Brazil 2014

Under & over goals

25 (66%) **Over 1.5** 13 (34%) ✓ ✗

14 (37%) **Over 2.5** 24 (63%) ✓ ✗

7 (18%) **Over 3.5** 31 (82%) ✓ ✗

2 (5%) **Over 4.5** 36 (95%) ✓ ✗

Both teams to score

17 (45%) **Both score** 21 (55%) ✓ ✗

4 (11%) **& win** 34 (89%) ✓ ✗

3 (8%) **& lose** 35 (92%) ✓ ✗

In 38 competitive games since Brazil 2014

Clean sheets

15 (39%) **Clean sheets** 23 (61%) ✓ ✗

11 (29%) **Win to nil** 27 (71%) ✓ ✗

10 (26%) **Fail to score** 28 (74%) ✓ ✗

6 (16%) **Lose to nil** 32 (84%) ✓ ✗

When they score

● For ● Against

Total match goals by half

17 (57%) **1st half** 13 (43%)
F ▬▬ A

28 (53%) **2nd half** 25 (47%)
F ▬▬ A

Goals for & against by half

17 (38%) **For** 28 (62%)
1st ▬▬ 2nd

13 (34%) **Against** 25 (66%)
1st ▬▬ 2nd

	4	3	2	2	6	5	7	4	3	9
	0-9	10-18	19-27	28-36	37-45	46-54	55-63	64-72	73-81	82-90
	3	1	2	2	5	6	2	5	5	7

Panama score first

They win	13	62%
They draw	7	33%
They lose	1	5%

Panama concede first

They win	2	15%
They draw	3	23%
They lose	8	62%

In 38 competitive games since Brazil 2014

GROUP G

Blaz Perez's two qualifying goals included a vital deflection in their final game that appeared not to cross the line

Top scorers in qualifying

	P	G	1st	AT	%	Jam 0-2 Pan	Pan 1-2 Cri	Hti 0-0 Pan	Pan 1-0 Hti	Pan 2-0 Jam	Cri 3-1 Pan	Hnd 0-1 Pan	Pan 0-0 Mex	Tto 1-0 Pan	Pan 1-1 USA	Cri 0-0 Pan	Pan 2-2 Hnd	Mex 1-0 Pan	Pan 3-0 Tto	USA 4-0 Pan	Pan 2-1 Cri
Abdiel Arroyo	9	2	0	2	13	ↄ	ↄ	ↄ		⌐1				-	ↄ				⌐1	ↄ	ↄ
Roman Torres	9	2	0	2	13						-		-	-	-	-	1		↺	-	1
Luis Tejada	10	2	0	2	13	⌐1		-		⌐1		ↄ	ↄ	-	-	ↄ	-				ↄ
Gabriel Torres	11	2	2	3	13				ↄ	⌐1		ↄ	ↄ	ↄ	↺		-	ↄ	1	-	↺
Blas Perez	13	2	0	2	13	-	-	ↄ	↺	-	ↄ	-	-		ↄ	⌐1		-	↺		1
Fidel Escobar	9	1	1	1	6					-	1	-			-	-	ↄ	-	ↄ	-	
Felipe Baloy	11	1	1	1	6	-	↺	-	1	-		-	-	-		-		-	ↄ	↺	
Armando Cooper	14	1	1	1	6	↺1	-	-	ↄ		↺		-	-	↺	-		ↄ	-	ↄ	ↄ
Gabriel Gomez	14	1	0	1	6	↺	↺	-	-	-		-	↺	↺1	↺	ↄ	-		↺	-	↺

G goals scored, **1st** first match goal (own goals don't count) **AT** goals at any time (ie. number of scoring appearances), **P** penalties, **%** percentage of total team goals scored by each player. Russia 2018 qualifying only. Game-by-game stats show goals scored, 1st goals are in red, dash did not score, ↄ substituted on, ↺ substituted off, blank did not play.

Bookings in World Cup qualifying

Played 16
Cards (28Y)

Avg make-up (☐10 ■25) 17.5

TUNISIA

Profile

Tunisia return to the World Cup finals after a 12-year absence and their dream is to qualify for the knockout stage for the first time after four previous group-stage exits.

The Carthage Eagles made World Cup history in 1978, beating Mexico to become the first African side to win a finals match, but they have not tasted success since.

How they qualified

It was squeaky-bum time for Tunisia, who edged out Democratic Republic of Congo by a point thanks to a 0-0 home draw with Libya in the final fixture of qualifying. They came back from two down late on against DR Congo in Kinshasa to nick a crucial point.

The manager

Nabil Maaloul was reappointed as Tunisia's manager in April 2017, replacing Henryk Kasperczak, who was sacked despite making a strong start to World Cup qualifying.

The Pole was given the boot after a quarter-final exit at the Africa Cup of Nations and subsequent friendly defeats by Morocco and Cameroon.

The squad

Tunisia have been attempting to strengthen their squad by registering new players but it has been a frustrating search. Sevilla's classy Wissam Ben Yedder has turned down the opportunity on five occasions and Rani Khedira, brother of German star Sami, followed suit.

Fousseny Coulibaly was rejected after it was reported he would not be registered by Fifa in time for the World Cup, although Montpellier's French-born Ellyes Skhiri has committed himself to Tunisia.

Maaloul seems set for a 4-2-3-1 formation and the three attacking players behind lone forward Taha Yassine Khenissi will be crucial if Tunisia are to make any impact.

Qatar-based Youssef Msakni will fancy his chances of enhancing his growing reputation, while Wahbi Khazri has

Factfile

FA founded 1957
www ftf.org.tn
Head coach Nabil Maaloul
Date qualified November 11, 2017

Strengths

☑ Squad unity – the group is referred to as a band of brothers
☑ Were rated Africa's top qualified team by Fifa for the draw

Weaknesses

☒ Is striker Khenissi good enough at this level?
☒ Not many European-based players in the squad reckoning

Star rating ★☆☆☆☆

Fixtures

1 June 18, 7pm v England, Volgograd
2 June 23, 1pm v Belgium, Otkrytie Arena, Moscow
3 June 28, 7pm v Panama, Saransk

Base Moscow
Total distance 1,800 miles

Youssef
Msakni

found some form at Rennes after a tough
time with Sunderland. Dijon's Naim Sliti
completes a tricky trio and they could
do more damage than Khenissi, who has
an excellent scoring record in Tunisia,
but failed to notch in qualifying.

Mohamed Amine Ben Amor of Al-Ahli will
be one of those charged with protecting a
defence where the centre-back choices are
slightly complicated by a lack of Ligue 1
minutes for Aymen Abdennour at Marseille.

Marauding left-back Ali Maaloul
is one to note. The Al Ahly man has
been linked with Premier League
clubs and reports claim Maaloul wants
a transfer after the World Cup.

Key man

It is surely a matter of time before
Msakni gives Europe a chance.

He is rampant in Qatar and
played a key role in a vital victory
in Guinea, scoring three goals and
providing the assist for the other.

Rising star

Bassem Srarfi did risk a move to Europe,
leaving home at 18 to join Nice. He has
worked hard to bulk up and the gym time
has been well spent with the 20-year-old
forcing his way into first-team reckoning.

Wildcard

Abdennour would ordinarily be a
certainty for the team but the former
Monaco man totally lost his form at
Valencia and has also struggled since
moving to Marseille last summer.

Prospects

They should finish third in Group G.

How to back them

Tunisia's clash with Panama on June
28 is a real chance to win a World Cup
match for the first time since 1978. Even
if it turns out to be a dead rubber, they
will be desperate for the victory and
look a value bet to take the points.

TUNISIA

World Cup record

World Cup record		Group stage(s)						Knockout rounds					
		P	W	D	L	F	A	P	W	D	L	F	A
Uruguay 1930	French protectorate	-	-	-	-	-	-	-	-	-	-	-	-
Italy 1934	French protectorate	-	-	-	-	-	-	-	-	-	-	-	-
France 1938	French protectorate	-	-	-	-	-	-	-	-	-	-	-	-
Brazil 1950	French protectorate	-	-	-	-	-	-	-	-	-	-	-	-
Switzerland 1954	French protectorate	-	-	-	-	-	-	-	-	-	-	-	-
Sweden 1958	Did not enter	-	-	-	-	-	-	-	-	-	-	-	-
Chile 1962	Did not qualify	-	-	-	-	-	-	-	-	-	-	-	-
England 1966	Withdrew	-	-	-	-	-	-	-	-	-	-	-	-
Mexico 1970	Did not qualify	-	-	-	-	-	-	-	-	-	-	-	-
Germany 1974	Did not qualify	-	-	-	-	-	-	-	-	-	-	-	-
Argentina 1978	Group stage	3	1	1	1	3	2	-	-	-	-	-	-
Spain 1982	Did not qualify	-	-	-	-	-	-	-	-	-	-	-	-
Mexico 1986	Did not qualify	-	-	-	-	-	-	-	-	-	-	-	-
Italy 1990	Did not qualify	-	-	-	-	-	-	-	-	-	-	-	-
USA 1994	Did not qualify	-	-	-	-	-	-	-	-	-	-	-	-
France 1998	Group stage	3	0	1	2	1	4	-	-	-	-	-	-
Korea/Japan 2002	Group stage	3	0	1	2	1	5	-	-	-	-	-	-
Germany 2006	Group stage	3	0	1	2	3	6	-	-	-	-	-	-
South Africa 2010	Did not qualify	-	-	-	-	-	-	-	-	-	-	-	-
Brazil 2014	Did not qualify	-	-	-	-	-	-	-	-	-	-	-	-
Totals		12	1	4	7	8	17	0	0	0	0	0	0

Continental championships (best perfomance)

Africa Cup of nations	Winners (1)	2004

World Cup head-to-heads

Tunisia v	P	W	D	L	F	A	Latest
Belgium	1	0	1	0	1	1	2002
Colombia	1	0	0	1	0	1	1998
England	1	0	0	1	0	2	1998
Germany	1	0	1	0	0	0	1978
Japan	1	0	0	1	0	2	2002
Mexico	1	1	0	0	3	1	1978
Poland	1	0	0	1	0	1	1978
Russia	1	0	0	1	0	2	2002
Saudi Arabia	1	0	1	0	2	2	2006
Spain	1	0	0	1	1	3	2006

90 mins only, includes games against West Germany

Raouf Bouzaiene (left) scored as Tunisia drew with Group G rivals Belgium in Japan in 2002

How they qualified

Round 2
Mauritania ..... (1) 1-2 (0) .... **Tunisia**
Tunisia .... (0) 2-1 (0) ...... Mauritania
Tunisia won 4-2 on aggregate

▶▶ Full qualifying results on pages 228-241

Round 3

Group A	P	W	D	L	F	A	GD	P
Tunisia	6	4	2	0	11	4	7	14
DR Congo	6	4	1	1	14	7	7	13
Libya	6	1	1	4	4	10	-6	4
Guinea	6	1	0	5	6	14	-8	3

Tunisia .... (0) 2-0 (0) .... Guinea
Libya .... (0) 0-1 (0) .... **Tunisia**
Tunisia .... (1) 2-1 (1) ...... DR Congo
DR Congo .... (1) 2-2 (0) .... **Tunisia**
Guinea .... (1) 1-4 (1) .... **Tunisia**
Tunisia .... (0) 0-0 (0) .... Libya

GROUP G

Players used in qualifying			Career		Qualification			
Pos	Club	Age	P	G	P	G	▢	▮
GK	Aymen Mathlouthi	Al-Batin	33	67	-	8	-	1	-
GK	Rami Jridi	CS Sfaxien	33	15	-	1	-	-	-
DEF	Abdelkader Ouelasti	Al-Fateh	26	8	-	1	-	-	-
DEF	Ali Maaloul	Al Ahly	28	41	-	8	-	-	-
DEF	Ammar Jemal	Etoile du Sahel	31	31	6	2	-	-	-
DEF	Aymen Abdennour	Marseille	28	55	2	2	1	-	-
DEF	Chamseddine Dhaouadi	Esperance Tunis	31	9	-	2	-	1	-
DEF	Hamdi Nagguez	Zamalek	25	14	-	5	-	-	-
DEF	Hamza Mathlouthi	CS Sfaxien	25	24	-	2	-	-	-
DEF	Oussama Haddadi	Dijon	26	6	-	1	-	-	-
DEF	Rami Bedoui	ES Sahel	28	10	-	3	-	-	-
DEF	Syam Ben Youssef	Kasimpasa	29	37	1	5	1	1	-
DEF	Yassine Meriah	CS Sfaxien	24	12	1	5	1	1	-
DEF	Zied Derbali	Muharraq	33	5	-	1	-	-	-
DEF	Bilel Mohsni	Dundee Utd	30	9	-	2	-	-	-
MID	Anis Ben-Hatira	Esperance Tunis	29	12	1	2	1	-	-
MID	Aymen Trabelsi	ES Sahel	25	1	-	1	-	-	-
MID	Ferjani Sassi	Al-Nasr	26	36	2	6	-	2	-
MID	Ghailan Chaalali	Esperance Tunis	24	5	1	4	1	1	-
MID	Hamza Lahmar	ES Sahel	28	12	2	1	-	-	-
MID	Issam Ben Khemis	Doncaster	22	1	-	1	-	-	-
MID	Karim Aouadhi	CS Sfaxien	32	7	1	3	-	-	-
MID	Mohamed Ali Manser	Esperance Tunis	27	15	3	2	-	1	-
MID	Mohamed Ben Amor	Al-Ahli	26	23	2	6	1	1	-
MID	Naim Sliti	Dijon	25	16	3	3	-	-	-
MID	Saad Bguir	Esperance Tunis	24	9	3	2	1	-	-
MID	Wahbi Khazri	Rennes	27	35	12	6	2	1	-
MID	Yassine Chikhaoui	Al Ahli	31	41	10	2	1	-	-
MID	Youssef Msakni	Al-Duhail	27	50	9	4	3	-	-
ATT	Ahmed Akaichi	Al-Ittihad	29	26	9	1	-	-	-
ATT	Anice Badri	Esperance Tunis	27	7	1	4	1	-	-
ATT	Fakhreddine Ben Youssef	Al-Ettifaq	27	33	4	5	-	1	-
ATT	Hamdi Harbaoui	Waregem	33	16	3	2	-	1	-
ATT	Taha Khenissi	Esperance Tunis	26	23	5	6	-	2	-
ATT	Yoann Touzghar	Sochaux	31	5	1	3	-	-	-

TUNISIA

Correct scores

	Competitive	Friendly
1-0	5	2
2-0	1	1
2-1	7	-
3-0	1	-
3-1	-	-
3-2	-	-
4-0	-	-
4-1	2	-
4-2	1	-
4-3	-	-
0-0	4	1
1-1	3	2
2-2	1	-
3-3	-	1
4-4	-	-
0-1	1	3
0-2	2	1
1-2	-	-
0-3	-	-
1-3	-	-
2-3	-	-
0-4	-	-
1-4	-	-
2-4	-	-
3-4	-	-
Other	1	-

Since Brazil 2014

Half-time/full-time double results

Win/Win	5	17%	Win 1st half	6	21%
Draw/Win	10	34%	Win 2nd half	17	59%
Lose/Win	3	10%	Win both halves	3	10%
Win/Draw	1	3%	Goal both halves	5	17%
Draw/Draw	6	21%			
Lose/Draw	1	3%	Overall		
Win/Lose	0	0%	● Win	62%	
Draw/Lose	2	7%	● Draw	28%	
Lose/Lose	1	3%	● Lose	10%	

Overall: W18, D8, L3 in 29 competitive games since Brazil 2014

Under & over goals

19 (66%) **Over 1.5** 10 (34%) ✓ ✗
13 (45%) **Over 2.5** 16 (55%) ✓ ✗
5 (17%) **Over 3.5** 24 (83%) ✓ ✗
4 (14%) **Over 4.5** 25 (86%) ✓ ✗

Both teams to score

15 (52%) **Both score** 14 (48%) ✓ ✗
11 (38%) **& win** 18 (62%) ✓ ✗
0 (0%) **& lose** 29 (100%) ✓ ✗

In 29 competitive games since Brazil 2014

Clean sheets

11 (38%) **Clean sheets** 18 (62%) ✓ ✗
7 (24%) **Win to nil** 22 (76%) ✓ ✗

7 (24%) **Fail to score** 22 (76%) ✓ ✗
3 (10%) **Lose to nil** 26 (90%) ✓ ✗

When they score

● For ● Against

Total match goals by half

16 (64%) **1st half** 9 (36%)
F A
33 (72%) **2nd half** 13 (28%)
F A

Goals for & against by half

16 (33%) **For** 33 (67%)
1st 2nd
9 (41%) **Against** 13 (59%)
1st 2nd

For: 3 3 3 3 4 7 5 6 10 5
Against: 1 2 1 1 4 2 2 3 3 3

0-9 10-18 19-27 28-36 37-45 46-54 55-63 64-72 73-81 82-90

Tunisia score first

They win	13		81%
They draw	3		19%
They lose	0		0%

Tunisia concede first

They win	5		56%
They draw	1		11%
They lose	3		33%

In 29 competitive games since Brazil 2014

GROUP G

Wahbi Khazri has found some form on loan at Rennes from Sunderland

Top scorers in qualifying

	P	G	1st	AT	%	Mrt 1-2 Tun	Tun 2-1 Mrt	Tun 2-0 Gin	Lby 0-1 Tun	Tun 2-1 Cod	Cod 2-2 Tun	Gin 1-4 Tun	Tun 0-0 Lby
Youssef Msakni	4	3	0	1	20					-	-	3	-
Wahbi Khazri	6	2	1	2	13	↺1	↺	↺	↺1		↪		↺
Aymen Abdennour	2	1	1	1	7					1	-		
Yassine Chikhaoui	2	1	0	1	7	1	-						
Saad Bguir	2	1	0	1	7		↺1			↪			
Anis Ben-Hatira	2	1	0	1	7			↺1	↺				
Ghilane Chalali	4	1	0	1	7						1	↺	-
Anice Badri	4	1	0	1	7					↪	↺1	↪	↺
Syam Ben Youssef	5	1	1	1	7	-	1			-	-		
Yassine Meriah	5	1	0	1	7	↺					1	-	-
Mohamed Ben Amor	6	1	0	1	7					-	-	-	1

G goals scored, **1st** first match goal (own goals don't count) **AT** goals at any time (ie. number of scoring appearances), **P** penalties, **%** percentage of total team goals scored by each player. Russia 2018 qualifying only. Game-by-game stats show goals scored, 1st goals are in red, dash did not score, ↪ substituted on, ↺ substituted off, blank did not play

Bookings in World Cup qualifying

Played 8 **Cards** (14Y) ▯▯▯▯▯▯▯▯▯▯▯▯▯▯   **Avg make-up** (▯10 ▮25) 17.5

ENGLAND

Profile

England were criticised for suffering successive World Cup eliminations at the quarter-final stage in 2002 and 2006 but most Three Lions supporters would settle for that respectability in Russia after the humiliating early bath in Brazil four years ago.

England's Euro 2016 exit at the hands of Iceland means expectations are fairly low.

How they qualified

Results were better than the performances as England went unbeaten in a soft section that produced the worst runner-up in Slovakia, who failed to qualify for the playoffs.

Sam Allardyce lasted one match as Euro 2016 flop Roy Hodgson's replacement before departing after a newspaper sting, to be replaced by Gareth Southgate.

The manager

Southgate talks a good game but was relegated with Middlesbrough in his only club job and his last Under-21 tournament with England resulted in a group-stage exit.

The squad

England are set to use a back three in Russia but many question marks remain over the the 23-man squad, never mind the starting 11.

Harry Kane, Premier League Golden Boot winner in 2016 and 2017, is the first name on the team sheet and was often England's saviour in qualifying, while Raheem Sterling should be booked for an advanced midfield role alongside Dele Alli or Jesse Lingard.

Central midfielders Jordan Henderson and Eric Dier were mainstays in qualifying, although both lack creativity.

The centre-back picture is murky with Gary Cahill of Chelsea and Michael Keane of Everton both out of form so it's probably John Stones, Harry Maguire and one other to fill the three places. Dier may even drop into the back three if a suitable midfield

Factfile

FA founded 1863
www thefa.com
Head coach Gareth Southgate
Date qualified October 5, 2017

Strengths

- ☑ Kane is one of the world's best strikers
- ☑ Excellent pace on the counter-attack

Weaknesses

- ☒ England's lack of goalkeeping options is a major concern
- ☒ Constantly turn over cheap possession in midfield

Star rating ★★★☆☆

Fixtures

1 June 18, 7pm v Tunisia, Volgograd
2 June 24, 1pm v Panama, Nizhny Novgorod
3 June 28, 7pm v Belgium, Kaliningrad

Base Saint Petersburg
Total distance 4,100 miles

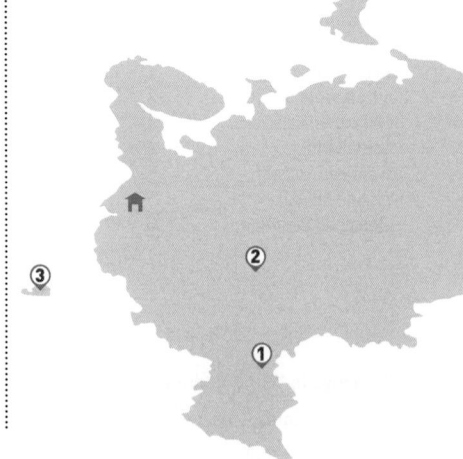

GROUP G

Raheem Sterling
Photo by Dean Mouhtaropoulos/ Getty Images

replacement can be found, while attack-minded full-back Kyle Walker was even tested as a centre-back in the 1-0 win over Holland in March and 1-1 draw with Italy.

It's even murkier in the goalkeeping position since Joe Hart lost his place at West Ham with Jordan Pickford favourite to wear the gloves.

Key man

Kane was woeful at the Euros but the Spurs striker has developed into one of the world's most feared forwards. He scored more goals than any other player in 2017, notching 56 times in 52 matches for club and country, finishing ahead of Lionel Messi (54 goals in 64), Robert Lewandowski (53 in 55), Cristiano Ronaldo (53 in 59) and Edinson Cavani (53 in 62).

Rising star

Sterling briefly went backwards after becoming England's most

expensive ever player after a £49m move to Manchester City in 2015.

However, Pep Guardiola has worked hard to develop him into one of Europe's most dangerous wide forwards.

Wildcard

He was on loan at Bournemouth last season and started this campaign as a Europa League skivvy, but Jack Wilshere has forced his way back into Arsenal's plans.

To some he is the answer to England's midfield passing problems, to others a vastly overrated injury-prone luxury.

Prospects

A kind draw means it may not take much to reach the last eight, but England tend to come up short against elite opponents.

How to back them

A straight forecast in Group G with Belgium first and England second.

ENGLAND

World Cup record		Group stage(s)						Knockout rounds					
		P	W	D	L	F	A	P	W	D	L	F	A
Uruguay 1930	Did not enter	-	-	-	-	-	-	-	-	-	-	-	-
Italy 1934	Did not enter	-	-	-	-	-	-	-	-	-	-	-	-
France 1938	Did not enter	-	-	-	-	-	-	-	-	-	-	-	-
Brazil 1950	Group stage	3	1	0	2	2	2	-	-	-	-	-	-
Switzerland 1954	Quarter-finals	2	1	1	0	5	3	1	0	0	1	2	4
Sweden 1958	Group stage	4	0	3	1	4	5	-	-	-	-	-	-
Chile 1962	Quarter-finals	3	1	1	1	4	3	1	0	0	1	1	3
England 1966	● Winners	3	2	1	0	4	0	3	2	1	0	5	3
Mexico 1970	Quarter-finals	3	2	0	1	2	1	1	0	1	0	2	2
Germany 1974	Did not qualify	-	-	-	-	-	-	-	-	-	-	-	-
Argentina 1978	Did not qualify	-	-	-	-	-	-	-	-	-	-	-	-
Spain 1982	2nd group stage	5	3	2	0	6	1	-	-	-	-	-	-
Mexico 1986	Quarter-finals	3	1	1	1	3	1	2	1	0	1	4	2
Italy 1990	Fourth place	3	1	2	0	2	1	4	0	3	1	4	5
USA 1994	Did not qualify	-	-	-	-	-	-	-	-	-	-	-	-
France 1998	Round of 16	3	2	0	1	5	2	1	0	1	0	2	2
Korea/Japan 2002	Quarter-finals	3	1	2	0	2	1	2	1	0	1	4	2
Germany 2006	Quarter-finals	3	2	1	0	5	2	2	1	1	0	1	0
South Africa 2010	Round of 16	3	1	2	0	2	1	1	0	0	1	1	4
Brazil 2014	Group stage	3	0	1	2	2	4	-	-	-	-	-	-
Totals		44	18	17	9	48	27	18	5	7	6	26	27

Continental championships (best perfomance)

Uefa European Championship	Semi-finals (1)	1996

World Cup head-to-heads

England v	P	W	D	L	F	A	Latest
Argentina	5	3	1	1	8	5	2002
Belgium	2	0	2	0	3	3	1990
Brazil	4	0	1	3	2	6	2002
Colombia	1	1	0	0	2	0	1998
Costa Rica	1	0	1	0	0	0	2014
Denmark	1	1	0	0	3	0	2002
Egypt	1	1	0	0	1	0	1990
France	2	2	0	0	5	1	1982
Germany	5	0	4	1	6	9	2010
Mexico	1	1	0	0	2	0	1966
Morocco	1	0	1	0	0	0	1986
Nigeria	1	0	1	0	0	0	2002
Poland	1	1	0	0	3	0	1986
Portugal	3	1	1	1	2	2	2006
Russia	2	0	1	1	2	3	1958
Spain	2	0	1	1	0	1	1982
Sweden	2	0	2	0	3	3	2006
Switzerland	1	1	0	0	2	0	1954
Tunisia	1	1	0	0	2	0	1998
Uruguay	3	0	1	2	3	6	2014

90 mins only, includes games against West Germany and USSR

David Platt produced an iconic England moment against Belgium at Italia 90

Picture by Albert Cooper/Mirrorpix

How they qualified

Group F	P	W	D	L	F	A	GD	P
England	10	8	2	0	18	3	15	26
Slovakia	10	6	0	4	17	7	10	18
Scotland	10	5	3	2	17	12	5	18
Slovenia	10	4	3	3	12	7	5	15
Lithuania	10	1	3	6	7	20	-13	6
Malta	10	0	1	9	3	25	-22	1

Slovakia .... (0) 0-1 (0) .... **England**
England .... (2) 2-0 (0) .... Malta
Slovenia .... (0) 0-0 (0) .... **England**
England .... (1) 3-0 (0) .... Scotland
England .... (1) 2-0 (0) .... Lithuania
Scotland .... (0) 2-2 (0) .... **England**
Malta .... (0) 0-4 (0) .... **England**
England .... (1) 2-1 (1) .... Slovakia
England .... (0) 1-0 (0) .... Slovenia
Lithuania .... (0) 0-1 (1) .... **England**

Results were better than performances in qualifying for Gareth Southgate's side

Players used in qualifying		Career			Qualification			
Pos		Club	Age	P	G	P	G	⬜ ◼
GK	Jack Butland	Stoke	25	7	-	1	-	- -
GK	Joe Hart	West Ham	31	75	-	9	-	- -
DEF	Aaron Cresswell	West Ham	28	3	-	1	-	- -
DEF	Chris Smalling	Man Utd	28	31	1	1	-	- -
DEF	Danny Rose	Tottenham	27	16	-	4	-	- -
DEF	Gary Cahill	Chelsea	32	58	4	8	1	2 -
DEF	Harry Maguire	Leicester	25	4	-	1	-	- -
DEF	John Stones	Man City	23	24	-	7	-	1 -
DEF	Kieran Trippier	Tottenham	27	5	-	1	-	- -
DEF	Kyle Walker	Man City	28	34	-	9	-	- -
DEF	Michael Keane	Everton	25	4	-	3	-	- -
DEF	Phil Jones	Man Utd	26	24	-	2	-	- -
DEF	Ryan Bertrand	Southampton	28	19	1	6	1	- -
MID	Adam Lallana	Liverpool	30	34	3	4	2	1 -
MID	Alex Oxlade-Chamberlain	Liverpool	24	32	6	5	1	- -
MID	Andros Townsend	Crystal Palace	26	13	3	1	-	- -
MID	Dele Alli	Tottenham	22	23	2	8	1	- -
MID	Eric Dier	Tottenham	24	25	3	7	1	3 -
MID	Harry Winks	Tottenham	22	1	-	1	-	- -
MID	Jake Livermore	West Brom	28	7	-	3	-	1 -
MID	Jesse Lingard	Man Utd	25	10	1	4	-	1 -
MID	Jordan Henderson	Liverpool	27	38	-	8	-	- -
ATT	Daniel Sturridge	Liverpool	28	26	8	5	2	1 -
ATT	Danny Welbeck	Arsenal	27	37	15	2	1	- -
ATT	Harry Kane	Tottenham	24	23	12	6	5	- -
ATT	Jamie Vardy	Leicester	31	21	7	4	1	- -
ATT	Jermain Defoe	Bournemouth	35	57	20	2	1	- -
ATT	Marcus Rashford	Man Utd	20	17	2	8	1	1 -
ATT	Raheem Sterling	Man City	23	37	2	7	-	- -
ATT	Theo Walcott	Everton	29	47	8	3	-	- -
ATT	Wayne Rooney	Everton	32	119	53	4	-	1 -

ENGLAND

Correct scores

	Competitive	Friendly
1-0	4	3
2-0	5	1
2-1	2	2
3-0	2	-
3-1	1	1
3-2	1	1
4-0	2	-
4-1	-	-
4-2	-	-
4-3	-	-
0-0	2	3
1-1	1	2
2-2	1	1
3-3	-	-
4-4	-	-
0-1	-	1
0-2	-	1
1-2	1	1
0-3	-	-
1-3	-	-
2-3	-	1
0-4	-	-
1-4	-	-
2-4	-	-
3-4	-	-
Other	2	-

Since Brazil 2014

Half-time/full-time double results

Win/Win	9	38%
Draw/Win	8	33%
Lose/Win	2	8%
Win/Draw	0	0%
Draw/Draw	4	17%
Lose/Draw	0	0%
Win/Lose	0	0%
Draw/Lose	0	0%
Lose/Lose	1	4%

Win 1st half	9	38%
Win 2nd half	17	71%
Win both halves	7	29%
Goal both halves	8	33%

Overall
- Win 79%
- Draw 17%
- Lose 4%

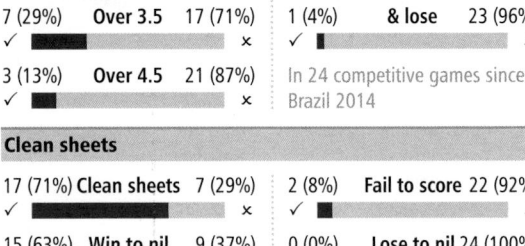

Overall: W19, D4, L1 in 24 competitive games since Brazil 2014

Under & over goals

18 (75%)	**Over 1.5**	6 (25%)
12 (50%)	**Over 2.5**	12 (50%)
7 (29%)	**Over 3.5**	17 (71%)
3 (13%)	**Over 4.5**	21 (87%)

Both teams to score

7 (29%)	**Both score**	17 (71%)
4 (17%)	**& win**	20 (83%)
1 (4%)	**& lose**	23 (96%)

In 24 competitive games since Brazil 2014

Clean sheets

17 (71%)	**Clean sheets**	7 (29%)
15 (63%)	**Win to nil**	9 (37%)

2 (8%)	**Fail to score**	22 (92%)
0 (0%)	**Lose to nil**	24 (100%)

When they score

● For ● Against

Total match goals by half

16 (76%)	**1st half**	5 (24%)
F		A
37 (88%)	**2nd half**	5 (12%)
F		A

Goals for & against by half

16 (30%)	**For**	37 (70%)
1st		2nd
5 (50%)	**Against**	5 (50%)
1st		2nd

	0-9	10-18	19-27	28-36	37-45	46-54	55-63	64-72	73-81	82-90
For	2	1	4	4	5	4	8	7	7	11
Against	2	1	0	0	2	0	1	0	0	4

England score first

They win	15	83%
They draw	2	11%
They lose	1	6%

England concede first

They win	4	100%
They draw	0	0%
They lose	0	0%

In 24 competitive games since Brazil 2014

England need a big tournament from Harry Kane

Top scorers in qualifying

	P	G	1st	AT	%	Svk 0-1 Eng	Eng 2-0 Mlt	Svn 0-0 Eng	Eng 3-0 Sco	Eng 2-0 Ltu	Sco 2-2 Eng	Mlt 0-4 Eng	Eng 2-1 Svk	Eng 1-0 Svn	Ltu 0-1 Eng
Harry Kane	6	5	3	4	28	↺					1	2	-	1	1
Adam Lallana	4	2	1	2	11	1			1	-	-				
Daniel Sturridge	5	2	2	2	11	↪	↪1	↺	↪1						↪
Jermain Defoe	2	1	1	1	6					↺1	↪				
Danny Welbeck	2	1	0	1	6								↪1	↪	
Jamie Vardy	4	1	0	1	6	↪			↪	↺1	↪				
Alex Oxlade-Chamberlain	5	1	1	1	6						-	↺1	↺	↺	↺
Ryan Bertrand	6	1	0	1	6	↺					-	-	1	-	-
Eric Dier	7	1	0	1	6	-		-	-	-	-		1	-	
Gary Cahill	8	1	0	1	6	-	-	-	1		-		-	-	
Dele Alli	8	1	0	1	6	↪	1	↺			-	↺	↺	↺	↺
Marcus Rashford	8	1	0	1	6		↪	↪		↪	↺	↪	↺1	-	↺

G goals scored, **1st** first match goal (own goals don't count) **AT** goals at any time (ie. number of scoring appearances), **P** penalties, **%** percentage of total team goals scored by each player. Russia 2018 qualifying only. Game-by-game stats show goals scored, 1st goals are in red, dash did not score, ↪ substituted on, ↺ substituted off, blank did not play

Bookings in World Cup qualifying

Played 10 **Cards** (12Y) ☐☐☐☐☐☐☐☐☐☐☐☐   **Avg make-up** (☐10 ◼25) 12

ENGLAND

Patriotic punters few and far between despite a kind draw for England

Four years ago England went off at 28-1 to win the World Cup – the biggest price in their history of international tournaments – and the Three Lions lived down to expectations by exiting the competition after just two matches following defeats to Italy and Uruguay.

This time, despite a more favourable draw, England are 18-1 – their second-largest price ever for a World Cup – and patriotic punters are nowhere near as slap-dash with their cash towards backing their own team as in years gone past.

Remember 2006?

England were just 15-2 second favourites to win the World Cup ante-post and bookmakers were beginning to sweat over a huge payout as Sven-Goran Eriksson's side marched to the quarter-finals before losing to Portugal on penalties.

Eriksson's men had been 11-10 to beat Portugal in normal time such was the confidence behind England in those days, something also evident in 1966 when, as tournament hosts, the Three Lions landed odds of 9-2 to lift the World Cup.

However, these days there seems to be a more realistic appreciation of where

England sit in the world pecking order, something acknowledged by former Coral head of football Nick Goff.

He told the Racing Post: "The market being more global is undoubtedly one of the reasons why there is not the same level of support for them in major tournaments, but it's also as if the public feel like they have bought into England's hopes one time too many only to have those hopes dashed, and refuse to make the same mistake again.

"That said England were still the third-biggest loser at Coral going into the 2014 World Cup but ten to 12 years ago it would have been disastrous had they won the World Cup. That is no longer the case."

England's ante-post World Cup odds

Year	Odds	Performance
2014	28-1	Group stage
2010	8-1	Last 16
2006	15-2	Quarter-finals
2002	14-1	Quarter-finals
1998	11-1	Last 16
1994	-	Did not qualify
1990	10-1	Semi-finals
1986	12-1	Quarter-finals
1982	14-1	Second group stage

GROUP G

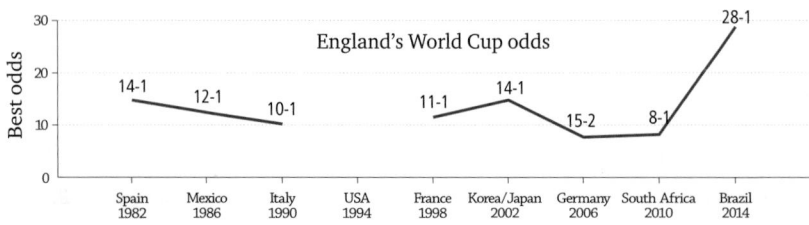

England's World Cup odds

Best odds

| | Spain 1982 | Mexico 1986 | Italy 1990 | USA 1994 | France 1998 | Korea/Japan 2002 | Germany 2006 | South Africa 2010 | Brazil 2014 |

14-1 · 12-1 · 10-1 · 11-1 · 14-1 · 15-2 · 8-1 · 28-1

Clockwise from top: England win it in 1966, Bryan Robson scores in 27 seconds in 1982, Maradona's 'hand of God' goal in 1986, Gazza's tears in the semi-final of Italia 90, Michael Owen's wonder goal at France 98, David Beckham celebrates scoring from the spot against Argentina in 2002, Steven Gerrard misses from the spot as England go out to Portugal in 2006, Frank Lampard's disallowed goal in 2010, Wayne Rooney is dejected as England crash out early in 2014

GROUP H

Japan set to pay the price for their lack of sparkle

The World Cup draw left the most fascinating group until last, *writes Mark Langdon*.

Group H has no standout favourite, no obvious two teams who should qualify and no clear minnows who are likely to finish bottom.

All six matches between Colombia, Poland, Senegal and Japan will be competitive and whoever reaches the last 16 will at least be combat-ready for the knockout stages knowing they will have done well just to make the next phase.

The market says Colombia to win from Poland but it would be wrong to dismiss Senegal, with the Africans capable of splitting the front two in the betting, so the best bet could be backing Japan to finish last in this fiendishly difficult punting puzzle.

There is a Japanese saying "Hana yori Dango" – dumplings over flowers – but unfortunately for Japan they may have too much substance and not enough beauty in comparison to their three rivals for the qualification berths.

Partly through design and partly because of the pool of players at his disposal, much-travelled Japan manager Vahid Halilhodzic has more dumplings than flowers and the few blossoming talents in the side have largely been dumped from the squad due to

an unsuitability to the approach demanded.

Halilhodzic was appointed as boss after a disastrous Asian Cup campaign in 2015 when Japan were eliminated by UAE at the quarter-final stage and not enough improvement has been made to suggest the Samurai Blue can cut down such illustrious opponents.

Colombia were quarter-finalists at the last World Cup and Copa America semi-finalists in 2016, Poland reached the quarter-finals of Euro 2016 when only beaten on penalties by eventual winners Portugal, and the same fate befell Senegal in last year's Afcon against Cameroon.

Japan cannot boast that level of form and they also fail to match the bunch of flowers possessed by their fellow Group H competitors.

Colombia have the wonderful talents of 2014 World Cup Golden Boot winner James Rodriguez, who is now at Bayern Munich on loan from Real Madrid; Poland can field one of the world's great strikers in Robert Lewandowski who, like Rodriguez, struts his stuff at the Allianz Arena, and Senegal sharpshooter Sadio Mane arguably makes the Lions of Teranga the strongest of the African challengers.

Photo by Clive Rose/Getty Images

Group H is tough and Japan could be disappointed

Recommendation

★☆☆☆☆ **Japan to finish bottom**

Group-stage performances since France 98

	Pot	P	W	Q	1998 Group	Pos	2002 Group	Pos	2006 Group	Pos	2010 Group	Pos	2014 Group	Pos
Poland	1	2	0	0	-	-	D	4	A	3	-	-	-	-
Colombia	2	2	1	1	G	3	-	-	-	-	-	-	C	1
Senegal	3	1	0	1	-	-	A	2	-	-	-	-	-	-
Japan	4	5	1	2	H	4	H	1	F	4	E	2	C	4

To win Group H

Win only

	Bet365	BtBrt	Betfair	Btfrd	Btwy	Boyle	Coral	Hills	Lads	P Power	Sky	188
Colombia	5-4	11-8	13-10	5-4	5-4	11-8	5-4	11-10	11-8	13-10	**6-4**	6-5
Poland	7-4	7-4	13-8	6-4	7-4	7-4	9-5	6-4	7-4	13-8	**15-8**	33-20
Senegal	5	9-2	4	**6**	9-2	9-2	9-2	11-2	4	4	4	5
Japan	7	7	17-2	7	8	15-2	7	**9**	7	17-2	5	7

Colombia v Japan

1pm, Tuesday June 19, BBC

	Bet365	BtBrt	Betfair	Btfrd	Btwy	Boyle	Coral	Hills	Lads	P Power	Sky	188
Colombia	**5-6**	4-5	4-5	4-5	4-5	3-4	4-5	**5-6**	4-5	3-4	**5-6**	9-11
Draw	**5-2**	9-4	**5-2**	12-5	9-4	11-5	9-4	12-5	9-4	12-5	12-5	**5-2**
Japan	10-3	10-3	4	18-5	15-4	10-3	18-5	3	18-5	4	18-5	62-17

Poland v Senegal

4pm, Tuesday June 19, ITV

	Bet365	BtBrt	Betfair	Btfrd	Btwy	Boyle	Coral	Hills	Lads	P Power	Sky	188
Poland	5-4	11-10	11-10	6-5	**5-4**	23-20	**5-4**	21-20	**5-4**	11-10	**5-4**	17-14
Draw	21-10	2	21-10	21-10	21-10	2	2	11-5	2	11-5	11-5	**40-17**
Senegal	12-5	23-10	**29-10**	12-5	23-10	11-5	9-4	5-2	9-4	13-5	23-10	40-17

Japan v Senegal

4pm, Sunday June 24, BBC

	Bet365	BtBrt	Betfair	Btfrd	Boyle	Coral	Hills	Lads	P Power	Sky	188
Senegal	**6-4**	7-5	7-5	**6-4**	7-5	**6-4**	7-5	**6-4**	13-10	**6-4**	22-15
Japan	2	9-5	**23-10**	19-10	7-4	9-5	9-5	9-5	21-10	19-10	13-7
Draw	2	2	21-10	21-10	2	2	9-4	2	15-8	11-5	**12-5**

Poland v Colombia

7pm, Sunday June 24, ITV

	Bet365	BtBrt	Betfair	Btfrd	Btwy	Boyle	Coral	Hills	Lads	P Power	Sky	188
Colombia	8-5	6-4	**13-8**	8-5	**13-8**	6-4	31-20	29-20	31-20	6-4	8-5	11-7
Poland	**19-10**	7-4	**19-10**	9-5	15-8	17-10	7-4	7-4	7-4	9-5	9-5	25-14
Draw	2	2	21-10	21-10	21-10	2	2	9-4	2	15-8	21-10	**23-10**

Japan v Poland

3pm, Thursday June 28, BBC

	Bet365	BetBright	Betfair	Betfred	Betway	Boyle	Hills	P Power	Sky Bet
Poland	10-11	17-20	20-23	17-20	5-6	5-6	**19-20**	4-5	5-6
Draw	12-5	9-4	12-5	12-5	12-5	11-5	11-5	9-4	**5-2**
Japan	3	3	**18-5**	16-5	14-5	3	16-5	10-3	10-3

Senegal v Colombia

3pm, Thursday June 28, BBC

	Bet365	BetBright	Betfair	Betfred	Betway	Boyle	Hills	P Power	Sky Bet
Colombia	Evs	10-11	Evs	Evs	19-20	10-11	10-11	10-11	Evs
Draw	**12-5**	11-5	9-4	23-10	21-10	11-5	23-10	21-10	23-10
Senegal	11-4	11-4	31-10	11-4	11-4	11-4	**16-5**	11-4	14-5

Prices correct March 28 2018

POLAND

Profile

Poland, semi-finalists in 1974 and 1982, have missed the last two World Cups but return rejuvenated.

They reached the Euro 2016 quarter-finals before a penalty shootout defeat by winners Portugal and arrive in Russia as a top seed.

How they qualified

Robert Lewandowski broke the Uefa goalscoring record with 16 goals but the sharpshooter needed to be at his best as Poland conceded 14 times, easily the highest of any European qualifier.

A 4-0 defeat in Denmark did not help those numbers but they still topped their group.

The manager

Adam Nawalka represented Poland at the 1978 World Cup and has helped the squad bond since taking the job in 2013 following a failed home Euros campaign.

That tournament controversially included the selection of four foreign-born Polish players but Nawalka has not chased those with tenuous passport links.

The squad

A number of the squad have overcome hardship, not least an 11-year-old Jakub Blaszczykowski, who witnessed his father stabbing his mother to death.

Kuba, as Blaszczykowski is known, had a bust-up with captain Robert Lewandowski over the armband but tends to still be an important figure in supplying the striker, while Hull's Kamil Grosicki is also charged with aiding Poland's goalscoring extraordinaire from the opposite flank.

Lewandowski could be partnered by Arkadiusz Milik in a 4-4-2 formation, although the Napoli hitman has been desperately unfortunate with serious injuries so Nawalka may be more tempted by a 4-2-3-1 formation with a strong spine.

Wojciech Szczesny and Lukasz Fabianski are fighting for the goalkeeping gloves, Monaco centre-back Kamil

Factfile

FA founded 1919

www pzpn.pl

Head coach Adam Nawalka

Date qualified October 8, 2017

Strengths

- ☑ The spine of the side is ultra-impressive
- ☑ Lewandowski is one of the world's best strikers

Weaknesses

- ☒ Supporting cast outside of the obvious names need to step up
- ☒ Poland kept only two clean sheets in ten qualifying matches

Star rating ★★★☆☆

Fixtures

1 June 19, 4pm v Senegal, Otkrytie Arena, Moscow

2 June 24, 7pm v Colombia, Kazan

3 June 28, 3pm v Japan, Volgograd

Base Sochi

Total distance 4,450 miles

GROUP H

Robert Lewandowski in action at Euro 2016
Photo by Alex Livesey/Getty Images

Glik is a warrior, and in midfield there is a trusted combination of Grzegorz Krychowiak and Piotr Zielinski. The emergence of Karol Linetty at Sampdoria means the switch to a five-man midfield could work in Poland's favour.

Key man

It's time for Lewandowski to deliver on the international stage. He has flopped with only one goal at each of his two European Championship tournaments but his last six full Bundesliga campaigns up to 2016-17 finished with tallies of 22-24-20-17-30-30.

Rising star

How is this for praise from Napoli boss Maurizio Sarri regarding Zielinski?

"He is an absolute talent, he also has great physical skills and if he grows in the level of personality, he can play in any area of the pitch – the new Kevin De Bruyne," said Sarri.

Wildcard

Dwight Yorke is the only player to have been selected for a World Cup side other than Australia and New Zealand while playing for an A-League side, but Sydney FC's attacking midfielder Adrian Mierzejewski has been in sensational scoring form after appearing to call time on his international career when he signed for Al Nasr in 2014.

Prospects

Their group is balanced but Poland would be tricky last-16 opponents for England should that potential match-up materialise. The quarter-finals would appear to be their limit.

How to back them

Lewandowski is a world-class striker but he looks a lay at extremely cramped odds to be Poland's top goalscorer. Milik as well as many midfielders could at least share top billing in a dead heat.

POLAND

World Cup record		Group stage(s)						Knockout rounds					
		P	W	D	L	F	A	P	W	D	L	F	A
Uruguay 1930	Did not enter	-	-	-	-	-	-	-	-	-	-	-	-
Italy 1934	Did not qualify	-	-	-	-	-	-	-	-	-	-	-	-
France 1938	First round	-	-	-	-	-	-	1	0	1	0	4	4
Brazil 1950	Did not enter	-	-	-	-	-	-	-	-	-	-	-	-
Switzerland 1954	Withdrew	-	-	-	-	-	-	-	-	-	-	-	-
Sweden 1958	Did not qualify	-	-	-	-	-	-	-	-	-	-	-	-
Chile 1962	Did not qualify	-	-	-	-	-	-	-	-	-	-	-	-
England 1966	Did not qualify	-	-	-	-	-	-	-	-	-	-	-	-
Mexico 1970	Did not qualify	-	-	-	-	-	-	-	-	-	-	-	-
Germany 1974	Third place	6	5	0	1	15	5	1	1	0	0	1	0
Argentina 1978	2nd group stage	6	3	1	2	6	6	-	-	-	-	-	-
Spain 1982	Third place	5	2	3	0	8	1	2	1	0	1	3	4
Mexico 1986	Round of 16	3	1	1	1	1	3	1	0	0	1	0	4
Italy 1990	Did not qualify	-	-	-	-	-	-	-	-	-	-	-	-
USA 1994	Did not qualify	-	-	-	-	-	-	-	-	-	-	-	-
France 1998	Did not qualify	-	-	-	-	-	-	-	-	-	-	-	-
Korea/Japan 2002	Group stage	3	1	0	2	3	7	-	-	-	-	-	-
Germany 2006	Group stage	3	1	0	2	2	4	-	-	-	-	-	-
South Africa 2010	Did not qualify	-	-	-	-	-	-	-	-	-	-	-	-
Brazil 2014	Did not qualify	-	-	-	-	-	-	-	-	-	-	-	-
Totals		26	13	5	8	35	26	5	2	1	2	8	12

Continental championships (best perfomance)

Uefa European Championship	Quarter-finals (1)	2016

World Cup head-to-heads

Poland v	P	W	D	L	F	A	Latest
Argentina	2	1	0	1	3	4	1978
Belgium	1	1	0	0	3	0	1982
Brazil	4	1	1	2	6	11	1986
Costa Rica	1	1	0	0	2	1	2006
Croatia	1	1	0	0	2	1	1974
England	1	0	0	1	0	3	1986
France	1	1	0	0	3	2	1982
Germany	3	0	1	2	0	2	2006
Mexico	1	1	0	0	3	1	1978
Morocco	1	0	1	0	0	0	1986
Peru	2	2	0	0	6	1	1982
Portugal	2	1	0	1	1	4	2002
Russia	1	0	1	0	0	0	1982
Serbia	1	1	0	0	2	1	1974
South Korea	1	0	0	1	0	2	2002
Sweden	1	1	0	0	1	0	1974
Tunisia	1	1	0	0	1	0	1978

90 mins only, includes games against Yugoslavia, West Germany and USSR

Gary Lineker got a hat-trick when Poland met potential last-16 opponents England in 1986

GROUP H

How they qualified

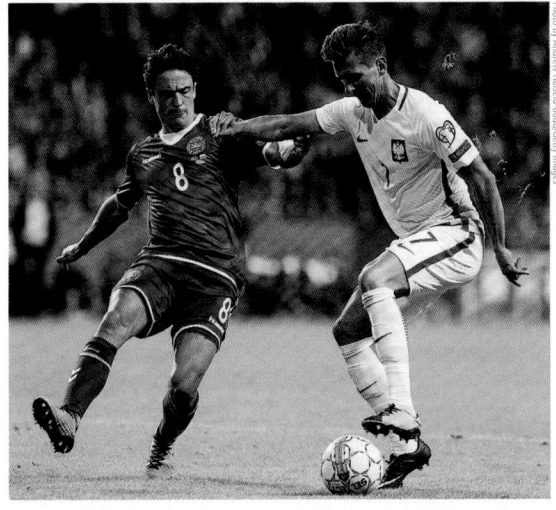

Group E	P	W	D	L	F	A	GD	P
Poland	10	8	1	1	28	14	14	25
Denmark	10	6	2	2	20	8	12	20
Montenegro	10	5	1	4	20	12	8	16
Romania	10	3	4	3	12	10	2	13
Armenia	10	2	1	7	10	26	-16	7
Kazakhstan	10	0	3	7	6	26	-20	3

Kazakhstan .... (0) 2-2 (2)............ **Poland**
Poland.......... (2) 3-2 (0)........**Denmark**
Poland.......... (0) 2-1 (0)............Armenia
Romania......... (0) 0-3 (1)............ **Poland**
Montenegro... (0) 1-2 (1)............ **Poland**
Poland.......... (1) 3-1 (0)......... Romania
Denmark ...... (2) 4-0 (0)............ **Poland**
Poland.......... (1) 3-0 (0).....Kazakhstan
Armenia .... (1) 1-6 (3)............ **Poland**
Poland.......... (2) 4-2 (0).... Montenegro

The 4-0 defeat by Denmark (left) was the only setback in Poland's qualifying campaign

Players used in qualifying		Career				Qualification			
Pos		**Club**	**Age**	**P**	**G**	**P**	**G**	☐	■
GK	Lukasz Fabianski	Swansea	33	43	-	7	-	-	-
GK	Wojciech Szczesny	Juventus	28	33	-	3	-	-	-
DEF	Artur Jedrzejczyk	Legia Warsaw	30	35	3	6	-	-	-
DEF	Bartosz Bereszynski	Sampdoria	25	6	-	2	-	-	-
DEF	Bartosz Salamon	Spal	27	9	-	1	-	-	-
DEF	Jan Bednarek	Southampton	22	1	-	1	-	-	-
DEF	Kamil Glik	Monaco	30	58	4	9	1	2	-
DEF	Lucasz Piszczek	B Dortmund	33	61	3	9	1	1	-
DEF	Michal Pazdan	Legia Warsaw	30	31	-	7	-	-	-
DEF	Thiago Cionek	Spal	32	17	-	6	-	2	-
MID	Maciej Rybus	Lok. Moscow	28	49	2	5	-	-	-
MID	Bartosz Kapustka	Freiburg	21	14	3	2	1	-	-
MID	Grzegorz Krychowiak	West Brom	28	48	2	7	-	-	-
MID	Jakub Blaszczykowski	Wolfsburg	32	97	17	10	1	1	-
MID	Kamil Grosicki	Hull	30	56	12	9	3	-	-
MID	Karol Linetty	Sampdoria	23	19	1	7	-	-	-
MID	Krzysztof Maczynski	Legia Warsaw	31	31	2	7	1	1	-
MID	Maciej Makuszewski	Lech Poznan	28	4	-	3	-	-	-
MID	Pawal Wszolek	QPR	26	11	2	1	-	-	-
MID	Piotr Zielinski	Napoli	24	31	4	10	-	1	-
MID	Rafal Wolski	Lechia Gdansk	25	7	1	2	1	-	-
MID	Slawomir Peszko	Lechia Gdansk	33	43	2	3	-	-	-
ATT	Arkadiusz Milik	Napoli	24	38	12	5	1	-	-
ATT	Kamil Wilczek	Brondby	30	3	-	1	-	-	-
ATT	Lukasz Teodorczyk	Anderlecht	27	15	4	5	-	-	-
ATT	Robert Lewandowski	B Munich	29	93	52	10	16	1	-

POLAND

Correct scores

	Competitive	Friendly
1-0	2	1
2-0	1	-
2-1	3	-
3-0	2	-
3-1	1	1
3-2	1	1
4-0	2	-
4-1	-	-
4-2	1	1
4-3	-	-
0-0	1	3
1-1	3	1
2-2	3	1
3-3	-	-
4-4	-	-
0-1	-	2
0-2	-	-
1-2	-	1
0-3	-	-
1-3	1	-
2-3	-	-
0-4	1	-
1-4	-	-
2-4	-	-
3-4	-	-
Other	3	1

Since Brazil 2014

Half-time/full-time double results

Win/Win	10	40%	Win 1st half	13	52%
Draw/Win	6	24%	Win 2nd half	12	48%
Lose/Win	0	0%	Win both halves	6	24%
Win/Draw	3	12%	Goal both halves	11	44%
Draw/Draw	4	16%			
Lose/Draw	0	0%	**Overall**		
Win/Lose	0	0%	● Win	64%	
Draw/Lose	0	0%	● Draw	28%	
Lose/Lose	2	8%	● Lose	8%	

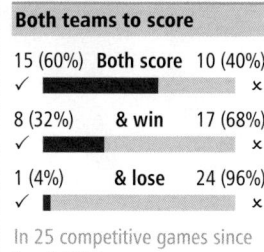

Overall: W16, D7, L2 in 25 competitive games since Brazil 2014

Under & over goals

22 (88%) **Over 1.5** 3 (12%) ✓ ✗

18 (72%) **Over 2.5** 7 (28%) ✓ ✗

13 (52%) **Over 3.5** 12 (48%) ✓ ✗

5 (20%) **Over 4.5** 20 (80%) ✓ ✗

Both teams to score

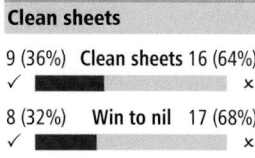

15 (60%) **Both score** 10 (40%) ✓ ✗

8 (32%) **& win** 17 (68%) ✓ ✗

1 (4%) **& lose** 24 (96%) ✓ ✗

In 25 competitive games since Brazil 2014

Clean sheets

9 (36%) **Clean sheets** 16 (64%) ✓ ✗

8 (32%) **Win to nil** 17 (68%) ✓ ✗

Fail to score

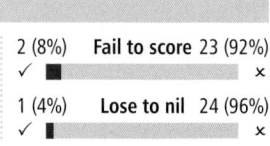

2 (8%) **Fail to score** 23 (92%) ✓ ✗

1 (4%) **Lose to nil** 24 (96%) ✓ ✗

When they score

● For ● Against

Total match goals by half

26 (74%) **1st half** 9 (26%)
F A

39 (70%) **2nd half** 17 (30%)
F A

Goals for & against by half

26 (40%) **For** 39 (60%)
1st 2nd

9 (35%) **Against** 17 (65%)
1st 2nd

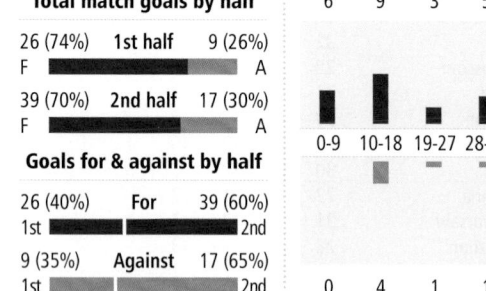

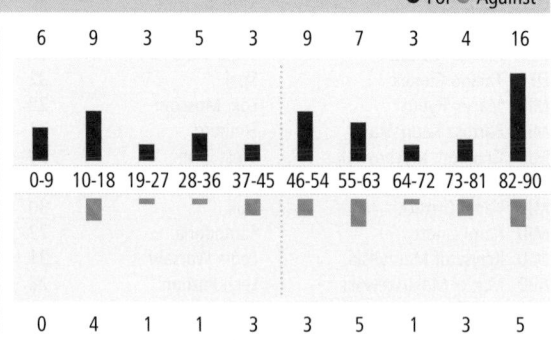

	0-9	10-18	19-27	28-36	37-45	46-54	55-63	64-72	73-81	82-90
For	6	9	3	5	3	9	7	3	4	16
Against	0	4	1	1	3	3	5	1	3	5

Poland score first

They win	16		73%
They draw	6		27%
They lose	0		0%

Poland concede first

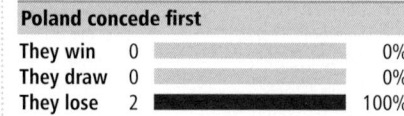

They win	0		0%
They draw	0		0%
They lose	2		100%

In 25 competitive games since Brazil 2014

GROUP H

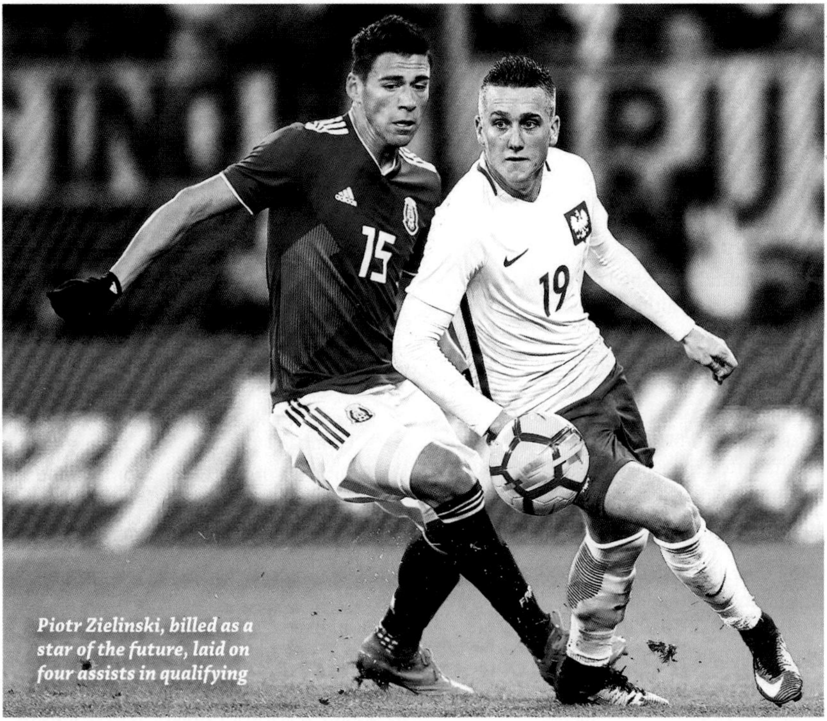

Piotr Zielinski, billed as a star of the future, laid on four assists in qualifying

Top scorers in qualifying

	P	G	1st	AT	%	Kaz 2-2 Pol	Pol 3-2 Dnk	Pol 2-1 Arm	Rou 0-3 Pol	Mne 1-2 Pol	Pol 3-1 Rou	Dnk 4-0 Pol	Pol 3-0 Kaz	Arm 1-6 Pol	Pol 4-2 Mne
Robert Lewandowski	10	16	3	9	57	1	3	1	2	1	3	-	1	3	1
Kamil Grosicki	9	3	2	3	11		⟲	⟲	⤷1	⟲	-		⟲	⤷1	⤷1
Bartosz Kapustka	2	1	1	1	4	⤷1	⤷								
Rafal Wolski	2	1	0	1	4									⤷1	⤷
Arkadiusz Milik	5	1	1	1	4	-	⟲				⤷	⤷	1		
Krzysztof Maczynski	7	1	1	1	4				⤷	⟲	⟲	-	⟲	⤷	⤷1
Lucasz Piszczek	9	1	0	1	4	-	-		-	1	-	⟲	-	-	⟲
Kamil Glik	9	1	0	1	4	-	-		-		-	-		1	-
Jakub Blaszczykowski	10	1	0	1	4	-	⟲	-	-	-		⟲	⤷	1	-

G goals scored, **1st** first match goal (own goals don't count) **AT** goals at any time (ie. number of scoring appearances), **P** penalties, **%** percentage of total team goals scored by each player. Russia 2018 qualifying only. Game-by-game stats show goals scored, 1st goals are in red, dash did not score, ⤷ substituted on, ⟲ substituted off, blank did not play

Bookings in World Cup qualifying

Played 10 **Cards** (9Y) ⬜⬜⬜⬜⬜⬜⬜⬜⬜   **Avg make-up** (⬜10 ⬛25) 9

SENEGAL

Profile

Senegal have only been to one World Cup but they made their mark, reaching the quarter-finals and stunning champions France with a 1-0 victory in the tournament opener. Big teams be warned – the Lions of Teranga are back.

How they qualified

They eventually finished five points clear of Burkina Faso, although that was due to replaying a match against South Africa which Senegal won having lost first time around. Fifa found original referee Joseph Lamptey guilty of breaching the rule relating to "unlawfully influencing match results" after giving a nonexistent penalty in a match with suspicious betting patterns.

The manager

Aliou Cisse, captain of that 2002 side, was promoted from managing the Under-23s in 2015 and led the seniors to the Afcon quarter-finals last year. They were beaten in a shootout by eventual champions Cameroon with Sadio Mane missing the decisive penalty.

The squad

Goalie Khadim N'Diaye is likely to be the only African-based player in a squad which has been boosted by striker M'Baye Niang, full-back Youssouf Sabaly and keeper Alfred Gomis committing to Senegal having represented France and Italy at various youth levels.

Cisse seems likely to use 4-3-3 and there is plenty of talent on the flanks with Mane and Monaco's Keita Balde. The main striking role will fall to either Niang or Diafra Sakho.

There is a strong English-based presence fighting for the three midfield slots with Idrissa Gana Gueye and Cheikhou Kouyate two almost definite starters. Stoke's recent signing Badou Ndiaye may join them, although Wolves' Alfred N'Diaye and Birmingham's Cheikh Ndoye are other options, along with Saint-

Factfile

FA founded 1960

www fsf.sn

Head coach Aliou Cisse

Date qualified November 10, 2017

Strengths

- ☑ Koulibaly and Mane give them real quality in both boxes
- ☑ Tremendous pace on the counter attack

Weaknesses

- ☒ Eccentric keeper N'Diaye plays in Guinea
- ☒ Difficult group with Colombia and Poland

Star rating ★★☆☆☆

Fixtures

1 June 19, 4pm v Poland, Otkrytie Arena, Moscow

2 June 24, 4pm v Japan, Yekaterinburg

3 June 28, 3pm v Colombia, Samara

Base Kaluga

Total distance 3,250 miles

Cheikhou Kouyate is a likely starter in a midfield with an English-based flavour

Etienne youngster Assane Diousse.

Napoli's rock Kalidou Koulibaly is one of the world's best and most underrated centre-backs, while Bordeaux's Sabala is an interesting addition to the defence. He was in the French squad that won the Under-20 World Cup in 2013.

Key man

Mane, part of a fab front three at Liverpool alongside Mo Salah and Roberto Firmino, can produce devastating quality and holds a burning desire for redemption having been the fall guy at the Africa Cup of Nations last year. He was in tears after fluffing his lines from 12 yards.

Rising star

It feels like Niang has had more car crashes than goals – he likes to live life in the fast lane with a number of high-profile prangs part of a colourful off-field career which has seen the Caen graduate sent on loan to Montpellier, Genoa, Watford and Torino since joining Milan in 2012.

The forward has talent – he became one of the youngest scorers in Milan's history – and represented France at youth levels from Under-16 to Under-21 but he was banned from the national team in 2012 after breaking a curfew when on Under-21 duty to visit a Paris nightclub alongside Antoine Griezmann and Wissam Ben Yedder.

Niang, whose girlfriend is Instagram model Emilie Fiorelli, will have to settle down if he is to avoid wasting his career. This could be his moment.

Wildcard

Pape Souare was not sure if he would ever recover from life-threatening injuries suffered in a car cash in 2016 but the Crystal Palace left-back was recalled to the Senegal squad in March.

Prospects

The group is difficult but don't underestimate Senegal.

How to back them

Draw no bet against an inferior Japan on June 24.

SENEGAL

World Cup record		Group stage(s)						Knockout rounds					
		P	W	D	L	F	A	P	W	D	L	F	A
Uruguay 1930	Did not enter	-	-	-	-	-	-	-	-	-	-	-	-
Italy 1934	Did not enter	-	-	-	-	-	-	-	-	-	-	-	-
France 1938	Did not enter	-	-	-	-	-	-	-	-	-	-	-	-
Brazil 1950	Did not enter	-	-	-	-	-	-	-	-	-	-	-	-
Switzerland 1954	Did not enter	-	-	-	-	-	-	-	-	-	-	-	-
Sweden 1958	Did not enter	-	-	-	-	-	-	-	-	-	-	-	-
Chile 1962	Did not enter	-	-	-	-	-	-	-	-	-	-	-	-
England 1966	Withdrew	-	-	-	-	-	-	-	-	-	-	-	-
Mexico 1970	Did not qualify	-	-	-	-	-	-	-	-	-	-	-	-
Germany 1974	Did not qualify	-	-	-	-	-	-	-	-	-	-	-	-
Argentina 1978	Did not qualify	-	-	-	-	-	-	-	-	-	-	-	-
Spain 1982	Did not qualify	-	-	-	-	-	-	-	-	-	-	-	-
Mexico 1986	Did not qualify	-	-	-	-	-	-	-	-	-	-	-	-
Italy 1990	Did not enter	-	-	-	-	-	-	-	-	-	-	-	-
USA 1994	Did not qualify	-	-	-	-	-	-	-	-	-	-	-	-
France 1998	Did not qualify	-	-	-	-	-	-	-	-	-	-	-	-
Korea/Japan 2002	Quarter-finals	3	1	2	0	5	4	2	0	2	0	1	1
Germany 2006	Did not qualify	-	-	-	-	-	-	-	-	-	-	-	-
South Africa 2010	Did not qualify	-	-	-	-	-	-	-	-	-	-	-	-
Brazil 2014	Did not qualify	-	-	-	-	-	-	-	-	-	-	-	-
Totals		3	1	2	0	5	4	2	0	2	0	1	1

Continental championships (best perfomance)

Africa Cup of nations	Beaten finalists (1)	2002

World Cup head-to-heads

Senegal produced one of the great upsets when they beat world champs France in the 2002 opener

Senegal v	P	W	D	L	F	A	Latest	Senegal v	P	W	D	L	F	A	Latest
Denmark	1	0	1	0	1	1	2002	Sweden	1	0	1	0	1	1	2002
France	1	1	0	0	1	0	2002	Uruguay	1	0	1	0	3	3	2002

90 mins only

How they qualified

Round 2
Madagascar... (1) 2-2 (0)......... **Senegal**
Senegal......... (1) 3-0 (0).....Madagascar
Senegal won 5-2 on aggregate

Round 3

Group D	P	W	D	L	F	A	GD	P
Senegal	6	4	2	0	10	3	7	14
Burkina Faso	6	2	3	1	10	6	4	9
Cape Verde	6	2	0	4	4	12	-8	6
South Africa	6	1	1	4	7	10	-3	4

Senegal......... (1) 2-0 (0).....Cape Verde
South Africa... (2) 2-1 (0)......... **Senegal**
Match annulled
Senegal......... (0) 0-0 (0)....Burkina Faso
Burkina Faso.. (1) 2-2 (1)......... **Senegal**
Cape Verde .... (0) 0-2 (0)......... **Senegal**
South Africa... (0) 0-2 (2)......... **Senegal**
Senegal......... (0) 2-1 (0).... South Africa

Coach Aliou Cisse captained Senegal's 2002 World Cup side

Players used in qualifying		Career			Qualification			
Pos	Club	Age	P	G	P	G	⬜	⬛
GK Abdoulaye Diallo	Rennes	26	16	-	3	-	-	-
GK Alfred Gomis	Spal	24	1	-	1	-	-	-
GK Khadim N'Diaye	Horoya AC	33	19	-	4	-	-	-
GK Pape Ndiaye	ASC Niary Tally	25	4	-	1	-	-	-
DEF Kara Mbodji	Anderlecht	28	43	5	7	1	2	-
DEF Adama Mbengue	Caen	24	5	-	1	-	-	-
DEF Kalidou Koulibaly	Napoli	26	23	-	6	-	1	1
DEF Lamine Gassama	Alanyaspor	28	34	-	5	-	2	-
DEF Lamine Sane	Orlando City	31	33	-	2	-	-	-
DEF Moussa Wague	KAS Eupen	19	8	-	4	-	-	-
DEF Salif Sane	Hannover	27	20	-	3	-	-	-
DEF Saliou Ciss	Angers	28	15	-	7	-	1	-
DEF Youssouf Sabaly	Bordeaux	25	3	-	2	-	-	-
DEF Zargo Toure	Lorient	28	18	-	1	-	-	-
MID Alfred N'Diaye	Wolves	28	17	1	2	-	-	-
MID Assane Diousse	St-Etienne	20	2	-	1	-	-	-
MID Papa Ndiaye	Stoke	27	15	1	4	-	1	-
MID Cheikh Ndoye	Birmingham	32	23	3	6	1	-	-
MID Cheikhou Kouyate	West Ham	28	42	2	8	1	-	-
MID Henri Saivet	Sivasspor	27	24	1	2	-	-	-
MID Idrissa Gueye	Everton	28	53	1	8	-	1	-
MID Ismaila Sarr	Rennes	20	12	2	2	1	-	-
MID Mohamed Diame	Newcastle	31	34	1	1	-	-	-
MID Pape Diop	Eibar	32	21	1	1	-	-	-
MID Younousse Sankhare	Bordeaux	28	6	1	2	-	-	-
ATT Mame Biram Diouf	Stoke	30	44	10	2	2	2	-
ATT Opa Nguette	Metz	23	4	1	2	1	1	-
ATT Diafra Sakho	Rennes	28	7	3	2	2	-	-
ATT Keita Balde	Monaco	23	16	3	4	1	-	-
ATT M'Baye Niang	Torino	23	4	-	3	-	1	-
ATT Moussa Konate	Amiens	25	25	9	4	1	1	-
ATT Moussa Sow	Bursaspor	32	47	18	4	1	-	-
ATT Oumar Niasse	Everton	28	6	3	1	-	-	-
ATT Sadio Mane	Liverpool	26	48	14	7	2	2	-

SENEGAL

Correct scores

	Competitive	Friendly
1-0	1	1
2-0	11	3
2-1	3	2
3-0	3	-
3-1	1	-
3-2	-	-
4-0	-	-
4-1	-	-
4-2	-	-
4-3	-	-
0-0	3	2
1-1	1	2
2-2	3	-
3-3	-	-
4-4	-	-
0-1	1	2
0-2	1	1
1-2	-	-
0-3	-	-
1-3	-	-
2-3	-	-
0-4	-	-
1-4	-	-
2-4	-	-
3-4	-	-
Other	-	1

Since Brazil 2014

Half-time/full-time double results

Win/Win	16	57%	Win 1st half	15	54%
Draw/Win	2	7%	Win 2nd half	12	43%
Lose/Win	1	4%	Win both halves	8	29%
Win/Draw	0	0%	Goal both halves	11	39%
Draw/Draw	6	21%			
Lose/Draw	1	4%	**Overall**		
Win/Lose	0	0%	● Win	68%	
Draw/Lose	1	4%	● Draw	25%	
Lose/Lose	1	4%	● Lose	7%	

Overall: W19, D7, L2 in 28 competitive games since Brazil 2014

Under & over goals

23 (82%) **Over 1.5** 5 (18%)
✓ ✗

10 (36%) **Over 2.5** 18 (64%)
✓ ✗

4 (14%) **Over 3.5** 24 (86%)
✓ ✗

0 (0%) **Over 4.5** 28 (100%)
✓ ✗

Both teams to score

8 (29%) **Both score** 20 (71%)
✓ ✗

4 (14%) **& win** 24 (86%)
✓ ✗

0 (0%) **& lose** 28 (100%)
✓ ✗

In 28 competitive games since Brazil 2014

Clean sheets

18 (64%) **Clean sheets** 10 (36%)
✓ ✗

15 (54%) **Win to nil** 13 (46%)
✓ ✗

5 (18%) **Fail to score** 23 (82%)
✓ ✗

2 (7%) **Lose to nil** 26 (93%)
✓ ✗

When they score

● For ● Against

Total match goals by half

25 (83%) **1st half** 5 (17%)
F A

23 (72%) **2nd half** 9 (28%)
F A

3	6	7	4	5	2	5	3	4	9
0-9	10-18	19-27	28-36	37-45	46-54	55-63	64-72	73-81	82-90
1	3	1	0	0	2	3	2	0	2

Goals for & against by half

25 (52%) **For** 23 (48%)
1st 2nd

5 (36%) **Against** 9 (64%)
1st 2nd

Senegal score first

They win	18	100%
They draw	0	0%
They lose	0	0%

Senegal concede first

They win	1	14%
They draw	4	57%
They lose	2	29%

In 28 competitive games since Brazil 2014

Sadio Mane will be desperate to make amends for missing his penalty as Senegal crashed out of the Africa Cup of Nations

Photo by Ian Mallan/Getty Images

Top scorers in qualifying

	P	G	1st	AT	%	Mdg 2-2 Sen	Sen 3-0 Mdg	Sen 2-0 Cpv	Sen 0-0 Bfa	Bfa 2-2 Sen	Cpv 0-2 Sen	Zaf 0-2 Sen	Sen 2-1 Zaf
Diafra Sakho	2	2	2	2	13						1	1	
Mame Biram Diouf	2	2	0	2	13	1	1						
Sadio Mane	7	2	0	2	13	1	-	-	-	1	↺	-	
Opa N'Guette	2	1	1	1	7						↳		1
Ismaila Sarr	2	1	0	1	7				↺		1		
Keita Balde	4	1	1	1	7				1	↳	↳	↺	
Moussa Sow	4	1	0	1	7				↺1	↺	↺		-
Moussa Konate	4	1	0	1	7	↳	↺1	↺				↳	
Cheikh N'Doye	6	1	0	1	7	↳	↳	↳				↺1	-	↳
Kara Mbodji	7	1	0	1	7	↺	-	-	-	-	-	-	1
Cheikhou Kouyate	8	1	1	1	7	↺	↺1	↺	↳	-		↺	-

G goals scored, **1st** first match goal (own goals don't count) **AT** goals at any time (ie. number of scoring appearances), **P** penalties, **%** percentage of total team goals scored by each player. Russia 2018 qualifying only. Game-by-game stats show goals scored, 1st goals are in red, dash did not score, ↳ substituted on, ↺ substituted off, blank did not play

Bookings in World Cup qualifying

Played 8 **Cards** (15Y, 1YR) □□□□□□□□□□□□□□□□ ▣   **Avg make-up** (□10 ▣25) 21.9

Note: Senegal's World Cup home kit had not been released when we went to press

COLOMBIA

Profile

Colombia were treated like heroes after returning from the 2014 World Cup, where they suffered heartbreak against hosts Brazil at the quarter-final stage, but they lost in the same round in a shootout in Argentina at the the 2015 Copa America and were eliminated in the semi-final in 2017 leaving many questioning whether Los Cafeteros are destined to be a nearly side.

How they qualified

A draw away in Peru on the final night secured nervy Colombia's spot. Given the quality of their attacking options it should come as a surprise to see Colombia scored just 21 goals in 18 qualifiers (James Rodriguez grabbed six of those), with Jose Pekerman using 45 players.

The manager

Pekerman teams are usually aesthetically pleasing. He did his best work as Argentina's youth manager, winning the Under-20 World Cup three times in 1995, 1997 and 2001.

The squad

David Ospina was the only player to start all 18 qualifiers and tends to be considered a more reliable last line of defence at international level than the jittery performances seen for Arsenal.

Rodriguez is the influential figure and his positioning will depend on whether Pekerman goes 4-4-2 or 4-2-3-1. In a two-pronged attack, Rodriguez starts on the left with Carlos Bacca or Luis Muriel alongside Radamel Falcao, although James is arguably at his best off one striker.

Falcao's minutes need to be managed due to long-standing knee problems but he will be desperate to impress after missing the last World Cup due to injury and Juventus's inconsistent Juan Cuadrado is a driving force down the right flank.

Aston Villa flop Carlos Sanchez sets the tone in midfield and the starting

Factfile

FA founded 1924

www fcf.com.co

Head coach Jose Pekerman

Date qualified October 10, 2017

Strengths

☑ James Rodriguez is a special talent when in the mood

☑ On paper they have many different goalscoring options

Weaknesses

☒ Falcao may struggle to play matches in quick succession

☒ Not a team to trust when the pressure is on

Star rating ★★★☆☆

Fixtures

1 June 19, 4pm v Japan, Saransk

2 June 24, 7pm v Poland, Kazan

3 June 28, 3pm v Senegal, Samara

Base Tartastan

Total distance 750 miles

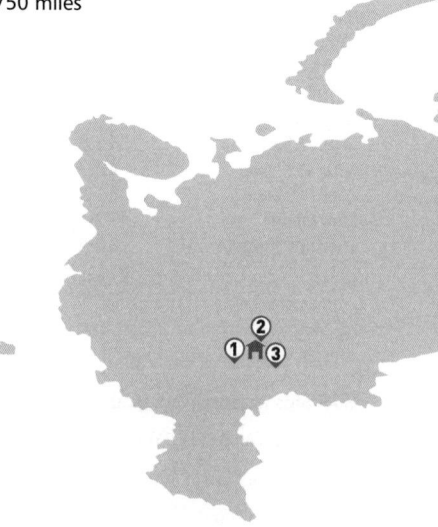

Knees permitting, Radamel Falcao will want to impress in Russia after missing out on Brazil 2014

centre-backs will be an interesting call for Pekerman, who began Conmebol qualifying with Jeison Murillo and Cristian Zapata but needs to weigh those up against emerging forces Davinson Sanchez (Tottenham) and Yerry Mina (Barcelona).

Key man

Rodriguez caused a stir at the last World Cup and not just because of his sensational strike against Uruguay in the last 16, one of the six goals that saw him land the Golden Boot. A move to Real Madrid followed, but after falling out of favour at the Bernabeu, a long-term loan switch to Bayern Munich has left James feeling peachy again.

Rising star

It has been a meteoric rise for Davinson Sanchez. The centre-back was signed by Ajax in 2016 after playing just over 20 matches for Nacional and one season in Amsterdam was enough to persuade Tottenham to break their transfer record to sign him. A robust,

quick and physical defender, Sanchez still needs to develop his positioning, decision making and distribution.

Wildcard

Jose Izquierdo was a regular scorer for Club Brugge and has forced his way into the squad since moving to Brighton. A skillful winger, he is capable of the spectacular.

Prospects

Colombia have probably missed their chance so close to home soil in South America in 2014. They are one of a number of sides who would regard reaching the quarter-finals as successful.

How to back them

Given the way they struggle under pressure, backing Colombia to start quickly might be the safest bet and Los Cafeteros look value to overcome Japan first up.

Looking further ahead, check out fancy prices on them to be eliminated on penalties.

COLOMBIA

World Cup record		Group stage(s)						Knockout rounds					
		P	W	D	L	F	A	P	W	D	L	F	A
Uruguay 1930	Not part of Fifa	-	-	-	-	-	-	-	-	-	-	-	-
Italy 1934	Not part of Fifa	-	-	-	-	-	-	-	-	-	-	-	-
France 1938	Withdrew	-	-	-	-	-	-	-	-	-	-	-	-
Brazil 1950	Did not enter	-	-	-	-	-	-	-	-	-	-	-	-
Switzerland 1954	Banned	-	-	-	-	-	-	-	-	-	-	-	-
Sweden 1958	Did not qualify	-	-	-	-	-	-	-	-	-	-	-	-
Chile 1962	Group stage	3	0	1	2	5	11	-	-	-	-	-	-
England 1966	Did not qualify	-	-	-	-	-	-	-	-	-	-	-	-
Mexico 1970	Did not qualify	-	-	-	-	-	-	-	-	-	-	-	-
Germany 1974	Did not qualify	-	-	-	-	-	-	-	-	-	-	-	-
Argentina 1978	Did not qualify	-	-	-	-	-	-	-	-	-	-	-	-
Spain 1982	Did not qualify	-	-	-	-	-	-	-	-	-	-	-	-
Mexico 1986	Did not qualify	-	-	-	-	-	-	-	-	-	-	-	-
Italy 1990	Round of 16	3	1	1	1	3	2	1	0	1	0	0	0
USA 1994	Group stage	3	1	0	2	4	5	-	-	-	-	-	-
France 1998	Group stage	3	1	0	2	1	3	-	-	-	-	-	-
Korea/Japan 2002	Did not qualify	-	-	-	-	-	-	-	-	-	-	-	-
Germany 2006	Did not qualify	-	-	-	-	-	-	-	-	-	-	-	-
South Africa 2010	Did not qualify	-	-	-	-	-	-	-	-	-	-	-	-
Brazil 2014	Quarter-finals	3	3	0	0	9	2	2	1	0	1	3	2
Totals		15	6	2	7	22	23	3	1	1	1	3	2

Continental championships (best perfomance)

Copa America	Winners (1)	2001

World Cup head-to-heads

Colombia v	P	W	D	L	F	A	Latest
Brazil	1	0	0	1	1	2	2014
Croatia	2	0	0	2	0	6	1990
England	1	0	0	1	0	2	1998
Germany	1	0	1	0	1	1	1990
Japan	1	1	0	0	4	1	2014
Russia	1	0	1	0	4	4	1962
Serbia	2	0	0	2	0	6	1990
Switzerland	1	1	0	0	2	0	1994
Tunisia	1	1	0	0	1	0	1998
Uruguay	2	1	0	1	3	2	2014

90 mins only, includes games against Yugoslavia, USSR and West Germany

Colombia beat Japan 4-1 at Brazil 2014

How they qualified

Top five	P	W	D	L	F	A	GD	P
Brazil	18	12	5	1	41	11	30	41
Uruguay	18	9	4	5	32	20	12	31
Argentina	18	7	7	4	19	16	3	28
Colombia	18	7	6	5	21	19	2	27
Peru	18	7	5	6	27	26	1	26

Colombia ...... (1) 2-0 (0) .... Peru

Uruguay .... (1) 3-0 (0) .... Colombia
Chile .... (1) 1-1 (0) .... Colombia
Colombia ...... (0) 0-1 (1) .... Argentina
Bolivia .... (0) 2-3 (2) .... Colombia
Colombia ...... (1) 3-1 (0) .... Ecuador
Colombia ...... (1) 2-0 (0) .... Venezuela
Brazil .... (1) 2-1 (1) .... Colombia
Paraguay .... (0) 0-1 (0) .... Colombia
Colombia ...... (1) 2-2 (1) .... Uruguay

Colombia ...... (0) 0-0 (0) .... Chile
Argentina ..... (2) 3-0 (0) .... Colombia
Colombia ...... (0) 1-0 (0) .... Bolivia
Ecuador .... (0) 0-2 (2) .... Colombia
Venezuela ...... (0) 0-0 (0) .... Colombia
Colombia ...... (0) 1-1 (1) .... Brazil
Colombia ...... (0) 1-2 (0) .... Paraguay
Peru .... (0) 1-1 (0) .... Colombia

Players used in qualifying		Career				Qualification			
Pos		Club	Age	P	G	P	G	🔲	⬛
GK	David Ospina	Arsenal	29	86	-	18	-	-	-
DEF	Oscar Murillo	Pachuca	30	12	-	9	-	3	-
DEF	Christian Zapata	Milan	31	55	2	10	-	4	-
DEF	Davison Sanchez	Tottenham	22	8	-	4	-	-	-
DEF	Eder Alvarez	Basel	25	7	-	1	-	1	-
DEF	Farid Diaz	Olimpia	34	13	-	8	-	1	-
DEF	Frank Fabra	Boca Juniors	27	18	1	8	-	1	-
DEF	Helibelton Palacios	Atletico Nacional	25	1	-	1	-	1	-
DEF	Jeison Murillo	Valencia	26	25	1	8	-	1	-
DEF	Pablo Armero	America de Cali	31	68	2	1	-	-	-
DEF	Santiago Arias	PSV Eindhoven	26	40	-	13	-	3	-
DEF	Steffan Medina	Monterrey	26	10	-	3	-	1	-
DEF	William Tesillo	Santa Fe	28	3	-	1	-	-	-
DEF	Yerry Mina	Barcelona	23	11	3	5	1	-	-
MID	Carlos Sanchez	Esmanyol	32	84	-	15	-	3	-
MID	Gustavo Cuellar	Flamengo	25	3	-	1	-	1	-
MID	Abel Aguilar	Cali	33	71	7	8	1	1	-
MID	Alexander Mejia	Leon	29	25	-	4	-	1	-
MID	Daniel Torres	Alaves	28	14	-	7	-	2	-
MID	Edwin Cardona	Boca Juniors	25	31	5	15	3	1	-
MID	Fabian Castillo	Trabzonspor	25	3	-	2	-	1	-
MID	Fredy Guarin	Shanghai Shenhua	31	58	4	2	-	-	-
MID	Giovanni Moreno	Shanghai Shenhua	31	22	3	2	-	-	-
MID	Guillermo Celis	V Guimaraes	25	6	-	1	-	-	-
MID	James Rodriguez	B Munich	26	62	21	13	6	1	-
MID	Jonathan Copete	Santos	29	2	-	1	-	-	-
MID	Juan Cuadrado	Juventus	30	68	7	15	1	3	1
MID	Macnelly Torres	Atletico Nacional	33	48	4	8	1	-	-
MID	Andres Mateus Uribe	America	27	7	-	2	-	-	-
MID	Orlando Berrio	Flamengo	27	4	-	3	-	-	-
MID	Sebastian Perez	Boca Juniors	25	8	1	2	1	-	-
MID	Wilmar Barrios	Boca Juniors	24	10	-	6	-	-	-
MID	Yimmi Chara	Junior	27	7	-	4	-	-	-
ATT	Roger Martinez	Villarreal	23	7	1	3	-	-	-
ATT	Adrian Ramos	Granada	32	37	4	2	-	-	-
ATT	Carlos Bacca	Villarreal	31	44	14	13	3	-	-
ATT	Duvan Zapata	Sampdoria	27	5	-	2	-	-	-
ATT	Felipe Pardo	Olympiakos	27	3	1	1	-	-	-
ATT	Jackson Martinez	Unattached	31	41	10	1	-	-	-
ATT	Luis Muriel	Sevilla	27	18	2	10	-	1	-
ATT	Luis Quinones	Toluca	26	1	-	1	-	-	-
ATT	Marlos Moreno	Flamengo	21	8	1	3	-	-	-
ATT	Miguel Borja	Palmeiras	25	6	2	2	-	-	-
ATT	Radamel Falcao	Monaco	32	73	29	8	2	1	-
ATT	Teofilo Gutierrez	Junior	33	52	15	5	1	1	-

COLOMBIA

Correct scores

	Competitive	Friendly
1-0	4	3
2-0	4	-
2-1	1	-
3-0	-	1
3-1	1	2
3-2	1	1
4-0	-	2
4-1	-	-
4-2	-	-
4-3	-	-
0-0	5	1
1-1	3	1
2-2	1	2
3-3	-	-
4-4	-	-
0-1	2	2
0-2	1	-
1-2	2	1
0-3	2	-
1-3	-	-
2-3	1	-
0-4	-	-
1-4	-	-
2-4	-	-
3-4	-	-
Other	-	1

Since Brazil 2014

Half-time/full-time double results

Win/Win	9	32%	Win 1st half	9	32%
Draw/Win	2	7%	Win 2nd half	7	25%
Lose/Win	0	0%	Win both halves	3	11%
Win/Draw	0	0%	Goal both halves	6	21%
Draw/Draw	7	25%			
Lose/Draw	2	7%	**Overall**		
Win/Lose	0	0%	● Win	39%	
Draw/Lose	3	11%	● Draw	32%	
Lose/Lose	5	18%	● Lose	29%	

Overall: W11, D9, L8 in 28 competitive games since Brazil 2014

Under & over goals

17 (61%) **Over 1.5** 11 (39%) ✓ ✗

9 (32%) **Over 2.5** 19 (68%) ✓ ✗

4 (14%) **Over 3.5** 24 (86%) ✓ ✗

2 (7%) **Over 4.5** 26 (93%) ✓ ✗

Both teams to score

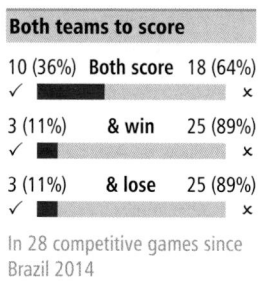

10 (36%) **Both score** 18 (64%) ✓ ✗

3 (11%) **& win** 25 (89%) ✓ ✗

3 (11%) **& lose** 25 (89%) ✓ ✗

In 28 competitive games since Brazil 2014

Clean sheets

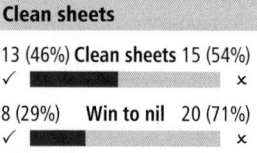

13 (46%) **Clean sheets** 15 (54%) ✓ ✗

8 (29%) **Win to nil** 20 (71%) ✓ ✗

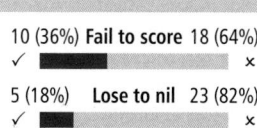

10 (36%) **Fail to score** 18 (64%) ✓ ✗

5 (18%) **Lose to nil** 23 (82%) ✓ ✗

When they score

● For ● Against

Total match goals by half

16 (57%) **1st half** 12 (43%)
F ▬▬▬▬▬ A

13 (48%) **2nd half** 14 (52%)
F ▬▬▬▬▬ A

Goals for & against by half

16 (55%) **For** 13 (45%)
1st ▬▬▬▬▬ 2nd

12 (46%) **Against** 14 (54%)
1st ▬▬▬▬▬ 2nd

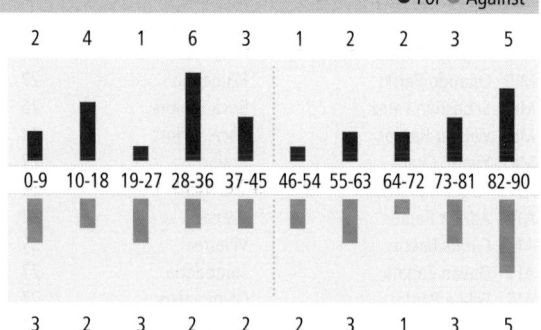

	2	4	1	6	3	1	2	2	3	5
	0-9	10-18	19-27	28-36	37-45	46-54	55-63	64-72	73-81	82-90
	3	2	3	2	2	2	3	1	3	5

Colombia score first

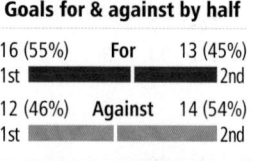

They win	11	79%
They draw	2	14%
They lose	1	7%

Colombia concede first

They win	0	0%
They draw	2	22%
They lose	7	78%

In 28 competitive games since Brazil 2014

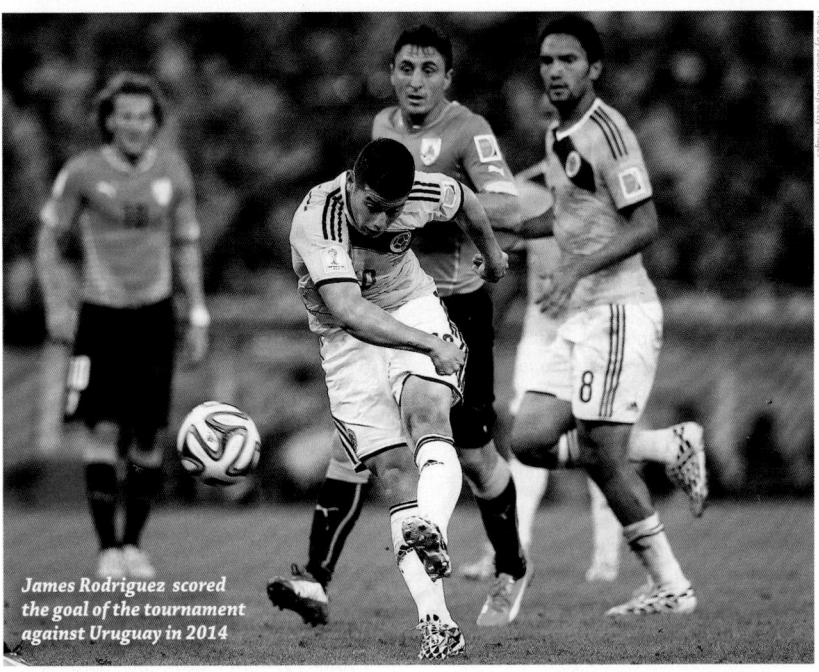

James Rodriguez scored the goal of the tournament against Uruguay in 2014

Top scorers in qualifying

	P	G	1st	AT	%	Ury 3-0 Col	Col 0-1 Arg	Col 3-1 Ecu	Col 2-0 Ven	Pry 0-1 Col	Col 0-0 Chi	Ecu 0-2 Col	Col 1-1 Bra	Per 1-1 Col	Col 2-0 Per	Chi 1-1 Col	Bol 2-3 Col	Bra 2-1 Col	Arg 3-0 Col	Col 1-0 Bol	Ven 0-0 Col	Col 1-2 Pry
James Rodriguez	13	6	5	6	29	-	-	1		-	1	-	↰1		1	1	-		-	1		-
Carlos Bacca	13	3	1	2	14	-	-	↰2	↰	-		↰		↰	↰	↰1	↰	↰	↰	↰		
Edwin Cardona	15	3	1	3	14	-	↰	-	↰	↰1	-	↰	↰	1		↰	↰1		↰		↰	↰
Radamel Falcao	8	2	1	2	10	↰				↰	-	1	↰	↰						↰	-	1
Juan Cuadrado	15	1	0	1	5	-		↰	↰	↰		1	↰	-	-		↰	↰	-	-	-	↰
Sebastian Perez	2	1	0	1	5		↰1							↰								
Tefilo Gutierrez	5	1	1	1	5	↰	↰						↰	↰1								↰
Yerry Mina	5	1	0	1	5				-	↰	-							1		-		
Abel Aguilar	8	1	1	1	5				-	-	↰	-	-					1			↰	↰
Macnelly Torres	8	1	0	1	5	↰	↰		1		↰						↰	-	↰	-		

G goals scored, **1st** first match goal (own goals don't count) **AT** goals at any time (ie. number of scoring appearances), **P** penalties, **%** percentage of total team goals scored by each player. Russia 2018 qualifying only. Game-by-game stats show goals scored, 1st goals are in red, dash did not score, ↰ substituted on, ↰ substituted off, blank did not play

Bookings in World Cup qualifying

Played 18 ▯▯▯▯▯▯▯▯▯▯▯▯▯▯▯▯▯▯▯▯▯▯▯▯▯▯▯▯▯ **Avg make-up** (▯10 ◼25) 19.7
Cards (33Y, 1R) ▯▯▯▯▯▯▯▯▯▯▯▯▯▯▯◼

Profile

Japan's Bosnian boss Vahid Halilhodzic is talking a good game ahead of the finals – "we can go to the World Cup as challengers, not tourists," he claimed after qualification was confirmed – and following the draw he admitted the group could have been worse. However, the confidence looks misplaced.

How they qualified

The Samurai Blue topped Group B in final qualifying without overly impressing and there was a suggestion at one stage that Halilhodzic was on the verge of the sack before a 2-0 home win over Australia booked a spot in Russia, Japan's sixth straight World Cup appearance.

The manager

Halilhodzic was a fabulous footballer in his time and has managed two other international sides, Ivory Coast and Algeria. He is not afraid to make big calls – his gamble on Riyad Mahrez, questioned in the lead-up to the 2014 World Cup given he had not produced consistently for Leicester at that point, worked out pretty well.

The Squad

A difficult one to read given Halilhodzic has said some of his biggest names such as Keisuke Honda, Shinji Kagawa and Shinji Okazaki are not certain to make the 23-man squad due to their perceived unsuitability to the formation (4-3-3) and counter-attacking approach.

Okazaki does not hold the ball up as well as Cologne's Yuya Osako and out wide there is a goal threat from Genki Haraguchi, who is in the German second division with Fortuna Dusseldorf. Haraguchi top-scored for Japan in final qualifying with six goals from the left wing. On the right Takuma Asano has shown a lack of confidence at Stuttgart, which could open the door for Yuya Kubo.

Takashi Inui is better than them all but does not appear to have

Factfile

FA founded 1921
www jfa.jp
Head coach Vahid Halilhodzic
Date qualified August 31, 2017

Strengths
- ☑ Halilhodzic took Algeria to the last 16 four years ago
- ☑ Avoided the big names in the draw

Weaknesses
- ☒ Halilhodzic has an uneasy relationship with the players and press
- ☒ Japan may not pick some of their top talents

Star rating ★☆☆☆☆

Fixtures

1 June 19, 4pm v Colombia, Saransk
2 June 24, 4pm v Senegal, Yekaterinburg
3 June 28, 3pm v Poland, Volgograd

Base Kazan
Total distance 2,350 miles

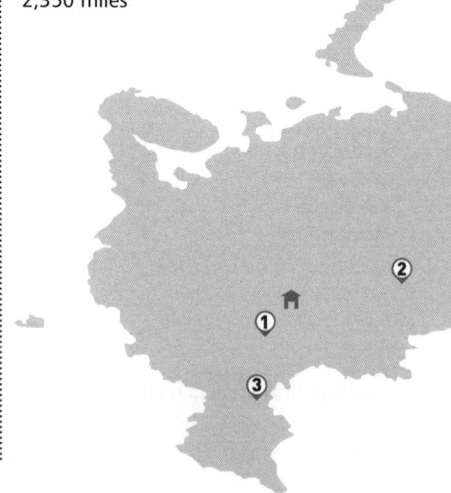

Keisuke Honda is capable of producing magic but is not guaranteed a place

Halilhodzic's full trust, unlike central midfield mainstays Hotaru Yamaguchi and captain Makoto Hasebe.

Kagawa falls into the same category as Inui, although there is more logic to the defensive picks, with the vastly experienced Yuto Nagatomo and Maya Yoshida vital.

Key man

Yoshida said of Halilhodzic "he is a bit of a weirdo" but the Southampton stopper will be influential seeing as the centre-back will probably be paired with either FC Tokyo's Masato Morishige or Kashima Antlers' Gen Shoji. Neither player has represented a club outside of Japan.

Rising star

The tiny Shoya Nakajima is having a fine season for Portimonense in Portugal on loan from FC Tokyo and scored on his debut against Mali in March.

Gent's Yuya Kubo is worth noting. He was nicknamed the Sushi Bomber as a result of his goalscoring exploits for Young Boys.

Wildcard

On paper Kagawa and Okazaki should walk into the squad and be in the starting 11. Kagawa is a nice passer in midfield for Borussia Dortmund and Okazaki is a Premier League title winner with Leicester. Honda has lost his way since being considered as the golden boy of Japanese football but the former CSKA Moscow and Milan man is still capable of producing magic from set-pieces with current Mexican club Pachuca.

Prospects

It could be an early bath for Japan.

How to back them

Discounting 2002 when they had home advantage, Japan have played 13 matches at the World Cup finals and won just twice, both in 2010. They should finish bottom of Group H.

World Cup record		Group stage(s)						Knockout rounds					
		P	W	D	L	F	A	P	W	D	L	F	A
Uruguay 1930	Did not enter	-	-	-	-	-	-	-	-	-	-	-	-
Italy 1934	Did not enter	-	-	-	-	-	-	-	-	-	-	-	-
France 1938	Withdrew	-	-	-	-	-	-	-	-	-	-	-	-
Brazil 1950	Banned	-	-	-	-	-	-	-	-	-	-	-	-
Switzerland 1954	Did not qualify	-	-	-	-	-	-	-	-	-	-	-	-
Sweden 1958	Did not enter	-	-	-	-	-	-	-	-	-	-	-	-
Chile 1962	Did not qualify	-	-	-	-	-	-	-	-	-	-	-	-
England 1966	Did not enter	-	-	-	-	-	-	-	-	-	-	-	-
Mexico 1970	Did not qualify	-	-	-	-	-	-	-	-	-	-	-	-
Germany 1974	Did not qualify	-	-	-	-	-	-	-	-	-	-	-	-
Argentina 1978	Did not qualify	-	-	-	-	-	-	-	-	-	-	-	-
Spain 1982	Did not qualify	-	-	-	-	-	-	-	-	-	-	-	-
Mexico 1986	Did not qualify	-	-	-	-	-	-	-	-	-	-	-	-
Italy 1990	Did not qualify	-	-	-	-	-	-	-	-	-	-	-	-
USA 1994	Did not qualify	-	-	-	-	-	-	-	-	-	-	-	-
France 1998	Group stage	3	0	0	3	1	4	-	-	-	-	-	-
Korea/Japan 2002	Round of 16	3	2	1	0	5	2	1	0	0	1	0	1
Germany 2006	Group stage	3	0	1	2	2	7	-	-	-	-	-	-
South Africa 2010	Round of 16	3	2	0	1	4	2	1	0	1	0	0	0
Brazil 2014	Group stage	3	0	1	2	2	6	-	-	-	-	-	-
Totals		15	4	3	8	14	21	2	0	1	1	0	1

Continental championships (best perfomance)

AFC Asian Cup	Winners (4)	1992, 2000, 2004, 2011

World Cup head-to-heads

Japan v	P	W	D	L	F	A	Latest	Japan v	P	W	D	L	F	A	Latest
Argentina	1	0	0	1	0	1	1998	Croatia	2	0	1	1	0	1	2006
Australia	1	0	0	1	1	3	2006	Denmark	1	1	0	0	3	1	2010
Belgium	1	0	1	0	2	2	2002	Russia	1	1	0	0	1	0	2002
Brazil	1	0	0	1	1	4	2006	Tunisia	1	1	0	0	2	0	2002
Colombia	1	0	0	1	1	4	2014								

90 mins only

How they qualified

Group E	P	W	D	L	F	A	GD	P
Japan	8	7	1	0	27	0	27	22
Syria	8	6	0	2	26	11	15	18
Singapore	8	3	1	4	9	9	0	10
Afghanistan	8	3	0	5	8	24	-16	9
Cambodia	8	0	0	8	1	27	-26	0

Japan............ (0) 0-0 (0)........ Singapore
Japan............ (1) 3-0 (0)........ Cambodia
Afghanistan ... (0) 0-6 (2)............. Japan
Syria .... (0) 0-3 (0)............. Japan
Singapore....... (0) 0-3 (2)............. Japan
Cambodia ...... (0) 0-2 (0)............. Japan

Japan............ (1) 5-0 (0).....Afghanistan
Japan............ (1) 5-0 (0)............... Syria

Group B	P	W	D	L	F	A	GD	P
Japan	10	6	2	2	17	7	10	20
Saudi Arabia	10	6	1	3	17	10	7	19
Australia	10	5	4	1	16	11	5	19
UAE	10	4	1	5	10	13	-3	13
Iraq	10	3	2	5	11	12	-1	11
Thailand	10	0	2	8	6	24	-18	2

Japan............ (1) 1-2 (1)................. UAE
Thailand........ (0) 0-2 (1)............. Japan
Japan............ (1) 2-1 (0)................. Iraq

Australia .... (0) 1-1 (1)............... Japan
Japan............ (1) 2-1 (0).. Saudi Arabia
UAE................. (0) 0-2 (1)............... Japan
Japan............ (2) 4-0 (0)........ Thailand
Iraq .... (0) 1-1 (0)............... Japan
Japan............ (1) 2-0 (0)........ Australia
Saudi Arabia. (0) 1-0 (0)............. Japan

▶▶ Full qualifying results on pages 228-241

GROUP H

Japan coach Vahid Halilhodzic led Algeria to the last 16, their best ever performance, at the 2014 World Cup

	Players used in qualifying		Career		Qualification			
Pos	**Club**	**Age**	**P**	**G**	**P**	**G**	🔲	⬛
GK	Eiji Kawashima	Metz	35	82	-	6	-	-	-
GK	Masaaki Higashiguchi	Gamba Osaka	32	4	-	1	-	-	-
GK	Shusaku Nishikawa	Urawa Red D.	31	31	-	11	-	1	-
DEF	Gen Shoji	Kashima Antlers	25	11	1	3	-	-	-
DEF	Genta Miura	Gamba Osaka	23	2	-	1	-	-	-
DEF	Gotoku Sakai	Hamburg	27	39	-	8	-	-	-
DEF	Hiroki Fujiharu	Gamba Osaka	29	3	-	1	-	-	-
DEF	Hiroki Sakai	Marseille	28	40	-	14	-	3	-
DEF	Kosuke Ota	FC Tokyo	30	7	-	1	-	-	-
DEF	Masato Morishige	FC Tokyo	31	41	2	12	1	2	-
DEF	Maya Yoshida	Southampton	29	79	10	18	4	2	-
DEF	Tomoaki Makino	Urawa Red D.	31	30	4	4	-	2	-
DEF	Wataru Endo	Urawa Red D.	25	11	-	3	-	-	-
DEF	Yuichi Maruyama	FC Tokyo	29	2	-	1	-	-	-
DEF	Yuto Nagatomo	Galatasaray	31	103	3	13	-	1	-
MID	Makoto Hasebe	E Frankfurt	34	108	2	13	-	-	-
MID	Gaku Shibasaki	Getafe	26	15	3	2	-	-	-
MID	Hiroshi Kiyotake	Cerezo Osaka	28	43	5	9	2	-	-
MID	Hotaru Yamaguchi	Cerezo Osaka	27	40	2	13	1	1	-
MID	Keisuke Honda	Pachuca	32	93	36	16	7	-	-
MID	Mu Kanazaki	Kashima Antlers	29	11	2	3	2	-	-
MID	Ryota Oshima	Kawasaki F	25	3	-	1	-	-	-
MID	Shinji Kagawa	B Dortmund	29	89	29	14	6	-	-
MID	Shinzo Koroki	Urawa Red D.	31	16	-	1	-	-	-
MID	Shu Kurata	Gamba Osaka	29	9	2	2	-	-	-
MID	Takashi Inui	Eibar	30	25	2	1	-	-	-
MID	Takashi Usami	F Dusseldorf	26	21	3	10	1	-	-
MID	Yasuyuki Konno	Gamba Osaka	35	93	4	2	1	-	-
MID	Yosuke Ideguchi	Cultural Leonesa	21	11	2	3	1	-	-
MID	Yosuke Kashiwagi	Urawa Red D.	30	11	-	4	-	-	-
ATT	Genki Haraguchi	Fortuna Dusseldorf	27	30	6	18	5	-	-
ATT	Kenyu Sugimoto	Cerezo Osaka	25	6	1	1	-	-	-
ATT	Mike Havenaar	Vissel Kobe	31	18	4	1	-	-	-
ATT	Shinji Okazaki	Leicester	32	111	50	14	5	-	-
ATT	Takumi Minamino	RB Salzburg	23	2	-	1	-	-	-
ATT	Takuma Asano	Stuttgart	23	17	3	6	2	-	-
ATT	Yoshinori Muto	Mainz	25	21	2	6	-	-	-
ATT	Yu Kobayashi	Kawasaki F.	30	12	2	4	-	-	-
ATT	Yuya Kubo	Gent	24	13	2	6	2	1	-
ATT	Yuya Osako	Cologne	28	26	7	5	1	1	-

Correct scores

	Competitive	Friendly
1-0	2	1
2-0	5	1
2-1	3	2
3-0	3	1
3-1	-	-
3-2	-	-
4-0	2	2
4-1	-	-
4-2	-	-
4-3	-	-
0-0	1	-
1-1	5	3
2-2	-	-
3-3	-	1
4-4	-	-
0-1	1	1
0-2	-	1
1-2	3	1
0-3	-	-
1-3	-	1
2-3	-	-
0-4	-	1
1-4	1	-
2-4	-	-
3-4	-	-
Other	4	2

Since Brazil 2014

Half-time/full-time double results

Win/Win	15	50%
Draw/Win	4	13%
Lose/Win	0	0%
Win/Draw	2	7%
Draw/Draw	3	10%
Lose/Draw	1	3%
Win/Lose	1	3%
Draw/Lose	3	10%
Lose/Lose	1	3%

Win 1st half	18	60%
Win 2nd half	17	57%
Win both halves	12	40%
Goal both halves	14	47%

Overall
- Win 63%
- Draw 20%
- Lose 17%

Overall: W19, D6, L5 in 30 competitive games since Brazil 2014

Under & over goals

26 (87%)	Over 1.5	4 (13%)	
16 (53%)	Over 2.5	14 (47%)	
7 (23%)	Over 3.5	23 (77%)	
5 (17%)	Over 4.5	25 (83%)	

Both teams to score

13 (43%)	Both score	17 (57%)	
4 (13%)	& win	26 (87%)	
4 (13%)	& lose	26 (87%)	

In 30 competitive games since Brazil 2014

Clean sheets

16 (53%)	Clean sheets	14 (47%)	
15 (50%)	Win to nil	15 (50%)	

2 (7%)	Fail to score	28 (93%)	
1 (3%)	Lose to nil	29 (97%)	

When they score

For ● Against ●

Total match goals by half

31 (79%)	1st half	8 (21%)
F		A
36 (73%)	2nd half	13 (27%)
F		A

Goals for & against by half

31 (46%)	For	36 (54%)
1st		2nd
8 (38%)	Against	13 (62%)
1st		2nd

	0-9	10-18	19-27	28-36	37-45	46-54	55-63	64-72	73-81	82-90
For	7	5	8	4	7	6	7	3	6	14
Against	1	2	3	2	0	2	3	3	1	4

Japan score first

They win	19		76%
They draw	2		8%
They lose	4		16%

In 30 competitive games since Brazil 2014

Japan concede first

They win	0		0%
They draw	3		75%
They lose	1		25%

Genki Haraguchi was Japan's leading scorer during the harder final phase of Asian qualification

Top scorers in qualifying

	P	G	1st	AT	%	Jpn 0-0 Sgp	Jpn 3-0 Khm	Afg 0-6 Jpn	Syr 0-3 Jpn	Sgp 0-3 Jpn	Khm 0-2 Jpn	Jpn 5-0 Afg	Jpn 5-0 Syr	Jpn 1-2 UAE	Tha 0-2 Jpn	Jpn 2-1 Irq	Aus 1-1 Jpn	Jpn 2-1 Sau	UAE 0-2 Jpn	Jpn 4-0 Tha	Irq 1-1 Jpn	Jpn 2-0 Aus	Sau 1-0 Jpn
Keisuke Honda	16	7	4	7	16	-	↺1	1	1	↺1	↺1		1	1	↳	↳	↳	↳	↳	↳	-		↳
Shinji Kagawa	14	6	3	4	14	↳	1	↺2	↳	↳	-	↳	2	-	-		-	↳	↳	↺1			
Shinji Okazaki	14	5	1	4	11	-	↳	2	↺1		↳	↺1	↳	↳		↳		↳	↳	1		↳	↳
Genki Haraguchi	18	5	3	5	11	↳	↳	-	↳	↳	-	-	↺1	↳	↺1	1	1	↺1	1	-	↳	↳	↳
Maya Yoshida	18	4	0	4	9	-	1	-	-	1	-	1	-	-	-	-	-	-	-	1	-	-	-
Mu Kanazaki	3	2	1	2	5							1	↺1	↳									
Takuma Asano	6	2	1	2	5											↳	↺1	↳	↳			↺1	↳
Yuya Kubo	6	2	1	2	5													↳	↺1	↺1	-	↳	↳
Hiroshi Kiyotake	9	2	1	2	5					↳	↳		1	↳	↳		-	↳	↺1		↳		
Yasuyuki Konno	2	1	0	1	2														1		↳		
Yosuke Ideguchi	3	1	0	1	2																↳	1	-
Yuya Osako	5	1	1	1	2	↳												↳	↳		1	↳	
Takashi Usami	10	1	0	1	2	↳	↳	↳	↺1	↳	↳		↳	↳	↳					↳			
Masato Morishige	12	1	0	1	2		-	1	-	-	-	-	-	-	-	-	-	-	-	-	-	-	-
Hotaru Yamaguchi	13	1	0	1	2		-	-	-		↳		-	↺1	-	-	-	-					

G goals scored, **1st** first match goal (own goals don't count) **AT** goals at any time (ie. number of scoring appearances), **P** penalties, **%** percentage of total team goals scored by each player. Russia 2018 qualifying only. Game-by-game stats show goals scored, 1st goals are in red, dash did not score, ↳ substituted on, ↺ substituted off, blank did not play.

Bookings in World Cup qualifying

Played 18 **Cards** (14Y) ▢▢▢▢▢▢▢▢▢▢▢▢▢▢   **Avg make-up** (▢10 ▮25) 7.8

HOW THEY QUALIFIED

It took 868 matches, played over more than two-and-a-half years, to whittle 208 nations down to the 31 who join hosts Russia at the World Cup, *writes Paul Charlton*.

South America provided both the first and the last qualifiers. Brazil booked their spot in Russia last March, but it took a change of coach to kickstart their campaign. After winning just two of their first six games and a group-stage exit from the Copa America, Dunga was replaced by Tite and eight straight wins saw the Selecao secure a top-four finish with four games to spare.

Peru became the final team to reach the finals courtesy of their playoff victory over New Zealand.

They claimed fifth place in the group at Chile's expense after the 2015 and 2016 Copa America winners appealed the result

of a goalless draw against Bolivia in which their opponents fielded an ineligible player. The South American champions were awarded a 3-0 victory, but Peru were also beneficiaries as their 2-0 loss to Bolivia was overturned. It proved crucial as Peru claimed the playoff spot on goal difference.

There were other upsets in qualifying too. The USA are absent for the first time since 1986 – eight World Cups ago – after a 2-1 defeat by Trinidad & Tobago in their final qualifier. The States scored an own goal and hit the woodwork and might still have made the playoffs with a defeat had results elsewhere gone their way.

In Europe, Holland, runners-up in 2010 and third in Brazil four years ago, followed up their unsuccessful bid to reach Euro 2016 by failing to get to Russia, and

Asia

How it works
Round 1 12 lowest-ranked teams play 6 two-legged ties, winners advance
Round 2 8 groups of 5, 8 winners and 4 best runners-up advance **Round 3** 2 groups of 6, winners and runners-up qualify for the finals, 3rd-placed teams advance to round 4 **Round 4** Two-legged tie, winners advance to intercontinental playoff

Round 1 first legs
Thursday, 12 March 2015
Cambodia ...... (0) 3-0 (0)............ Macau
Chinese Taipei (0) 0-1 (1).............Brunei
India.............. (0) 2-0 (0).............Nepal
Sri Lanka .... (0) 0-1 (0)............Bhutan
Timor-Leste.... (2) 4-1 (0)........Mongolia
Yemen .... (3) 3-1 (0)..........Pakistan

Round 1 second legs
Tuesday, 17 March 2015
Bhutan .... (1) 2-1 (1).........Sri Lanka
    Bhutan won 3-1 on aggregate
Brunei .... (0) 0-2 (1). Chinese Taipei
    Chinese Taipei 2-1 on aggregate
Macau............ (0) 1-1 (1).......Cambodia
    Cambodia won 4-1 on aggregate
Mongolia .... (0) 0-1 (1)..... Timor-Leste
    Timor Leste won 5-1 on aggregate
Nepal .... (0) 0-0 (0)............... India
    India won 2-0 on aggregate
Monday, 23 March 2015
Pakistan .... (0) 0-0 (0)............Yemen
    Yemen won 3-1 on aggregate

Round 2

Group A	P	W	D	L	F	A	GD	P
Saudi Arabia	8	6	2	0	28	4	24	20
UAE	8	5	2	1	27	4	23	17
Palestine	8	4	2	2	24	5	19	14
Malaysia	8	2	0	6	7	29-22	6	
Timor-Leste	8	0	0	8	0	44-44	0	

Thursday, 11 June 2015
Malaysia .... (1) 1-1 (0)..... Timor-Leste
    Match awarded 3-0 to Malaysia
Saudi Arabia. (1) 3-2 (0).........Palestine
Tuesday, 16 June 2015
Timor-Leste.... (0) 0-1 (0)................ UAE
    Match awarded 3-0 to UAE
Malaysia .... (0) 0-6 (3).........Palestine
Thursday, 3 September 2015
UAE................ (7) 10-0 (0) ....Malaysia
Saudi Arabia. (5) 7-0 (0)..... Timor-Leste
Tuesday, 8 September 2015
Malaysia .... (0) 1-2 (0).. Saudi Arabia
    Match awarded 3-0 to Saudi Arabia
Palestine .... (0) 0-0 (0)................ UAE
Thursday, 8 October 2015
Timor-Leste.... (0) 1-1 (0).........Palestine
    Match awarded 3-0 to Palestine
Saudi Arabia. (1) 2-1 (1)................ UAE
Tuesday, 13 October 2015
Timor-Leste.... (0) 0-1 (1).........Malaysia
    Match awarded 3-0 to Malaysia
Monday, 9 November 2015
Palestine .... (0) 0-0 (0).. Saudi Arabia
Thursday, 12 November 2015
Palestine .... (3) 6-0 (0).........Malaysia
UAE................ (3) 8-0 (0).... Timor-Leste

Tuesday, 17 November 2015
Timor-Leste.... (0) 0-10 (4).. Saudi Arabia
Malaysia .... (0) 1-2 (1)................ UAE
Thursday, 24 March 2016
UAE.............. (1) 2-0 (0).........Palestine
Saudi Arabia. (0) 2-0 (0).........Malaysia
Tuesday, 29 March 2016
Palestine .... (4) 7-0 (0)..... Timor-Leste
UAE............... (0) 1-1 (1).. Saudi Arabia

Group B	P	W	D	L	F	A	GD	P
Australia	8	7	0	1	29	4	25	21
Jordan	8	5	1	2	21	7	14	16
Kyrgyzstan	8	4	2	2	10	8	2	14
Tajikistan	8	1	2	5	9	20-11	5	
Bangladesh	8	0	1	7	2	32-30	1	

Thursday, 11 June 2015
Bangladesh.... (1) 1-3 (3)......Kyrgyzstan
Tajikistan .... (0) 1-3 (1)............. Jordan
Tuesday, 16 June 2015
Bangladesh.... (0) 1-1 (1).........Tajikistan
Kyrgyzstan..... (0) 1-2 (1).........Australia
Thursday, 3 September 2015
Australia .... (4) 5-0 (0).....Bangladesh
Jordan............ (0) 0-0 (0).....Kyrgyzstan
Tuesday, 8 September 2015
Bangladesh.... (0) 0-4 (2)............. Jordan
Tajikistan .... (0) 0-3 (0)........Australia
Thursday, 8 October 2015
Jordan............ (0) 2-0 (0).......Australia
Kyrgyzstan..... (1) 2-2 (0).........Tajikistan
Tuesday, 13 October 2015
Kyrgyzstan..... (1) 2-0 (0).....Bangladesh
Jordan............ (0) 3-0 (0).........Tajikistan

228 **RACING POST** RUSSIA 2018 GUIDE

Italy missed out for the first time since 1958 after losing their playoff 1-0 on aggregate to the hosts in 1958, Sweden. It was the Swedes who finished ahead of the Dutch in their qualifying group, too.

The less generous allocation of places saw some of the heroes of Euro 2016 – Hungary and Wales – miss out, but Iceland made it through, building on their run to the quarter-finals in France by securing a first World Cup appearance. They lost out to Croatia in the playoffs in qualification for Brazil 2014 but made sure of things this time, winning their group ahead of the 1998 semi-finalists.

Asia almost provided another tale of plucky underdogs as Syria, who had to play their home games in Oman and Malaysia due to the civil war that has devastated their country, missed out on a place in the intercontinental playoffs only after an extra-time defeat by Australia in the final round of games in Asia.

Robert Lewandowski set a new scoring record in European Qualifying, finishing with 16 goals, one ahead of Cristiano Ronaldo, who also beat the tally set by Predrag Mijatovic in the preliminaries for France 98. Lewandowski's tally was matched in Asia by Saudi Arabian striker Mohammad Al-Sahlawi and Ahmed Khalil of UAE.

Only Karim Bagheri, ahead of the 1998 World Cup, has ever scored more in a qualifying campaign, but it's worth noting that the last man to top score both in qualifying and at the finals was the great Gerd Muller back in 1970.

Thursday, 12 November 2015
Australia ...... (1) 3-0 (0)......Kyrgyzstan
Tajikistan .... (2) 5-0 (0)......Bangladesh
Tuesday, 17 November 2015
Bangladesh.... (0) 0-4 (4)......**Australia**
Kyrgyzstan ..... (0) 1-0 (0)............. Jordan
Thursday, 24 March 2016
Australia ...... (2) 7-0 (0)......... Tajikistan
Jordan .... (5) 8-0 (0)......Bangladesh
Tuesday, 29 March 2016
Australia ...... (3) 5-1 (0)............. Jordan
Tajikistan .... (0) 0-1 (1)......Kyrgyzstan

Group C	P	W	D	L	F	A	GD	P
Qatar	8	7	0	1	29	4	25	21
China	8	5	2	1	27	1	26	17
Hong Kong	8	4	2	2	13	5	8	14
Maldives	8	2	0	6	8	20	-12	6
Bhutan	8	0	0	8	5	52	-47	0

Thursday, 11 June 2015
Hong Kong.... (4) 7-0 (0)............Bhutan
Maldives .... (0) 0-1 (0)............... Qatar
Tuesday, 16 June 2015
Bhutan .... (0) 0-6 (1).............. China
Hong Kong..... (0) 2-0 (0).........Maldives
Thursday, 3 September 2015
China............ (0) 0-0 (0)..... Hong Kong
Qatar............ (8) 15-0(0) ....Bhutan
Tuesday, 8 September 2015
Maldives .... (0) 0-3 (1).............China
Hong Kong..... (0) 2-3 (1)............ Qatar
Thursday, 8 October 2015
Bhutan .... (0) 3-4 (3).........Maldives
Qatar............ (1) 1-0 (0).............. China

Tuesday, 13 October 2015
Bhutan .... (0) 0-1 (0)..... Hong Kong
Qatar............. (1) 4-0 (0).........Maldives
Thursday, 12 November 2015
Maldives .... (0) 0-1 (1)..... Hong Kong
China............ (7) 12-0(0).........Bhutan
Tuesday, 17 November 2015
Bhutan .... (0) 0-3 (2).............. Qatar
Hong Kong..... (0) 0-0 (0).............. China
Thursday, 24 March 2016
China............ (2) 4-0 (0).........Maldives
Qatar............. (1) 2-0 (0)..... Hong Kong
Tuesday, 29 March 2016
China............ (0) 2-0 (0)............. Qatar
Maldives .... (1) 4-2 (1).........Bhutan

Group D	P	W	D	L	F	A	GD	P
Iran	8	6	2	0	26	3	23	20
Oman	8	4	2	2	11	7	4	14
Turkmenistan	8	4	1	3	10	11	-1	13
Guam	8	2	1	5	3	16	-13	7
India	8	1	0	7	5	18	-13	3

Thursday, 11 June 2015
Guam .... (1) 1-0 (0)...Turkmenistan
India............ (1) 1-2 (2)............Oman
Tuesday, 16 June 2015
Guam .... (1) 2-1 (0).............. India
Turkmenistan. (1) 1-1 (1)................ **Iran**
Thursday, 3 September 2015
Iran.............. (4) 6-0(0)............Guam
Oman .... (2) 3-1 (0)...Turkmenistan
Tuesday, 8 September 2015
Guam .... (0) 0-0 (0)............Oman
India............ (0) 0-3 (1)................ **Iran**

Thursday, 8 October 2015
Turkmenistan. (1) 2-1 (1)................India
Oman .... (0) 1-1 (0)................ **Iran**
Tuesday, 13 October 2015
Turkmenistan. (1) 1-0 (0).............Guam
Oman .... (0) 3-0 (0)................India
Thursday, 12 November 2015
Iran.............. (1) 3-1 (0)...Turkmenistan
India............. (1) 1-0 (0).............Guam
Tuesday, 17 November 2015
Guam .... (0) 0-6 (2)................ **Iran**
Turkmenistan. (1) 2-1 (0)............Oman
Thursday, 24 March 2016
Iran.............. (1) 4-0 (0)................India
Oman .... (0) 1-0 (0).............Guam
Tuesday, 29 March 2016
India............. (1) 1-2 (1)...Turkmenistan
Iran.............. (2) 2-0 (0)............Oman

Group E	P	W	D	L	F	A	GD	P
Japan	8	7	1	0	27	0	27	22
Syria	8	6	0	2	26	11	15	18
Singapore	8	3	1	4	9	9	0	10
Afghanistan	8	3	0	5	8	24	-16	9
Cambodia	8	0	0	8	1	27	-26	0

Thursday, 11 June 2015
Cambodia ...... (0) 0-4 (3)........ Singapore
Afghanistan ... (0) 0-6 (3)................ Syria
Tuesday, 16 June 2015
Japan............ (0) 0-0 (0)........ Singapore
Cambodia ...... (0) 0-1 (0).....Afghanistan
Thursday, 3 September 2015
Japan............ (1) 3-0 (0).......Cambodia

Syria .... (0) 1-0 (0)........ Singapore
Tuesday, 8 September 2015
Cambodia ...... (0) 0-6 (4)............... Syria
Afghanistan ... (0) 0-6 (2)............. **Japan**
Thursday, 8 October 2015
Singapore....... (0) 1-0 (0).....Afghanistan
Syria .... (0) 0-3 (0)............. **Japan**
Tuesday, 13 October 2015
Singapore....... (1) 2-1 (0).......Cambodia
Syria .... (3) 5-2 (1).....Afghanistan
Thursday, 12 November 2015
Singapore....... (0) 0-3 (2)............. **Japan**
Afghanistan ... (1) 3-0 (0)......Cambodia
Tuesday, 17 November 2015
Singapore....... (0) 1-2 (1)............... Syria
Cambodia ...... (0) 0-2 (0)............. **Japan**
Thursday, 24 March 2016
Japan............ (1) 5-0 (0)....Afghanistan
Syria .... (2) 6-0 (0).......Cambodia
Tuesday, 29 March 2016
Afghanistan ... (1) 2-1 (0).......Singapore
Japan............ (1) 5-0 (0)............... Syria

Group F	P	W	D	L	F	A	GD	P
Thailand	6	4	2	0	14	6	8	14
Iraq	6	3	3	0	13	6	7	12
Vietnam	6	2	1	3	7	8	-1	7
Chinese Taipei	6	0	0	6	5	19	-14	0

Sunday, 24 May 2015
Thailand......... (0) 1-0 (0)...........Vietnam
Tuesday, 16 June 2015
Chinese Taipei (0) 0-2 (2)......... Thailand
Thursday, 3 September 2015
Iraq .... (1) 5-1 (0). Chinese Taipei
Tuesday, 8 September 2015
Chinese Taipei (0) 1-2 (0)...........Vietnam
Thailand......... (0) 2-2 (1)...................Iraq
Thursday, 8 October 2015
Vietnam .... (1) 1-1 (0)..................Iraq
Tuesday, 13 October 2015
Vietnam .... (0) 0-3 (1)......... Thailand
Thursday, 12 November 2015
Thailand......... (1) 4-2 (1). Chinese Taipei
Tuesday, 17 November 2015
Chinese Taipei (0) 0-2 (1)..................Iraq
Thursday, 24 March 2016
Vietnam .... (3) 4-1 (1). Chinese Taipei
Iraq .... (0) 2-2 (1)......... Thailand
Tuesday, 29 March 2016
Iraq .... (1) 1-0 (0)...........Vietnam

Group G	P	W	D	L	F	A	GD	P
South Korea	8	8	0	0	27	0	27	24
Lebanon	8	3	2	3	12	6	6	11
Kuwait	8	3	1	4	12	10	2	10
Myanmar	8	2	2	4	9	21	-12	8
Laos	8	1	1	6	6	29	-23	4

Thursday, 11 June 2015
Laos .... (0) 2-2 (1)...........Myanmar
Lebanon......... (0) 0-1 (0)............. Kuwait
Tuesday, 16 June 2015
Myanmar........ (0) 0-2 (1)... **South Korea**
Laos .... (0) 0-2 (1)......... Lebanon

Thursday, 3 September 2015
South Korea.. (3) 8-0 (0)................Laos
Kuwait .... (3) 9-0 (0)...........Myanmar
Tuesday, 8 September 2015
Laos .... (0) 0-2 (1)............Kuwait
Lebanon......... (0) 0-3 (2)... **South Korea**
Thursday, 8 October 2015
Myanmar........ (0) 0-2 (1)......... Lebanon
Kuwait .... (0) 0-1 (1)... **South Korea**
Tuesday, 13 October 2015
Myanmar........ (2) 3-1 (1)................Laos
Kuwait .... (0) 0-0 (0)......... Lebanon
Thursday, 12 November 2015
South Korea.. (2) 4-0 (0)......... Myanmar
Lebanon......... (4) 7-0 (0)................Laos
Tuesday, 17 November 2015
Laos .... (0) 0-5 (4)... **South Korea**
Myanmar......... P-P .... Kuwait
Match awarded 3-0 to Myanmar
Thursday, 24 March 2016
South Korea.. (0) 1-0 (0)......... Lebanon
Kuwait .... P-P ....Laos
Match awarded 3-0 to Laos
Tuesday, 29 March 2016
Lebanon......... (0) 1-1 (0)......... Myanmar
South Korea.... P-P ....Kuwait
Match awarded 3-0 to South Korea

Group H	P	W	D	L	F	A	GD	P
Uzbekistan	8	7	0	1	20	7	13	21
North Korea	8	5	1	2	14	8	6	16
Philippines	8	3	1	4	8	12	-4	10
Bahrain	8	3	0	5	10	10	0	9
Yemen	8	1	0	7	2	17	-15	3

Thursday, 11 June 2015
Philippines ..... (0) 2-1 (0)...........Bahrain
Yemen .... (0) 0-1 (0).....North Korea
Match awarded 3-0 to North Korea
Tuesday, 16 June 2015
North Korea ... (4) 4-2 (0)...... Uzbekistan
Yemen .... (0) 0-2 (0)......Philippines
Thursday, 3 September 2015
Uzbekistan..... (0) 1-0 (0)............ Yemen
Bahrain .... (0) 0-1 (1).....North Korea
Tuesday, 8 September 2015
Philippines ..... (0) 1-5 (3)...... Uzbekistan
Yemen .... (0) 0-4 (2)...........Bahrain
Thursday, 8 October 2015
North Korea ... (0) 0-0 (0).......Philippines
Bahrain .... (0) 0-4 (0)...... Uzbekistan
Tuesday, 13 October 2015
North Korea ... (1) 1-0 (0)............ Yemen
Bahrain .... (0) 2-0 (0)......Philippines
Thursday, 12 November 2015
Philippines ..... (0) 0-1 (0)............ Yemen
Uzbekistan..... (1) 3-1 (1).....North Korea
Tuesday, 17 November 2015
North Korea ... (1) 2-0 (0)...........Bahrain
Yemen .... (0) 1-3 (2)..... Uzbekistan
Thursday, 24 March 2016
Uzbekistan..... (0) 1-0 (0).......Philippines
Bahrain .... (1) 3-0 (0)............ Yemen
Tuesday, 29 March 2016
Philippines ..... (1) 3-2 (1).....North Korea
Uzbekistan..... (0) 1-0 (0)...........Bahrain

Round 3

Group A	P	W	D	L	F	A	GD	P
Iran	10	6	4	0	10	2	8	22
South Korea	10	4	3	3	11	10	1	15
Syria	10	3	4	3	9	8	1	13
Uzbekistan	10	4	1	5	6	7	-1	13
China	10	3	3	4	8	10	-2	12
Qatar	10	2	1	7	8	15	-7	7

Thursday, 1 September 2016
South Korea.. (1) 3-2 (0)...............China
Uzbekistan..... (0) 1-0 (0)............... Syria
Iran................ (0) 2-0 (0)............. Qatar

Left to right: fans of Thailand, Saudi Arabia, Japan and China support their teams during World Cup qualifying

China.............. (0) 0-0 (0).................. **Iran**
Syria.............. (0) 0-0 (0)... **South Korea**
Qatar.............. (0) 0-1 (0)..... **Uzbekistan**
Thursday, 6 October 2016
South Korea.. (1) 3-2 (2).............. Qatar
China.............. (0) 0-1 (0)................ **Syria**
Uzbekistan..... (0) 0-1 (1)................ **Iran**
Tuesday, 11 October 2016
Uzbekistan..... (0) 2-0 (0).............. China
Iran.............. (1) 1-0 (0)... South Korea
Qatar.............. (1) 1-0 (0)................ Syria
Tuesday, 15 November 2016
South Korea.. (0) 2-1 (1)..... Uzbekistan

China.............. (0) 0-0 (0).............. Qatar
Syria.............. (0) 0-0 (0)................ **Iran**
Thursday, 23 March 2017
China.............. (1) 1-0 (0)... **South Korea**
Syria.............. (0) 1-0 (0)..... Uzbekistan
Qatar.............. (0) 0-1 (0)................ **Iran**
Tuesday, 28 March 2017
South Korea.. (1) 1-0 (0).............. Syria
Iran.............. (0) 1-0 (0)................China
Uzbekistan..... (0) 1-0 (0).............. Qatar
Monday, 12 June 2017
Iran.............. (1) 2-0 (0)..... Uzbekistan
Tuesday, 13 June 2017
Syria.............. (1) 2-2 (0)................China
Qatar.............. (1) 3-2 (0)... **South Korea**

Thursday, 31 August 2017
China.............. (0) 1-0 (0)..... Uzbekistan
South Korea.. (0) 0-0 (0)................ **Iran**
Syria.............. (1) 3-1 (1).............. Qatar
Tuesday, 5 September 2017
Qatar.............. (0) 1-2 (0)..............China
Iran.............. (1) 2-2 (1)................ Syria
Uzbekistan..... (0) 0-0 (0)... **South Korea**

Group B	P	W	D	L	F	A	GD	P
Japan	10	6	2	2	17	7	10	20
Saudi Arabia	10	6	1	3	17	10	7	19
Australia	10	5	4	1	16	11	5	19
UAE	10	4	1	5	10	13	-3	13
Iraq	10	3	2	5	11	12	-1	11
Thailand	10	0	2	8	6	24	-18	2

Thursday, 1 September 2016
Australia...... (0) 2-0 (0)..............Iraq
Japan.............. (1) 1-2 (1).................. UAE
Saudi Arabia.(0) 1-0 (0)......... Thailand
Tuesday, 6 September 2016
Iraq.............. (1) 1-2 (0). **Saudi Arabia**
Thailand........ (0) 0-2 (1)..............**Japan**
UAE.............. (0) 0-1 (0)........**Australia**
Thursday, 6 October 2016
Japan.............. (1) 2-1 (0)..................Iraq
UAE.............. (1) 3-1 (0)........ Thailand
Saudi Arabia. (1) 2-2 (1)........**Australia**
Tuesday, 11 October 2016
Australia...... (0) 1-1 (1)..............**Japan**
Iraq .... (2) 4-0 (0)........ Thailand
Saudi Arabia. (0) 3-0 (0)................ UAE
Tuesday, 15 November 2016
Japan.............. (1) 2-1 (0). Saudi Arabia
Thailand........ (1) 2-2 (1)........**Australia**
UAE.............. (1) 2-0 (0)..................Iraq
Thursday, 23 March 2017
Iraq .... (0) 1-1 (1)........**Australia**
Thailand........ (0) 0-3 (1). **Saudi Arabia**
UAE.............. (0) 0-2 (1)..............**Japan**
Tuesday, 28 March 2017
Australia...... (1) 2-0 (0)................ UAE
Japan.............. (2) 4-0 (0)......... Thailand
Saudi Arabia. (0) 1-0 (0)..................Iraq
Thursday, 8 June 2017
Australia...... (2) 3-2 (2). **Saudi Arabia**
Tuesday, 13 June 2017
Thailand........ (0) 1-1 (0)................ UAE
Iraq .... (0) 1-1 (1)..............**Japan**
Tuesday, 29 August 2017
UAE.............. (1) 2-1 (1). **Saudi Arabia**
Thursday, 31 August 2017
Japan.............. (1) 2-0 (0)........**Australia**
Thailand........ (0) 1-2 (1)..................Iraq
Tuesday, 5 September 2017
Australia...... (1) 2-1 (0)......... Thailand
Iraq .... (1) 2-1 (0)................ UAE
Saudi Arabia. (0) 1-0 (0)..............**Japan**

Round 4
Thursday, 5 October 2017
Syria.............. (0) 1-1 (1)........**Australia**
Tuesday, 10 October 2017
Australia...... (1) 2-1 (1).............. Syria
AET – 1-1 after 90 minutes
Australia won 3-2 on aggregate

Australia's Tim Cahill scores against Syria in the second leg of their qualifying playoff
Photo by Cameron Spence/Getty Images

How it works
Round 1 26 lowest-ranked teams play 13 two-legged ties, winners advance Round 2 20 two-legged ties, winners advance Round 3 5 groups of 4, winners qualify for the finals

Round 1 first legs
Wednesday, 7 October 2015
Comoros .... (0) 0-0 (0)...........Lesotho
Mauritius ...... (0) 2-5 (2).............. Kenya
Seychelles ..... (0) 0-1 (1)...........Burundi
South Sudan .. (1) 1-1 (1)......Mauritania
Tanzania........ (2) 2-0 (0)... Malawi
Thursday, 8 October 2015
Liberia........... (1) 1-1 (0). Guinea-Bissau
Sao Tome & P. (0) 1-0 (0).......... Ethiopia
Friday, 9 October 2015
Djibouti......... (0) 0-6 (1).......Swaziland
Gambia .... (0) 1-1 (0).......Namibia
Somalia .... (0) 0-2 (0).............. Niger
Saturday, 10 October 2015
Cent African Rep(0) 0-3 (2).....Madagascar
Chad .... (0) 1-0 (0).... Sierra Leone
Eritrea........... (0) 0-2 (1)....... Botswana

Round 1 second legs
Sunday, 11 October 2015
Ethiopia......... (1) 3-0 (0).. Sao Tome & P
Ethiopia won 3-1 on aggregate
Kenya .... (0) 0-0 (0)........Mauritius
Kenya won 5-2 on aggregate
Malawi........... (1) 1-0 (0)......... Tanzania
Tanzania won 2-1 on aggregate
Tuesday, 13 October 2015
Botswana....... (2) 3-1 (1).............Eritrea
Botswana won 5-1 on aggregate
Burundi .... (0) 2-0 (0).......Seychelles
Burundi won 3-0 on aggregate
Guinea-Bissau (1) 1-3 (2)............. Liberia
Liberia won 4-2 on aggregate
Lesotho .... (1) 1-1 (0).........Comoros
1-1 agg. Comoros won on away goals
Madagascar ... (2) 2-2 (2)Cent African Rep
Madagascar won 5-2 on aggregate
Mauritania ..... (1) 4-0 (0).... South Sudan
Mauritania won 5-1 on aggregate
Namibia .... (1) 2-1 (1).........Gambia
Namibia won 3-2 on aggregate
Niger .... (3) 4-0 (0).......... Somalia
Niger won 6-0 on aggregate
Sierra Leone... (0) 2-1 (1)...............Chad
2-2 agg. Chad won on away goals
Saturday, 17 October 2015
Swaziland ...... (2) 2-1 (1).......... Djibouti
Swaziland won 8-1 on aggregate

Round 2 first legs
Wednesday, 11 November 2015
Mozambique.. (0) 1-0 (0).............Gabon
Sudan............ (0) 0-1 (1)........... Zambia
Thursday, 12 November 2015
Benin............. (1) 2-1 (0)....Burkina Faso
Burundi .... (1) 2-3 (1).......DR Congo
Morocco........ (1) 2-0 (0).......Eq Guinea
Namibia .... (0) 0-1 (1)...........Guinea
Togo.............. (0) 0-1 (1)...........Uganda

Friday, 13 November 2015
Angola .... (1) 1-3 (2).... South Africa
Comoros .... (0) 0-0 (0)...........Ghana
Kenya .... (1) 1-0 (0)......Cape Verde
Liberia........... (0) 0-1 (1)...... Ivory Coast
Libya .... (0) 1-0 (0)............. Rwanda
Madagascar... (1) 2-2 (0)........ Senegal
Mauritania ..... (1) 1-2 (0)........... Tunisia
Niger.............. (0) 0-3 (3)........Cameroon
Swaziland ...... (0) 0-0 (0)...........Nigeria
Saturday, 14 November 2015
Botswana....... (2) 2-1 (0)............... Mali
Chad .... (0) 1-0 (0).............. Egypt
Ethiopia......... (1) 3-4 (1).............Congo
Tanzania........ (1) 2-2 (0)...........Algeria

Round 2 second legs
Saturday, 14 November 2015
Gabon .... (1) 1-0 (0)... Mozambique
AET – 1-0 after 90 minutes. 1-1 agg.
Gabon 4-3 pens
Sunday, 15 November 2015
DR Congo....... (1) 2-2 (1)...........Burundi
Match awarded 3-0 to DR Congo.
DR Congo won 6-2 on aggregate
Eq Guinea ...... (1) 1-0 (0)........... Morocco
Morocco won 2-1 on aggregate
Guinea .... (1) 2-0 (0)...........Namibia
Guinea won 3-0 on aggregate
Uganda .... (3) 3-0 (0)............... Togo
Uganda won 4-0 on aggregate
Zambia........... (0) 2-0 (0)............. Sudan
Zambia won 3-0 on aggregate
Tuesday, 17 November 2015
Algeria .... (3) 7-0 (0)...........Tanzania
Algeria won 9-2 on aggregate
Burkina Faso .. (1) 2-0 (0).............. Benin
Burkina Faso won 3-2 on aggregate
Cameroon ...... (0) 0-0 (0)............... Niger
Cameroon won 3-0 on aggregate
Cape Verde .... (1) 2-0 (0)............. Kenya
Cape Verde won 2-1 on aggregate
Congo .... (0) 2-1 (1)........... Ethiopia
Congo won 6-4 on aggregate
Egypt............. (4) 4-0 (0)............... Chad
Egypt won 4-1 on aggregate
Ghana .... (1) 2-0 (0).........Comoros
Ghana won 2-0 on aggregate
Ivory Coast..... (2) 3-0 (0)........... Liberia
Ivory Coast won 4-0 on aggregate
Mali................ (2) 2-0 (0)....... Botswana
Mali won 3-2 on aggregate
Nigeria........... (0) 2-0 (0)....... Swaziland
Nigeria won 2-0 on aggregate
Rwanda.......... (1) 1-3 (1)................Libya
Libya won 4-1 on aggregate
Senegal .... (1) 3-0 (0)....Madagascar
Senegal won 5-2 on aggregate
South Africa... (0) 1-0 (0)..............Angola
South Africa won 4-1 on aggregate
Tunisia........... (0) 2-1 (0).......Mauritania
Tunisia won 4-2 on aggregate

Round 3

Group A	P	W	D	L	F	A	GD	P
Tunisia	6	4	2	0	11	4	7	14
DR Congo	6	4	1	1	14	7	7	13
Libya	6	1	1	4	4	10	-6	4
Guinea	6	1	0	5	6	14	-8	3

Saturday, 8 October 2016
DR Congo....... (2) 4-0 (0)...............Libya
Sunday, 9 October 2016
Tunisia........... (0) 2-0 (0)............Guinea
Friday, 11 November 2016
Libya .... (0) 0-1 (0)....... Tunisia
Sunday, 13 November 2016
Guinea .... (1) 1-2 (0)....... DR Congo
Thursday, 31 August 2017
Guinea .... (2) 3-2 (0)...............Libya
Friday, 1 September 2017
Tunisia........... (1) 2-1 (1)....... DR Congo
Monday, 4 September 2017
Libya .... (1) 1-0 (0)............Guinea
Tuesday, 5 September 2017
DR Congo....... (1) 2-2 (0)...........Tunisia
Saturday, 7 October 2017
Guinea .... (1) 1-4 (1)....... Tunisia
Libya .... (0) 1-2 (0)....... DR Congo
Saturday, 11 November 2017
Tunisia........... (0) 0-0 (0)...............Libya
DR Congo....... (0) 3-1 (0)...........Guinea

Group B	P	W	D	L	F	A	GD	P
Nigeria	6	4	1	1	11	6	5	13
Zambia	6	2	2	2	8	7	1	8
Cameroon	6	1	4	1	7	9	-2	7
Algeria	6	1	1	4	6	10	-4	4

Sunday, 9 October 2016
Zambia........... (0) 1-2 (2)...........Nigeria
Algeria .... (1) 1-1 (1).......Cameroon
Saturday, 12 November 2016
Cameroon ...... (1) 1-1 (1) .... Zambia
Nigeria........... (2) 3-1 (0)............Algeria
Friday, 1 September 2017
Nigeria........... (4) 4-0 (0).......Cameroon
Saturday, 2 September 2017
Zambia........... (2) 3-1 (0)............Algeria
Monday, 4 September 2017
Cameroon ...... (0) 1-1 (1)...........Nigeria
Tuesday, 5 September 2017
Algeria .... (0) 0-1 (0) .... Zambia
Saturday, 7 October 2017
Nigeria........... (0) 1-0 (0) .... Zambia
Cameroon ...... (1) 2-0 (0)............Algeria
Friday, 10 November 2017
Algeria .... (0) 1-1 (0)...........Nigeria
Match awarded 3-0 to Algeria
Saturday, 11 November 2017
Zambia........... (1) 2-2 (1).......Cameroon

Group C	P	W	D	L	F	A	GD	P
Morocco	6	3	3	0	11	0	11	12
Ivory Coast	6	2	2	2	7	5	2	8
Gabon	6	1	3	2	7	7	-5	6
Mali	6	0	4	2	1	9	-8	4

Saturday, 8 October 2016
Gabon .... (0) 0-0 (0)....... Morocco
Ivory Coast..... (3) 3-1 (1)............... Mali
Saturday, 12 November 2016
Mali................ (0) 0-0 (0)...........Gabon
Morocco........ (0) 0-0 (0)...... Ivory Coast
Friday, 1 September 2017
Morocco........ (2) 6-0 (0)............... Mali

Saturday, 2 September 2017
Gabon .... (0) 0-3 (0) ...... Ivory Coast
Tuesday, 5 September 2017
Ivory Coast..... (0) 1-2 (2).............Gabon
Mali................ (0) 0-0 (0)......... **Morocco**
Friday, 6 October 2017
Mali................ (0) 0-0 (0)...... Ivory Coast
Saturday, 7 October 2017
Morocco........ (1) 3-0 (0).............Gabon
Saturday, 11 November 2017
Gabon .... (0) 0-0 (0)................ Mali
Ivory Coast..... (0) 0-2 (2)......... **Morocco**

Group D	P	W	D	L	F	A	GD	P
Senegal	6	4	2	0	10	3	7	14
Burkina Faso	6	2	3	1	10	6	4	9
Cape Verde	6	2	0	4	4	12	-8	6
South Africa	6	1	1	4	7	10	-3	4

Saturday, 8 October 2016
Burkina Faso .. (0) 1-1 (0).... South Africa
Senegal........ (1) 2-0 (0)......Cape Verde
Saturday, 12 November 2016
South Africa... (2) 2-1 (0)......... **Senegal**
Match annulled
Cape Verde ... (0) 0-2 (2)....Burkina Faso
Friday, 1 September 2017
Cape Verde .... (2) 2-1 (1)... South Africa
Saturday, 2 September 2017
Senegal........ (0) 0-0 (0)....Burkina Faso
Tuesday, 5 September 2017
South Africa... (0) 1-2 (0)......Cape Verde
Burkina Faso .. (1) 2-2 (1).......... **Senegal**

Saturday, 7 October 2017
South Africa... (3) 3-1 (0)....Burkina Faso
Cape Verde .... (0) 0-2 (0)......... **Senegal**
Friday, 10 November 2017
South Africa... (0) 0-2 (2)......... **Senegal**
Tuesday, 14 November 2017
Burkina Faso .. (1) 4-0 (0)......Cape Verde
Senegal........ (0) 2-1 (0).... South Africa

Group E	P	W	D	L	F	A	GD	P
Egypt	6	4	1	1	8	4	4	13
Uganda	6	2	3	1	3	2	1	9
Ghana	6	1	4	1	7	5	2	7
Congo	6	0	2	4	5	12	-7	2

Friday, 7 Octo ber 2016
Ghana .... (0) 0-0 (0)..........Uganda
Sunday, 9 October 2016
Congo .... (1) 1-2 (1)............. **Egypt**
Saturday, 12 November 2016
Uganda .... (1) 1-0 (0).............Congo
Sunday, 13 November 2016
Egypt............. (1) 2-0 (0).............Ghana
Thursday, 31 August 2017
Uganda .... (0) 1-0 (0)............. **Egypt**
Friday, 1 September 2017
Ghana .... (0) 1-1 (1).............Congo
Tuesday, 5 September 2017
Congo .... (1) 1-5 (3).............Ghana
Egypt............. (1) 1-0 (0)..........Uganda
Saturday, 7 October 2017
Uganda .... (0) 0-0 (0).............Ghana
Sunday, 8 October 2017
Egypt............. (0) 2-1 (0).............Congo

Sunday, 12 November 2017
Congo .... (1) 1-1 (1)..........Uganda
Ghana .... (0) 1-1 (0)............. **Egypt**

North & Central America

How it works

Round 1 14 lowest-ranked teams play 7 two-legged ties, winners advance **Round 2** round 1 winners and 13 next lowest-ranked teams play 10 two-legged ties, winners advance **Round 3** round 2 winners and 2 next lowest-ranked teams play 10 two-legged ties, winners advance **Round 4** 3 groups of 4, winners and runners-up advance **Round 5** 1 group of 6, top 3 qualify for the finals, 4th-placed team advances to intercontinental playoff

Round 1 first legs
Sunday, 22 March 2015
Barbados........ (0) 0-1 (1)....... US Virgin I
Monday, 23 March 2015
Nicaragua ...... (4) 5-0 (0)..........Anguilla
St Kitts & Nevis. (3) 6-2 (1).Turks & Caicos
Wednesday, 25 March 2015
Bahamas........ (0) 0-5 (3).........Bermuda
Belize .... (0) 0-0 (0).........Caymans
Thursday, 26 March 2015
British Virgin I (1) 2-3 (1)........ Dominica
Friday, 27 March 2015
Curacao.......... (2) 2-1 (1)...... Montserrat

Despite Christian Pulisic's goal, a final-game defeat by Trinidad & Tobago saw the USA miss out

Round 1 second legs
Thursday, 26 March 2015
Turks & Caicos. (2) 2-6 (3). St Kitts & Nevis
St Kitts & Nevis won 12-4 on aggregate
US Virgin I....... (0) 0-4 (2)........ Barbados
Barbados won 4-1 on aggregate
Sunday, 29 March 2015
Anguilla ...... (0) 0-3 (2).......Nicaragua
Nicaragua won 8-0 on aggregate
Bermuda .... (0) 3-0 (0).........Bahamas
Bermuda won 8-0 on aggregate
Caymans .... (1) 1-1 (1)...............Belize
1-1 agg. Belize won on away goals
Dominica........ (0) 0-0 (0). British Virgin I
Dominica won 3-2 on aggregate
Tuesday, 31 March 2015
Montserrat..... (0) 2-2 (1)........... Curacao
Curacao won 4-3 on aggregate

Round 2 first legs
Sunday, 7 June 2015
Nicaragua ...... (1) 1-0 (0)........ Suriname
Wednesday, 10 June 2015
Antigua/Barbuda(1) 1-3 (1)............St Lucia
Aruba............ (0) 0-2 (2)........Barbados
Curacao......... (0) 0-0 (0)................Cuba
St Vincent & G (0) 2-2 (1)............Guyana
Thursday, 11 June 2015
Dominica........ (0) 0-2 (1)............ Canada
Dominican Rep (0)1-2 (1)...............Belize
St Kitts & Nevis(0) 2-2 (1)...... El Salvador
Friday, 12 June 2015
Guatemala ..... (0) 0-0 (0).........Bermuda
Puerto Rico .... (1) 1-0 (0)..........Grenada

Round 2 second legs
Sunday, 14 June 2015
Barbados........ (0) 1-0 (0)............. Aruba
Match awarded 3-0 to Aruba –
Aruba won 3-2 on aggregate
Belize .... (2) 3-0 (0)Dominican Rep
Belize won 5-1 on aggregate
Cub a .... (1) 1-1 (1)........... Curacao
1-1 agg. Curacao won on away goals
Guyana .... (1) 4-4 (2). St Vincent & G
6-6 agg. St Vincent & G won on away goals
St Lucia .... (0) 1-4 (0)Antigua/Barbuda
Anitigua/Barbuda won 5-4 on aggregate
Monday, 15 June 2015
Bermuda .... (0) 0-1 (1).......Guatemala
Guatemala won 1-0 on aggregate
Tuesday, 16 June 2015
Canada........... (2) 4-0 (0)........ Dominica
Canada won 6-0 on aggregate
El Salvador..... (1) 4-1 (0)St Kitts & Nevis
El Salvador won 6-3 on aggregate
Grenada .... (1) 2-0 (0).....Puerto Rico
Grenada won 2-1 on aggregate
Suriname....... (1) 1-3 (1).........Nicaragua
Nicaragua won 4-1 on aggregate

Round 3 first legs
Friday, 4 September 2015
Curacao......... (0) 0-1 (1)....... El Salvador
Canada........... (1) 3-0 (0)...............Belize
Grenada .... (1) 1-3 (2)................Haiti
Jamaica......... (0) 2-3 (2).......Nicaragua

St Vincent & G (0) 2-0 (0)............. Aruba
Antigua/Barbuda(0) 1-0 (0)......Guatemala
Round 3 second legs
Tuesday, 8 September 2015
Aruba............ (1) 2-1 (0). St Vincent & G
St Vincent & G won 3-2 on aggregate
Belize .... (1) 1-1 (1)............Canada
Canada won 4-1 on aggregate
El Salvador..... (1) 1-0 (0)...........Curacao
El Salvador won 2-0 on aggregate
Guatemala ..... (0) 2-0 (0)Antigua/Barbuda
Guatemala won 2-1 on aggregate
Haiti .... (2) 3-0 (0)...........Grenada
Haiti won 6-1 on aggregate
Nicaragua ...... (0) 0-2 (1)........... Jamaica
Jamaica won 4-3 on aggregate

Round 4

Group A	P	W	D	L	F	A	GD	P
Mexico	6	5	1	0	13	1	12	16
Honduras	6	2	2	2	6	6	0	8
Canada	6	2	1	3	5	8	-3	7
El Salvador	6	0	2	4	4	13	-9	2

Friday, 13 November 2015
Canada........... (1) 1-0 (0).........Honduras
Mexico .... (2) 3-0 (0)..... El Salvador
Tuesday, 17 November 2015
El Salvador..... (0) 0-0 (0)...........Canada
Honduras .... (0) 0-2 (0)...........Mexico
Friday, 25 March 2016
Canada........... (0) 0-3 (2)...........Mexico
El Salvador..... (1) 2-2 (1).......Honduras
Tuesday, 29 March 2016
Honduras .... (0) 2-0 (0)..... El Salvador
Mexico .... (2) 2-0 (0)........... Canada
Friday, 2 September 2016
El Salvador..... (1) 1-3 (0)...........Mexico
Honduras .... (1) 2-1 (1)............Canada
Tuesday, 6 September 2016
Canada........... (1) 3-1 (0)..... El Salvador
Mexico .... (0) 0-0 (0)........Honduras

Group B	P	W	D	L	F	A	GD	P
Costa Rica	6	5	1	0	11	3	8	16
Panama	6	3	1	2	7	5	2	10
Haiti	6	1	1	4	2	4	-2	4
Jamaica	6	1	1	4	2	10	-8	4

Friday, 13 November 2015
Costa Rica..... (1) 1-0 (0)................Haiti
Jamaica........ (0) 0-2 (1).........Panama
Tuesday, 17 November 2015
Haiti .... (0) 0-1 (0)........... Jamaica
Panama......... (1) 1-2 (0)..... Costa Rica
Friday, 25 March 2016
Haiti .... (0) 0-0 (0)........... Panama
Jamaica........ (1) 1-1 (0)..... Costa Rica
Tuesday, 29 March 2016
Costa Rica..... (2) 3-0 (0)........... Jamaica
Panama......... (1) 2-0 (0)................Haiti
Friday, 2 September 2016
Haiti .... (0) 0-1 (0)..... Costa Rica
Panama......... (1) 2-0 (0)........... Jamaica

Tuesday, 6 September 2016
Costa Rica..... (1) 3-1 (0)......... Panama
Jamaica.......... (0) 0-2 (0)................Haiti

Group C	P	W	D	L	F	A	GD	P
USA	6	4	1	1	20	3	17	13
Trin & Tobago	6	3	2	1	13	9	4	11
Guatemala	6	3	1	2	18	11	7	10
St Vincent & G	6	0	0	6	6	34	-28	0

Friday, 13 November 2015
Guatemala ..... (0) 1-2 (0).. Trin & Tobago
USA................ (3) 6-1 (1). St Vincent & G
Tuesday, 17 November 2015
St Vincent & G (0) 0-4 (2)......Guatemala
Trin & Tobago (0) 0-0 (0).................USA
Friday, 25 March 2016
Guatemala ..... (2) 2-0 (0).................USA
St Vincent & G (1) 2-3 (0).. Trin & Tobago
Tuesday, 29 March 2016
Trin & Tobago (1) 6-0 (0). St Vincent & G
USA................ (2) 4-0 (0)......Guatemala
Friday, 2 September 2016
St Vincent & G (0) 0-6 (3).................USA
Trin & Tobago (1) 2-2 (1)......Guatemala
Tuesday, 6 September 2016
Guatemala ..... (4) 9-3 (2). St Vincent & G
USA................ (1) 4-0 (0).. Trin & Tobago

Round 5

	P	W	D	L	F	A	GD	P
Mexico	10	6	3	1	16	7	9	21
Costa Rica	10	4	4	2	14	8	6	16
Panama	10	3	4	3	9	10	-1	13
Honduras	10	3	4	3	13	19	-6	13
USA	10	3	3	4	17	13	4	12
Trin & Tobago	10	2	0	8	7	19	-12	6

Friday, 11 November 2016
Honduras .... (0) 0-1 (1)......... Panama
Trin & Tobago (0) 0-2 (0)..... Costa Rica
USA................ (0) 1-2 (1)...........Mexico
Tuesday, 15 November 2016
Costa Rica..... (1) 4-0 (0).................USA
Honduras .... (2) 3-1 (0).. Trin & Tobago
Panama......... (0) 0-0 (0)...........Mexico
Friday, 24 March 2017
Mexico .... (2) 2-0 (0)..... Costa Rica
Trin & Tobago (0) 0-1 (0)......... Panama
USA................ (3) 6-0 (0)........Honduras
Tuesday, 28 March 2017
Honduras .... (1) 1-1 (0)..... Costa Rica
Panama......... (1) 1-1 (1).................USA
Trin & Tobago (1) 2-1 (0)...........Mexico
Thursday, 8 June 2017
Costa Rica..... (0) 0-0 (0)......... Panama
Mexico .... (3) 3-0 (0)........Honduras
USA................ (0) 2-0 (0).. Trin & Tobago
Sunday, 11 June 2017
Mexico .... (1) 1-1 (1).................USA
Tuesday, 13 June 2017
Costa Rica..... (2) 2-1 (1).. Trin & Tobago
Panama......... (1) 2-2 (1)........Honduras

Friday, 1 September 2017
Mexico .... (0) 1-0 (0)......... Panama
Trin & Tobago (0) 1-2 (2).........Honduras
USA............... (0) 0-2 (1)...... Costa Rica
Tuesday, 5 September 2017
Costa Rica..... (0) 1-1 (1)...........Mexico
Honduras .... (1) 1-1 (0)................USA
Panama......... (1) 3-0 (0).. Trin & Tobago
Friday, 6 October 2017
Mexico .... (0) 3-1 (0).. Trin & Tobago
USA............... (3) 4-0 (0)......... Panama
Saturday, 7 October 2017
Costa Rica..... (0) 1-1 (0)........Honduras
Tuesday, 10 October 2017
Honduras .... (1) 3-2 (2)..........Mexico
Panama......... (0) 2-1 (1)..... Costa Rica
Trin & Tobago (2) 2-1 (0)................USA

Oceania

How it works
Round 1 lowest-ranked teams contest 1 group of 4, winners advance **Round 2** 2 groups of 4, winners and runners-up advance (this is the group stage of the OFC Nations Cup) **Round 3** 2 groups of 3, winners contest a two-legged tie, winners advance to intercontinental playoff

Round 1

	P	W	D	L	F	A	GD	P
Samoa	3	2	0	1	6	3	3	6
US Samoa	3	2	0	1	6	4	2	6
Cook Islands	3	2	0	1	4	2	2	6
Tonga	3	0	0	3	1	8	-7	0

Monday, 31 August 2015
Tonga............ (0) 0-3 (1)....Cook Islands
Samoa........... (3) 3-2 (1)........US Samoa
Wednesday, 2 September 2015
Cook Islands .. (1) 1-0 (0)............. Samoa
Tonga............ (0) 1-2 (0)........US Samoa
Friday, 4 September 2015
Tonga............ (0) 0-3 (2)............. Samoa
US Samoa....... (0) 2-0 (0)....Cook Islands

Round 2

Group A	P	W	D	L	F	A	GD	P
Pap New Guinea	3	1	2	0	11	3	8	5
New Caledonia	3	1	2	0	9	2	7	5
Tahiti	3	1	2	0	7	3	4	5
Samoa	3	0	0	3	0	19	-19	0

Sunday, 29 May 2016
Pap New Guinea(1) 1-1 (0)New Caledonia
Tahiti............. (4) 4-0 (0)............. Samoa
Wednesday, 1 June 2016
Pap New Guinea(1)2-2 (0).............. Tahiti
New Caledonia(4) 7-0 (0)............ Samoa
Sunday, 5 June 2016
Pap New Guinea(2)8-0 (0)............ Samoa
Tahiti............. (0) 1-1 (0)New Caledonia

Marco Rojas scores in New Zealand's 2-0 win over New Caledonia

Group B	P	W	D	L	F	A	GD	P
New Zealand	3	3	0	0	9	1	8	9
Solomon I	3	1	0	2	1	2	-1	3
Fiji	3	1	0	2	4	6	-2	3
Vanuatu	3	1	0	2	3	8	-5	3

Saturday, 28 May 2016
New Zealand.. (2) 3-1 (1)...................Fiji
Vanuatu .... (0) 0-1 (1)........ Solomon I
Tuesday, 31 May 2016
Vanuatu .... (0) 0-5 (5)... New Zealand
Solomon I...... (0) 0-1 (0)...................Fiji
Saturday, 4 June 2016
Fiji .... (0) 2-3 (2)..........Vanuatu
New Zealand.. (0) 1-0 (0)........ Solomon I

Round 2 semi-finals
Wednesday, 8 June 2016
New Zealand.. (0) 1-0 (0)New Caledonia
Pap New Guinea(1) 2-1 (1)........ Solomon I

Round 2 final
Saturday, 11 June 2016
New Zealand.. (0) 0-0 (0)Pap New Guinea
AET – New Zealand won 4-2 on penalties

Round 3

Group A	P	W	D	L	F	A	GD	P
New Zealand	4	3	1	0	6	0	6	10
New Caledonia	4	1	2	1	4	5	-1	5
Fiji	4	0	1	3	3	8	-5	1

Saturday, 12 November 2016
New Zealand.. (1) 2-0 (0)New Caledonia
Tuesday, 15 November 2016
New Caledonia(0) 0-0 (0)... New Zealand

Saturday, 25 March 2017
Fiji .... (0) 0-2 (0)... New Zealand
Tuesday, 28 March 2017
New Zealand.. (1) 2-0 (0)...................Fiji
Wednesday, 7 June 2017
Fiji .... (1) 2-2 (2)New Caledonia
Sunday, 11 June 2017
New Caledonia(1) 2-1 (0)...................Fiji

Group B	P	W	D	L	F	A	GD	P
Solomon I	4	3	0	1	6	6	0	9
Tahiti	4	2	0	2	7	4	3	6
Pap New Guinea	4	1	0	3	6	9	-3	3

Monday, 7 November 2016
Tahiti............. (0) 1-0 (0)........ Solomon I
Match awarded 3-0 to Tahiti
Sunday, 13 November 2016
Solomon I...... (0) 1-0 (0).............. Tahiti
Thursday, 23 March 2017
Pap New Guinea(1) 1-3 (0).............. Tahiti
Tuesday, 28 March 2017
Tahiti............. (0) 1-2 (0)Pap New Guinea
Friday, 9 June 2017
Solomon I...... (2) 3-2 (0)Pap New Guinea
Tuesday, 13 June 2017
Pap New Guinea(1)1-2 (2)........ Solomon I

Final round first leg
Friday, 1 September 2017
New Zealand.. (3) 6-1 (0)........ Solomon I

Final round second leg
Tuesday, 5 September 2017
Solomon I...... (1) 2-2 (2)... New Zealand
New Zealand won 8-3 on aggregate

Europe

How it works
Round 1 9 groups of 6, winners qualify for the finals, 8 best runners-up advance to round 2 **Round 2** 4 two-legged ties, winners qualify for the finals

Round 1

Group A	P	W	D	L	F	A	GD	P
France	10	7	2	1	18	6	12	23
Sweden	10	6	1	3	26	9	17	19
Holland	10	6	1	3	21	12	9	19
Bulgaria	10	4	1	5	14	19	-5	13
Luxembourg	10	1	3	6	8	26	-18	6
Belarus	10	1	2	7	6	21	-15	5

Tuesday, 6 September 2016
Belarus........... (0) 0-0 (0)........... France
Bulgaria .... (1) 4-3 (0).... Luxembourg
Sweden .... (1) 1-1 (0)........... Holland
Friday, 7 October 2016
France .... (3) 4-1 (1)....... Bulgaria
Luxembourg... (0) 0-1 (0)......... **Sweden**
Holland .... (2) 4-1 (0)........... Belarus
Monday, 10 October 2016
Belarus........... (0) 1-1 (0).... Luxembourg
Holland .... (0) 0-1 (1)........... **France**
Sweden .... (2) 3-0 (0)....... Bulgaria
Friday, 11 November 2016
France .... (0) 2-1 (0)......... Sweden
Sunday, 13 November 2016
Bulgaria .... (1) 1-0 (0)......... Belarus
Luxembourg... (1) 1-3 (1)........... Holland
Saturday, 25 March 2017
Sweden .... (1) 4-0 (0)......... Belarus
Bulgaria .... (2) 2-0 (0)......... Holland
Luxembourg... (1) 1-3 (2)........... France
Friday, 9 June 2017
Belarus........... (1) 2-1 (0)....... Bulgaria
Holland .... (2) 5-0 (0).... Luxembourg
Sweden .... (1) 2-1 (1)........... France
Thursday, 31 August 2017
Bulgaria .... (2) 3-2 (2)......... **Sweden**
France .... (1) 4-0 (0)........... Holland
Luxembourg... (0) 1-0 (0)......... Belarus
Sunday, 3 September 2017
Belarus........... (0) 0-4 (3)......... **Sweden**
Holland .... (1) 3-1 (0)....... Bulgaria
France .... (0) 0-0 (0).... Luxembourg
Saturday, 7 October 2017
Sweden .... (3) 8-0 (0).... Luxembourg
Belarus........... (0) 1-3 (1)........... Holland
Bulgaria .... (0) 0-1 (1)........... France
Tuesday, 10 October 2017
France .... (2) 2-1 (1)....... Belarus
Luxembourg... (1) 1-0 (0)....... Bulgaria
Holland .... (2) 2-0 (0)......... **Sweden**

Group B	P	W	D	L	F	A	GD	P
Portugal	10	9	0	1	32	4	28	27
Switzerland	10	9	0	1	23	7	16	27
Hungary	10	4	1	5	14	14	0	13
Faroe Islands	10	2	3	5	4	16	-12	9
Latvia	10	2	1	7	7	18	-11	7
Andorra	10	1	1	8	2	23	-21	4

Tuesday, 6 September 2016
Andorra.......... (0) 0-1 (0)............. Latvia
Faroe Islands.. (0) 0-0 (0)......... Hungary
Switzerland .. (2) 2-0 (0)........ Portugal
Friday, 7 October 2016
Hungary .... (0) 2-3 (0)....Switzerland
Latvia............. (0) 0-2 (1)... Faroe Islands
Portugal........ (3) 6-0 (0)........... Andorra
Monday, 10 October 2016
Andorra.......... (0) 1-2 (1)....Switzerland
Faroe Islands.. (0) 0-6 (3)........ **Portugal**
Latvia............. (0) 0-2 (1)......... Hungary
Sunday, 13 November 2016
Hungary .... (2) 4-0 (0)......... Andorra
Switzerland .. (1) 2-0 (0)... Faroe Islands
Portugal........ (1) 4-1 (0)............. Latvia
Saturday, 25 March 2017
Andorra.......... (0) 0-0 (0)... Faroe Islands
Switzerland .. (0) 1-0 (0)............. Latvia
Portugal........ (2) 3-0 (0)......... Hungary
Friday, 9 June 2017
Andorra.......... (1) 1-0 (0)......... Hungary
Faroe Islands.. (0) 0-2 (1)....Switzerland
Latvia............. (0) 0-3 (1)........ Portugal
Thursday, 31 August 2017
Hungary .... (2) 3-1 (1)............. Latvia
Portugal........ (2) 5-1 (1)... Faroe Islands
Switzerland .. (1) 3-0 (0)......... Andorra
Sunday, 3 September 2017
Faroe Islands.. (1) 1-0 (0)......... Andorra
Hungary .... (0) 0-1 (0)........ **Portugal**
Latvia............. (0) 0-3 (1)....Switzerland

France goalkeeper Hugo Lloris looks on as a halfway-line lob by Ola Toivonen finds the net to give Sweden a 93rd-minute winner

Saturday, 7 October 2017
Faroe Islands.. (0) 0-0 (0)............. Latvia
Andorra.......... (0) 0-2 (0)........ **Portugal**
Switzerland .. (3) 5-2 (0)......... Hungary
Tuesday, 10 October 2017
Hungary .... (0) 1-0 (0)... Faroe Islands
Latvia............. (2) 4-0 (0)......... Andorra
Portugal........ (1) 2-0 (0)....Switzerland

Group C	P	W	D	L	F	A	GD	P
Germany	10	10	0	0	43	4	39	30
N Ireland	10	6	1	3	17	6	11	19
Czech Rep	10	4	3	3	17	10	7	15
Norway	10	4	1	5	17	16	1	13
Azerbaijan	10	3	1	6	10	19	-9	10
San Marino	10	0	0	10	2	51	-49	0

Sunday, 4 September 2016
San Marino .... (0) 0-1 (1)...... Azerbaijan
Czech Rep ...... (0) 0-0 (0)........ N Ireland
Norway .... (0) 0-3 (2)........ **Germany**
Saturday, 8 October 2016
Azerbaijan...... (1) 1-0 (0)........... Norway
Germany .... (1) 3-0 (0)....... Czech Rep
N Ireland........ (1) 4-0 (0)..... San Marino
Tuesday, 11 October 2016
Czech Rep ...... (0) 0-0 (0)...... Azerbaijan
Germany .... (2) 2-0 (0)......... N Ireland
Norway .... (1) 4-1 (0)..... San Marino
Friday, 11 November 2016
Czech Rep ...... (1) 2-1 (0)........... Norway
N Ireland........ (2) 4-0 (0)...... Azerbaijan
San Marino .... (0) 0-8 (3)........ **Germany**

Sunday, 26 March 2017
Azerbaijan...... (1) 1-4 (3)........**Germany**
San Marino .... (0) 0-6 (5)......**Czech Rep**
N Ireland........ (2) 2-0 (0)..........Norway
Saturday, 10 June 2017
Azerbaijan...... (0) 0-1 (0).... N Ireland
Germany .... (4) 7-0 (0).....San Marino
Norway.......... (0) 1-1 (1)......Czech Rep
Friday, 1 September 2017
Czech Rep ...... (0) 1-2 (1)........**Germany**
Norway .... (1) 2-0 (0)......Azerbaijan
San Marino .... (0) 0-3 (0)........ N Ireland
Monday, 4 September 2017
Azerbaijan...... (2) 5-1 (0).....San Marino
Germany .... (4) 6-0 (0)............Norway
N Ireland........ (2) 2-0 (0)......Czech Rep
Thursday, 5 October 2017
Azerbaijan...... (0) 1-2 (1)......Czech Rep
N Ireland........ (0) 1-3 (2)........**Germany**
San Marino .... (0) 0-8 (4)..........Norway
Sunday, 8 October 2017
Czech Rep ...... (3) 5-0 (0).....San Marino
Germany .... (1) 5-1 (1).....Azerbaijan
Norway .... (0) 1-0 (0)........ N Ireland

Group D	P	W	D	L	F	A	GD	P
Serbia	10	6	3	1	20	10	10	21
Rep of Ireland	10	5	4	1	12	6	6	19
Wales	10	4	5	1	13	6	7	17
Austria	10	4	3	3	14	12	2	15
Georgia	10	0	5	5	8	14	-6	5
Moldova	10	0	2	8	4	23	-19	2

Monday, 5 September 2016
Georgia .... (0) 1-2 (2).............Austria
Serbia............. (0) 2-2 (1)..Rep of Ireland
Wales.............. (2) 4-0 (0).........Moldova
Thursday, 6 October 2016
Austria .... (1) 2-2 (2)............. Wales
Moldova.......... (0) 0-3 (2)............ **Serbia**
Rep of Ireland .. (0) 1-0 (0).......... Georgia
Sunday, 9 October 2016
Wales.............. (1) 1-1 (0).......... Georgia
Moldova.......... (1) 1-3 (1)..Rep of Ireland
Serbia............. (2) 3-2 (1)...........Austria
Saturday, 12 November 2016
Austria .... (0) 0-1 (0)..Rep of Ireland
Georgia.......... (1) 1-1 (0)...........Moldova
Wales.............. (1) 1-1 (0)............ **Serbia**
Friday, 24 March 2017
Georgia .... (1) 1-3 (1)............ **Serbia**

Austria .... (0) 2-0 (0)......... Moldova
Rep of Ireland (0) 0-0 (0)............. Wales
Sunday, 11 June 2017
Moldova.......... (2) 2-2 (0).......... Georgia
Rep of Ireland (0) 1-1 (1)............Austria
Serbia............. (0) 1-1 (1).............. Wales
Saturday, 2 September 2017
Georgia .... (1) 1-1 (1)..Rep of Ireland
Serbia............. (2) 3-0 (0).........Moldova
Wales.............. (0) 1-0 (0)............Austria
Tuesday, 5 September 2017
Austria .... (1) 1-1 (1).......... Georgia
Moldova.......... (0) 0-2 (0)............. Wales
Rep of Ireland (0) 0-1 (0)............ **Serbia**
Friday, 6 October 2017
Georgia .... (0) 0-1 (0).............. Wales
Austria .... (1) 3-2 (1)............ **Serbia**
Rep of Ireland (2) 2-0 (0).......... Moldova
Monday, 9 October 2017
Moldova.......... (0) 0-1 (0)............Austria
Serbia............. (0) 1-0 (0).......... Georgia
Wales.............. (0) 0-1 (0)..Rep of Ireland

Group E	P	W	D	L	F	A	GD	P
Poland	10	8	1	1	28	14	14	25
Denmark	10	6	2	2	20	8	12	20
Montenegro	10	5	1	4	20	12	8	16
Romania	10	3	4	3	12	10	2	13
Armenia	10	2	1	7	10	26	-16	7
Kazakhstan	10	0	3	7	6	26	-20	3

Sunday, 4 September 2016
Denmark....... (1) 1-0 (0)..........Armenia
Kazakhstan .... (0) 2-2 (2)............ **Poland**
Romania.......... (0) 1-1 (0)..... Montenegro
Saturday, 8 October 2016
Armenia .... (0) 0-5 (4).......... Romania
Montenegro... (1) 5-0 (0).....Kazakhstan
Poland........... (2) 3-2 (0)........**Denmark**
Tuesday, 11 October 2016
Kazakhstan .... (0) 0-0 (0)........... Romania
Denmark....... (0) 0-1 (1).... Montenegro
Poland........... (0) 2-1 (0)..........Armenia
Friday, 11 November 2016
Armenia .... (0) 3-2 (2)..... Montenegro
Denmark....... (2) 4-1 (1).....Kazakhstan
Romania.......... (0) 0-3 (1)............ **Poland**
Sunday, 26 March 2017
Armenia .... (0) 2-0 (0)....Kazakhstan
Montenegro... (0) 1-2 (1)........... **Poland**
Romania.......... (0) 0-0 (0)..........**Denmark**

Saturday, 10 June 2017
Kazakhstan .... (0) 1-3 (1)........**Denmark**
Montenegro... (2) 4-1 (0)..........Armenia
Poland........... (1) 3-1 (0)........... Romania
Friday, 1 September 2017
Kazakhstan .... (0) 0-3 (1).... Montenegro
Denmark....... (2) 4-0 (0)........... Poland
Romania.......... (0) 1-0 (0)..........Armenia
Monday, 4 September 2017
Armenia .... (1) 1-4 (2)........**Denmark**
Montenegro... (0) 1-0 (0).......... Romania
Poland........... (1) 3-0 (0).....Kazakhstan
Thursday, 5 October 2017
Armenia .... (1) 1-6 (3)........... **Poland**
Montenegro... (0) 0-1 (1)........**Denmark**
Romania.......... (2) 3-1 (0).....Kazakhstan
Sunday, 8 October 2017
Denmark....... (0) 1-1 (0).......... Romania
Kazakhstan .... (0) 1-1 (1)..........Armenia
Poland........... (2) 4-2 (0)... Montenegro

Group F	P	W	D	L	F	A	GD	P
England	10	8	2	0	18	3	15	26
Slovakia	10	6	0	4	17	7	10	18
Scotland	10	5	3	2	17	12	5	18
Slovenia	10	4	3	3	12	7	5	15
Lithuania	10	1	3	6	7	20	-13	6
Malta	10	0	1	9	3	25	-22	1

Sunday, 4 Sept ember 2016
Lithuania........ (2) 2-2 (0)..........Slovenia
Slovakia .... (0) 0-1 (0)............ **England**
Malta .... (1) 1-5 (1)......... Scotland
Saturday, 8 October 2016
England........ (2) 2-0 (0).............Malta
Scotland.......... (0) 1-1 (0)......... Lithuania
Slovenia .... (0) 1-0 (0)......... Slovakia
Tuesday, 11 October 2016
Lithuania......... (0) 2-0 (0)..............Malta
Slovakia .... (1) 3-0 (0)......... Scotland
Slovenia .... (0) 1-0 (0)............ **England**
Friday, 11 November 2016
England........ (1) 3-0 (0)......... Scotland
Malta .... (0) 0-1 (0)..........Slovenia
Slovakia .... (3) 4-0 (0)......... Lithuania
Sunday, 26 March 2017
England........ (1) 2-0 (0)......... Lithuania
Malta .... (1) 1-3 (2).........Slovakia
Scotland.......... (0) 1-0 (0).........Slovenia
Saturday, 10 June 2017
Scotland.......... (0) 2-2 (0)............ **England**
Slovenia .... (1) 2-0 (0)..............Malta
Lithuania......... (0) 1-2 (1).........Slovakia
Friday, 1 September 2017
Lithuania........ (0) 0-3 (2)......... Scotland
Malta .... (0) 0-4 (0)............ **England**
Slovakia .... (0) 1-0 (0).........Slovenia
Monday, 4 September 2017
England........ (1) 2-1 (1)..........Slovakia
Scotland.......... (1) 2-0 (0)..............Malta
Slovenia .... (1) 4-0 (0)......... Lithuania
Thursday, 5 October 2017
England........ (0) 1-0 (0).........Slovenia
Malta .... (1) 1-0 (0)......... Lithuania
Scotland.......... (0) 1-0 (0).........Slovenia
Sunday, 8 October 2017
Lithuania........ (0) 0-1 (1)......... **England**

Despair for Ireland as Denmark celebrate their playoff victory

Slovakia .... (1) 3-0 (0).............Malta
Slovenia .... (0) 2-2 (1)........... Scotland

Group G	P	W	D	L	F	A	GD	P
Spain	10	9	1	0	36	3	33	28
Italy	10	7	2	1	21	8	13	23
Albania	10	4	1	5	10	13	-3	13
Israel	10	4	0	6	10	15	-5	12
Macedonia	10	3	2	5	15	15	0	11
Liechtenstein	10	0	0	10	1	39	-38	0

Monday, 5 September 2016
Albania .... (1) 2-1 (0)...... Macedonia
Match suspended – completed on Sep 6
Israel .... (1) 1-3 (2).............. Italy
Spain .... (1) 8-0 (0)... Liechtenstein
Thursday, 6 October 2016
Italy................ (0) 1-1 (0)..............Spain
Liechtenstein . (0) 0-2 (1)............Albania
Macedonia..... (0) 1-2 (2).............. Israel
Sunday, 9 October 2016
Israel .... (2) 2-1 (0)..... Liechtenstein
Albania .... (0) 0-2 (0)...........Spain
Macedonia..... (0) 2-3 (1)................Italy
Saturday, 12 November 2016
Albania .... (0) 0-3 (1)............. Israel
Liechtenstein . (0) 0-4 (4)................Italy
Spain .... (1) 4-0 (0)..... Macedonia
Friday, 24 March 2017
Italy................ (1) 2-0 (0)...........Albania
Liechtenstein . (0) 0-3 (1)..... Macedonia
Spain .... (2) 4-1 (0)............... Israel
Sunday, 11 June 2017
Israel .... (0) 0-3 (2)...........Albania
Italy................ (1) 5-0 (0)... Liechtenstein
Macedonia..... (0) 1-2 (2).............Spain
Saturday, 2 September 2017
Albania .... (0) 2-0 (0)... Liechtenstein
Israel .... (0) 0-1 (0)..... Macedonia
Spain .... (2) 3-0 (0)................Italy
Tuesday, 5 September 2017
Italy................ (0) 1-0 (0)......... Israel
Liechtenstein . (0) 0-8 (4)..............Spain
Macedonia..... (0) 1-1 (0)...........Albania
Friday, 6 October 2017
Italy................ (1) 1-1 (0)..... Macedonia
Liechtenstein . (0) 0-1 (1)............. Israel
Spain .... (3) 3-0 (0)...........Albania
Monday, 9 October 2017
Albania .... (0) 0-1 (0)................Italy
Israel .... (0) 0-1 (0)...........Spain
Macedonia..... (2) 4-0 (0)... Liechtenstein

Group H	P	W	D	L	F	A	GD	P
Belgium	10	9	1	0	43	6	37	28
Greece	10	5	4	1	17	6	11	19
Bosnia-Hz	10	5	2	3	24	13	11	17
Estonia	10	3	2	5	13	19	-6	11
Cyprus	10	3	1	6	9	18	-9	10
Gibraltar	10	0	0	10	3	47	-44	0

Tuesday, 6 September 2016
Bosnia-Hz....... (2) 5-0 (0)........... Estonia
Cyprus............ (0) 0-3 (1)...........Belgium
Gibraltar......... (1) 1-4 (4)............Greece

Friday, 7 October 2016
Belgium.......... (2) 4-0 (0)....... Bosnia-Hz
Estonia............ (0) 4-0 (0)..........Gibraltar
Greece............. (2) 2-0 (0)............. Cyprus
Monday, 10 October 2016
Bosnia-Hz....... (0) 2-0 (0)............. Cyprus
Estonia............ (0) 0-2 (1)............. Greece
Gibraltar......... (0) 0-6 (3)........Belgium
Sunday, 13 November 2016
Cyprus............ (1) 3-1 (0)..........Gibraltar
Belgium.......... (3) 8-1 (1)........ Estonia
Greece............. (0) 1-1 (1)........ Bosnia-Hz
Saturday, 25 March 2017
Bosnia-Hz....... (2) 5-0 (0)..........Gibraltar
Cyprus............ (0) 0-0 (0)............ Estonia
Belgium.......... (0) 1-1 (0)........ Greece
Friday, 9 June 2017
Bosnia-Hz....... (0) 0-0 (0)........... Greece
Estonia............ (0) 0-2 (1)........Belgium
Gibraltar......... (1) 1-2 (1)............. Cyprus
Thursday, 31 August 2017
Belgium.......... (6) 9-0 (0)..........Gibraltar
Cyprus............ (0) 3-2 (2)........Bosnia-Hz
Greece............. (0) 0-0 (0)............ Estonia
Sunday, 3 September 2017
Estonia............ (0) 1-0 (0)............. Cyprus
Greece............. (0) 1-2 (0)........Belgium
Gibraltar......... (0) 0-4 (1)........ Bosnia-Hz
Saturday, 7 October 2017
Gibraltar......... (0) 0-6 (3)........ Estonia
Bosnia-Hz....... (2) 3-4 (1)........Belgium
Cyprus............ (1) 1-2 (1)........ Greece
Tuesday, 10 October 2017
Belgium.......... (1) 4-0 (0)............. Cyprus
Estonia............ (0) 1-2 (0)........ Bosnia-Hz
Greece............. (1) 4-0 (0)..........Gibraltar

Group I	P	W	D	L	F	A	GD	P
Iceland	10	7	1	2	16	7	9	22
Croatia	10	6	2	2	15	4	11	20
Ukraine	10	5	2	3	13	9	4	17
Turkey	10	4	3	3	14	13	1	15
Finland	10	2	3	5	9	13	-4	9
Kosovo	10	0	1	9	3	24	-21	1

Monday, 5 September 2016
Croatia .... (1) 1-1 (1)...........Turkey
Finland............ (1) 1-1 (1)............Kosovo
Ukraine .... (1) 1-1 (1)..........Iceland
Thursday, 6 October 2016
Iceland .... (1) 3-2 (2)........... Finland
Kosovo .... (0) 0-6 (3)..........Croatia
Turkey .... (1) 2-2 (2)...........Ukraine
Sunday, 9 October 2016
Finland............ (0) 0-1 (1)...........Croatia
Ukraine .... (1) 3-0 (0)...........Kosovo
Iceland .... (2) 2-0 (0)...........Turkey
Saturday, 12 November 2016
Croatia .... (1) 2-0 (0)...........Iceland
Turkey .... (0) 2-0 (0)...........Kosovo
Ukraine .... (1) 1-0 (0)........... Finland
Friday, 24 March 2017
Turkey .... (2) 2-0 (0)........... Finland
Croatia .... (1) 1-0 (0)...........Ukraine
Kosovo .... (0) 1-2 (2)...........Iceland

From top: French fans get cocky, Scotland go close to their first finals since 1998, family fun in Sweden, Serbian flags, ponchos in Lithuania, Germany's mascot Paule meets a young supporter

Sunday, 11 June 2017
Finland............ (0) 1-2 (0)...........Ukraine
Iceland .... (0) 1-0 (0)...........**Croatia**
Kosovo .... (1) 1-4 (2).............Turkey
Saturday, 2 September 2017
Finland........... (1) 1-0 (0)...........**Iceland**
Croatia .... (0) 1-0 (0)...........Kosovo
Match suspended – completed on Sep 3
Ukraine .... (2) 2-0 (0).............Turkey
Tuesday, 5 September 2017
Iceland .... (0) 2-0 (0)...........Ukraine
Kosovo .... (0) 0-1 (0)............ Finland
Turkey .... (0) 1-0 (0)...........**Croatia**
Friday, 6 October 2017
Croatia .... (0) 1-1 (0)............ Finland
Kosovo .... (0) 0-2 (0)...........Ukraine
Turkey .... (0) 0-3 (2)...........**Iceland**
Monday, 9 October 2017
Finland........... (0) 2-2 (0)...........Turkey
Iceland .... (1) 2-0 (0)...........Kosovo
Ukraine .... (0) 0-2 (0)...........**Croatia**

Playoffs first legs
Thursday, 9 November 2017
Croatia .... (3) 4-1 (1)............ Greece
N Ireland........ (0) 0-1 (0)....**Switzerland**
Friday, 10 November 2017
Sweden .... (0) 1-0 (0)................ Italy
Saturday, 11 November 2017
Denmark ...... (0) 0-0 (0)..Rep of Ireland

Playoffs second legs
Sunday, 12 November 2017
Greece............ (0) 0-0 (0)...........**Croatia**
Croatia won 4-1 on aggregate
Switzerland .. (0) 0-0 (0)......... N Ireland
Switzerland won 1-0 on aggregate
Monday, 13 November 2017
Italy................ (0) 0-0 (0)...........**Sweden**
Sweden won 1-0 on aggregate
Tuesday, 14 November 2017
Rep of Ireland (1) 1-5 (2)........**Denmark**
Denmark won 5-1 on aggregate

South America

How it works
1 group of 10, top 4 qualify for the finals, 5th-placed team advances to intercontinental playoff

	P	W	D	L	F	A	GD	P
Brazil	18	12	5	1	41	11	30	41
Uruguay	18	9	4	5	32	20	12	31
Argentina	18	7	7	4	19	16	3	28
Colombia	18	7	6	5	21	19	2	27
Peru	18	7	5	6	27	26	1	26
Chile	18	8	2	8	26	27	-1	26
Paraguay	18	7	3	8	19	25	-6	24
Ecuador	18	6	2	10	26	29	-3	20
Bolivia	18	4	2	12	16	38	-22	14
Venezuela	18	2	6	10	19	35	-16	12

Thursday, 8 October 2015
Bolivia............ (0) 0-2 (1).........**Uruguay**
Colombia ...... (1) 2-0 (0)............... **Peru**

Joshua Kimmich: nine assists in qualifying

Venezuela ...... (0) 0-1 (0)......... Paraguay
Chile............. (0) 2-0 (0)..............**Brazil**
Argentina ..... (0) 0-2 (0).......... Ecuador
Tuesday, 13 October 2015
Ecuador.......... (0) 2-0 (0)............. Bolivia
Uruguay .... (1) 3-0 (0)......**Colombia**
Paraguay........ (0) 0-0 (0)......**Argentina**
Brazil .... (2) 3-1 (0).........Venezuela
Peru .... (2) 3-4 (3)............... Chile
Thursday, 12 November 2015
Bolivia............ (3) 4-2 (1).......Venezuela
Ecuador.......... (1) 2-1 (0).........**Uruguay**
Chile............... (1) 1-1 (0).......**Colombia**
Friday, 13 November 2015
Argentina ..... (1) 1-1 (0)..............**Brazil**
Peru .... (1) 1-0 (0)......... Paraguay
Tuesday, 17 November 2015
Colombia ...... (0) 0-1 (1)......**Argentina**
Venezuela ...... (0) 1-3 (2).......... Ecuador
Paraguay........ (0) 2-1 (0)............. Bolivia
Uruguay .... (1) 3-0 (0)................ Chile
Brazil .... (1) 3-0 (0)................ **Peru**
Thursday, 24 March 2016
Bolivia............ (0) 2-3 (2).......**Colombia**
Ecuador.......... (1) 2-2 (1)......... Paraguay
Chile............... (1) 1-2 (2).......**Argentina**
Peru .... (0) 2-2 (1).......Venezuela
Friday, 25 March 2016
Brazil .... (2) 2-2 (1).........**Uruguay**
Tuesday, 29 March 2016
Colombia ...... (1) 3-1 (0).......... Ecuador
Uruguay .... (1) 1-0 (0)................ **Peru**
Venezuela ..... (1) 1-4 (1)................ Chile
Argentina ..... (2) 2-0 (0)............. Bolivia
Paraguay........ (1) 2-2 (0)..............**Brazil**
Thursday, 1 September 2016
Bolivia............ (1) 2-0 (0)................ **Peru**
Match awarded 3-0 to Peru
Colombia ...... (1) 2-0 (0).......Venezuela
Ecuador.......... (0) 0-3 (0)..............**Brazil**
Argentina ..... (1) 1-0 (0).........**Uruguay**
Paraguay........ (2) 2-1 (1)................ Chile
Tuesday, 6 September 2016
Uruguay .... (3) 4-0 (0)......... Paraguay
Chile............... (0) 0-0 (0)............. Bolivia
Match awarded 3-0 to Chile
Venezuela ...... (1) 2-2 (0)......**Argentina**
Brazil .... (1) 2-1 (1).........**Colombia**
Peru .... (1) 2-1 (1).......... Ecuador
Thursday, 6 October 2016
Ecuador.......... (2) 3-0 (0)............ Chile
Uruguay .... (1) 3-0 (0).......Venezuela
Paraguay........ (0) 0-1 (0)........**Colombia**
Brazil .... (4) 5-0 (0)............. Bolivia
Peru .... (0) 2-2 (1)......**Argentina**
Tuesday, 11 October 2016
Bolivia............ (2) 2-2 (0).......... Ecuador
Colombia ...... (1) 2-2 (1).........**Uruguay**
Argentina ..... (0) 0-1 (1).......... Paraguay
Chile............... (1) 2-1 (0)................ **Peru**
Venezuela ...... (0) 0-2 (1)..............**Brazil**
Thursday, 10 November 2016
Colombia ...... (0) 0-0 (0)................ Chile
Uruguay .... (2) 2-1 (1).......... Ecuador

Brazil's talisman Neymar puts Chile's defence through their paces

Paraguay........ (1) 1-4 (0)................ **Peru**
Brazil .... (2) 3-0 (0).......**Argentina**
Venezuela ...... (2) 5-0 (0)......... Bolivia
Tuesday, 15 November 2016
Bolivia............ (0) 1-0 (0)......... Paraguay
Ecuador.......... (0) 3-0 (0).......Venezuela
Argentina ..... (2) 3-0 (0)........**Colombia**
Chile............... (1) 3-1 (1).........**Uruguay**
Peru .... (0) 0-2 (0)..............**Brazil**
Thursday, 23 March 2017
Colombia ...... (1) 1-0 (0)......... Bolivia
Paraguay........ (1) 2-1 (0)......... Ecuador
Uruguay .... (1) 1-4 (1)..............**Brazil**
Argentina ..... (1) 1-0 (0)................ Chile
Venezuela ...... (2) 2-2 (0)................ **Peru**

Tuesday, 28 March 2017
Bolivia............ (1) 2-0 (0)......**Argentina**
Ecuador.......... (0) 0-2 (2).......**Colombia**
Chile............... (3) 3-1 (0).......Venezuela
Brazil .... (1) 3-0 (0)......... Paraguay
Peru .... (1) 2-1 (1).........**Uruguay**
Thursday, 31 August 2017
Venezuela ...... (0) 0-0 (0).......**Colombia**
Chile............... (0) 0-3 (1)......... Paraguay
Uruguay .... (0) 0-0 (0)......**Argentina**
Brazil .... (0) 2-0 (0).......... Ecuador
Peru .... (0) 2-1 (0)............. Bolivia
Tuesday, 5 September 2017
Bolivia............ (0) 1-0 (0)................ Chile

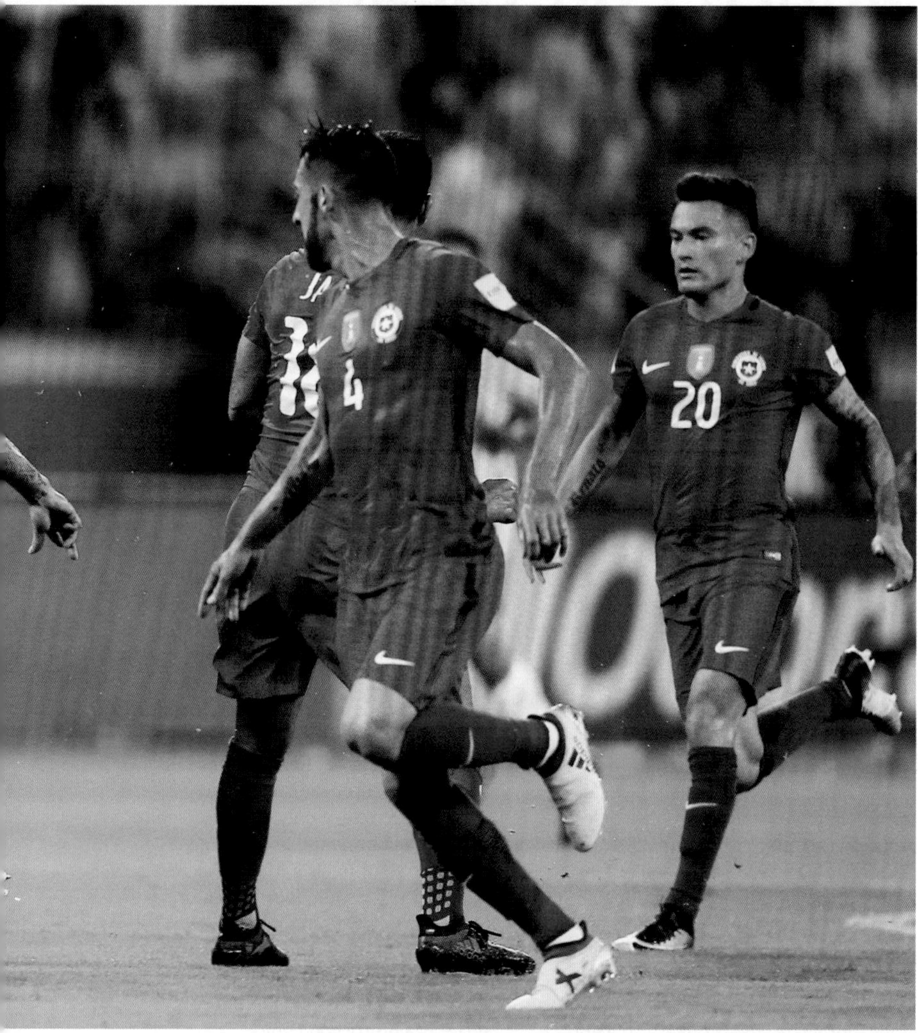

Photo by Alexandre Schneider/Getty Images

Colombia	(0)	1-1	(1)	**Brazil**
Ecuador	(0)	1-2	(0)	**Peru**
Argentina	(0)	1-1	(0)	Venezuela
Paraguay	(0)	1-2	(0)	**Uruguay**
Thursday, 5 October 2017				
Bolivia	(0)	0-0	(0)	**Brazil**
Venezuela	(0)	0-0	(0)	**Uruguay**
Argentina	(0)	0-0	(0)	**Peru**
Chile	(1)	2-1	(0)	Ecuador
Colombia	(0)	1-2	(0)	Paraguay
Tuesday, 10 October 2017				
Brazil	(0)	3-0	(0)	Chile
Ecuador	(1)	1-3	(2)	**Argentina**
Paraguay	(0)	0-1	(0)	Venezuela
Peru	(0)	1-1	(0)	**Colombia**
Uruguay	(2)	4-2	(1)	Bolivia

Photo by Hagen Hopkins/Getty Images

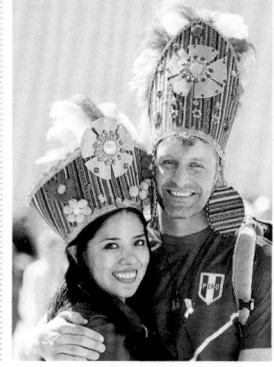

Inter-continental playoffs

Playoffs first legs				
Friday, 10 November 2017				
Honduras	(0)	0-0	(0)	**Australia**
Saturday, 11 November 2017				
New Zealand	(0)	0-0	(0)	**Peru**
Playoffs second legs				
Wednesday, 15 November 2017				
Australia	(0)	3-1	(0)	Honduras
Australia won 3-1 on aggregate				
Peru	(1)	2-0	(0)	New Zealand
Peru won 2-0 on aggregate				

Peru fans pose before the second leg of their playoff

WORLD CUP TRENDS

Germany can buck holders' dismal recent record

The obvious place to look for hints towards what might happen in Russia is what happened at previous World Cups, *writes Paul Charlton*.

There are a few constants – at least one of Brazil and Germany have made it at least as far as the semi-finals at every World Cup since 1934 – but there are also always a few surprises.

The record of World Cup finalists four years on has been patchy since Brazil made three finals in a row from 1994 to 2002. The USA 94 winners were beaten finalists at France 98, the first World Cup to be contested in the current 32-team format, and won it again in 2002 before defeat in the quarter-finals in 2006.

Only Italy in 1938 and Brazil in 1962 have won back-to-back World Cups but, Brazil aside, the record of recent champions is abject with France, Italy and Spain, the three other winners since 1994, all failing to get out of the group stage four years later. France also went out in the group stage in 2010 after losing the 2006 final to Italy on penalties.

However, if anyone can break the hoodoo for defending European World Cup winners, it's probably Germany, who have reached at least the semi-finals in every World Cup this century and, going back to their tournament debut in Italy in 1934, reached at least the last four in 13 of the 18 World Cups they have taken part in.

They've crashed out at the first hurdle only once, in France in 1938, when the competition kicked off with a knockout round rather than a group stage.

The last time Germany failed to win a group they contested at a World Cup was at Mexico 86, and you have to go back to the 1978 World Cup in Argentina to find the last time they failed to qualify from a group, when they finished behind Holland and Italy in the second group stage.

Continental champions have been quite disappointing in recent years too, with Spain the only team to follow a regional championship with World Cup victory in the current format, although Brazil lifted the Copa America trophy in 1997 before reaching the final of France 98.

Reigning European champions Portugal are one of only two other teams to reach a continental final and get as far as the semi-finals in the subsequent World Cup. They did it in 2006 and Germany followed suit in 2010.

The group stage tends to be a little more predictable than the final stages of the tournament, and Fifa's seedings serve as a pretty good guide.

Spain were the only team in Pot 1 to fail to get out of the group stage in 2014, with five of the top seeds winning their groups. That took the total top-seeded group winners to 28 teams out of 40 for the five World Cups post USA 94, with seven in 1998, five in 2002 and 2006 and six in 2010.

Six of the remaining 12 seeded sides failed to get out of the group stage – France and Argentina in 2002, South Africa and Italy in 2010 and Spain in both 1998 and 2014.

There are some interesting trends to consider in the match goal markets, too.

Records of tournament winners at subsequent World Cups since 1998

Tournament	DNQ	GS	R16	QF	SF	RU	W	Current champions
World Cup	-	3	-	1	-	1	-	Germany
European Championship	1	2	-	1	-	-	1	Portugal
Copa America	1	-	1	2	-	1	-	Chile (DNQ)
Concacaf Gold Cup	-	1	3	1	-	-	-	USA (DNQ)
Asian Cup	1	3	1	-	-	-	-	Australia
Africa Cup of Nations	3	1	1	-	-	-	-	Cameroon (DNQ)
Confederations Cup	-	1	-	2	1	1	-	Germany

GS group stage, R16 round of 16, QF quarters, SF semis, RU runners-up, W winners, DNQ did not qualify

Average goals per game

	GS	R16	QF	SF	3rd/4th	F
1998	2.6	2.8	2.8	2.5	3.0	3.0
2002	2.7	1.9	1.0	1.0	5.0	2.0
2006	2.4	1.8	1.5	0.5	4.0	2.0
2010	2.1	2.6	2.5	3.0	5.0	0.0
2014	2.8	1.4	1.3	4.0	3.0	0.0
Games	240	40	20	10	5	5
Goals	610	83	36	22	20	7
Average	2.5	2.1	1.8	2.2	4.0	1.4

Final tournaments since France 98. 90 mins only

Average goals per game

	Teams	Games	Total goals	Avg goals per game
1998	32	64	171	2.7
2002	32	64	161	2.5
2006	32	64	147	2.3
2010	32	64	145	2.3
2014	32	64	171	2.7
Totals		320	795	2.5

Final tournaments since France 98. Includes goals scored in extra time

Over 2.5 goals

	GS	R16	QF	SF	3rd/4th	F
1998	52%	63%	75%	50%	100%	100%
2002	44%	13%	25%	0%	100%	0%
2006	44%	25%	25%	0%	100%	0%
2010	35%	63%	50%	50%	100%	0%
2014	65%	13%	25%	50%	100%	0%
Totals	48%	35%	40%	30%	100%	20%

Final tournaments since France 98. 90 mins only

Both teams to score

	GS	R16	QF	SF	3rd/4th	F
1998	52%	63%	50%	100%	100%	0%
2002	52%	38%	25%	0%	100%	0%
2006	38%	25%	25%	0%	100%	100%
2010	40%	63%	50%	50%	100%	0%
2014	56%	38%	25%	50%	0%	0%
Totals	48%	45%	35%	40%	80%	20%

Final tournaments since France 98. 90 mins only

After a couple of tournaments where total match goals averaged out at 2.3 goals-per-game in 2006 and 2010, Brazil saw a rise to 2.7, with 171 goals scored during the tournament.

Overall, goal averages have tended to be higher during the group stage than the knockout rounds, with averages in 90 minutes declining as the tournament nears a conclusion. Germany's 7-1 mauling of Brazil in 2014 massaged the semi-final figures – remove that outlier, and the remaining nine matches averaged 1.4 goals.

The one exception is the third-place playoff match, which has averaged four goals since France 98. All five games would have landed an over 2.5 goals bet and four of the five would have copped in the both teams to score market.

If the playoff is usually full of goals, the final is the polar opposite – unders and 'no' in both teams to score would both have landed in six of the last seven. The 2006 final was the only one since Mexico 86 in which both teams scored and the 1998 final was the most recent to feature three goals.

Gulf Cup of Nations 2014

Saudi Arabia, November 13-26 2014

Group A	P	W	D	L	F	A	GD	P
Saudi Arabia	3	2	1	0	5	1	4	7
Qatar	3	0	3	0	1	1	0	3
Yemen	3	0	2	1	0	1	-1	2
Bahrain	3	0	2	1	0	3	-3	2

Thursday, November 13 2014
Saudi Arabia. (1) 1-1 (0)............... Qatar
Yemen .... (0) 0-0 (0)..........Bahrain
Sunday, November 16 2014
Yemen .... (0) 0-0 (0).............Qatar
Saudi Arabia. (1) 3-0 (0)...........Bahrain
Wednesday, November 19 2014
Saudi Arabia. (1) 1-0 (0)............Yemen
Bahrain .... (0) 0-0 (0)............Qatar

Group B	P	W	D	L	F	A	GD	P
Oman	3	1	2	0	6	1	5	5
UAE	3	1	2	0	4	2	2	5
Kuwait	3	1	1	1	3	7	-4	4
Iraq	3	0	1	2	1	4	-3	1

Friday, November 14 2014
UAE............... (0) 0-0 (0)..............Oman
Iraq .... (0) 0-1 (0)..............Kuwait
Monday, November 17 2014
UAE............... (2) 2-2 (2)............Kuwait
Iraq .... (1) 1-1 (0)............Oman
Thursday, November 20 2014
UAE............... (0) 2-0 (0)................Iraq
Kuwait .... (0) 0-5 (2)............Oman

Semi-finals
Sunday, November 23 2014
Oman .... (1) 1-3 (1).............. Qatar
Saudi Arabia. (2) 3-2 (0)............... UAE

Third place
Tuesday, November 25 2014
UAE............... (0) 1-0 (0)..............Oman

Final
Wednesday, November 26 2014
Saudi Arabia. (1) 1-2 (1).............. Qatar

Africa Cup of Nations 2015

Equatorial Guinea, Jan 17-Feb 8 2015

Group A	P	W	D	L	F	A	GD	P
Congo	3	2	1	0	4	2	2	7
Eq Guinea	3	1	2	0	3	1	2	5
Gabon	3	1	0	2	2	3	-1	3
Burkina Faso	3	0	1	2	1	4	-3	1

Saturday, 17 January 2015
Eq Guinea ...... (1) 1-1 (0).............Congo
Burkina Faso.. (0) 0-2 (1)............Gabon
Wednesday, 21 January 2015
Eq Guinea ...... (0) 0-0 (0)....Burkina Faso
Gabon .... (0) 0-1 (0)............Congo
Sunday, 25 January 2015
Gabon .... (0) 0-2 (0)......Eq Guinea
Congo .... (0) 2-1 (0)....Burkina Faso

Group B	P	W	D	L	F	A	GD	P
Tunisia	3	1	2	0	4	3	1	5
Congo DR	3	0	3	0	2	2	0	3
Cape Verde	3	0	3	0	1	1	0	3
Zambia	3	0	2	1	2	3	-1	2

Sunday, 18 January 2015
Zambia........... (1) 1-1 (0)....... DR Congo
Tunisia........... (0) 1-1 (0)....Cape Verde
Thursday, 22 January 2015
Zambia........... (0) 1-2 (0)....... Tunisia
Cape Verde .... (0) 0-0 (0)......... DR Congo
Monday, 26 January 2015
Cape Verde .... (0) 0-0 (0)........... Zambia
DR Congo....... (0) 1-1 (1)............Tunisia

Group C	P	W	D	L	F	A	GD	P
Ghana	3	2	0	1	4	3	1	6
Algeria	3	2	0	1	5	2	3	6
Senegal	3	1	1	1	3	4	-1	4
South Africa	3	0	1	2	3	6	-3	1

Monday, 19 January 2015
Ghana .... (1) 1-2 (0)......... Senegal
Algeria .... (0) 3-1 (0).... South Africa
Friday, 23 January 2015
Ghana .... (0) 1-0 (0)..........Algeria
South Africa... (0) 1-1 (0)......... Senegal
Tuesday, 27 January 2015
South Africa... (1) 1-2 (0)...........Ghana
Senegal......... (0) 0-2 (1)............Algeria

Group D	P	W	D	L	F	A	GD	P
Ivory Coast	3	1	2	0	3	2	1	5
Guinea	3	0	3	0	3	3	0	3
Mali	3	0	3	0	3	3	0	3
Cameroon	3	0	2	1	2	3	-1	2

Tuesday, 20 January 2015
Ivory Coast..... (0) 1-1 (1).............Guinea
Mali.............. (0) 1-1 (0).......Cameroon
Saturday, 24 January 2015
Ivory Coast..... (0) 1-1 (1)................Mali
Cameroon ...... (1) 1-1 (1)...........Guinea
Wednesday, 28 January 2015
Cameroon ...... (0) 0-1 (1)...... Ivory Coast
Guinea .... (1) 1-1 (0)............Mali

Quarter-finals
Saturday, 31 January 2015
Congo .... (0) 2-4 (0)....... DR Congo
Tunisia........... (0) 1-2 (0).......Eq Guinea
AET. 1-1 90 mins
Sunday, 1 February 2015
Ghana .... (2) 3-0 (0).............Guinea
Ivory Coast..... (1) 3-1 (0)............Algeria

Semi-finals
Wednesday, 4 February 2015
DR Congo........ (1) 1-3 (2)... Ivory Coast
Thursday, 5 February 2015
Ghana .... (2) 3-0 (0).......Eq Guinea

Third place
Saturday, 7 February 2015
DR Congo....... (0) 0-0 (0).......Eq Guinea
AET. DR Congo 4-2 pens

Final
Sunday, 8 February 2015
Ivory Coast..... (0) 0-0 (0).............Ghana
AET. Ivory Coast 9-8 pens

Asian Cup 2015

Australia, January 9-31 2015

Group A	P	W	D	L	F	A	GD	P
South Korea	3	3	0	0	3	0	3	9
Australia	3	2	0	1	8	2	6	6
Oman	3	1	0	2	1	5	-4	3
Kuwait	3	0	0	3	1	6	-5	0

Friday, 9 January 2015
Australia .... (2) 4-1 (1)............Kuwait
Saturday, 10 January 2015
South Korea.. (1) 1-0 (0)..............Oman
Tuesday, 13 January 2015
Kuwait .... (0) 0-1 (1)... South Korea
Oman .... (0) 0-4 (3)........Australia
Saturday, 17 January 2015
Australia .... (0) 0-1 (1)... South Korea
Oman .... (0) 1-0 (0)..........Kuwait

Group B	P	W	D	L	F	A	GD	P
China	3	3	0	0	5	2	3	9
Uzbekistan	3	2	0	1	5	3	2	6
Saudi Arabia	3	1	0	2	5	5	0	3
North Korea	3	0	0	3	2	7	-5	0

Saturday, 10 January 2015
Uzbekistan..... (0) 1-0 (0).....North Korea
Saudi Arabia. (0) 0-1 (0).............. China
Wednesday, 14 January 2015
North Korea ... (1) 1-4 (1).. Saudi Arabia
China.............. (0) 2-1 (1)...... Uzbekistan
Sunday, 18 January 2015
Uzbekistan..... (1) 3-1 (0).. Saudi Arabia
China.............. (2) 2-1 (0)....North Korea

Group C	P	W	D	L	F	A	GD	P
Iran	3	3	0	0	4	0	4	9
UAE	3	2	0	1	6	3	3	6
Bahrain	3	1	0	2	3	5	-2	3
Qatar	3	0	0	3	2	7	-5	0

Sunday, 11 January 2015
UAE............... (1) 4-1 (1)..............Qatar
Iran................ (1) 2-0 (0)...........Bahrain
Thursday, 15 January 2015
Bahrain .... (1) 1-2 (1)................UAE
Qatar.............. (0) 0-1 (0)................Iran
Monday, 19 January 2015
Iran................ (0) 1-0 (0)................UAE
Qatar.............. (0) 1-2 (1)............Bahrain

Group D	P	W	D	L	F	A	GD	P
Japan	3	3	0	0	7	0	7	9
Iraq	3	2	0	1	3	1	2	6
Jordan	3	1	0	2	5	4	1	3
Palestine	3	0	0	3	1	11	-10	0

Monday, 12 January 2015
Japan............. (3) 4-0 (0).........Palestine
Jordan .... (0) 0-1 (0)................Iraq

Australia celebrate their 2015 Asian Cup final win over South Korea at the ANZ Stadium, Sydney

Friday, 16 January 2015
Palestine .... (0) 1-5 (3)............ Jordan
Iraq .... (0) 0-1 (1)............**Japan**
Tuesday, 20 January 2015
Japan............ (1) 2-0 (0)............ Jordan
Iraq .... (0) 2-0 (0).......Palestine

Quarter-finals
Thursday, 22 January 2015
South Korea.. (0) 2-0 (0)...... Uzbekistan
AET. 0-0 90 mins
China............. (0) 0-2 (0)........**Australia**
Friday, 23 January 2015
Iran............... (1) 3-3 (0)................Iraq
AET. 1-1 90 mins. Iraq 7-6 pens
Japan............ (0) 1-1 (1)................ UAE
AET. UAE 5-4 pens

Semi-finals
Monday, 26 January 2015
South Korea.. (1) 2-0 (0)................Iraq
Tuesday, 27 January 2015
Australia ...... (2) 2-0 (0)................ UAE

Third place
Friday, 30 January 2015
Iraq .... (2) 2-3 (1)................ UAE

Final
Saturday, 31 January 2015
South Korea.. (0) 1-2 (1).........**Australia**
AET. 1-1 90 mins

Copa America 2015
Chile, June 11-July 4 2015

Group A	P	W	D	L	F	A	GD	P
Chile	3	2	1	0	10	3	7	7
Bolivia	3	1	1	1	3	7	-4	4
Ecuador	3	1	0	2	4	6	-2	3
Mexico	3	0	2	1	4	5	-1	2

Thursday, 11 June 2015
Chile.............. (0) 2-0 (0).......... Ecuador
Friday, 12 June 2015
Mexico .... (0) 0-0 (0)............ Bolivia
Monday, 15 June 2015
Ecuador.......... (0) 2-3 (3)............ Bolivia
Chile.............. (2) 3-3 (2).......**Mexico**
Friday, 19 June 2015
Mexico .... (0) 1-2 (1).......... Ecuador
Chile.............. (2) 5-0 (0)............ Bolivia

Group B	P	W	D	L	F	A	GD	P
Argentina	3	2	1	0	4	2	2	7
Paraguay	3	1	2	0	4	3	1	5
Uruguay	3	1	1	1	2	2	0	4
Jamaica	3	0	0	3	0	3	-3	0

Saturday, 13 June 2015
Uruguay .... (0) 1-0 (0).......... Jamaica
Argentina ..... (2) 2-2 (0)......... Paraguay
Tuesday, 16 June 2015
Paraguay .... (1) 1-0 (0).......... Jamaica
Argentina ..... (0) 1-0 (0).........**Uruguay**
Saturday, 20 June 2015
Uruguay .... (1) 1-1 (1)......... Paraguay
Argentina ..... (1) 1-0 (0).......... Jamaica

Group C	P	W	D	L	F	A	GD	P
Brazil	3	2	0	1	4	3	1	6
Peru	3	1	1	1	2	2	0	4
Colombia	3	1	1	1	1	1	0	4
Venezuela	3	1	0	2	2	3	-1	3

Sunday, 14 June 2015
Colombia ...... (0) 0-1 (0).......Venezuela
Brazil............ (1) 2-1 (1)................ Peru
Wednesday, 17 June 2015
Brazil............ (0) 0-1 (1).......Colombia
Thursday, 18 June 2015
Peru............... (0) 1-0 (0).......Venezuela

Sunday, 21 June 2015
Colombia ...... (0) 0-0 (0).............. Peru
Brazil............ (1) 2-1 (0).......Venezuela

Quarter-finals
Wednesday, 24 June 2015
Chile.............. (0) 1-0 (0).........**Uruguay**
Thursday, 25 June 2015
Bolivia........... (0) 1-3 (2).............. Peru
Friday, 26 June 2015
Argentina ..... (0) 0-0 (0).......**Colombia**
AET. Argentina 5-4 pens
Saturday, 27 June 2015
Brazil............ (1) 1-1 (0)........ Paraguay
AET. Paraguay 4-3 pens

Semi-finals
Monday, 29 June 2015
Chile.............. (1) 2-1 (0).............. Peru
Tuesday, 30 June 2015
Argentina ..... (2) 6-1 (1)........ Paraguay

Third place
Friday, 3 July 2015
Peru............... (0) 2-0 (0)........ Paraguay

Final
Saturday, 4 July 2015
Chile.............. (0) 0-0 (0).......**Argentina**
AET. Chile 4-1 pens

Concacaf Gold Cup 2015
USA & Canada, July 7-26 2015

Group A	P	W	D	L	F	A	GD	P
USA	3	2	1	0	4	2	+2	7
Haiti	3	1	1	1	2	2	0	4
Panama	3	0	3	0	3	3	0	3
Honduras	3	0	1	2	2	4	-2	1

Tuesday, 7 July 2015
Panama.........(0) 1-1 (0).................Haiti
USA................(1) 2-1 (0)...........Honduras
Friday, 10 July 2015
Honduras.......(0) 1-1 (1)......... Panama
USA................(0) 1-0 (0)...............Haiti
Monday, 13 July 2015
Haiti..............(1) 1-0 (0).......Honduras
Panama.........(1) 1-1 (0)...................USA

Group B	P	W	D	L	F	A	GD	P
Jamaica	3	2	1	0	4	2	+2	7
Costa Rica	3	0	3	0	3	3	0	3
El Salvador	3	0	2	1	1	2	-1	2
Canada	3	0	2	1	0	1	-1	2

Wednesday, 8 July 2015
Costa Rica.....(2) 2-2 (1)........... Jamaica
El Salvador.....(0) 0-0 (0).......... Canada
Saturday, 11 July 2015
Jamaica.........(0) 1-0 (0)...........Canada
Costa Rica.....(0) 1-1 (0)......... El Salvador
Tuesday, 14 July 2015
Jamaica.........(0) 1-0 (0)...... El Salvador
Canada..........(0) 0-0 (0)..... Costa Rica

Group C	P	W	D	L	F	A	GD	P
Trin & Tobago	3	2	1	0	9	5	+4	7
Mexico	3	1	2	0	10	4	+6	5
Cuba	3	1	0	2	1	8	-7	3
Guatemala	3	0	1	2	1	4	-3	1

Thursday, 9 July 2015
Trin & Tobago (3) 3-1 (0)......Guatemala
Mexico ....(4) 6-0 (0)................Cuba
Sunday, 12 July 2015
Trin & Tobago (2) 2-0 (0)................Cuba
Guatemala .....(0) 0-0 (0)..............Mexico
Wednesday, 15 July 2015
Cuba ....(0) 1-0 (0)........Guatemala
Mexico ....(1) 4-4 (0)..Trin & Tobago

Quarter-finals
Saturday, July 18 2015
USA................(4) 6-0 (0)................Cuba
Haiti ....(0) 0-1 (1)....... Jamaica
Sunday, July 19 2015
Trin & Tobago (0) 1-1 (1)......... Panama
AET. Panama 6-5 pens
Mexico ....(0) 1-0 (0)..... Costa Rica
AET. 0-0 90 mins

Semi-finals
Wednesday, July 22 2015
USA................(0) 1-2 (2)........... Jamaica
Panama.........(0) 1-2 (0)..............Mexico
AET. 1-1 90 mins

Third place
Saturday, July 25 2015
USA................(0) 1-1 (0)......... Panama
AET. Panama 3-2 pens

Final
Monday, July 27 2015
Jamaica ....(0) 1-3 (1)...........Mexico

African Nations Championship 2016

Rwanda, Jan 16-Feb 7 2016
Note: only players active in their national team's domestic league were eligible for this tournament

Group A	P	W	D	L	F	A	GD	P
Rwanda	3	2	0	1	4	5	-1	6
Ivory Coast	3	2	0	1	5	2	3	6
Morocco	3	1	1	1	4	2	2	4
Gabon	3	0	1	2	2	6	-4	1

Saturday, January 16 2016
Rwanda..........(1) 1-0 (0)...... Ivory Coast
Gabon ....(0) 0-0 (0).......... Morocco
Wednesday, January 20 2016
Rwanda..........(1) 2-1 (0)............Gabon
Morocco......(0) 0-1 (1)..... Ivory Coast
Sunday, January 24 2016
Morocco........(4) 4-1 (1)......... Rwanda
Ivory Coast.....(1) 4-1 (0)...........Gabon

Group B	P	W	D	L	F	A	GD	P
Cameroon	3	2	1	0	4	1	3	7
DR Congo	3	2	0	1	8	5	3	6
Angola	3	1	0	2	4	6	-2	3
Ethiopia	3	0	1	2	1	5	-4	1

Sunday, January 17 2016
DR Congo.......(1) 3-0 (0)........... Ethiopia
Angola ....(0) 0-1 (1)............Cameroon
Thursday, January 21 2016
DR Congo.......(3) 4-2 (0)...........Angola
Cameroon ......(0) 0-0 (0).......... Ethiopia
Monday, January 25 2016
Cameroon ......(1) 3-1 (0)....... DR Congo
Ethiopia.........(0) 1-2 (0)...........Angola

Group C	P	W	D	L	F	A	GD	P
Tunisia	3	1	2	0	8	3	5	5
Guinea	3	1	2	0	5	4	1	5
Nigeria	3	1	1	1	5	3	2	4
Niger	3	0	1	2	3	11	-8	1

Monday, January 18 2016
Tunisia..........(1) 2-2 (1)...........Guinea
Nigeria ....(0) 4-1 (0)............... Niger
Friday, January 22 2016
Tunisia..........(0) 1-1 (0)...........Nigeria
Niger.............(1) 2-2 (1)...........Guinea
Tuesday, January 26 2016
Niger.............(0) 0-5 (2)...........Tunisia
Guinea ....(1) 1-0 (0)...........Nigeria

Group D	P	W	D	L	F	A	GD	P
Zambia	3	2	1	0	2	0	2	7
Mali	3	1	2	0	3	2	1	5
Uganda	3	0	2	1	3	4	-1	2
Zimbabwe	3	0	1	2	1	3	-2	1

Tuesday, January 19 2016
Zimbabwe......(0) 0-1 (0)...........Zambia
Mali................(1) 2-2 (2)...........Uganda
Saturday, January 23 2016
Zimbabwe......(0) 0-1 (0)................Mali
Uganda..........(0) 0-1 (1)...........Zambia
Wednesday, January 27 2016
Uganda ....(0) 1-1 (0)...... Zimbabwe
Zambia..........(0) 0-0 (0)............... Mali

Quarter-finals
Saturday, January 30 2016
Rwanda..........(0) 1-2 (1)........ DR Congo
AET. 1-1 90 mins
Cameroon ......(0) 0-3 (0)..... Ivory Coast
AET. 0-0 90 mins
Sunday, January 31 2016
Tunisia............(1) 1-2 (0)................. Mali
Zambia...........(0) 0-0 (0)............Guinea
AET. Guinea 5-4 pens

Semi-finals
Wednesday, February 3 2016
DR Congo.......(0) 1-1 (0)............Guinea
AET. 0-0 90 mins DR Congo 5-4 pens
Thursday, February 4 2016
Mali................(0) 1-0 (0)..... Ivory Coast

Third place
Sunday, February 7 2016
Guinea ....(0) 1-2 (2)..... Ivory Coast

Final
Sunday, February 7 2016
DR Congo.......(1) 3-0 (0)................ Mali

Kirin Cup Soccer 2016

Japan, June 3-7 2016

Semi-finals
Friday, June 3 2016
Bosnia-Hz.......(0) 2-2 (2)........Denmark
AET. Bosnia-Hz 4-3 pens
Japan.............(4) 7-2 (0)........Bulgaria

Third place
Tuesday, June 7 2016
Denmark.......(1) 4-0 (0)..........Bulgaria

Final
Tuesday, June 7 2016
Bosnia-Hz.......(1) 2-1 (1)..............Japan

Copa America 2016

USA, June 3-26 2016

Group A	P	W	D	L	F	A	GD	P
USA	3	2	0	1	5	2	3	6
Colombia	3	2	0	1	6	4	2	6
Costa Rica	3	1	1	1	3	6	-3	4
Paraguay	3	0	1	2	1	3	-2	1

Friday, June 3 2016
USA................(0) 0-2 (2).......Colombia
Saturday, June 4 2016
Costa Rica.....(0) 0-0 (0)..... Paraguay
Tuesday, June 7 2016
USA................(3) 4-0 (0)..... Costa Rica
Colombia ......(2) 2-1 (0)........ Paraguay
Saturday, June 11 2016
USA................(1) 1-0 (0)..... Paraguay
Colombia ......(1) 2-3 (2)..... Costa Rica

Group B	P	W	D	L	F	A	GD	P
Peru	3	2	1	0	4	2	2	7
Ecuador	3	1	2	0	6	2	4	5
Brazil	3	1	1	1	7	2	5	4
Haiti	3	0	0	3	1	12-11	0

Saturday, June 4 2016
Haiti ....(0) 0-1 (0)............... Peru

Brazil .... (0) 0-0 (0) .... Ecuador
Wednesday, June 8 2016
Brazil .... (3) 7-1 (0) ....Haiti
Ecuador......... (1) 2-2 (2) .... Peru
Sunday, June 12 2016
Ecuador......... (2) 4-0 (0) ....Haiti
Brazil .... (0) 0-1 (0) .... Peru

Group C	P	W	D	L	F	A	GD	P
Mexico	3	2	1	0	6	2	4	7
Venezuela	3	2	1	0	3	1	2	7
Uruguay	3	1	0	2	4	4	0	3
Jamaica	3	0	0	3	0	6	-6	0

Sunday, June 5 2016
Jamaica.......... (0) 0-1 (1) ....Venezuela
Mexico .... (1) 3-1 (0) ....Uruguay
Thursday, June 9 2016
Uruguay .... (0) 0-1 (1) ....Venezuela
Mexico .... (1) 2-0 (0) .... Jamaica
Monday, June 13 2016
Mexico .... (0) 1-1 (1) ....Venezuela
Uruguay .... (1) 3-0 (0) .... Jamaica

Group D	P	W	D	L	F	A	GD	P
Argentina	3	3	0	0	10	1	9	9
Chile	3	2	0	1	7	5	2	6
Panama	3	1	0	2	4	10	-6	3
Bolivia	3	0	0	3	2	7	-5	0

Monday, June 6 2016
Panama........ (1) 2-1 (0) .... Bolivia

Argentina ..... (0) 2-1 (0) .... Chile
Friday, June 10 2016
Chile............... (0) 2-1 (0) .... Bolivia
Argentina ..... (1) 5-0 (0) .... Panama
Tuesday, June 14 2016
Chile............... (2) 4-2 (1) .... Panama
Argentina ..... (3) 3-0 (0) .... Bolivia

Quarter-finals
Thursday, June 16 2016
USA................ (1) 2-1 (0) .... Ecuador
Friday, June 17 2016
Peru............... (0) 0-0 (0) ....Colombia
AET. Colombia 4-2 pens
Saturday, June 18 2016
Argentina ..... (2) 4-1 (0) ....Venezuela
Mexico .... (0) 0-7 (2) .... Chile

Semi-finals
Tuesday, June 21 2016
USA................ (0) 0-4 (2) ....Argentina
Wednesday, June 22 2016
Colombia ..... (0) 0-2 (2) .... Chile

Third place
Saturday, June 25 2016
USA................ (0) 0-1 (1) ....Colombia

Final
Sunday, June 26 2016
Argentina ..... (0) 0-0 (0) .... Chile
AET. Chile 4-2 pens

Euro 2016
France, June 10-July 10 2016

Group A	P	W	D	L	F	A	GD	P
France	3	2	1	0	4	1	3	7
Switzerland	3	1	2	0	2	1	1	5
Albania	3	1	0	2	1	3	-2	3
Romania	3	0	1	2	2	4	-2	1

Friday, June 10 2016
France .... (0) 2-1 (0) .... Romania
Saturday, June 11 2016
Albania .... (0) 0-1 (1) ....Switzerland
Wednesday, June 15 2016
Romania........ (1) 1-1 (0) ....Switzerland
France .... (0) 2-0 (0) ....Albania
Sunday, June 19 2016
Romania........ (0) 0-1 (1) ....Albania
Switzerland .. (0) 0-0 (0) ....France

Group B	P	W	D	L	F	A	GD	P
Wales	3	2	0	1	6	3	3	6
England	3	1	2	0	3	2	1	5
Slovakia	3	1	1	1	3	3	0	4
Russia	3	0	1	2	2	6	-4	1

Saturday, June 11 2016
Wales............. (1) 2-1 (0) ....Slovakia
England......... (0) 1-1 (0) ....Russia
Wednesday, June 15 2016
Russia............ (0) 1-2 (2) ....Slovakia
Thursday, June 16 2016
England......... (0) 2-1 (1) .... Wales
Monday, June 20 2016
Russia............ (0) 0-3 (2) .... Wales
Slovakia .... (0) 0-0 (0) .... England

Group C	P	W	D	L	F	A	GD	P
Germany	3	2	1	0	3	0	3	7
Poland	3	2	1	0	2	0	2	7
N Ireland	3	1	0	2	2	2	0	3
Ukraine	3	0	0	3	0	5	-5	0

Sunday, June 12 2016
Poland........... (0) 1-0 (0) .... N Ireland
Germany .... (1) 2-0 (0) ....Ukraine
Thursday, June 16 2016
Ukraine .... (0) 0-2 (0) .... N Ireland
Germany .... (0) 0-0 (0) .... Poland
Tuesday, June 21 2016
Ukraine .... (0) 0-1 (0) .... Poland
N Ireland........ (0) 0-1 (1) ....Germany

Group D	P	W	D	L	F	A	GD	P
Croatia	3	2	1	0	5	3	2	7
Spain	3	2	0	1	5	2	3	6
Turkey	3	1	0	2	2	4	-2	3
Czech Republic	3	0	1	2	2	5	-3	1

Sunday, June 12 2016
Turkey .... (0) 0-1 (1) ....Croatia
Monday, June 13 2016
Spain .... (0) 1-0 (0) ....Czech Rep
Friday, June 17 2016
Czech Rep ...... (0) 2-2 (1) ....Croatia
Spain .... (2) 3-0 (0) ....Turkey

Argentina have lost two Copa America finals on penalties to Chile since the last World Cup – they last won it in 1993

Tuesday, June 21 2016
Czech Rep ..... (0) 0-2 (1).............Turkey
Croatia .... (1) 2-1 (1)..............**Spain**

Group E	P	W	D	L	F	A	GD	P
Italy	3	2	0	1	3	1	2	6
Belgium	3	2	0	1	4	2	2	6
Rep of Ireland	3	1	1	1	2	4	-2	4
Sweden	3	0	1	2	1	3	-2	1

Monday, June 13 2016
Rep of Ireland (0) 1-1 (0).........Sweden
Belgium........ (0) 0-2 (1)...............Italy
Friday, June 17 2016
Italy............... (0) 1-0 (0).........Sweden
Saturday, June 18 2016
Belgium........ (0) 3-0 (0)..Rep of Ireland
Wednesday, June 22 2016
Italy............... (0) 0-1 (0)..Rep of Ireland
Sweden .... (0) 0-1 (0).........**Belgium**

Group F	P	W	D	L	F	A	GD	P
Hungary	3	1	2	0	6	4	2	5
Iceland	3	1	2	0	4	3	1	5
Portugal	3	0	3	0	4	4	0	3
Austria	3	0	1	2	1	4	-3	1

Tuesday, June 14 2016
Austria .... (0) 0-2 (0).........**Hungary**
Portugal........ (1) 1-1 (0)............Iceland
Saturday, June 18 2016
Iceland .... (1) 1-1 (0).........Hungary
Portugal........ (0) 0-0 (0)............Austria
Wednesday, June 22 2016
Iceland .... (1) 2-1 (0)...........Austria
Hungary .... (1) 3-3 (1)........**Portugal**

Round of 16
Saturday, June 25 2016
Switzerland .. (0) 1-1 (1)............Poland
AET. 1-1 90 mins Poland 5-4 pens
Wales............. (0) 1-0 (0)......... N Ireland
Croatia .... (0) 0-1 (0)........ **Portugal**
AET. 0-0 90 mins
Sunday, June 26 2016
France .... (0) 2-1 (0)..Rep of Ireland
Germany .... (2) 3-0 (0).........Slovakia
Hungary .... (0) 0-4 (1).........**Belgium**
Monday, June 27 2016
Italy............... (1) 2-0 (0).............Spain
England......... (1) 1-2 (2)............**Iceland**

Quarter-finals
Thursday, June 30 2016
Poland........... (1) 1-1 (1)........**Portugal**
AET. 1-1 90 mins Portugal 5-3 pens
Friday, July 1 2016
Wales............. (1) 3-1 (1).........Belgium
Saturday, July 2 2016
Germany .... (0) 1-1 (0)...............Italy
AET. 1-1 90 mins Germany 6-5 pens
Sunday, July 3 2016
France .... (4) 5-2 (0)............Iceland

Semi-finals
Wednesday, July 6 2016
Portugal........ (2) 2-0 (0)............. Wales

Hugo Lloris can't keep out Eder's shot in the Euro 2016 final
Photo by Matthias Hangst/Getty Images

Thursday, July 7 2016
Germany .... (0) 0-2 (1)............**France**
Final
Sunday, July 10 2016
Portugal........ (0) 1-0 (0)............France
AET. 0-0 90 mins

Copa Centroamericana 2017
Panama, January 13-22 2017

Group A	P	W	D	L	F	A	GD	P
Honduras	5	4	1	0	7	3	4	13
Panama	5	3	1	1	4	2	2	10
El Salvador	5	2	1	2	5	4	1	7
Costa Rica	5	1	3	1	4	2	2	6
Nicaragua	5	1	1	3	5	6	-1	4
Belize	5	0	1	4	2	10	-8	1

Friday, January 13 2017
Honduras .... (1) 2-1 (1).......Nicaragua
Costa Rica..... (0) 0-0 (0)...... El Salvador
Panama.......... (0) 0-0 (0)..............Belize
Sunday, January 15 2017
Belize .... (0) 0-3 (1).... **Costa Rica**
El Salvador..... (1) 1-2 (0)........**Honduras**
Panama.......... (2) 2-1 (1).......Nicaragua
Tuesday, January 17 2017
El Salvador..... (3) 3-1 (0)............Belize
Costa Rica..... (0) 0-0 (0).......Nicaragua
Panama......... (0) 0-1 (1).......**Honduras**
Friday, January 20 2017
Nicaragua ...... (1) 3-1 (0).........Belize
Honduras .... (1) 1-1 (0).... **Costa Rica**
Panama.......... (1) 1-0 (0)..... El Salvador
Sunday, January 22 2017
Belize .... (0) 0-1 (1).......**Honduras**
El Salvador..... (1) 1-0 (0)........Nicaragua
Panama......... (0) 1-0 (0)..... **Costa Rica**

Africa Cup of Nations 2017
Gabon, Jan 14-Feb 5 2017

Group A	P	W	D	L	F	A	GD	P
Burkina Faso	3	1	2	0	4	2	2	5
Cameroon	3	1	2	0	3	2	1	5
Gabon	3	0	3	0	2	2	0	3
Guinea-Bissau	3	0	1	2	2	5	-3	1

Saturday, January 14 2017
Gabon .... (0) 1-1 (0). Guinea-Bissau
Burkina Faso .. (0) 1-1 (1).......Cameroon
Wednesday, January 18 2017
Gabon .... (1) 1-1 (1)....Burkina Faso
Cameroon ...... (0) 2-1 (0). Guinea-Bissau
Sunday, January 22 2017
Cameroon ...... (0) 0-0 (0).............Gabon
Guinea-Bissau (0) 0-2 (1)....Burkina Faso

Group B	P	W	D	L	F	A	GD	P
Senegal	3	2	1	0	6	2	4	7
Tunisia	3	2	0	1	6	5	1	6
Algeria	3	0	2	1	4	6	-1	2
Zimbabwe	3	0	1	2	4	8	-4	1

Sunday, January 15 2017
Algeria........... (1) 2-2 (2)...... Zimbabwe
Tunisia.......... (0) 0-2 (2)......... Senegal
Thursday, January 19 2017
Algeria .... (0) 1-2 (1)........ **Tunisia**
Senegal .... (2) 2-0 (0)....... Zimbabwe
Monday, January 23 2017
Senegal......... (1) 2-2 (1)...........Algeria
Zimbabwe...... (2) 2-4 (4).......... **Tunisia**

Group C	P	W	D	L	F	A	GD	P
DR Congo	3	2	1	0	6	3	3	7
Morocco	3	2	0	1	4	2	2	6
Ivory Coast	3	0	2	1	2	3	-1	2
Togo	3	0	1	2	2	6	-4	1

Monday, January 16 2017
Ivory Coast..... (0) 0-0 (0)............... **Togo**
DR Congo....... (0) 1-0 (0)........ **Morocco**
Friday, January 20 2017
Ivory Coast..... (1) 2-2 (2)....... DR Congo
Morocco........ (2) 3-1 (1)............... Togo
Tuesday, January 24 2017
Morocco........ (0) 1-0 (0)..... Ivory Coast
Togo............. (0) 1-3 (1)....... DR Congo

Group D	P	W	D	L	F	A	GD	P
Egypt	**3**	**2**	**1**	**0**	**2**	**0**	**2**	**7**
Ghana	3	2	0	1	2	1	1	6
Mali	3	0	2	1	1	2	-1	2
Uganda	3	0	1	2	1	3	-2	1

Tuesday, January 17 2017
Ghana .... (1) 1-0 (0)..........Uganda
Mali............. (0) 0-0 (0)............ Egypt
Saturday, January 21 2017
Ghana .... (1) 1-0 (0)............... Mali
Egypt........... (0) 1-0 (0)..........Uganda
Wednesday, January 25 2017
Egypt........... (1) 1-0 (0)............Ghana
Uganda .... (0) 1-1 (0)............... Mali

Quarter-finals
Saturday, January 28 2017
Burkina Faso .. (0) 2-0 (0)..........**Tunisia**
Senegal .... (0) 0-0 (0)........**Cameroon**
AET. Cameroon 5-4 pens
Sunday, January 29 2017
DR Congo....... (0) 1-2 (0).............**Ghana**
Egypt........... (0) 1-0 (0)........ **Morocco**

Semi-finals
Wednesday, February 1 2017
Burkina Faso .. (0) 1-1 (0)............. **Egypt**
AET. 1-1 90 mins Egypt 4-3 pens
Thursday, February 2 2017
Cameroon ...... (0) 2-0 (0).............Ghana

Third place
Saturday, February 4 2017
Burkina Faso .. (0) 1-0 (0).............Ghana

Final
Sunday, February 5 2017
Egypt........... (1) 1-2 (0)......**Cameroon**

Confederations Cup 2017
Russia, June 17-July 2 2017

Group A	P	W	D	L	F	A	GD	P
Portugal	**3**	**2**	**1**	**0**	**7**	**2**	**5**	**7**
Mexico	**3**	**2**	**1**	**0**	**6**	**4**	**2**	**7**
Russia	**3**	**1**	**0**	**2**	**3**	**3**	**0**	**3**
New Zealand	3	0	0	3	1	8	-7	0

Saturday, June 17 2017
Russia............ (1) 2-0 (0)... New Zealand
Sunday, June 18 2017
Portugal........ (1) 2-2 (1)..........**Mexico**
Wednesday, June 21 2017
Russia........... (0) 0-1 (1)........ **Portugal**
Mexico .... (0) 2-1 (1)... New Zealand

Saturday, June 24 2017
Mexico .... (1) 2-1 (1)............ **Russia**
New Zealand.. (0) 0-4 (2)........ **Portugal**

Group B	P	W	D	L	F	A	GD	P
Germany	**3**	**2**	**1**	**0**	**7**	**4**	**3**	**7**
Chile	3	1	2	0	4	2	2	5
Australia	3	0	2	1	4	5	-1	2
Cameroon	3	0	1	2	2	6	-4	1

Sunday, June 18 2017
Cameroon ...... (0) 0-2 (0)............... Chile
Monday, June 19 2017
Australia .... (1) 2-3 (2)........**Germany**
Thursday, June 22 2017
Cameroon ...... (1) 1-1 (0)......**Australia**
Germany .... (1) 1-1 (1)............... Chile
Sunday, June 25 2017
Germany .... (0) 3-1 (0)......Cameroon
Chile............. (0) 1-1 (1)......**Australia**

Semi-finals
Wednesday, June 28 2017
Portugal........ (0) 0-0 (0)............... Chile
AET. Chile 3-0 pens
Thursday, June 29 2017
Germany .... (2) 4-1 (0)..........**Mexico**

Third place
Sunday, July 2 2017
Portugal........ (0) 2-1 (0)..........**Mexico**
AET. 1-1 90 mins

Final
Sunday, July 2 2017
Chile............. (0) 0-1 (1)........**Germany**

Concacaf Gold Cup 2017
USA, July 7-26 2017

Group A	P	W	D	L	F	A	GD	P
Costa Rica	**3**	**2**	**1**	**0**	**5**	**1**	**4**	**7**
Canada	3	1	2	0	5	3	2	5
Honduras	3	1	1	1	3	1	2	4
French Guyana	3	0	0	3	2	10	-8	0

Friday, July 7 2017
French Guiana (0) 2-4 (2)..........Canada
Honduras .... (0) 0-1 (1)..... **Costa Rica**

Tuesday, July 11 2017
Costa Rica..... (1) 1-1 (1)...........Canada
Honduras .... (0) 0-0 (0). French Guiana
Match awarded 3-0 to Honduras
Friday, July 14 2017
Costa Rica..... (1) 3-0 (0). French Guiana
Canada.......... (0) 0-0 (0)...........Honduras

Group B	P	W	D	L	F	A	GD	P
USA	**3**	**2**	**1**	**0**	**7**	**3**	**4**	**7**
Panama	**3**	**2**	**1**	**0**	**6**	**2**	**4**	**7**
Martinique	3	1	0	2	4	6	-2	3
Nicaragua	3	0	0	3	1	7	-6	0

Saturday, July 8 2017
USA .... (0) 1-1 (0)......... **Panama**
Martinique ..... (1) 2-0 (0)......Nicaragua
Wednesday, July 12 2017
Panama......... (0) 2-1 (0).......Nicaragua
USA .... (0) 3-2 (0)..... Martinique
Saturday, July 15 2017
Panama......... (1) 3-0 (0)..... Martinique
Nicaragua ...... (0) 0-3 (1).................USA

Group C	P	W	D	L	F	A	GD	P
Mexico	**3**	**2**	**1**	**0**	**5**	**1**	**+4**	**7**
Jamaica	3	1	2	0	3	1	+2	5
El Salvador	3	1	1	1	4	4	0	4
Curacao	3	0	0	3	0	6	-6	0

Sunday, July 9 2017
Curacao.......... (0) 0-2 (0).......... Jamaica
Mexico .... (2) 3-1 (1)..... El Salvador
Thursday, July 13 2017
El Salvador..... (2) 2-0 (0)........ Curacao
Mexico .... (0) 0-0 (0)......... Jamaica
Sunday, July 16 2017
Jamaica.......... (0) 1-1 (1)..... El Salvador
Curacao.......... (0) 0-2 (1).........**Mexico**

Quarter-finals
Wednesday, July 19 2017
Costa Rica..... (0) 1-0 (0)......... Panama
USA .... (2) 2-0 (0)..... El Salvador
Thursday, July 20 2017
Jamaica.......... (1) 2-1 (0)...........Canada
Mexico .... (1) 1-0 (0)...........Honduras

Lars Stindl celebrates scoring in the Confederations Cup final

Semi-finals
Saturday, July 22 2017
Costa Rica..... (0) 0-2 (0).................USA
Sunday, July 23 2017
Mexico .... (0) 0-1 (0).......... Jamaica

Final
Wednesday, July 26 2017
USA............... (1) 2-1 (0).......... Jamaica

Gulf Cup of Nations 2017
Kuwait, Dec 22 2017-Jan 5 2018

Group A	P	W	D	L	F	A	GD	P
Oman	3	2	0	1	3	1	2	6
UAE	3	1	2	0	1	0	1	5
Saudi Arabia	3	1	1	1	2	3	-1	4
Kuwait	3	0	1	2	1	3	-2	1

Friday, December 12 2017
Kuwait .... (0) 1-2 (1).. Saudi Arabia
Oman .... (0) 0-1 (1)................ UAE
Monday, December 25 2017
UAE............... (0) 0-0 (0).. Saudi Arabia
Kuwait .... (0) 0-1 (0)..............Oman
Thursday, December 28 2017
Kuwait .... (0) 0-0 (0)................ UAE
Saudi Arabia. (0) 0-2 (0)..............Oman

Group B	P	W	D	L	F	A	GD	P
Iraq	3	2	1	0	6	2	4	7
Bahrain	3	1	2	0	3	2	1	5
Qatar	3	1	1	1	6	3	3	4
Yemen	3	0	0	3	0	8	-8	0

Saturday, December 23 2017
Qatar.............. (3) 4-0 (0)............ Yemen
Bahrain .... (0) 1-1 (0)................Iraq
Tuesday, December 26 2017
Yemen .... (0) 0-1 (1)...........Bahrain
Iraq .... (1) 2-1 (1)............ Qatar
Friday, December 29 2017
Iraq .... (0) 3-0 (0)............ Yemen
Qatar.............. (1) 1-1 (0)...........Bahrain

Semi-finals
Tuesday, January 2 2018
Oman .... (1) 1-0 (0)...........Bahrain
Iraq .... (0) 0-0 (0)............ UAE
AET. UAE 4-2 pens

Final
Friday, January 5 2018
Oman .... (0) 0-0 (0)................ UAE
AET. Oman 5-4 pens

African Nations Championship 2018
Morocco, Jan 13-Feb 4 2018
Note: only players active in their national team's domestic league were eligible for this tournament

Group A	P	W	D	L	F	A	GD	P
Morocco	3	2	1	0	7	1	6	7
Sudan	3	2	1	0	3	1	2	7
Guinea	3	1	0	2	3	5	-2	3
Mauritania	3	0	0	3	0	6	-6	0

Saturday, January 13 2018
Morocco........ (0) 4-0 (0)......Mauritania
Sunday, January 14 2018
Guinea .... (0) 1-2 (1)............. Sudan
Wednesday, January 17 2018
Morocco........ (1) 3-1 (1)...........Guinea
Sudan............. (1) 1-0 (0)......Mauritania
Sunday, January 21 2018
Mauritania ..... (0) 0-1 (1).............Guinea
Sudan............. (0) 0-0 (0)........ Morocco

Group B	P	W	D	L	F	A	GD	P
Zambia	3	2	1	0	6	2	4	7
Namibia	3	2	1	0	3	1	2	7
Uganda	3	0	1	2	1	4	-3	1
Ivory Coast	3	0	1	2	0	3	-3	1

Sunday, January 14 2018
Ivory Coast..... (0) 0-1 (0)..........Namibia
Zambia........... (1) 3-1 (1)..........Uganda
Thursday, January 18 2018
Ivory Coast..... (0) 0-2 (1).......... Zambia
Uganda........... (0) 0-1 (0)..........Namibia
Monday, January 22 2018
Namibia .... (1) 1-1 (0).......... Zambia
Uganda .... (0) 0-0 (0)...... Ivory Coast

Group C	P	W	D	L	F	A	GD	P
Nigeria	3	2	1	0	4	1	3	7
Libya	3	2	0	1	4	1	3	6
Rwanda	3	1	1	1	1	1	0	4
Eq Guinea	3	0	0	3	1	7	-6	0

Monday, January 15 2018
Libya .... (2) 3-0 (0).......Eq Guinea
Nigeria........... (0) 0-0 (0).......... Rwanda
Friday, January 19 2018
Libya .... (0) 0-1 (0)...........Nigeria
Rwanda........... (0) 1-0 (0).......Eq Guinea
Tuesday, January 23 2018
Eq Guinea .... (1) 1-3 (0)...........Nigeria
Rwanda........... (0) 0-1 (0)..............Libya

Group D	P	W	D	L	F	A	GD	P
Congo	3	2	1	0	3	0	3	7
Angola	3	1	2	0	1	0	1	5
Burkina Faso	3	0	2	1	1	3	-2	2
Cameroon	3	0	1	2	1	3	-2	1

Tuesday, January 16 2018
Angola .... (0) 0-1 (0)....Burkina Faso
Cameroon ...... (0) 0-1 (0)...........Congo
Saturday, January 20 2018
Angola .... (1) 1-0 (0).......Cameroon
Congo .... (0) 2-0 (0)....Burkina Faso
Wednesday, January 24 2018
Burkina Faso.. (1) 1-1 (0)...........Cameroon
Congo .... (0) 0-0 (0)...........Angola

Quarter-finals
Saturday, January 27 2018
Morocco........ (1) 2-0 (0)..........Namibia
Zambia........... (0) 0-1 (1)............. Sudan
Sunday, January 28 2018
Nigeria........... (0) 2-1 (0)............Angola
AET. 1-1 90 mins
Congo .... (1) 1-1 (1)..............Libya
AET. 1-1 90 mins Libya 5-3 pens

Semi-finals
Wednesday, January 31 2018
Morocco........ (0) 3-1 (0)...............Libya
AET. 1-1 90 mins
Sudan............. (0) 0-1 (1)...........**Nigeria**

Third place playoff
Saturday, February 3 2018
Libya .... (0) 1-1 (1).............. Sudan
AET. 1-1 90 mins Sudan 4-2 pens

Final
Sunday, February 4 2018
Morocco........ (1) 4-0 (0)...........**Nigeria**

Last five Under-17 World Cups

India 2017
Final: England 5-2 Spain
Semi-finals: Brazil, Mali

Chile 2015
Final: Nigeria 2-0 Mali
Semi-finals: Belgium, Mexico

UAE 2013
Final: Nigeria 3-0 Mexico
Semi-finals: Sweden, Argentina

Mexico 2011
Final: Mexico 2-0 Uruguay
Semi-finals: Germany, Brazil

Nigeria 2009
Final: Switzerland 1-0 Nigeria
Semi-finals: Spain, Colombia

England U20 captain Lewis Cook with the World Cup

Last five Under-20 World Cups

South Korea 2017
Final: England 1-0 Venezuela
Semi-finals: Italy, Uruguay

New Zealand 2015
Final: Serbia 2-1 (aet) Brazil
Semi-finals: Mali, Senegal

Turkey 2013
Final: France 0-0 Uruguay (France 4-1 pens)
Semi-finals: Ghana, Iraq

Colombia 2011
Final: Brazil 3-2 (aet) Portugal
Semi-finals: Mexico, France

Egypt 2009
Final: Ghana 0-0 Brazil (Ghana 4-3 pens)
Semi-finals: Hungary, Costa Rica

England's Jamie Vardy celebrates his friendly goal against Italy

Friendly results since qualifying

Thursday, October 5 2017
Iran.............. (0) 2-0 (0)............... **Togo**
Friday, October 6 2017
Japan............ (0) 2-1 (0)... New Zealand
Saturday, October 7 2017
Russia........... (1) 4-2 (0)... **South Korea**
Tuesday, October 10 2017
Japan............. (2) 3-3 (1)................**Haiti**
Russia........... (0) 1-1 (0)................ **Iran**
South Korea.. (0) 1-3 (2)......... **Morocco**
Wednesday, October 25 2017
Grenada........ (0) 0-5 (3).......... **Panama**
Tuesday, November 7 2017
Saudi Arabia. (1) 2-0 (0)............. Latvia
Wednesday, November 8 2017
Iceland......... (0) 1-2 (1).......Czech Rep
Thursday, November 9 2017
Iran............... (2) 2-1 (1)......... **Panama**
Friday, November 10 2017
Belgium........ (1) 3-3 (1)..........**Mexico**
China............. (0) 0-2 (1)............. **Serbia**
England........ (0) 0-0 (0).......**Germany**
France .... (1) 2-0 (0)............. Wales
Japan............. (0) 1-3 (3)............**Brazil**
Poland........... (0) 0-0 (0).......**Uruguay**
Portugal........ (1) 3-0 (0).. **Saudi Arabia**
South Korea.. (1) 2-1 (0).........**Colombia**
Saturday, November 11 2017
Russia........... (0) 0-1 (0)......**Argentina**
Spain .... (2) 5-0 (0).... **Costa Rica**
Monday, November 13 2017
Bulgaria .... (0) 1-0 (0).. **Saudi Arabia**
Poland........... (0) 0-1 (1)..........**Mexico**
Venezuela ..... (0) 0-1 (0)............. **Iran**
Tuesday, November 14 2017
Argentina ..... (2) 2-4 (1)..........**Nigeria**
Austria .... (1) 2-1 (1)..........**Uruguay**
Belgium........ (0) 1-0 (0)............**Japan**

China............. (0) 0-4 (1)......**Colombia**
England........ (0) 0-0 (0).............**Brazil**
Germany....... (0) 2-2 (1)............**France**
Hungary........ (1) 1-0 (0)..... **Costa Rica**
Portugal........ (1) 1-1 (1)..................USA
Qatar............. (0) 1-1 (1)............**Iceland**
Russia............ (1) 3-3 (2)..............**Spain**
South Korea.. (0) 1-1 (0)............. **Serbia**
Wales............. (0) 1-1 (0)......... **Panama**
Sunday, January 7 2018
Sweden .... (0) 1-1 (0)........... Estonia
Thursday, January 11 2018
Indonesia ...... (0) 0-6 (1)..........**Iceland**
Sweden .... (0) 1-0 (0).......**Denmark**
Sunday, January 14 2018
Indonesia ...... (1) 1-4 (1)..........**Iceland**
Monday, January 15 2018
Denmark .... (0) 2-3 (1)............. Jordan
Saturday, January 27 2018
South Korea.. (0) 1-0 (0).........Moldova
Tuesday, January 30 2018
South Korea.. (0) 2-2 (1).......... Jamaica
Thursday, February 1 2018
Mexico .... (0) 1-0 (0)...... Bosnia-Hz
Saturday, February 3 2018
South Korea.. (1) 1-0 (0)............. Latvia
Monday, February 26 2018
Saudi Arabia. (1) 3-0 (0).........Moldova
Wednesday, February 28 2018
Iraq .... (1) 4-1 (0).. **Saudi Arabia**
Saturday, March 17 2018
Iran............... (3) 4-0 (0).... Sierra Leone
Thursday, March 22 2018
Denmark .... (0) 1-0 (0)......... **Panama**
Friday, March 23 2018
Argentina ..... (0) 2-0 (0)...............Italy
France .... (2) 2-3 (1)....**Colombia**
Germany....... (1) 1-1 (1)..............**Spain**
Greece........... (0) 0-1 (1)....**Switzerland**
Holland .... (0) 0-1 (0)....... **England**

Japan............. (0) 1-1 (1)................ Mali
Norway .... (1) 4-1 (1).......**Australia**
Poland........... (0) 0-1 (0).........**Nigeria**
Portugal........ (0) 2-1 (0)............ **Egypt**
Russia............ (0) 0-3 (0)..............**Brazil**
Saudi Arabia. (1) 1-1 (1).......Ukraine
Scotland........ (0) 0-1 (1).... **Costa Rica**
Senegal......... (0) 1-1 (1)...... Uzbekistan
Serbia............ (1) 1-2 (2)....... **Morocco**
Tunisia........... (0) 1-0 (0)............. **Iran**
Uruguay .... (2) 2-0 (0)......Czech Rep
Saturday, March 24 2018
Mexico .... (1) 3-0 (0)..........**Iceland**
N Ireland......... (1) 2-1 (1)... **South Korea**
Peru .... (1) 2-0 (0)..........**Croatia**
Sweden .... (1) 1-2 (1)............. Chile
Monday, March 26 2018
Portugal........ (0) 0-3 (3)..........Holland
Wales............. (0) 0-1 (0).......**Uruguay**
Tuesday, March 27 2018
Belgium........ (2) 4-0 (0).. **Saudi Arabia**
Colombia....... (0) 0-0 (0).......**Australia**
Denmark .... (0) 0-0 (0)............. Chile
Egypt............. (0) 0-1 (1)............Greece
England........ (1) 1-1 (0)...............Italy
Germany....... (0) 0-1 (0)..............**Brazil**
Iran............... (2) 2-1 (0)...........Algeria
Japan............. (1) 1-2 (1)...........Ukraine
Morocco........ (2) 2-0 (0)... Uzbekistan
Nigeria.......... (0) 0-2 (0)............ **Serbia**
Poland........... (2) 3-2 (0)... **South Korea**
Romania......... (1) 1-0 (0)...........**Sweden**
Russia............ (0) 1-3 (0)............**France**
Senegal......... (0) 0-0 (0)....... Bosnia-Hz
Spain .... (2) 6-1 (1).....**Argentina**
Switzerland .. (4) 6-0 (0)....... **Panama**
Tunisia........... (1) 1-0 (0)..... **Costa Rica**
Wednesday, March 28 2018
Iceland.......... (1) 1-3 (1)............... **Peru**
Mexico .... (0) 0-1 (0)...........**Croatia**

THE REFEREES

Revolution in Russia as VAR ushers in a new era

A World Cup usually heralds the introduction of new rules or sees regional innovations gain widespread adoption, *writes Paul Charlton*.

From red and yellow cards in 1970, to outlawing the tackle from behind in 1998, clamping down on feints by penalty takers in 2010 or giving referees a can of vanishing spray in 2014, there are usually tweaks to the regulations at the finals, some of which have far-reaching implications for the game.

Video assistant referees (VAR) will be the big change in Russia, following experiments all over the world since 2016.

There were mixed results last summer in the Confederations Cup. In the first semi-final, Chile were denied what seemed a clear-cut penalty in extra time when referee Alireza Faghani awarded a goal kick without reviewing the footage.

Then, in the final, Chile's Gonzalo Jara appeared to get off lightly with an elbow on Germany's Timo Werner, even after a three-minute delay while Milorad Mazic consulted replays and conferred with his assistants and the two VARs.

On the other hand, before either of those incidents, the chance to watch a replay spared Wilmar Roldan's blushes after he had initially booked the wrong player and upgraded the booking to a red card before finally getting the right man in Germany's 3-1 group-stage win over Cameroon.

Overall, the two-year experimentation period run by Ifab, the body responsible for the laws of the game, has been judged a success by football's rule makers.

An analysis of 804 matches run by 20 national and international bodies, including domestic matches in Belgium, Brazil, England, France, Germany, Holland,

Italy, Portugal, and the USA as well as internationals overseen by Conmebol and Fifa, Ifab concluded that the accuracy of decisions in reviewable categories increased by 5.9 percentage points to 98.9 per cent.

They also found that in eight per cent of matches the VAR had a decisive effect on the result, with a futher 24 per cent "positively affected" with an initial wrong decision by the referee corrected.

The VAR can only be used in the event of a 'clear and obvious error' or a 'serious missed incident' affecting the award of a goal, a penalty, a straight red card or a case of mistaken identity when the referee is showing a red or yellow card to a player. These types of incident are reviewed in the background and the VAR tells the ref if a check has shown an incident. It's then up to the arbiter to decide whether to act on the VAR's advice, watch the footage themselves or just carry on.

Disruption has not been as great as many feared – 68.8 per cent of games in Ifab's study had no review and less than one per cent of playing time was lost overall – but in matches where it has caused a delay, many feel that it does impact on the flow of the game. Tottenham's FA Cup replay victory over Rochdale in February might be the worst example so far – six minutes were added for video review delays in the first half alone.

Uefa president Aleksander Ceferin has ruled out its use in the Champions League next season, citing "confusion", although he also said he is sure it will happen eventually.

While VAR may lead to fewer errors within its narrow scope, there is still room for error, potential for controversy and plenty of the confusion that Ceferin talked about.

Referee stats

		S Africa 2010					Brazil 2014					2018 qualifying				
Asia (Afc)		G	□	⚑	■	LR	G	□	⚑	■	LR	G	□	⚑	■	Avg
Mohamed Abdulla	UAE											3	13			43.3
Alireza Faghani	Iran											6	23			38.3
Nawaf Shukralla	Bahrain						2	7			GS	5	15		1	35.0
Ravshan Irmatov	Uzbekistan	5	16			SF	4	12		1	QF	5	14			28.0
Ryuji Sato	Japan											4	10		1	31.3
Fahad Al-Mirdasi	Saudi Arabia											3	8			26.7
Africa (Caf)																
Janny Sikazwe	Zambia											5	17	1	1	44.0
Malang Diedhiou	Senegal											5	19		1	43.0
Mehdi Abid Charef	Algeria											3	8		1	35.0
Bakary Gassama	Gambia						1	2			GS	5	16			32.0
Ghead Grisha	Egypt											5	15			30.0
Bamlak Tessema Weyesa	Ethiopia											3	6		1	28.3
North & Central America and the Caribbean (Concacaf)																
Joel Aguilar	El Salvador						2	6		1	GS	6	27		1	49.2
Mark Geiger	USA						3	7			R16	3	13			43.3
Jair Marrufo	USA											3	8		1	35.0
Cesar Arturo Ramos	Mexico											4	14			35.0
John Pitti	Panama											5	15		1	35.0
Ricardo Montero	Costa Rica											5	17			34.0
South America (Conmebol)																
Nestor Pitana	Argentina						4	8			QF	7	37	1	2	63.6
Wilmar Roldan	Colombia						2	5			GS	6	30	1	2	62.5
Enrique Caceres	Paraguay											6	32		2	61.7
Julio Bascunan	Chile											6	30		2	58.3
Sandro Ricci	Brazil						3	8		1	R16	6	29		1	52.5
Andres Cunha	Uruguay											4	15			37.5
Oceania (OFC)																
Matthew Conger	New Zealand											3	18		1	68.3
Norbert Hauata	French Polynesia											6	19			31.7
Europe (Uefa)																
Felix Brych	Germany						2	6		1	GS	4	21		2	65.0
Antonio Mateu Lahoz	Spain											5	21		1	47.0
Gianluca Rocchi	Italy											4	13	1	1	45.0
Damir Skomina	Slovenia											3	12			40.0
Cuneyt Cakir	Turkey	3	11			SF						5	15		1	35.0
Milorad Mazic	Serbia						2	3		1	GS	5	12		2	34.0
Sergei Karasev	Russia											4	11		1	33.8
Clement Turpin	France											4	13			32.5
Bjorn Kuipers	Holland						3	5			R16	5	15			30.0
Szymon Marciniak	Poland											5	14			28.0

Referee stats include all World Cup finals appearances and qualifying matches for Russia 2018. **G** games, **LR** shows the latest stage of the finals the referee appeared at – **GS** group, **R16** round of 16, **QF** quarter-finals, **SF** semi-finals. **Avg** shows average bookings make-ups in qualifying, □ 10pts ■ 25pts, max 35pts per player. 90 minutes only

HOW THEY BET

World Cup winner

Win or each-way. See individual bookmakers for terms

	Bet365	BtBrt	Betfair	Btfrd	Btwy	Boyle	Coral	Hills	Lads	Power	Sky	188
Brazil	4	9-2	9-2	9-2	9-2	9-2	9-2	9-2	9-2	9-2	9-2	**23-5**
Germany	9-2	9-2	9-2	9-2	9-2	9-2	9-2	9-2	9-2	9-2	9-2	**23-5**
France	**13-2**	11-2	11-2	11-2	**13-2**	11-2	6	11-2	6	11-2	11-2	**13-2**
Spain	6	**7**	6	13-2	13-2	6	6	6	6	6	6	13-2
Argentina	**10**	8	9	9	**10**	8	9	9	9	9	9	**10**
Belgium	11	11	10	10	11	**12**	11	11	**12**	10	**12**	**12**
England	**18**	16	16	16	16	16	14	16	14	16	16	**18**
Portugal	**25**	**25**	20	**25**	**25**	**25**	22	**25**	20	20	**25**	**25**
Uruguay	33	28	33	25	33	28	28	25	25	33	28	**35**
Croatia	33	33	33	33	33	33	33	28	33	33	33	**40**
Colombia	**40**	33	33	28	**40**	28	33	33	33	33	**40**	**40**
Russia	40	33	40	33	40	40	33	**50**	40	40	40	40
Poland	**50**	40	**50**	40	**50**	**50**	33	**50**	40	**50**	**50**	**50**
Denmark	**100**	80	80	**100**	80	80	80	**100**	80	80	80	**100**
Switzerland	**100**	66	80	80	**100**	80	66	**100**	**100**	70	**100**	**100**
Mexico	100	66	100	80	**125**	66	66	100	80	100	100	100
Sweden	**150**	66	100	80	125	80	100	**150**	80	80	100	100
Senegal	**200**	125	125	150	125	150	150	150	125	125	**200**	150
Serbia	**200**	125	150	100	150	100	125	150	150	125	**200**	150
Nigeria	200	150	150	150	200	150	200	150	150	150	**250**	200
Iceland	200	150	100	200	200	150	125	**250**	150	175	**250**	200
Peru	200	200	125	200	150	200	200	200	150	125	**250**	**250**
Egypt	150	150	250	150	200	250	125	150	150	**275**	200	250
Japan	**300**	200	250	200	**300**	200	200	250	150	250	200	**300**
Costa Rica	**500**	250	300	400	400	250	250	300	250	425	**500**	**500**
Morocco	**500**	250	400	**500**	400	400	250	300	250	325	**500**	**500**
Australia	300	250	300	500	300	250	500	500	500	275	**750**	**750**
Iran	500	300	**750**	500	500	250	500	500	500	425	500	500
S Korea	**750**	250	500	400	500	500	250	300	250	500	500	**750**
Tunisia	**750**	500	**750**	500	500	500	500	**750**	500	500	**750**	**750**
Panama	1000	1000	1000	1000	750	1000	1000	1000	1000	500	**2000**	1500
S Arabia	1000	750	1000	1000	750	1000	1000	1000	1000	500	**2000**	1500

Odds conversion

Odds-on As %	Decimal	Fractional	Odds-against Decimal	As %	Odds-on As %	Decimal	Fractional	Odds-against Decimal	As %
50.00%	2.00	Evens	2.00	50.00%	73.33%	1.36	**11-4**	3.75	26.67%
52.38%	1.91	**11-10**	2.10	47.62%	73.68%	1.36	**14-5**	3.80	26.32%
54.55%	1.83	**6-5**	2.20	45.45%	75.00%	1.33	**3-1**	4.00	25.00%
55.56%	1.80	**5-4**	2.25	44.44%	76.92%	1.30	**10-3**	4.33	23.08%
57.89%	1.73	**11-8**	2.38	42.11%	77.78%	1.29	**7-2**	4.50	22.22%
60.00%	1.67	**6-4**	2.50	40.00%	80.00%	1.25	**4-1**	5.00	20.00%
61.90%	1.62	**13-8**	2.63	38.10%	81.82%	1.22	**9-2**	5.50	18.18%
63.64%	1.57	**7-4**	2.75	36.36%	83.33%	1.20	**5-1**	6.00	16.67%
65.22%	1.53	**15-8**	2.88	34.78%	84.62%	1.18	**11-2**	6.50	15.38%
66.67%	1.50	**2-1**	3.00	33.33%	85.71%	1.17	**6-1**	7.00	14.29%
69.23%	1.44	**9-4**	3.25	30.77%	86.67%	1.15	**13-2**	7.50	13.33%
71.43%	1.40	**5-2**	3.50	28.57%	87.50%	1.14	**7-1**	8.00	12.50%
72.22%	1.38	**13-5**	3.60	27.78%	88.24%	1.13	**15-2**	8.50	11.76%

Top goalscorer (selected)

Win or each-way. See individual bookmakers for terms. Rules may vary. Others available

	Bet365	Betfair	Betfred	Boyle	Coral	Hills	Lads	P Power	Sky Bet	188
L Messi	9	8	9	9	8	9	8	9	10	10
Neymar	10	7	10	10	8	10	9	10	10	12
A Griezmann	14	14	14	16	14	14	16	14	16	16
H Kane	16	16	16	16	16	16	16	16	16	16
C Ronaldo	14	12	12	12	12	10	10	12	20	14
T Werner	12	10	16	14	14	16	14	14	20	20
G Jesus	20	16	20	20	12	14	14	16	20	20
R Lukaku	18	18	20	20	20	16	20	16	20	20
S Aguero	25	20	25	25	16	20	25	25	25	25
L Suarez	25	25	25	25	20	20	20	20	25	25
T Muller	25	20	28	25	18	16	20	20	20	25
E Cavani	25	25	28	25	20	20	20	25	33	30
A Morata	25	12	20	20	20	16	18	20	33	20
R Lewandowski	25	33	33	33	28	33	25	33	33	35
G Higuain	33	25	33	28	20	20	25	25	28	35
K Mbappe	33	33	33	25	40	25	40	33	40	40
O Giroud	40	40	40	40	28	25	25	40	40	40
D Costa	33	20	40	33	28	20	25	20	25	40
A Lacazette	40	40	40	40	33	25	25	40	40	40
R Falcao	33	40	50	40	40	33	40	40	50	40
E Hazard	40	40	40	40	33	33	33	40	50	50
A Silva	50	50	50	50	50	40	50	40	50	50
S Wagner	50	33	40	40	40	40	40	33	33	50
M Salah	50	40	50	50	40	50	40	40	50	50
P Dybala	33	40	40	40	40	33	40	40	40	50
D Mertens	50	20	50	50	40	50	40	33	66	60
J Rodriguez	66	50	50	50	50	33	50	50	66	60
Isco	40	50	50	50	66	50	66	60	66	60
M Icardi	50	40	40	33	50	40	50	40	66	50
R Firmino	33	50	66	50	40	25	40	50	66	70
J Vardy	50	66	80	66	50	50	50	66	66	80
P Coutinho	80	66	66	66	66	40	66	66	50	70
K De Bruyne	100	100	80	100	66	50	66	100	80	100
C Eriksen	80	100	100	80	66	66	66	100	100	100

Prices correct March 28 2018

Correct scores & total goals

Scores	GS	R16	QF	SF	3rd/4th	F
1-0	47	8	5	4	-	-
2-0	30	5	-	-	-	1
2-1	36	5	4	1	1	-
3-0	15	3	2	-	1	1
3-1	17	2	-	-	1	-
3-2	8	-	1	1	2	-
4-0	8	-	1	-	-	-
4-1	4	3	-	-	-	-
4-2	2	-	-	-	-	-
4-3	-	-	-	-	-	-
0-0	21	6	5	2	-	2
1-1	27	7	2	1	-	1
2-2	15	1	-	-	-	-
3-3	1	-	-	-	-	-
4-4	-	-	-	-	-	-
Other	9	-	-	1	-	-
Games	240	40	20	10	5	5

Overs	GS	R16	QF	SF	3rd/4th	F
<1.5	28%	35%	50%	60%	0%	40%
>1.5	72%	65%	50%	40%	100%	60%
<2.5	52%	65%	60%	70%	0%	80%
>2.5	48%	35%	40%	30%	100%	20%
<3.5	73%	85%	90%	80%	40%	100%
>3.5	27%	15%	10%	20%	60%	0%
<4.5	90%	93%	95%	80%	60%	100%
>4.5	10%	7%	5%	20%	40%	0%

BTTS	GS	R16	QF	SF	3rd/4th	F
Yes	48%	45%	35%	40%	80%	20%
No	52%	55%	65%	60%	20%	80%

Final tournaments since France 98. 90 mins only

World Cup penalty shootout records

	W	L		Win %
Germany*	4	0		100%
Argentina	4	1		80%
Brazil	3	1		75%
France	2	2		50%
Belgium	1	0		100%
Portugal	1	0		100%
South Korea	1	0		100%
Sweden	1	0		100%
Uruguay	1	0		100%
Costa Rica	1	1		50%
Spain	1	2		33%
Croatia*	0	1		0%
Japan	0	1		0%
Serbia*	0	1		0%
Switzerland	0	1		0%
Mexico	0	2		0%
England	0	3		0%

All-time records sorted by wins. Table includes countries playing at Russia 2018 who have contested at least one penalty shootout at a previous World Cup finals. Penalty shootout records are from World Cup final tournaments only.

*Croatia and Serbia's records include matches played as Yugoslavia, Germany's includes games played as West Germany

Top scorers in qualifying by team

	Goals	Player(s)
Argentina	7	Lionel Messi
Australia	11	Tim Cahill
Belgium	11	Romelu Lukaku
Brazil	7	Gabriel Jesus
Colombia	6	James Rodriguez
Costa Rica	4	Cristian Bolanos, Marco Urena
Croatia	5	Mario Mandzukic
Denmark	11	Christian Eriksen
Egypt	5	Mohamed Salah
England	5	Harry Kane
France	4	Olivier Giroud, Antoine Griezmann
Germany	5	Thomas Muller, Sandro Wagner
Iceland	4	Gylfi Sigurdsson
Iran	11	Sardar Azmoun
Japan	7	Keisuke Honda
Mexico	4	Hirving Lozano

	Goals	Player(s)
Morocco	4	Khalid Boutaib
Nigeria	3	Victor Moses
Panama	2	Abdiel Arroyo, Blas Perez, Luis Tejada, Gabriel Torres, Roman Torres
Peru	5	Edison Flores, Paolo Guerrero
Poland	16	Robert Lewandowski
Portugal	15	Cristiano Ronaldo
South Korea	7	Heung-Min Son
Saudi Arabia	16	Mohammad Al-Sahlawi
Senegal	2	Mame Biram Diouf, Sadio Mane, Diafra Sakho
Serbia	6	Aleksandar Mitrovic
Spain	5	Diego Costa, Isco, Alvaro Morata, David Silva
Sweden	8	Marcus Berg
Switzerland	4	Haris Seferovic
Tunisia	3	Youssef Msakni
Uruguay	10	Edinson Cavani